The Murder of Charles the Good

RECORDS OF WESTERN CIVILIZATION

RECORDS OF WESTERN CIVILIZATION

The Murder of Charles the Good

GALBERT OF BRUGES

Translated and edited by James Bruce Ross

COLUMBIA UNIVERSITY PRESS
NEW YORK

Columbia University Press
Publishers Since 1893
New York   Chichester, West Sussex
Copyright © 1959, 2005 Columbia University Press

Library of Congress Cataloging-in-Publication Data
Galbert, de Bruges, d. 1134.
   [De multro, traditione, et occisione gloriosi Karoli
comitis Flandriarum. English]
   The murder of Charles the Good / Galbert of
Bruges ; translated and edited by James Bruce Ross.
      p.   cm. — (Records of Western civilization)
   Includes bibliographical references and index.
   ISBN 978-0-231-13670-9 (cloth : alk. paper)
   ISBN 978-0-231-13671-6 (pbk : alk. paper)
   1. Charles, Count of Flanders, d. 1127 — Death
and burial. 2. Flanders (Belgium) — Kings and
rulers — Biography. 3. Flanders (Belgium) —
Politics and government. I. Ross, James Bruce,
1902– II. Title. III. Series

   DH801.F46G313 2005
   949.3'101'092 — dc22
   [B]   2004061383

Columbia University Press books are printed on
permanent and durable acid-free paper.
Printed in the United States of America
c 10 9 8 7 6 5 4 3 2
p 10 9 8 7

Records of Western Civilization is a series published under the auspices of the Interdepartmental Committee on Medieval and Renaissance Studies of the Columbia University Graduate School. The Western Records are, in fact, a new incarnation of a venerable series, the Columbia Records of Civilization, which, for more than half a century, published sources and studies concerning great literary and historical landmarks. Many of the volumes of that series retain value, especially for their translations into English of primary sources, and the Medieval and Renaissance Studies Committee is pleased to cooperate with Columbia University Press in reissuing a selection of those works in paperback editions, especially suited for classroom use, and in limited clothbound editions.

Committee for the Records of Western Civilization

Caroline Walker Bynum

oan M. Ferrante

Carmela Vircillo Franklin

Robert Hanning

Robert Somerville, editor

Contents

NOTE TO THE PREFACE, 1967

To the many reviewers of this book, at home and abroad, I am grateful for criticisms and suggestions which have aided me in correcting and amending the text in preparation for its appearance in Torchbooks, and in adding a Supplement to the Bibliography. It has not seemed necessary or desirable to make major changes in the Introduction or annotations although new items noted in the Supplement to the Bibliography illumine minor points. The import of these items is easily discernible to those who are interested.

The fullness of annotation which some scholars have praised and others lamented was the result of a conscious effort to meet the needs of the American undergraduate and the general reader as well as those of the medievalist. Concerning the absence of a Latin text, which was regretted by some European scholars, it should be said that the Records of Civilization for which this translation was prepared is primarily a series of English translations of sources unaccompanied by texts in the original languages, unlike the Nelson's Medieval Texts in England and similar series published in France and Germany. As for the use of Pirenne's edition without substantial revision as a basis for the present translation, I can only say that the value of the late, probably seventeenth-century, manuscript overlooked by Pirenne (Ms. Bruges, Bibliothèque Publique, 570) is debatable even among Belgian scholars. A thorough revision of Galbert's text awaits another hand.

It is my hope that this new version will restore Galbert's record to the popularity it deserves and which it once achieved in the small, abridged French paperback issued in 1853 by the *Bibliothèque des chemins de fer*.

Washington, D.C.   *J.B.R.*
April, 1967

PREFACE

"Few events created such a stir in their time as the murder at Bruges of Charles, count of Flanders, on March 2, 1127." With these words Henri Pirenne in 1891 opened his preface to the definitive edition of the narrative of Galbert, notary of Bruges, by all odds the fullest and most reliable record of the act and its impact upon Flemish society.[1] Unique in its day-by-day reporting, and in its revelation of profound social crisis, this account has been studied by a long line of distinguished Belgian scholars, especially by those of Flanders, for whom it bears a significance comparable to that of the Venerable Bede among the English or *The Russian Primary Chronicle* among the Russians in its concern with a decisive phase of "national" history.

It has, however, received little notice in modern times outside Belgium, except in Germany,[2] and is little known in the English-speaking world. No translation in a modern language has been made since two French versions of the early nineteenth century, both based on the original seventeenth-century edition of the Bollandists, and yet the popular appeal of this narrative can be gauged by its inclusion in the mid-nineteenth century in an abridged French version designed to entertain travelers, in the *Bibliothèque des chemins de fer.*[3]

---

[1] *Histoire du meurtre de Charles le Bon, comte de Flandre (1127-1128) par Galbert de Bruges* (Paris, 1891). ("Collection de textes pour servir à l'étude et à l'enseignement de l'histoire.") The present English title follows Pirenne's model, based on the title of the manuscripts he used, *De multro, traditione et occisione gloriosi Karoli comitis Flandriarum.* The excellent contemporary biography by Walter of Therouanne, *Vita Karoli comitis Flandriae,* ed. by R. Köpke, MGH, SS XII, 537-61, supplements Galbert's account, as the notes to the text will show. Next in importance is the material found in Herman of Tournai's *Liber de restauratione monasterii S. Martini Tornacensis,* ed. by G. Waitz, MGH, SS XIV, 284–89, to which frequent reference is made in the notes. Brief contemporary accounts will be referred to in the notes as they are drawn upon.

[2] See H. Sproemberg, "Das Erwachen des Staatsgefühls in den Niederlanden. Galbert von Brügge," in *L'Organisation corporative du Moyen Âge à la fin de l'Ancien Régime,* II (Louvain, 1939), 31-88.

[3] In 1853; these translations are listed in the bibliography.

There is obviously need for a modern translation and commentary, though none for a new text. Pirenne's masterly edition, on which this translation is based, has been subjected to only slight correction[4] and will not require revision unless new manuscripts are discovered. By the use of the only surviving manuscripts, two closely related ones of the sixteenth century, Pirenne was able to correct many readings in the Bollandist text of 1668, which was based on four manuscripts now lost, and to add several passages (in chapters 113, 114, 115, and 118) not included in that edition.[5] The original Bollandist text was, in fact, the only previous edition, since all other versions, including that by R. Köpke,[6] were simply reproductions, more or less accurate, of the original. But Pirenne's text has been out of print for many years and is now a collector's item. As a Latin text it is, moreover, a closed book to many modern students. And Pirenne's notes, indispensable though they remain, are in many respects out of date in view of the great progress in historical scholarship since 1891 and the acceleration of interest in the investigation and interpretation of social history which his own work did so much to stimulate.[7] Countless scholars have by their probings brought forth new evidence, as they have also laid bare new problems, in their efforts to understand those common western European trends which underlay the dramatic events of 1127-28 in Flanders: the increase in population, the expansion of trade, the rise of towns, the changes in social structure, the state-

[4] The changes suggested by P. Thomas, "Notes sur Galbert de Bruges," in *Mélanges d'histoire offerts à Henri Pirenne* (Brussels, 1926), II, 515-17, are incorporated in the present translation.

[5] *Vita B. Caroli boni comitis Flandriae, auctore Galberto notario ex aliquot mss,* AASS, March I (Antwerp, 1668), pp. 179-219. The correspondence between Pirenne and the Bollandists, inspired by his suggestion (in the preface to his edition, p. xxiv, n. 1) that these passages had been deliberately omitted by the seventeenth-century Bollandist editors because of their anti-clerical tone, is to be found in the *Revue générale* for February and March, 1892. In this debate Pirenne stood his ground, adding that the Bollandist editors had also certainly suppressed two obscene words in chapter 29. He admitted, however, that he had probably erred in one reading in chapter 115.

[6] *Passio Karoli comitis auctore Galberto,* ed. by R. Köpke, MGH, SS XII, 561-619.

[7] The same is true of the essay on Flemish society as revealed in Galbert's account by H. Van Houtte, *Essai sur la civilisation flamande au commencement du XIIe siècle d'après Galbert de Bruges* (Louvain, 1898).

building of princes, and the growth of collective consciousness. And the historians of "the School of Ghent" in particular have, in their writings on Belgian history, made exhaustive use of Galbert's narrative in illuminating various aspects of Flemish history. The masterly studies of Professors Dhondt, Ganshof, and Van Werveke, to name only a few, have, in fact, created the necessity for a new commentary on Galbert's account. And the superb edition of the cartulary of the counts of Flanders from 1071-1128 prepared by Professor Vercauteren, as well as such works as the comprehensive ecclesiastical history of Belgium by the late Reverend Father de Moreau, which were not available to Pirenne, have provided aids now essential to any student of Flemish history.

The aim of the present translation of Galbert's narrative, therefore, is to present to the English-speaking world a readable version equipped with an up-to-date commentary and notes which will give greater depth and meaning to an account of murder, pursuit, and vengeance, worth reading for its own sake, however, simply as a story. Because Galbert was thinking in Flemish, while recording the words and acts of Flemings in Latin,[8] it seems proper to translate much of his day-by-day account in words of Anglo-Saxon origin and in simple English locutions, and also to reveal, if possible, his conscious efforts, in the parts written at greater leisure, to clothe his thoughts in a more "literary" and therefore more cumbersome style.

Place names have been given in the forms in which they are most familiar today, whether Flemish or French, and the Latinized names of persons have been given in the forms best known to modern readers, Anglicized for the most part but occasionally Gallicized, for example, "Thierry" for "Theodoricus." Certain names, such as "Isaac" and "Hacket," remain unchanged for obvious reasons. Common sense rather than consistency has been the guiding principle.

The divisions into "chapters," which for the most part coincide

---

[8] The problems posed by this prevailing linguistic dualism, both for the writer and his translator, are analyzed by Marc Bloch in *La Société féodale: la formation des liens de dépendance* (Paris, 1939), pp. 121-26.

with the events of one day, are in accordance with the text of Pirenne, who followed Köpke's usage, an improvement on that of the Bollandists. Since Köpke skipped one number (59) in his series, the numbers given by Pirenne to his chapters are, from that point on, one less than those of Köpke. The chapter headings are my own.

The quotations that head sections II, III, and IV of my Introduction are free translations of verses from the texts of Latin poems, written soon after Count Charles's death; these are included in the appendix to Pirenne's edition of Galbert (pp. 177 ff.).

The notes to the present translation are intended to elucidate the text for the curious reader so that he may proceed independently, if he wishes, of the Introduction, which is concerned to interpret the murder and its aftermath in the broader framework of Flemish society and history. The contents of Pirenne's notes have been absorbed rather than reproduced. His evidence has, in rare cases, been corrected, and his interpretations frequently modified and expanded in the light of subsequent scholarship—his own as well as that of others. Both his notes and introduction remain invaluable, however, to the student of Galbert and of Flemish society.

JAMES BRUCE ROSS

Vassar College
Poughkeepsie, New York
April 15, 1959

ACKNOWLEDGMENTS

Thanks to the extraordinary kindness and courtesy of several Flemish scholars a number of graphic aids have been added to this translation which will make the text more vivid to modern readers. The fine map of Flanders, showing the coastline as it was *ca.*1127 and noting all the places named by Galbert as well as the lines of communication which existed in his time, was drawn by Dr. A. Verhulst of the University of Ghent, an expert in the historical topography of Flanders. The plans of Bruges and of the castle at Bruges were drawn under the supervision of Professor Jan Dhondt of the University of Ghent, whose recent study of the early topography of Bruges, based to a considerable extent upon Galbert's testimony, has corrected many errors and clarified many disputed points on this subject. The scene of the most dramatic action in Galbert's account, the castral church of Saint Donatian at Bruges, has been illuminated by the special appendix written by Dr. J. Mertens of the University of Louvain. His remarkable excavations in 1955 on the site of this Carolingian church have revealed a lost monument of great historical and artistic interest and, incidentally, confirmed the accuracy of Galbert's literary evidence. To these special contributors to the present translation of Galbert I cannot adequately express my appreciation. I hope it will be a satisfaction to them to know that twelfth-century Flanders will come alive to English readers through their efforts.

What I owe to the learning and wisdom of Professors Jan Dhondt and François L. Ganshof will be obvious to the reader. It is a privilege to serve as a medium through which their profound understanding of early Flemish history can be made accessible to a wider public. To Professor Dhondt in particular my indebtedness and my gratitude are immeasurable. His critical reading of the whole manuscript was the latest of many services he has performed; in countless ways he has helped me bring to bear on the text of Galbert the rich resources of Belgian scholarship, past and present, and shared with me his insight into the processes of social change.

I should like also to pay tribute to the memory of the late Professor James Westfall Thompson, who first introduced me to the works of Henri Pirenne and to the text of Galbert in his seminar at the University of Chicago.

I acknowledge with thanks the permission of the Viking Press to use an excerpt from Galbert's work published in *The Portable Medieval Reader,* ed. by J. B. Ross and M. M. McLaughlin (New York, 1949).

My warm thanks go to the staff members of the Vassar College Library and of the Widener Library of Harvard College, where I have received unfailing help and courtesy. I owe a special debt of gratitude to Miss Eleanor Rogers of the Vassar College Library for the meticulous care with which she typed the manuscript.

To the President, the Trustees, and the Faculty of Vassar College I wish to express my appreciation for the award of Faculty Fellowships which enabled me to pursue my investigations in Belgium and to enjoy the freedom from teaching necessary for the completion of this work. I am grateful also to many of my colleagues at Vassar College for advice on particular points. With this book, I should like to honor Vassar College on the occasion of its forthcoming Centennial in 1961.

J. B. R.

List of Abbreviations Used in Footnotes

AASS	*Acta sanctorum quotquot toto orbe coluntur*
AHES	*Annales d'histoire économique et sociale*
ASEB	*Annales de la Société d'émulation de Bruges*
ASRA	*Annales de la Société royale d'archéologie de Bruxelles*
HMGG	*Handelingen der maatschappij voor geschiedenis en oudheidkunde te Gent*
MGH	*Monumenta Germaniae historica* (SS = *Scriptores*)
NH	*Nederlandsche Historiebladen*
PL	*Patrologiae cursus completus, series latina,* ed. by J. P. Migne
RB	*Revue belge de philologie et d'histoire*
RBA	*Revue belge d'archéologie et d'histoire de l'art*
RHC	*Recueil des historiens des croisades* (Occ. = *Historiens occidentaux*)
RHD	*Revue d'histoire du droit*
RHF	*Recueil des historiens des Gaules et de la France*
RHDF	*Revue historique de droit français et étranger*
RN	*Revue du Nord*

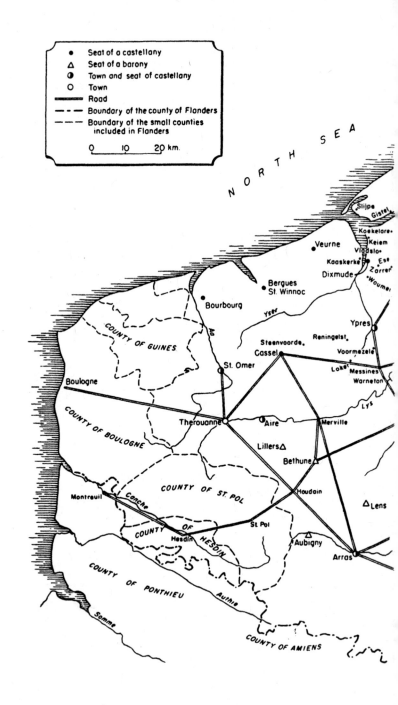

Seat of a castellany
Seat of a barony
Town and seat of castellany
Town
Road
Boundary of the county of Flanders
Boundary of the small counties
included in Flanders

0   10   20 km.

NORTH SEA

Slijpe
Gistel
Koekelare
Keiem
Veurne
Vladslo
Kaaskerke
Ese
Zarren
Dixmude
Woumen
Bergues
St. Winnoc
Bourbourg
Yser
Ypres
COUNTY OF GUINES
Steenvoorde
Reningelst
Aa
Voormezele
Cassel
Loker
Messines
St. Omer
Warneton
Boulogne
Lys
COUNTY OF BOULOGNE
Therouanne
Aire
Merville
Lillers
Bethune
Montreuil
Canche
COUNTY OF ST. POL
Houdain
Lens
COUNTY   OF
St. Pol
COUNTY   OF   HESDIN
Hesdin
Aubigny
COUNTY OF PONTHIEU
Arras
Authie
Somme
COUNTY OF AMIENS

COUNTY OF FLANDERS

Middelburg

HONT

Wulpen
Cadzand
Oostburg
Ijzendijke
Axel

ZWIN
Aardenburg
Lapscheure
Boekhoute

Lissewege
Uitkerke
Oostkerke
Praat
Maldegem
Raverschoot

WAAS

Rupelmonde

Bruges
Ouden-
burg
Jabbeke
Straten
(St. Andries)
Oostkamp
Beernem
Zomergem

Aartrijke
Ruddervoorde
Aalter
Ghent
Dendermonde

Wijnendale
Wingene
Torhout

BRABANT

Lichtervelde
Tielt
Axspoele
Deinze
Scheldt
Aalst

Staden
Gavere

Roeselare

Eine
Ninove
Oudenaarde
Dender

Leie
Courtrai
Scheldt
Boelare

Wervik

Tourcoing

Lille
Tournai

Deule

Mons

Douai

Scarpe
Escaut
HAINAUT

Cambrai

PLAN OF BRUGES, WITH DETAIL
SHOWING PLAN OF THE CASTLE

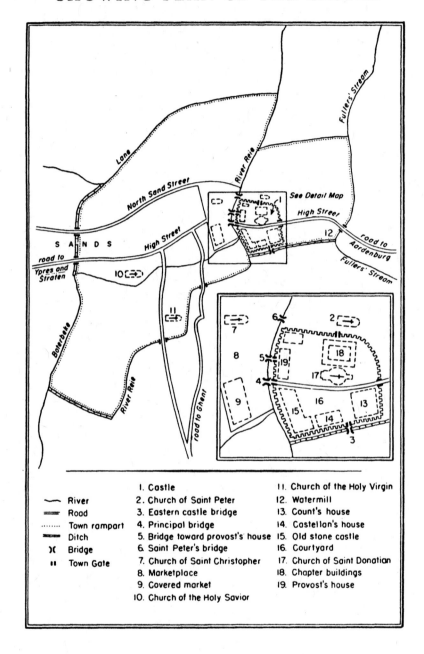

～	River	1. Castle
＝	Road	2. Church of Saint Peter
………	Town rampart	3. Eastern castle bridge
＝	Ditch	4. Principal bridge
)(	Bridge	5. Bridge toward provost's house
ıı	Town Gate	6. Saint Peter's bridge
		7. Church of Saint Christopher
		8. Marketplace
		9. Covered market
		10. Church of the Holy Savior

11. Church of the Holy Virgin
12. Watermill
13. Count's house
14. Castellan's house
15. Old stone castle
16. Courtyard
17. Church of Saint Donation
18. Chapter buildings
19. Provost's house

The Murder of Charles the Good

NOTE TO
THE INTRODUCTION, 1967

In his review of the present work (*Medium Aevum*, XXXII [1963], 51–53), Professor K. Leyser has called attention in admirably succinct words to significant parallels to Galbert's story in the early twelfth century:

For the Erembald clan had become in the government of Flanders what the family of Roger of Salisbury was in Henry I's England and the Garlandes in Louis VI's France, a new caste of princes' agents with immense opportunities to rise in the world under the patronage of their employers and to shuffle off their modest beginnings.

These strikingly similar cases certainly "deserve a mention"; with Galbert's Erembalds, they might well form the basis of a substantial comparative study. For a deeper analysis of the Flemish case than could be included in the Introduction to this translation, see my essay, "Rise and Fall of a Twelfth-Century Clan," listed in the Supplement to the Bibliography.

In an effort to enlarge the reader's understanding of Galbert's society as well as the limits of his own sensitivity to the major currents of his age, I noted briefly in the Introduction the absence of allusions to some of its most significant religious movements. As Dom Huyghebaert has pointed out in his review (*Revue belge de philologie et d'histoire*, XL [1962], 483–86), recent studies of Tanchelm have modified Pirenne's view, emphasizing both the untrustworthiness of the sources and the fact that this stormy figure began his career, at least, as "un adversaire déclaré des clercs simoniaques." Whether or not Tanchelm himself was actually a "heretic," he was certainly one of those powerful preachers of reform whose activities pose very sharply the problems of distinguishing between heresy and orthodoxy in the diverse movements that were transforming the religious life of the early twelfth century. A helpful guide to the problems of interpretation posed by these movements in general, and by Tanchelm's case in particular, is H. Grundmann's recent judicious survey, *Die Ketzergeschichte des Mittelalters* in "Die Kirche in ihrer Geschichte," Band II, Lieferung G, Göttingen, 1963, especially pages 15–18.

J.B.R.

INTRODUCTION

[I] *The fivefold question*

"Whom did you slay, and why, and when, and where, and how, you most evil Borsiard?" asks Walter of Therouanne[1] of the man, then dead, whose sword first struck Count Charles as he knelt in prayer on March 2, 1127. And his own brief reply follows: "Your lord, because of his concern for justice, in Lent, in church, and in violation of the reverence due him," adding, "Your crime was worse than that of the Jews!"

A much more detailed answer to this fivefold question is given by two acute observers of the events of 1127; Walter himself, archdeacon of Therouanne,[2] at a distance from the scene, and Galbert, notary of Bruges, on the spot. The excellence of their sources of information and their obvious integrity as recorders enabled them to give their contemporaries substantial and accurate accounts of "when, where, and how" Count Charles was slain, and to explain "why" in so far as it lay within their power. Their very proximity to the events, however, and their necessarily restricted vision of the society in which they were immersed, made it difficult for them to comprehend the dynamic social forces which were transforming their world and which alone could explain the "why" of the murder. The questions asked by Walter can be answered by the modern student only by posing much broader and more complex problems and by attempting to solve

---

[1] *Vita Karoli*, c. 26, MGH, SS XII, 549: "O nefandissime Burcharde, . . . quem, quare, quando, ubi, et quomodo occidistis?"

[2] At the request of his bishop, John, "in order to strengthen the good and warn the evil," Walter wrote, probably late in 1127, his *Vita Karoli*, an admirably objective account, apparently from eye-witnesses, of events up to early May, 1127. Unlike Galbert, he begins with an account of Charles's ancestors and gives a much fuller picture of his early life, succession, and rule before 1127. Walter's elegant style and sincere religious feeling lend dignity to his work, but it lacks the vitality and movement of Galbert's more direct and immediate record.

them in the light of the unconscious revelations, as well as the recorded facts, of Walter's and Galbert's accounts, and with the aid of modern methods of historical inquiry and the fruits of recent scholarship.

The present-day questioner is led inevitably into an investigation of basic aspects of Flemish society in the early twelfth century. The murdered man was the count, the successor of a line of able and ruthless princes who had gradually created out of disparate elements of land, race, and language a remarkable entity, the county of Flanders. The viability of this state was proved by the events of 1127-28 still to rest upon the strength of its ruler, his ability to control the conflicting social groups within his lands, and his capacity to exploit to his own advantage the economic resources of his age. How had the counts of Flanders attained their eminent position as rulers of a unified, rich, and virtually independent state, and their reputation for maintaining peace and justice? What had Count Charles done to strengthen or weaken this tradition? And why did his sudden death precipitate such an acute crisis?

Within this apparently stable and well-ordered society a ferment was at work. Restless individuals and groups could be found, both among the older noble class whose appetite for aggression was thwarted by the reign of law and justice, and within the amorphous but vital communities of townspeople whose taste for liberties had received only slight recognition from the counts up to this point. This pervasive restlessness, not unique to Flanders in the early twelfth century, was given a focus and an opportunity for expression by a peculiar situation in Flanders, the extensive influence exerted by a single family, the Erembald clan, vassals of the count, who hated him to the death. Implicated in the plot and murder with them were other members of the knightly class, and many others of various classes proved ready to lend them aid and comfort after the murder. What lay at the root of this ferment in Flemish society? What did these restless, dissatisfied men want? How far would their opportunity for self-assertion carry them down the paths of disloyalty, treason, and social revolution?

The brutality of the murder, carried out by many swordsmen against one defenseless man at prayer, reveals the violence and insecurity that were close to the surface even in a society famed for its peace and justice. The act itself unleashed the most lawless elements in society and opened a period of killing and counter-killing which culminated in a frightful punishment of the captured traitors and was followed soon after by a period of civil war. What aspects of the environment and social order contributed to the perpetual precariousness of life even at a time when the sanctions against lawlessness were growing stronger, and when the civilizing influences of religion and learning and town life were becoming more pervasive?

The murder was committed at Bruges, a curious juxtaposition of castle and town, within the very castle of the count and within his own castral church of Saint Donatian. What kind of a place was Bruges, what functions did it serve, who were its inhabitants, and why did it become the scene of the murder? And how did it become and remain a focal point of contact and interaction between the manifold avenging forces, urban, baronial, regional, "national," and royal, as well as an important center in the determination of the larger issues at stake, the selection of a new count and the pacification of Flanders?

[II] *Whom?*

> *"When you were alive, Charles,*
> *Flanders shone in fame and peace and wealth."*

Although Galbert writes, not so much as a conscious historian, or even as a biographer, but rather as a day-by-day reporter of events which seemed to be destroying his fatherland, his use of titles and names unconsciously illuminates the long process by which Flanders as he knew it had been made by the predecessors of Count Charles.[1] It was a purely artificial unity, the creation

---

[1] For admirable summary accounts of the early history of Flanders see especially F. L. Ganshof, *La Flandre sous les premiers comtes* (3d ed., rev.; Brussels, 1949), and his recent chapter "La Flandre" in *Histoire des institutions françaises au moyen*

of an extraordinarily vital dynasty over a period of nearly three centuries.[2] The title of "count," most frequently applied to Count Charles by Galbert, and found almost exclusively in the charters of the count,[3] was first borne by his remote Carolingian ancestor Baldwin I, "Iron-Arm," a functionary of the West Frankish king Charles the Bald, whose fortunes rose after his abduction of the latter's daughter Judith in 862. Among the group of *pagi* or "counties"[4] which he administered in the name of the king was the *pagus Flandrensis,* a strip of coastal plain between the deep estuaries of the Zwin and Yser, which soon gave its name to the whole complex of counties, lands, offices, and rights gathered up by his son Baldwin II (879-918) as the royal power waned during the Viking invasions. This bundle of inherited and usurped rights was transformed into a legitimate personal authority in 888 when Odo, first of the Robertian kings of France, recognized Baldwin II as his vassal.

But Galbert also frequently refers to Count Charles as "marquis" of Flanders, a title which was first regularly added to that of count by Arnold I (918-65), the son of Baldwin II, doubtless because an essential part of his lands had once formed the northern stretch of the Carolingian maritime march.[5] After long persistence, however, this honorific title was becoming archaic in Galbert's time, and his use of it, as well as his occasional employment of "consul,"[6] both rarely found in the charters of the time,[7] is doubtless simply a token of his profound respect for

âge, ed. by F. Lot and R. Fawtier, I (Paris, 1957), 343-426.

[2] The classic study of Flemish geography, however, insists upon the essential unity of "la plaine flamande"; see R. Blanchard, *La Flandre, étude géographique* (Paris, 1906), pp. 4-5.

[3] See *Actes des comtes de Flandre, 1071-1128,* ed. by F. Vercauteren (Brussels, 1938), pp. lxviii-lxix (hereafter referred to as *Actes*).

[4] For a map showing the Carolingian *pagi* and the probable coastline of *ca.* 900, see J. Lestocquoy, *Histoire de la Flandre et de l'Artois* (Paris, 1949), p. 26.

[5] See J. Dhondt, *Études sur la naissance des principautés territoriales en France, IXe-Xe siècle* (Bruges, 1948), pp. 277-84.

[6] "Consul," unlike marquis, seems to have no historical basis. Galbert uses it, perhaps as a literary device, especially in his more carefully written introductory chapters (1-14), added later to the running account of events.

[7] In the charters the last use of "marquis," applied to Baldwin VII, occurs in 1119 (*Actes,* no. 87, p. 195), except for a dubious charter of 1123 attributed to Charles (*Actes,* no. 115, p. 265). The last use of "consul" appears in 1094-95 (*Actes,* no. 18, p. 59), applied to Robert II.

his lord, whom he deemed worthy of all the honorable titles borne by his forebears. The original title of count had become the prevailing title, and it is as the "good count" that Galbert's hero was known to posterity.

As "our natural lord and prince," ruling by hereditary right, Count Charles reigned over what Galbert calls indifferently a "land" or "realm" or "county" characterized by extreme diversity, a composite of lands and peoples which had expanded, and at times contracted, throughout the course of centuries but which was gradually acquiring in Galbert's time a sense of community supplementing the dynastic bond. There is no doubt that in 1127 "la Flandre apparaît à ses habitants comme un ensemble territorial et une collectivité humaine."[8] To Galbert this "Flanders" or "land of Flanders" was "our fatherland," but his frequent use of the plural form of Flanders[9] reveals the persistence of the identity of the various parts which had been brought together by successive counts to make up the whole inherited by Count Charles. By his push to the south Count Arnold I had added to the Germanic-speaking peoples of the northern plain richer and more populous areas of Romance-speaking inhabitants,[10] and, after a period of crisis, the dynasty had resumed its expansive course under Baldwin IV and Baldwin V (988-1067), now to the east, into imperial territory. And so to "Flanders," fief of the French crown, already mixed in character, was added "Imperial Flanders,"[11] east of the Scheldt, held by the counts from 1056 as a fief of the Empire and enfeoffed by them in turn to a number of powerful barons with local interests. This eastward

[8] J. Dhondt, *Les Origines des États de Flandre* (Louvain, 1950), p. 6, n. 8.

[9] In the translation only the form "Flanders" is given because of the impossibility of distinguishing singular from plural in English. The singular form is used throughout by Petrus Pictor, canon of Saint Omer, in his poem *De laude Flandriae*, written *ca.*1100, an extraordinary expression of patriotic pride and devotion. See M. Manitius, *Geschichte der lateinischen Literatur des Mittelalters* (3 vols.; Munich, 1911-31), III, 880-81.

[10] The density of the Gallo-Roman population in the south at the time of the Frankish invasion, as contrasted to its paucity in the north, was the fundamental factor in the determination of the linguistic frontier, according to J. Dhondt, "Essai sur l'origine de la frontière linguistique," *L'Antiquité Classique*, XVI (1947), 280-86.

[11] See F. L. Ganshof, "Les Origines de la Flandre impériale," ASRA, XLVI (1942-43), 99-137.

expansion also increased the ecclesiastical diversity of Flanders by bringing under the rule of the count lands which lay within the diocese of Cambrai in the province of Rheims (as did the other Flemish dioceses of Therouanne, Noyon-Tournai, and Arras after 1094), as well as territory in the diocese of Utrecht in the province of Cologne.[12]

When Galbert speaks of "Flanders," therefore, whether in the singular or plural,[13] he encompasses this extraordinary complex of lands and peoples; but it is notable that he reserves the name of "Flemings"[14] for the inhabitants of that coastal plain, the original "county" of Flanders, which gave its name to the later state and whose people still possessed some sense of solidarity, as is apparent in the crisis of 1127 following the count's death. For "all the people" he apparently knows no appropriate name and must refer to them simply as "inhabitants"[15] or in the several social categories to which they belonged, as "knights and barons and citizens,"[16] or loosely as "clergy and people."

In characterizing "such a great prince" Galbert fixes upon those attributes and qualities which conform to the ideal conception of a secular ruler in Latin Christendom at this time. His "power and piety" combined to make him a "defender of the fatherland," "lord and father of his people," "sustainer of the poor," "advocate of the churches of God," ready to die for the "justice of God and the welfare of his people."[17] If Count Charles had proved able to realize this ideal to a high degree in his brief reign, it was thanks to the strong foundations of the realm he inherited and, especially, to the policies of his predecessors from the time of Baldwin V (1035-67) who had saved

[12] See É. de Moreau, *Histoire de l'Église en Belgique* (3 vols.; Brussels, 1945), I (2d ed.), 6, and the "Carte générale des circonscriptions ecclésiastiques avant 1559" in the *Tome complémentaire I: cartes.*

[13] In the charters of Count Charles the singular occurs more frequently than the plural form; see *Actes*, p. lxix. On the remaining seals of his reign he is called "Karolus comes Flandriae"; *Actes*, p. cvii.

[14] See for example c. 16, 25,. 51; several versions are used in the Latin text, generally *Flandrenses.*

[15] See c. 14.

[16] See c. 106.

[17] See especially Galbert's Introduction and c. 4, 6.

Flanders from a fate common to many feudal states at this time.[18] Security against the encroachment of external enemies had been achieved by the aggression of the early counts and by 1100 was embodied in military effectives of one thousand knights, a force of extraordinary size.[19] Both the king of France and the "Roman" emperor had learned to respect the frontiers of their powerful vassal, and the king of England, Henry I, had found it desirable to neutralize his potential enemy, Count Robert II, by the secret treaty of Dover in 1101. "The defender of the fatherland" could thus afford to gain military fame by tourneys and deeds of knighthood rather than on the field of battle, except when summoned to perform the military service he owed to his liege lord, the king of France.[20] His two immediate predecessors, Robert II and Baldwin VII, had lost their lives in performance of this duty and so brought the direct male line to an end.

And Count Charles could act as "lord and father" of his people, the instrument of peace and justice, because of the controls over men and resources achieved by his forebears. He owed much to the energy of Count Baldwin V, whom Galbert, with some justice, calls "the first father of the line,"[21] in whose reign the great feudal court of the count seems to have been shaped,[22] the reorganization of the domain into castellanies completed,[23] and the position of the count as superior-advocate over most of the ecclesiastical establishments within Flanders systematically affirmed.[24] Baldwin V had not only arrested the natural centri-

[18] Such as Anjou, for example; see J. Boussard, "La Vie en Anjou au XIe et XIIe siècle," *Le Moyen Âge*, LVI (1950), 36.

[19] J. F. Verbruggen, *De krijgskunst in West-Europa in de middeleeuwen* (Brussels, 1954), p. 546. The effectives of the king of France numbered between five and seven hundred at this time, those of the count of Hainaut seven hundred.

[20] According to the Treaty of Dover (*Actes*, no. 30, pp. 88 ff.) the count could fulfill this duty by the service of only twenty knights, while promising the king of England service with a thousand knights under certain conditions. See n. 34 below.

[21] See c. 68.

[22] See R. Monier, *Les Institutions centrales du comté de Flandre* (Paris, 1943), p. 40.

[23] See J. Dhondt, "Note sur les châtelains de Flandre," in *Études historiques dédiées à la mémoire de M. Roger Rodière* (Calais, 1947), pp. 43-51. "Domain" here refers to the lands directly under the count's jurisdiction; it does not include the autonomous counties and baronies of southern and eastern Flanders.

[24] Moreau, *Histoire de l'Église*, II (2d ed.), 226-28; Monier, *Les Institutions centrales*, pp. 16-17.

fugal tendencies of his time but had also bound the core of his
state, the domain, together more firmly by stimulating the growth
of towns and trade within this central strip lying between the
coastal plain and the Scheldt valley.[25] New mercantile agglomerations appeared and new fairs were established alongside
newly founded or strengthened castles within this area, and the
castles were provided with chapters of collegiate clergy and other
clerics who could serve as functionaries of the count's administration.

The substantial authority exercised by the counts in the late
eleventh century sprang not only from the effective administration they had devised but from their capacity to take advantage
of the "economic revolution" which was transforming their
world. The pressure of increasing population was leading to
intensified reclamation of land from the sea, and from marsh
and wastelands, and consequently to a considerable enlargement
of the count's private domain, especially in the coastal area, since
all "new lands" belonged by right to him.[26] Increasing revenues
from tolls levied on the circulation and sale of goods, as well as
payments in money and kind from the count's estates, were
swelling the count's strong boxes and granaries. It became
necessary in 1089 to create a permanent chancellor as receiver-
general of all the domanial revenues, with supervision over all
the notaries, chaplains, and clerics serving the count's court.[27] A
fatal outcome of this act, the boundless ambition of the holder of
this powerful office from 1091, Bertulf, provost of Bruges, forms
a major theme in Galbert's narrative. The amazing wealth of
the count is revealed in the frenzied hunt for Count Charles's
treasure by all parties, including the king of France, after his
murder.

[25] See J. Dhondt, "Développement urbain et initiative comtale en Flandre au
XIe siècle," RN, XXX (1948), 133 ff., especially pp. 151-56.
[26] See F. L. Ganshof, "Medieval Agrarian Society in its Prime," Section I, in
The Cambridge Economic History, I (Cambridge, 1941), 278 ff. The charters of
the late eleventh and early twelfth centuries contain innumerable references to
"new lands"; see *Actes, passim*. "Domain" here refers to the lands directly exploited
by the count within the larger "domain."
[27] See *Actes*, no. 9 ,1089, pp. 23 ff., also the analysis by Vercauteren, *Actes*,
pp. xlix ff.

The urgent need of the new class of traders and burghers for security of person and property reinforced the growing ecclesiastical demand for internal peace which was formally expressed in the Peace and Truce of God. From at least 1030 the counts cooperated with the Church in proclaiming such measures, but the "peace of God" gradually assumed the form of the "peace of the count"[28] in Flanders, enforced so ruthlessly by punitive measures and by judicial processes that Galbert could say with conviction in 1127 that "none of the counts since the beginning of the realm had permitted such depredations" as those private wars which aroused the anger of Count Charles.[29]

In the period between the dynastic crisis of 1071 when Robert the Frisian treacherously seized the countship from his young nephew, Arnold, and the treacherous murder of Count Charles in 1127—an inevitable consequence in Galbert's eyes[30]—the power and fame of the counts reached new heights. Their security and wealth enabled them to undertake long and costly foreign adventures and enter into a network of daring foreign alliances. The impressive pilgrimage of Count Robert I to the Holy Land in 1086[31] and the crusading zeal and piety of his son, Robert II,[32] added that world prestige to the dynasty which is reflected in the reputation of Count Charles.

The alarming growth of the Anglo-Norman domain after 1066 strained the earlier friendly relationship with William the Conqueror and led *ca.* 1079 to a Danish-Flemish alliance[33] against

[28] See below, pp. 43-46.

[29] See c. 9.

[30] See c. 70-71.

[31] He probably left Flanders in 1086 and returned in 1090. See Vercauteren, *Actes,* p. xvi. The emperor Alexis Comnenus was so impressed by Robert's following that he asked Robert to send him five hundred knights, who, together with one hundred and fifty horses, were received with honor on their arrival; see Anna Comnena, *Alexiade,* lib. VII, c. 6, 7, ed. by B. Leib (3 vols.; Paris, 1937-45), II, 105, 109. Robert may have had as many as six hundred knights, according to S. Runciman, *History of the Crusades* (3 vols.; Cambridge, 1951-54), I, 339.

[32] En route to the First Crusade he preferred gifts of relics to gold and silver from his brother-in-law, Roger Borsa, in Apulia, "since he was rich and lacked nothing." See "Charta Clementiae," in *Epistulae et chartae,* ed. by H. Hagenmeyer (Innsbruck, 1901), pp. 142-43.

[33] Robert the Frisian in 1085 added over six hundred boats to King Canute's thousand for the projected invasion of England. The effort crumbled, however, on Canute's assassination in 1086, according to William of Malmesbury, *Gesta*

William   as well as a strengthening of the feudal bond between
the Flemish counts and the king of France. But after the death
of the Conqueror, Count Robert II secretly renewed the Anglo-
Flemish alliance in the form of a feudal bond,[34] receiving from
Henry I an enormous money-fief in return for the promise of
military aid under certain circumstances. Reversing this policy,
his son Baldwin VII supported the claims of Henry's nephew
William Clito to the duchy of Normandy, from which his father,
Robert Curthose, had been dispossessed by Henry. The outcome
of these intricate maneuvers[35] is demonstrated in Galbert's narrative. Count Charles was born of the Danish alliance; he
acceded to the countship when his cousin Baldwin VII was killed
while serving in the host of the king of France; and it was the
unfortunate William Clito whom the king chose to succeed
Charles as count of Flanders and forced upon the barons and
burghers.

The "good Count Charles" succeeded to the rule of a state
which only the duchy of Normandy, the kingdom of England,
and the Norman duchy of Apulia and Calabria under Robert
Guiscard could rival in the apparent solidity of its institutions
and the wealth and prestige of its rulers. But the structure of
such a state was only as strong as the ruler himself, as the experience of England during the Anarchy, or Apulia under Roger
Borsa and his son William,[36] or Flanders during the crisis follow-

---

regum Anglorum, lib. III, § 261, ed. by W. Stubbs (2 vols.; London, 1887), II, 319.

[34] The Treaty of Dover, March 10, has been dated 1103 by most historians
following Rymer's *Foedera*; see for example Vercauteren, *Actes*, pp. 88-89. The
date 1103 should be changed to 1101 in the judgment of British scholars; see the
Regesta regum anglo-normannorum 1066-1154, Vol. II, *Regesta Henrici primi
1100-1135*, ed. by C. Johnson and H. A. Cronne (Oxford, 1956), No. 515, p. 7;
and also the forthcoming *Diplomatic Documents*, Vol. I (1101-1307), Public
Record Office, in which "the Anglo-Fleming alliance of 1101" will be the first item.
Examples of such use of the feudal bond in "international agreements" are discussed by F. L. Ganshof, *Le Moyen Âge* (Paris, 1953), pp. 135-36. See also L. Ver-
cauteren-Desmet, "Étude sur les rapports politiques de l'Angleterre et de la Flandre
sous le règne du comte Robert II," in *Études d'histoire dédiées à la mémoire de
Henri Pirenne* (Brussels, 1937), pp. 413-23. The treaty was renewed in 1110. The
date 1101 for the Treaty of Dover has recently been accepted and further substantiated by F. L. Ganshof in a careful study of the treaty, its date, provisions, and
significance; "Note sur le premier traité anglo-normand de Douvres," RN, XL
(1958), 245-57.

[35] See the analysis of G. Dept, *Les influences anglaise et française dans le comté
de Flandre au début du XIIIᵉ siècle* (Ghent, 1928), pp. 18-19 and of B. Lyon,
From Fief to Indenture (Cambridge, 1957), pp. 33-35.

ing the murder of Count Charles was to prove.

Only a few meager facts concerning the infancy and youth of Charles can be gathered from the Flemish and Danish sources. Born in Denmark, probably between 1080 and 1086,[37] he was carried off to Flanders in 1086 by his mother, Adele, who had been instructed by her husband to take this step in case he was assassinated.[38] A "very little boy"[39] on his arrival at his grandfather's court, he grew up during the reign of his uncle, Robert II, in the company of his younger cousin, the future Baldwin VII. The boy was soon separated from his mother, who in 1092 was sent off to Apulia by her father to marry Duke Roger.[40]

Adele was one of those remarkably adaptable noble ladies whose successive marriages to princes in various parts of Europe did so much to create social bonds among the ruling class. Chosen as a mere girl[41] for her "nobility" by a warrior king of the far north who cast off his concubines to content himself with her alone,[42] she was forced to flee for her life when about twenty, abandoning two small daughters, and after only a few years with her son in Flanders to proceed to the far south. Surviving her Mediterranean as well as her Baltic husband, in her forties she became regent (1111-15) for her only Apulian son, William, like his father a pious but ineffectual ruler,[43] and she witnessed the creeping anarchy in this disordered realm.[44] William died without heirs in 1127, presumably of grief on hearing the news

[36] See F. Chalandon, *Histoire de la domination normande en Italie et Sicile* (2 vols.; Paris, 1907), I, 301 ff., 325.

[37] *Actes*, p. xviii, n. 7.

[38] Saxo grammaticus, *Gesta Danorum*, lib. XI, MGH, SS XXIX, 69. Concerning Canute see *Vita S. Canuti*, AASS, July III, 121-36.

[39] Walter, c. 2. The only glimpses of the child and his mother come from a Danish saga of the thirteenth century; *Knytlingasaga*, c. 68, MGH, SS XXIX, 283-84.

[40] C. Verlinden, *Robert Ier le Frison* (Antwerp, 1935), p. 24, believes Robert may have met Roger Borsa on his way to Jerusalem and arranged the marriage at that time, for reasons which remain obscure.

[41] She was born between 1065 and 1071, probably married to Canute *ca.*1080; see *Actes*, p. xviii, n. 7.

[42] Aelnoth, *Vita Canuti regis*, c. 8, MGH, SS XXIX, 6.

[43] Romoald, *Salernitati annales*, MGH, SS XIX, 414-18.

[44] Only a few links with her life in the north are known. She begged her brother, Count Robert II, to spend the winter with her as he passed through Apulia on the First Crusade; *Gesta francorum*, c. 4, RHC, Occ. III, 493. And she sent gifts to adorn her sainted husband's relics; Aelnoth, *Vita Canuti*, c. 34, MGH, SS XXIX, 6.

of Count Charles's death.[45] It is hard to know what either mother
or son knew of Count Charles, whom Adele had left in Flanders
as a small child and whom William had probably never seen.

Galbert tells us nothing about Charles's parents except their
names and nothing about his early years, and Walter of Therouanne says little although he is purportedly writing a biography
of Charles. Of his youth and young manhood we learn only of
his prowess as a knight, his pilgrimage to Jerusalem,[46] and his
relationship to Count Baldwin VII (1111-19). As a young man
he seems to have been a person of little importance in the court
of Robert II (1087-1111). His name never appears as witness or
signer in the count's charters. He may, however, have been sent
to Germany on some mission for Count Robert, because his name
is recorded as a witness to a charter of Henry, bishop of Pader-
born, on November 1, 1101.[47] Perhaps the Countess Clemence
was already hostile to the influence which he must have gained
over her son and which becomes evident in the charters of
Baldwin VII. From 1112 to Baldwin's death in 1119 Charles's
name appears frequently, either as first lay witness or as first
lay signer of documents, designated at first as "son of the king
of the Danes" but from 1113 on generally called "kinsman or
cousin" of the count, and in the last charter, probably of early
1119, when Baldwin was dying, "kinsman and successor of Count
Baldwin."[48] Baldwin's confidence in his cousin, about ten years
his senior, who soon became his adviser,[49] was such that he
entrusted Flanders to him while he was fighting on the Norman
frontier,[50] and he endowed him in 1115 with a castle, Encre,
taken from his aggressive vassal Hugh of Saint Pol,[51] and, probably in 1118, a suitable wife, Marguerite of Clermont, who
brought him the county of Amiens as her dower from her mother,

[45] According to Walter, c. 2. Chalandon, *Histoire*, I, 311-12, doubts Walter's
statement that William left everything to the Holy See. The duchy was soon
absorbed by Count Roger of Sicily.
[46] See Galbert, c. 1, 12, and notes.
[47] See N. Schaten, *Annales Paderbornenses* (2 vols.; Neuhaus, 1693-94), I, 651.
[48] *Actes*, nos. 58, 59, 61, 70, 74, 76, 79, 85, 86, 87, 88 (false), 92.
[49] Walter, c. 5.
[50] Herman of Tournai, c. 26.
[51] *Sigeberti continuatio Valcellensis*, A. 1115, MGH, SS VI, 459.

Adele of Vermandois.[52] Despite the opposition of his mother, Clemence, Baldwin designated his cousin, "whose integrity and industry he had tested," as his heir[53] after his fatal wound in September, 1118, and during the months of illness before his death, June 17, 1119.[54] Charles was present at his cousin's funeral, together with a great crowd of the barons, at the abbey of Saint Bertin, where Baldwin had died in the monastic habit of the house.[55]

The first charters of the new reign of Charles, "count of Flanders by the grace of God," date from July 17, 1119, at Bruges;[56] and his first court was held at the Abbey of Saint Omer in 1120, perhaps because the count was on his way to destroy the castle of Saint Pol where the rebellious Hugh and many "bandits" were hiding out.[57] For his accession was challenged by a rebellion involving various nobles of the south, supported openly by Baldwin III of Hainaut, secretly by the king of France, and led by the rich and influential Clemence, who had violated the peace with Charles forced upon her by her son on his death-bed[58] and, now strengthened by her marriage to Godfrey, duke of Lower Lorraine, was supporting the claims of the illegitimate William of Ypres.[59] Charles seems to have crushed this first revolt easily; he tamed Hugh of Saint Pol, expelled Walter of Hesdin, forced Clemence to give up four of the twelve strongholds she held as her dower in Flanders, and drove out his external enemies.[60]

Despite its relevance to his own subject, Galbert completely ignores this first indication of disaffection among Charles's vassals and the unique problem of succession which arose in

---

[52] See L. Vanderkindere, *La Formation territoriale des principautés belges au moyen âge* (2 vols.; Brussels, 1902), I, 152-53. The house of Vermandois did not acquire Amiens until 1117, when Louis VI took it from Coucy.

[53] Walter, c. 7; *Actes*, no. 92.

[54] Walter, c. 6; Herman, c. 26; *Actes*, p. xviii.

[55] Simon, *Gesta abbatum S. Bertini*, lib. II, c. 104; MGH, SS XIII, 656.

[56] *Actes*, no. 93, 94, pp. 209, 211.

[57] Lambert, *Genealogia comitum Flandriae*, c. 10, MGH, SS IX, 311-12.

[58] Walter, c. 8.

[59] Walter, c. 7.

[60] Walter, c. 9.

1119, that is, the death without direct heirs of a reigning count.[61] But since the normal procedure of succession in Flanders had been followed, designation by the reigning count and confirmation by the barons,[62] the legality of Charles's position seems not to have been seriously challenged by other claimants, several of whom had hereditary claims as good as his or better.[63] The multiplicity of claimants in 1127 was due to the fact that Charles, also without heirs, had not designated a successor, and the open intervention of Louis VI of France can be explained in the same terms.

Both Galbert and Walter portray Charles primarily as count, after 1119, a mature man in his thirties and early forties, as a ruler concerned above all with the maintenance of internal peace and justice, determined to punish aggression and abase the rich and proud, even at the risk of his own life.[64] He apparently had no interest in conquest, and he had no occasion to defend his lands from invaders, but he maintained the honor of his county by serving in the host of his liege lord, the king of France, on the Norman frontier in 1119, soon after his accession,[65] and by leading a large contingent to the French host assembling at Rheims for the defense of the kingdom against the emperor in 1124.[66] "The very powerful count of Flanders" participated also in an expedition against the count of Auvergne in 1126;[67] his absence was to prove dangerous to himself and to Flanders. He was punctilious in acknowledging by legates in 1127 his vassalage to the new emperor, Lothair, the only one of the princes of Lorraine to do so.[68] In contrast to Baldwin VII, his relations

---

[61] The vital statistics of the dynasty are given by P. Feuchère, "Histoire sociale et généalogie; la noblesse duNord de la France," *Annales,* VI (1951), 317-18.

[62] Monier, *Les Institutions centrales,* pp. 30 ff.

[63] His foreign birth was a weakness, however; see Galbert, c. 8.

[64] See the comments of Marc Bloch on the fundamental duties of the medieval ruler, *La Société féodale: les classes et le gouvernement des hommes* (Paris, 1940), pp. 194-98. Many of the charters seem to echo Charles's preoccupation with "peace and justice"; see, for example, *Actes,* nos. 106, 107.

[65] Suger, *Vie de Louis VI le gros,* c. 26, ed. and trans. by H. Waquet (Paris, 1929), p. 200.

[66] *Ibid.,* c. 28, p. 224; hardly ten thousand men as Suger suggests.

[67] *Ibid.,* c. 29, p. 236.

[68] *Anselmi continuatio Sigeberti,* A. 1127, MGH, SS VI, 380.

with the king of England seem to have been friendly.[69] At Henry I's court at Rouen in 1124 he spoke up freely,[70] and he seems to have renewed the earlier feudal bond with the king of England.[71] Galbert says almost nothing about these relationships, but he insists proudly on Charles's prestige in foreign lands, his military prowess in tournaments abroad, and the "invitations" he received to become ruler of the empire in 1125 and king of Jerusalem in 1123.[72]

Persuaded in both cases by his advisors that his desertion of Flanders would be its ruin, he devoted himself to the arts of peace and good government. His personal devoutness is attested by all contemporaries, but it was not inconsistent with a firm control over the clergy. When, on the day of Epiphany, the abbot of Saint Bertin appeared at his court to complain of the aggression of a knight, Charles told him sharply that his function was to stay home and pray; it was the count's function to defend and protect the Church. And he threatened the knight with a punishment once inflicted by Baldwin VII, "boiling in a cauldron."[73] But he protected the clergy systematically by attempting to check the abuses suffered by the abbeys at the hands of such powerful lower-advocates as Baldwin of Aalst and Daniel of Dendermonde,[74] and of others whose deeds, like those of wolves, "belied their role as protector,"[75] and, in some cases, by strongly reasserting his own traditional role as advocate.[76] He took measures also against the encroachment of domanial officers of the abbeys and against their greedy vassals.[77] "In his

[69] But in 1122, after Henry I's marriage to Alix, daughter of Godfrey of Lorraine, he forbade Mathilda, daughter of Henry and wife of the emperor Henry V, to cross his lands. See *Annales Waverleienses*, A. 1122, MGH, SS XXVII, 458.

[70] Ordericus Vitalis, *Historia ecclesiastica*, lib. XII, c. 39, ed. by A. le Prévost (5 vols.; Paris, 1835-55), IV, 460-61.

[71] William of Malmesbury, *Gesta regum*, lib. V, § 403, ed. by Stubbs, II, 479; see also Galbert, c. 122.

[72] Galbert, c. 4, 5, and notes.

[73] Herman of Tournai, c 22. This form of punishment, regularly inflicted on counterfeiters from the thirteenth century, seems to have been a "morbid fantasy" on the part of Baldwin VII, according to R. C. Van Caenegem, *Geschiedenis van het strafrecht in Vlaanderen van de XIe tot de XIVe eeuw* (Brussels, 1954), p. 165

[74] *Actes*, no. 106, pp. 240 ff.; no. 107, pp. 243 ff.

[75] *Ibid.*, no. 119, p. 272.

[76] *Ibid.*, no. 124, pp. 287, 290.

[77] *Ibid.*, no. 108, pp. 247 ff.

peace is the peace of the Church," said a contemporary abbot.[78]

The charters record his many benefactions to churches and abbeys, especially in the form of "new lands" and tithes to the newer abbeys of maritime Flanders, such as the abbey of Bourbourg.[79] His humility in relation to the clergy and his consideration in hearing their cases first in his court are noted by his biographer.[80] Nonetheless he forced upon the canons of Tournai the election as bishop of his brother-in-law, the adolescent Simon of Vermandois, already chosen by the canons of Noyon for this dual bishopric.[81] Little is known about his relations with the saintly bishop of Therouanne, John of Warneton.

To Suger he was the "illustrious champion of the Church of God, generous donor of alms and distinguished guardian of justice."[82] His capacity in this last role was, of course, limited by the means at his disposal. Direct punitive action in person against malefactors such as that employed by his cousin Baldwin was still perhaps the most effective, but Charles seems to have preferred the renewal and extension of the regulations of peace promulgated by his ancestors,[83] and to have relied on the increased functioning of the territorial courts, the sessions of which the count himself often attended,[84] and on the broad judicial competence, both civil and criminal, of the great court of higher clergy, great barons, and officials, which he called at will and presided over in person.[85] The fact that he used only judicial procedures against the Erembald clan only stimulated their arrogance.[86] Despite their persistent aggression he took no punitive

[78] *Liber de restauratione S. Martini Tornacensis continuatio*, c. 13, MGH, SS XIV, 323.

[79] For example, *Actes,* nos. 100, 101, 102, 103, 104.

[80] Walter, c. 10, 12.

[81] Herman, c. 10.

[82] Suger, c. 30, ed. by Waquet, p. 242.

[83] Galbert, c. 1; Vercauteren, *Actes,* p. xlii, believes Galbert is here referring to specific enactments. See also Walter, c. 12.

[84] Galbert, c. 1, 7.

[85] Concerning the various courts and their competence, see F. L. Ganshof, "Les Transformations de l'organisation judiciaire dans le comté de Flandre," RB, XVIII (1939), 43-61, a synthesis of all his earlier works on this subject.

[86] Walter, c. 18. Fear as an effective sanction of the count's authority is again emphasized by Walter in c. 43, where he says that malefactors had been restrained "more by fear of Charles than of God."

step against them until February 28, 1127, and then only after consulting his court. His strict sense of justice undoubtedly turned many of the knightly class against him and made him "either loved or feared."[87]

He was certainly revered as a father by the poor whom he sustained out of compassion for their sufferings[88] and by the common people in town and country whom he saved during the awful famine years by strict measures of economic control,[89] but he must have been a stern and lonely figure, trusting few and loved by few even at his court. His impressive stature, perhaps a Danish inheritance, must have set him off from the Flemings.[90] He was in one sense a foreigner, as his enemies recalled.[91] His wife remains a shadowy figure, not even named by Galbert, and referred to only three times in the charters, in connection with pious donations.[92] There is no evidence she ever lived with him. He had no children, no relatives close at hand. Galbert refers cryptically to him as "once a sinner"[93] but that may be only a conventional expression. That he was capable of giving and receiving affection, however, is clear. Galbert speaks of his personal servant, John, as "his best-loved servant,"[94] and of the notary, Fromold Junior, as one intimate with the count and returning the count's love for himself.[95] Fromold's grief over his

---

[87] *Ibid.*, c. 12.

[88] *Ibid.*, c. 21; Galbert, c. 12.

[89] Galbert, c. 3.

[90] What did Count Charles look like? Little can be learned from the four surviving seals of two similar types which dimly reveal a tall figure on horseback, clothed in a long tunic, wearing a conical helmet; he holds a long sword in the right hand and a shield in the left. (See Vercauteren, *Actes*, p. cvii, Planches XII and XIII). The height of the figure is impressive, as compared with that of the other counts similarly represented on seals, and this is confirmed by the comment made when his bones were exhumed in 1794 shortly before Saint Donatian was torn down: "He was a man of extraordinary stature, to be exact, nine feet in length." See A. Sanderus, *Hagiologium Flandriae*, in *Flandria illustrata* (3 vols.; The Hague, 1732), Vol. III, Book IX, p. 51. Concerning later representations see J. M. De Smet, "Bijdrage tot de iconographie van de Glz. Karel de Goede, Graaf van Vlaanderen," *Album English*, 1952, pp. 117-57.

[91] Galbert, c. 8.

[92] *Actes*, nos. 100, 103, 116. Her chaplain, Salomo, is named in three charters of 1123 and 1124; *Actes*, pp. 262, 265, 267.

[93] Galbert, c. 6.

[94] *Ibid.*, c. 16.

[95] *Ibid.*, c. 19, 24.

lord's death seems convincing.[96] Lavishly favored by his lord, he seems to have been one of an inner group at the court, familiars or intimates, who had the count's ear and influenced his policies, "little men" who depended wholly on his friendship and enjoyed his confidence more than the great barons or officers of the land. They paid for it dearly on his death: Fromold by exile; Walter of Loker, knight, by death; and Gervaise, knight and chamberlain, by flight.[97] And even this group contained a traitor; Isaac, "chamberlain, vassal, and intimate" of the count, was the "head of the treachery."[98]

Charles's devotion to religion seems to have expressed itself in conventional forms of piety rather than in spiritual fervor, and perhaps his real and consuming passion was for law and justice. Legalism rather than compassion seems to have inspired the argument of his protest to Henry I against the blinding of the minstrel, Luke of Barre, who had written scurrilous songs against the king, that "you are doing what is abhorrent to our usages when you mutilate captives taken in the service of their lords," and he was silenced by the king's reply that he was doing "what was right."[99]

[III] *Why?*

> "Oh faithless Flanders!
> Why did you commit this crime?"

The confusion and anarchy suddenly engulfing Flanders on the murder of Count Charles were such that "even the most simple-minded could understand how much authority that one prince had exercised."[1] The contrast between the state of peace, justice, and order that prevailed before the murder, and the violence, iniquity, and confusion that followed it, fills the verses of the

[96] *Ibid.*, c. 64.
[97] *Ibid.*, c. 24, 17, 16.
[98] *Ibid.*, c. 28.
[99] Ordericus Vitalis, *Historia ecclesiastica*, lib. XII, c. 39, ed. by Prévost, IV, 461.

[1] Herman, c. 30.

many laments and epitaphs written soon after the crime.[2] When the shepherd is dead, the flocks are seized; when the head is cut off, the members are at war with each other, mourns a monk.[3] And the authors of these poems are impelled to ask the same question that arises in the minds of later generations. "Why did you commit such a crime? Why did you overturn the laws of peace, violate justice, slay your father?"[4] And one questioner probes more deeply. "What did you lack when he was count? Not gold or garments, or lands or abundance of horses!"[5]

Looking back on the events of March, April, and May, 1127, as he hopefully completed his account later in the year, Galbert himself seeks an answer to this fundamental question and finds it in a combination of factors, divine and secular. In his introductory chapters he sees the ultimate cause of the tragedy in the work of the devil[6] and in the consequent iniquity prevailing among the people of Flanders, whom God tried in vain to save by warnings and punishments.[7] The impious traitors are described by him as "full of the demon."[8] Their act of treason against their lord, likened to that of the Jews[9] or of Judas[10] by other contemporaries, was regarded as a sin against God in its violation of the oath of fealty sworn on the relics of the saints. It was also, of course, a crime against the social order, the stability of which depended greatly on respect for the oath[11]

---

[2] See "Poésies latines sur le meurtre du comte Charles le Bon," appendix to Pirenne's edition of Galbert, *Histoire du meurtre de Charles le Bon*, pp. 177 ff.

[3] In "Huc ades, Calliope," *ibid.*, p. 187, attributed to Galbert, a monk of Marchiennes, by J. M. de Smet, "Bij de latijnsche gedichten over den moord op den Glz. Karel den Goede Graaf van Vlaanderen," in *Miscellanea historica in honorem Alberti de Meyer* (2 vols.; Louvain and Brussels, 1946), I, 418-30.

[4] "Lamentatio," in "Poésies latines," Pirenne, p. 178.

[5] *Ibid.*

[6] Galbert, at the end of his own introduction. Concerning the stages of composition of the work see my Introduction, VI.

[7] *Ibid.*, c. 1, 2, 3, 14.

[8] *Ibid.*, c. 5, 6.

[9] Walter, c. 26.

[10] "Huc ades," in "Poésies latines," Pirenne, p. 188.

[11] On the general significance of the oath in medieval society see J. Dhondt, "Petit-Dutaillis et les communes françaises," *Annales*, VII (1952), 381: "Lien élémentaire, mais qui annexe l'Infini. Le serment, c'est Dieu pris à témoin, Dieu élu pour vengeur." John of Salisbury warns that no one should kill a tyrant to whom he is bound by oath or the obligation of fealty. *Policraticus*, lib. VIII, c. 20,

which bound men together not only vertically as vassals and lords but also horizontally as members of "sworn associations" or in simple compacts between individuals.

In an interpolation added at the same time, Galbert finds a more specific explanation of the crime and its consequences in divine punishment for the deeds of earlier generations in both the families concerned, now visited simultaneously upon their respective descendants, Count Charles and the provost, Bertulf, and his clan.[12] The treachery of Robert the Frisian in 1071 was finally expiated by his innocent grandson, the count, and two separate acts of treason on the part of the ancestors of Bertulf were ultimately avenged by the "precipitation" of the traitors. In his efforts at this time to explain the murder of the count in human terms, however, Galbert, like Walter,[13] fixes upon fatal weaknesses in the character of the archtraitor, Bertulf, especially his overweening pride and excessive ambition for his whole clan.[14] The villainy of the leaders of this family, Bertulf the provost, Didier Hacket the castellan, and Isaac the chamberlain, all of whom were both vassals and officials of the count, had been stimulated by the count's attempt to prove that they were legally his serfs, and hence the defense of "liberty" against servitude, so dramatically stated by Bertulf,[15] appears to Galbert as a secular cause of the crime. Still another immediate factor that Galbert seems to regard primarily as an occasion for the treachery[16] was the private war, incited by Bertulf,[17] which raged between his nephews and those of Thancmar, leader of a rival clan, and which finally drove the count to harsh punitive measures against Borsiard, nephew of Bertulf.

---

in Migne, PL, Vol. CXCIX, col. 796. Concerning the oath in Flemish society, see below, Introduction, IV.

[12] Galbert, c. 69, 71, 75; see also c. 11, 13, concerning the dispensation of God. The theme of God's direct intervention in the first sentence of c. 26, and in c. 27, of the day-by-day account sounds as if it might have been added at this time.

[13] Walter, c. 14.

[14] Galbert, in the introductory material, c. 8, 13.

[15] *Ibid.*, c. 8.

[16] *Ibid.*, c. 9; but note Galbert's version of the popular interpretation in c. 45, where direct responsibility is fixed upon Thancmar and his nephews.

[17] *Ibid.*, c. 13.

But at the very end of his introductory chapters[18] Galbert suddenly shifts the responsibility for the crime from the shoulders of the Erembald clan to a wider group, the barons of the land, and in so doing he reveals the appalling conclusion to which he had gradually been driven as he witnessed and recorded the events of March, April, and May, 1127, day by day. His own evidence in his running account affords a more convincing explanation of the crime than his efforts at interpretation added later; and his own disclosure of widespread complicity with the traitors among peers and barons, as well as knights and even townsmen, was confirmed by the inquest held in September, 1127, on order of the new count, William Clito.[19] The number of those named as guilty of murder, pillage, seizure of treasure, and active support to the traitors before or after the murder is 118, and many more must be implied in the nameless group of "hangers-on" referred to at the end. Galbert's own figures of those guilty are even larger.[20]

It seems clear, therefore, that disaffection pervaded all parts and ranks of Flemish society, that there were many disgruntled and unsatisfied persons in this apparently stable and prosperous state; some so hated the count that they conspired to slay him, and others were ready to give either secret or open support to those bold enough to do away with him. The story of the murder and its aftermath becomes a kind of window through which we can see, though at a distance and imperfectly, certain aspects of this society which alone can make comprehensible the deed and its sequel.

Flanders was a society in flux. Even its physical contours were changing as the great estuaries of the Zwin and the Yser, and lesser gulfs created by the marine inundations of the fourth century, gradually shrank, thanks both to natural dessication and the toil of men.[21] Tangible evidence of the increase in population

[18] *Ibid.*, the last sentence in c. 13 and in c. 14.
[19] Incorporated in French translation in the *Chronicon Hanoniense*, attributed to Baldwin of Avesnes, MGH, SS XXV, 441-43 (hereafter cited as the Inquest).
[20] Galbert, c. 87.
[21] After another great inundation in the tenth century the work of dike-building began, probably the first such effort in western Europe. From the middle of the eleventh century evidence of the rise of urban agglomerations and of the creation

in the late eleventh and twelfth century fills the narrative and documentary sources, although it offers little statistical basis[22] for a critical evaluation of this general European phenomenon so much studied and still so little understood by modern scholars.[23] An increase in land was one of the significant concomitants of the increase in people in what Suger calls "the very populous land of Flanders."[24] By lavish donations to newly founded abbeys and chapters of clergy in maritime Flanders, as well as by direct exploitation, the counts were engaged in a deliberate policy of drainage and clearance. The "new lands" won from the sea or marshes were being converted by stages into sheepruns and goosegreens, pasturage for cattle, and in some cases arable acreage by tenants of privileged status known as *hospites*.[25] Baldwin V was lavishly praised by a contemporary for bringing fertility to once unprofitable lands and for introducing to his people even the "gifts of Bacchus."[26]

But still there was insufficient land to meet the needs of peasants for tenures and knights for fiefs. Landless workers emigrated to northern Germany under favorable arrangements with bishops eager to secure their skills in reclamation and willing to grant them the privileges of *hospites*.[27] Others must

---

of new parishes reveals a notable increase in the population of the coastal plain; see M. K. E. Gottschalk, *Historische geografie van westelijk Zeeuws-Vlaanderen* (Assen, 1955), pp. 212-14.

[22] This period belongs to the age of "demographic prehistory" which lasts until the fourteenth century for northern Europe, according to the collective report of Cipolla, Dhondt, Postan, and Wolff in *IXe Congrès International des sciences historiques:* I, *Rapports* (Paris, 1950), 56.

[23] See L. Génicot, "Sur les témoignages d'accroissement de la population en occident du XIe au XIIIe siècle," *Cahiers d'histoire mondiale*, I (1953), 446-62; R. Delatouche, "Agriculture médiévale et population," *Études sociales*, XXVIII (1955), 13-23; J. C. Russell, *Late Ancient and Medieval Population* (Philadelphia, 1958).

[24] Suger, *Vie de Louis VI le gros*, c. 30, ed. by Waquet, p. 242.

[25] See Ganshof, "Medieval Agrarian Society in Its Prime," in *The Cambridge Economic History*, II, 278-82; Bryce Lyon, "Medieval Real Estate Developments and Freedom," *American Historical Review*, LXIII (1957-58), 50-54.

[26] See the letter of Gervaise, archbishop of Rheims, to Baldwin (between 1055 and 1067), in the *Miraculi S. Donatiani*, MGH, SS XV², 854-56.

[27] The earliest evidence of this movement is the charter of 1106, granted by Frederick I, bishop of Bremen-Hamburg (1104-23), to men of the Low Countries. It is in the form of a contract between the bishop and representatives of the emigrants who were granted extensive legal and economic privileges as free men. Similar arrangements were made later by other north German bishops. See É. de Borchgrave,

have flocked to the mercantile agglomerations springing up all over Flanders in the eleventh century. The hundreds of landless knights available for foreign expeditions in the conquest of England, in pilgrimage and crusade, or in mercenary service at Constantinople, indicate the pressure upon the land of this class, some of whom may even have been absorbed into the mercantile centers.[28]

Both growing population and expanding cultivation are reflected in the appearance of new communities, new monastic foundations for both men and women,[29] and new mercantile settlements of merchants and burghers like the town of Bruges, which forms the focus of Galbert's narrative. The impact of the economic revolution was creating groups of townspeople whose origins were diverse but whose needs and desires were markedly different from those of "country-dwellers," whether monks or peasants or knights. But, like the other nonmilitary groups, they were wholly dependent upon the count's "peace" for their security of person and goods whether at home, at fairs, or in transit, and upon his policies for their mobility in this period of "active commerce" when merchants went in person to seek goods and markets. The foreign merchants flee at the very rumor of Count Charles's death,[30] and the native merchants at Ypres immediately suffer oppression at the hands of lawless knights and William of Ypres.[31] During the uneasy reign of Count William the merchants of Bruges complain bitterly that they are shut up in their land and forced to consume their substance because of the hostility of Henry I of England.[32] Certainly the merchants of Flanders seemed to have nothing to gain and everything to lose by the count's murder and the interruption of their orderly life.

Histoire des colonies belges qui s'établirent en Allemagne pendant le douzième et le treizième siècle (Brussels, 1865); charter, pp. 334-35, discussion, pp. 54-67.

[28] See J. Lestocquoy, *Les Villes de Flandre et d'Italie* (Paris, 1952), pp. 19-21.

[29] Concerning the increasing numbers of nuns at this time, see Moreau, *Histoire de l'Église*, III, 507-10. At first their needs were met in the dual houses of the Premonstratensians, later in separate Cistercian houses.

[30] Galbert, c. 16.

[31] *Ibid.*, c. 20, 25.

[32] *Ibid.*, c. 95, 106.

The townsmen of Flanders, however, were a mixed and rest-less lot as we see them in Galbert's account. Whether sprung from local peasants or knights, from the entourage of count or abbey, or from wandering merchants,[33] they formed neither ho-mogeneous nor egalitarian collectivities.[34] The "men from Ghent" prove to be not only law-abiding burghers, welcomed by their counterparts at Bruges, but also expert bowmen and builders of siege machinery, together with a rabble from the environs.[35] The citizens of Bruges also seem to be a composite group of traders and miscellaneous artisans such as carpenters and masons.[36] No textile workers appear, probably because Bruges was less develop-ed as an industrial center than other Flemish towns at this time.[37] There must have been great inequalities of wealth and position between the mass of townspeople and those burghers of Ghent[38] and Bruges[39] whose names appear as witnesses to charters of the counts, or those "wiser ones"[40] who act as leaders of the com-munity at Bruges in critical moments. And although there is no evidence of an urban "proletariat" at Bruges, there are plenty of "poor" who are not afraid to speak up at critical moments.[41]

[33] The classic theory of Henri Pirenne that the original population of the urban nucleus was composed solely of wandering merchants has been hotly debated and is no longer generally accepted, though it was stoutly defended by the late Georges Espinas. See, for example, the comments of J. Lestocquoy, "Les Dynasties bour-geoises d'Arras du XIe au XVe siècle," *Mémoires de la Commission historique du Pas-de-Calais,* V (1945), 172 ff. and "Les Origines du patriciat urbain. Henri Pirenne s'est-il trompé? La thèse," *Annales,* I (1946), 143-48; É Perroy, "Les Origines urbaines en Flandre," RN, XXIX (1947), 49-63; J. Massiet du Biest, "Les Origines de la population et du patriciat urbain à Amiens (1109-XIVe siècle)", RN, XXX (1948), 113-32; and Georges Espinas, reply to Lestocquoy in *Annales,* I (1946), 148-53, and general rebuttal of his opponents in "Les Origines urbaines en Flandre," *Le Moyen Âge,* LIV (1948), 37-56.
[34] See H. Van Werveke, "Les Villes belges," in *La Ville* (3 vols.; Brussels, 1954-56), II, 551-56; Perroy, "Les Origines urbaines," RN, XXIX (1947), 58.
[35] Galbert, c. 33.
[36] *Ibid.,* c. 9, 40, 59.
[37] See E. Coornaert, "Draperies rurales, draperies urbaines, l'évolution de l'in-dustrie flamande au moyen âge," RB, XXVIII (1950), 59 ff. The production of cloth, however, was probably widespread in the country regions throughout Flanders.
[38] *Actes,* no. 95, 1120, p. 216; the arrogance of a rich citizen of Ghent, one Everwacker, is clearly seen in this charter.
[39] *Ibid.,* no. 61, 1113, p. 147; see the remarks of F. L. Ganshof, "Iets over Brugge gedurende de preconstitutionelle periode van haar geschiedenis," NH, I (1938), 301, n. 61.
[40] Called *sapientiores, meliores,* or *prudentiores* by Galbert, c. 27, 33, 51, 53, 100, 106.   [41] *Ibid.,* c. 22.

Although it is difficult to determine what their attitude towards the count was before the murder, and there is no evidence of actual complicity in the plot on the part of the burghers of Bruges, no burning spirit of revenge seems to color their attitude towards the traitors. When the killing begins, "one of our citizens," a mercenary, joins in.[42] The citizens obey the provost's order to fortify the town and enter openly into the councils of the traitors.[43] When avengers arrive, first the knight Gervaise and then the barons, they are compelled to swear oaths to the citizens before being admitted to the town to begin the seige of the traitors.[44] They take no action against the traitors until persuaded by Gervaise to do so.[45] They show more concern about keeping the valuable body of the martyred count, and their fellow-burghers in Ghent show more interest in stealing it, than either group does in avenging his death.[46] They remain enamored of Robert the Young,[47] whose obvious guilt they refuse to believe, and they show real feeling for the plight of their "lords," the Erembald clan.[48] It is obvious that some citizens were confined in the castle with the traitors, whether willingly or not. Some townsmen maintain connections with their relatives inside, despite stern prohibitions.[49] Once inside the castle, they concentrate on looting, at the expense of pursuing the enemy, and force the barons to share the booty with them.[50] They respond to the gestures of the traitors on the ramparts, who are urging them to attack their common enemy, Thancmar and his nephews.[51]

Perhaps many of them would have gladly accepted a new regime under William of Ypres,[52] guided or supported by the Erembald clan, if they could have got what they wanted, just as

[42] *Ibid.*, c. 16.
[43] *Ibid.*, c. 25.
[44] *Ibid.*, c. 27, 31.
[45] *Ibid.*, c. 27.
[46] *Ibid.*, c. 22, 43.
[47] *Ibid.*, c. 41, 60, 65, 74, 82.
[48] *Ibid.*, c. 45, 75. The Erembalds are their lords by virtue of the fact that they constitute the family of the castellan of Bruges.
[49] *Ibid.*, c. 59.
[50] *Ibid.*, c. 41.
[51] *Ibid.*, c. 45.
[52] This seems to be implied by Galbert, c. 86, 90.

they eventually accept William Clito in return for a charter, and later shift to Thierry of Alsace when he offers them even more, confirming and enlarging their gains. For it becomes clear after the murder that these dynamic communities are beginning to want more than simply the "peace and justice" afforded by a strong ruler. The burghers of Bruges and Ghent, Saint Omer and Aardenburg, at any rate, are quick to seize the opportunity created by the count's death to demand a variety of privileges for themselves, economic, legal, and judicial, which would make them freer as individuals and more autonomous as communities, and they are successful in selling their support to successive claimants at a stiff price, in the form of charters of liberties[53] and mercantile privileges.[54] Their appetite for self-assertion grows as the crisis lengthens; it assumes the extraordinary form of claiming a rightful share in the election of a count and even of sitting in judgment on his merits.[55] Their gains as individual communities actually both reduced the count's revenues and encroached upon his rights, and their larger claims, if embodied in institutions, would have established the principle of "popular sovereignty" in Flanders and the virtual autonomy of the county in relation to the French crown.

Realistic and opportunistic in almost all situations, in Galbert's account the burghers of Flanders seem to be guided primarily by self-interest, whether they are acting as individuals or in urban groups or as an embryonic "order." The count's murder, though probably not plotted by them or even consciously desired, proved to be of immense advantage, affording them their first occasion for claiming and exercising, both individually and collectively, a significant role in Flemish society.

But when the poet asks "What did you lack when he was count?" and answers by saying "Not goods or garments, not lands or horses," he was doubtless addressing the upper class

---

[53] *Ibid.*. c. 55, 102. See the masterly analysis of F. L. Ganshof, "Le Droit urbain en Flandre au début de la première phase de son histoire (1127)," RHD. XIX (1951), 387-416.

[54] Galbert, c. 99.

[55] *Ibid.*, c. 95, 106. See F. L. Ganshof, "Les Origines du concept de souveraineté nationale en Flandre," RHD, XVIII (1950), 135-58; J. Dhondt, *Les Origines des États de Flandre*, pp. 16-19.

of society, barons and knights, not townsmen or peasants. Whatever may have been the source of the "nobility," whether it sprang originally from the possession of land or the monopoly of arms,[56] the members of this "first nobility"[57] in Flanders were by no means a homogeneous group in Galbert's time, although they shared a common "noble way of life" and already enjoyed a privileged juridical status.[58]

The highest rank was clearly enjoyed by those whom Galbert calls "peers," or "princes" or "barons"[59] at times, always sharply differentiating them from the knights (*milites*). The composition of this small and select group is not entirely clear. Galbert actually names as "peers" only Ivan and Baldwin of Aalst,[60] Daniel of Dendermonde,[61] and the butler Walter of Vladslo,[62] but by association he includes Robert of Bethune and Roger, castellan of Lille.[63] Perhaps this élite also comprised other leaders of the avenging forces, such as Richard of Woumen,[64] Thierry,[65] castellan of Dixmude, and Wenemar,[66] castellan of Ghent, who arrived at the siege with the peers named above, and such strong men as Hugh of Saint Pol,[67] Arnold of Grenbergen,[68] the butler Razo of Gavere,[69] and Stephen of Boelare,[70] who acted in con-

[56] See the valuable summary of this current controversy by L. Génicot, "Sur les origines de la noblesse dans le Namurois, premiers jalons," RHD, XX (1952), 143-44, and by G. Despy, RB, XXXI (1953), 890; also R. Boutruche, "Histoire de France au moyen âge," *Revue historique*, CCXII (1955), 57-58.

[57] See P. Feuchère, "Histoire sociale et généalogie: la noblesse du Nord de la France," *Annales*, VI (1951), 312 ff., concerning the "first nobility," born, he believes, in the eleventh century and reaching its height in the thirteenth century.

[58] See M. Bloch, *La Société féodale: les classes et le gouvernement des hommes*, pp. 16-45, for a classic description of "la vie noble." His thesis that the "noblesse de fait" did not become a "noblesse de droit" until the thirteenth century is no longer considered tenable, however. In Galbert's account, knights in Flanders are justiciable only in the court of the count, while those of inferior rank are justiciable in the courts of the *échevins*; see c. 102, 110.

[59] Galbert, c. 4, 47, 52, 101 among other examples.

[60] *Ibid.*, c. 91, 101, 102

[61] *Ibid.*, c. 31, 101.

[62] *Ibid.*, c. 89, 102; he was lord of the barony of Eine near Oudenaarde.

[63] *Ibid.*, c. 52.

[64] *Ibid.*, c. 31, 114.

[65] *Ibid.*, c. 31.

[66] *Ibid.*, c. 30.

[67] *Ibid.*, c. 67.

[68] *Ibid.*, c. 65.

[69] *Ibid.*, c. 33, 67.

[70] *Ibid.*, c. 100.

cert with them. It seems to include most of those who enjoyed
rights of "high-justice" in the baronies and counties of eastern
and southern Flanders,[71] and to constitute the group of greater
vassals who claimed and exercised the right of electing the
count[72] in the crisis of 1127-28. Their names appear often as
witnesses and signers in the charters of the counts, together with
those of abbots, bishops, and provosts.

Galbert is horrified as he gradually discovers relations between
the traitors and members of this small group, practically all of
whom he comes to suspect of complicity even in the plot.[73] They
are surprisingly slow to take measures against the Erembald clan,
with whom some of them had been in close relationship before
the murder, for example, Walter the butler and Daniel of Dendermonde.[74] They maintain illicit connections during the siege
with the traitors, who at first seem sure of their support;[75] they
receive money and gifts from them,[76] and Walter the butler even
helps Bertulf to escape.[77] Some intervene with the king on behalf
of Robert the Young.[78] To Galbert the most shocking cases are
those of Baldwin[79] and Walter the butler,[80] the latter "next to
the count" in power, whom no one dared to lay hands on even
after the inquest had established his guilt. But God punished
these two peers by sudden death from trivial causes!

What could such men as these, the rich and powerful of the land,
hope to gain by helping the traitors, if not before the murder, certainly afterwards? What did they want? Probably greater influ-

---

[71] As well as leading men in the region of Veurne such as Richard of Woumen.
See J. Dhondt, "Les Solidarités médiévales: une société en transition, la Flandre
en 1127-1128," *Annales*, XII (1957), 549, n. 2; also Dhondt, *Les Origines des
États de Flandre*, pp. 10-12 and notes 19 and 20; and P. Feuchère, "Pairs de principauté et pairs de château," RB, LI (1955), 977, n. 4, and 997 ff.

[72] Galbert, c. 47, 52, 106.

[73] *Ibid.*, c. 20, 29, 44, 45; in c. 13 and 14, added later, he affirms this conviction
even more strongly.

[74] *Ibid.*, c. 21, 31, 38.

[75] *Ibid.*, c. 44.

[76] *Ibid.*, c. 29.

[77] *Ibid.*, c. 42, 46.

[78] *Ibid.*, c. 65.

[79] *Ibid.*, c. 91; his complicity, however, seems specifically limited to harboring
Hacket after the murder, and this is confirmed by the Inquest, MGH, SS XXV, 442.

[80] *Ibid.*, c. 89; in addition to helping Bertulf escape (c. 42, 46), he harbored one
of the murderers of the count, according to the Inquest (p. 441).

ence at the court than they exercised under Charles, who seems to have trusted his inner circle of "new men" as counselors more than he trusted them. They were also avid for money, to judge from their pursuit of the count's treasure, much of which they seem to have extorted from the traitors early in the siege.[81] But whatever promises some may have made to the traitors before the murder, and whatever their plans to use them or cooperate with them immediately after the murder, they are quick to realize the great opportunities of the situation and the advantages of playing the leading role of avengers as "barons of the siege." They soon form a "sworn association,"[82] consult as a group with the king concerning candidates for the office of count,[83] conduct the siege, and in general act as if they, and they alone, constitute the knightly class and in fact the real authority in Flanders, until they are forced to share their new power with the burghers.[84] They demand—and secure—from the king and count, under oath, the lands and goods of the traitors[85] and prove able to hold the king to his promise.[86] Two of them, Ivan and Daniel, later play the role of "king-makers"[87] in relation to Thierry of Alsace, betraying their new lord, William Clito, whom they had recently "elected," as well as the interests of another lord, the duke of Lorraine, in return for English money.[88]

Whether these men, a dozen or more, formed the whole of those loosely and confusingly called by a variety of names— usually peers, princes, barons[89]—by Galbert is not clear. But he sharply distinguishes the upper crust of the military aristocracy from the hundreds of knights with whom they were closely associated in function and way of life. These knights themselves seem to be a heterogeneous lot in Galbert's time, unequal in position and wealth and consequence. Some are vassals of the

[81] *Ibid.*, c. 29.
[82] *Ibid.*, c. 34; renewed in c. 85.
[83] *Ibid.*, c. 52.
[84] See Dhondt, *Les Origines des États*, pp. 14-16.
[85] Galbert, c. 52.
[86] *Ibid.*, c. 65.
[87] *Ibid.*, c. 95, 101, 102.
[88] *Ibid.*, c. 101.
[89] Also *nobiles* (c. 4), *primates* (c. 11, 49, 52), *proceres* (c. 1, 31, 44).

counts, some vassals of his vassals. Some are lords of estates comprising fortified houses, demesne, and tenures, such as Thancmar, Isaac, Borsiard, Robert, and Folk.[90] Others are knights of the castle at Bruges with quarters inside;[91] Borsiard may also have been one of these. Some appear in the followings of their castellans, or of their feudal lords,[92] others as individuals of importance.[93] Some as representatives of the castellany confer with the citizens of Bruges.[94] Some form part of the household of other knights, for example, of Borsiard's *familia,* hired to slay the count, and of Gervaise's.[95] Some are simply mercenaries.[96] There is also a class of squires.[97]

Galbert pictures them all engaged in the same activity, fighting and killing and looting, whether for themselves or their lords, in single acts of violence, in private wars between clans, or in sieges and battles of larger proportions, and all motivated by desire for vengeance, display of prowess, or gain in the shape of booty or pay. Fighting was their métier and their means of livelihood. They had always been, and still were, the most anarchic force in the land, the scourge of all peaceful folk, peasants and clergy, merchants and artisans, whose lawless ways neither counts nor clergy had been able wholly to curb or deflect. They had seized every chance in the past to weaken the authority of the counts.[98] Though temporarily terrorized by the harsh punishments inflicted on aggressors by Baldwin VII, they had doubtless served in the forces of the rebellious barons in 1119, and it is clear that in 1127 many were in league with Bertulf and his kin,[99] most of whom were knights themselves. Among the actual murderers were knights of Borsiard's household, paid

[90] See for example Thancmar's estate in Galbert, c. 9.
[91] *Ibid.,* c. 11.
[92] *Ibid.,* c. 100.
[93] *Ibid.,* c. 98.
[94] *Ibid.,* c. 53.
[95] *Ibid.,* c. 11, 59.
[96] *Ibid.,* for example, c. 49, 120; the mercenary Benkin (c. 75, 77) was a citizen of Bruges (c. 16).
[97] *Ibid.,* c. 9, 30, 39.
[98] Dhondt, *Les Origines des États,* p. 8.
[99] Galbert, c. 9, 20.

four marks apiece for the deed;[100] perhaps Eric, "an evil knight," [101] and George, "the strongest knight of the traitors," [102] belonged to this group. More influential knights who had married Bertulf's nieces were Guy of Steenvoorde, "famous and strong, of the count's counsel," [103] and Walter Crommelin, "rich and distinguished." [104] The knights Ingran and William of Wervik were members of the original plot.[105] According to the inquest, many joined the traitors after the murder and gave "aid and comfort" to them in a variety of ways.[106] The skill and strength of certain knights in the castle, Benkin and Weriot,[107] aroused even Galbert's admiration. Most of those precipitated on May 5, 1127,[108] seem to have been knights whose guilt had made it unwise for them to come out earlier.[109]

But there is no solidarity among them, as there was among the burghers and even temporarily among the barons. Those bound to the traitors before the murder doubtless expected advantages for themselves under a new régime dominated by the Erembalds, as well as opportunities for fighting and looting during an interim; and those who joined them later did so for a price.[110] Among the many who came out of the castle when offered a chance[111] were probably knights who saw they had chosen the wrong side. But regardless of sides, knights stood to gain in a period of anarchy like that of 1127-28. Gervaise used it adroitly to gain and hold for himself the office of castellan of Bruges.[112] The knight Walter was able to act as spokesman for the besiegers and as leader in breaking faith with the besieged.[113] Knights played a leading part in the storming of the castle, but,

[100] *Ibid.*, c. 11.
[101] *Ibid.*, c. 16.
[102] *Ibid.*, c. 29.
[103] *Ibid.*, c. 58.
[104] *Ibid.*, c. 54.
[105] *Ibid.*, c. 11.
[106] MGH, SS XXV, 442.
[107] Galbert, c. 36.
[108] *Ibid.*, c. 81.
[109] *Ibid.*, c. 37.
[110] *Ibid.*, c. 36.
[111] *Ibid.*, c. 37.
[112] *Ibid.*, c. 54, 100, 104.
[113] *Ibid.*, c. 38.

once inside, competition among themselves for honors and spoils, and rivalry with the citizens for booty, absorbed their attention.[114] The lure of treasure and loot seemed to Galbert the driving motive.[115] Count William, dependent on their support, soon found the knights turning against him when he remitted to the burghers the tolls with which the knights were enfeoffed.[116] The disciplined force of Count William's knights prevailed over Thierry's mixed army of knights and townsmen in the battle of Axspoele, and they followed up their victory by seizing the burghers who tried to pick up their dead.[117] Many knights shifted sides as they saw Thierry gaining ground.[118]

As for the so-called "knight-serfs" or ministerials, it is difficult to tell whether there actually was such a class in Flemish society. Since the chief evidence for their existence seems to be the alleged servile origin of the high-placed Erembald clan, their case may well be a rare or even unique phenomenon, rather than a type.[119] Their motive for the murder was personal survival. Although Galbert refers to them frequently as *servi*, they had nothing in common with the other *servi* and *servientes*,[120] who were apparently household servants and represented as simply obeying their masters' orders even though murder was involved.

The agrarian workers, never called "serfs" by Galbert but always "rustics" or country-dwellers[121] as opposed to townspeople or "castle people," appear only as sufferers and victims of military aggression. It is impossible to tell exactly what their status was; to Galbert, at any rate, what matters is the kind of life they led. Less articulate than burghers or clergy, and without the strength of association enjoyed by those groups, their voices are rarely heard. It is remarkable, therefore, that two hundred of them dared to come to the count's court at Ypres to protest against the injuries they had suffered during the private war

[114] *Ibid.*, c. 40, 45, 46.
[115] *Ibid.*, c. 41, 63, 75.
[116] *Ibid.*, c. 88.
[117] *Ibid.*, c. 114.
[118] *Ibid.*, c. 101.
[119] See c. 7, n. 10 in the text.
[120] Galbert, c. 11, 29, 30.
[121] *Rustici* generally; *ibid.*, c. 10, 55, 110, 112.

between the two clans, but they came "secretly and by night," even to their protector, the count.[122] "No one in the country was secure" during the "civil war" of 1128; all fled to the woods or towns for refuge.[123]

Dependent upon the counts' protection, like the burghers and peasants, and long inured to their firm control, the clergy (with one notable exception) were not apparently implicated in the plot against Count Charles, "advocate of the churches of God."[124] The upper clergy barely appear in the events of 1127-28. Simon, bishop of Noyon, it is true, at once excommunicates the murderers of his brother-in-law,[125] and he comes later to perform the final funeral rites, together with three abbots whom Galbert does not even name.[126] The abbot of Saint Peter's in Ghent tries but fails, despite the aid of Bertulf, to get hold of the martyred count's body.[127] Only the castral clergy of Bruges are important actors in the events. Their loyalty to the count and dependence upon him are revealed in the plight of the clerics and chaplains hiding just after the murder in the sanctuary of Saint Donatian from the bloodthirsty nephews of the provost.[128] Though subordinate to the provost in their functions, they are clearly the count's men, not his. The canons proper seem to be a more independent and fearless lot in their dealings with the provost and his nephews after the murder,[129] and the provost finds it necessary to offer excuses to them.[130] But the dean, Helias, proves to be a tool of the provost, rewarded with 300 marks for his services[131] while several other canons also profited from the count's treasure.[132] And the canons, like the burghers, use the crisis following the murder to secure for themselves sworn con-

[122] *Ibid.*, c. 10.
[123] *Ibid.*, c. 112.
[124] *Ibid.*, c. 6. It was the clergy, monks, peasants and poor who mourned the count, according to Walter, c. 43.
[125] *Ibid.*, c. 21.
[126] *Ibid.*, c. 77.
[127] *Ibid.*, c. 22.
[128] *Ibid.*, c. 18.
[129] *Ibid.*, c. 21, 22, 35.
[130] *Ibid.*, c. 20.
[131] *Ibid.*, c. 83.
[132] *Ibid.*, c. 85.

firmation and possibly some extension of their privileges from the king and Count William in 1127[133] and similar guarantees from Thierry of Alsace before receiving him formally as count in 1128.[134] Their primary concern is for the church of Saint Donatian, the confirmation of the liberties of its chapter, the preservation and restoration of its structure,[135] and the honoring of its precious new martyr.[136]

It is true that the archvillain Bertulf, as provost of Bruges, was one of the highest ecclesiastics in the land, and that it was his fear of losing his office at the Easter Court which probably precipitated the murder.[137] But his real power, which the count was trying to undermine, sprang not from his spiritual or ecclesiastical functions but from his dual administrative role as chancellor of the realm and receiver of the domanial revenues. For him, the plot was a desperate effort to save his whole clan from social abasement and ruin. What he intended to do after the murder is not clear. His first efforts to gain supporters outside Bruges seem impromptu,[138] rather than well planned. Although William of Ypres was ready to act as his partner in a new régime, the support he had apparently expected from the barons fails him, and they seize the initiative by becoming avengers, filling the vacuum of authority which he had hoped to use to his own advantage.

The question "why" the count was slain, therefore, is highly complex and answers are multiple. The motives of persons and groups in supporting the Erembald clan before or after the murder must be analyzed largely in terms of what they actually did during and after the murder and in the light of what certain contemporaries, writing soon after the murder, believed to have been the causes of the plot. It was natural for the latter to stress personalities rather than processes, but both must be considered. The dynamic forces of change in Flemish society had generated

[133] *Ibid.,* c. 55.
[134] *Ibid.,* c. 103.
[135] *Ibid.,* c. 22, 64.
[136] *Ibid.,* c. 77.
[137] *Ibid.,* c. 19.
[138] *Ibid.,* c. 21, 25.

a kind of obscure triangular struggle between a stern, just ruler determined to exert effective control, the older "vested interests" of the baronage resolved to affirm and extend their own power, and emergent elements on the fringes of the established order, living under new economic and social conditions and determined to acquire a recognized place for themselves within the old framework.[139]

The structure of Flemish society was not yet sufficiently firm to endure such stresses and strains without collapse under the impact of sudden crisis but the Flemish people proved resourceful in evolving new forms of solidarity. As we see the social order in motion through Galbert's eyes, it is not a clear-cut hierarchy of homogeneous orders but rather a confused agglomeration of groups and persons in shifting relations to one another.[140] Self-interest often prevails over sense of class. Social distinctions do not preclude association and joint effort. Knights and barons form sworn compacts with each other but also with burghers. The burghers of Bruges enter into a succession of sworn compacts. They agitate together with canons, receive knights like brothers and fight alongside them. Serfs and knights act together as murderers. Intermarriage between knightly and burgher classes seems commonplace.[141] In Flanders, "la réalité, surtout sociale et économique, se rit de la symétrie."[142]

In this crisis the customary social bonds proved to be both unreliable and variable. The most primitive bond, blood kinship, was still potent: consider Bertulf's aggrandizement of his clan and Hacket's reluctant loyalty to his guilty nephews.[143] The feud between the Erembald clan and Thancmar's clan bears the mark of a *faida*[144] as well as of private feudal warfare. But the bond of blood failed to ensure solidarity among the Erembald

---

[139] See J. Dhondt, "Petit-Dutaillis et les communes françaises," *Annales,* VII (1952), 381.

[140] See Marc Bloch, "Un Problème d'histoire comparée," RHDF, VII (1928), 79-80.

[141] Galbert, c. 59.

[142] Perroy, "Les Origines urbaines," RN, XXIX, 58.

[143] Galbert, c. 38.

[144] See Marc Bloch, *La Société féodale: la formation des liens de dépendance,* (Paris, 1939), pp. 195-203.

clan immediately following the murder,[145] or even loyalty among the besieged in their desperate plight.[146] The tie of vassalage, which may have evolved because of the very inadequacies of the kinship bond,[147] reveals its own contradictions in Galbert's account. In fact, treachery, not fealty towards one's lord, whether king, count, baron, or knight, pervades the whole crisis of 1127-28 "like a stench," as one chronicler says.[148]

Homage and fealty, moreover, are not restricted to the establishment of bonds between members of the noble class in Flemish society. Generally accompanied in Flanders by a special pledge of "loyalty," [149] these acts are widely used in the crisis of 1127 to bind non-noble individuals and groups of such persons, merchants and burghers, to members of the noble class, sometimes forcibly, as in the case of the homage of merchants at Ypres to William of Ypres,[150] but for the most part voluntarily, as for example the homage of groups of burghers or their representatives to Count William and later to Count Thierry.[151] Whether this practice represents a resort, in moments of crisis, to the form of feudal usage as the most binding link between men or whether it marks a resurgence in current feudal "disguise" of something essentially different, "territorial allegiance," once due a ruler from all his subjects and now re-emerging in western Europe,[152] is not clear. It was probably not a customary procedure, despite Galbert's efforts to represent it as such,[153] but it was not unique[154] in Europe at this time, and it confirms the general

[145] Galbert, for example, c. 29, 103.

[146] *Ibid.*, c. 29, 42, 54, 61.

[147] According to Bloch, *La Société féodale: la formation*, p. 221, but this has been challenged, for example, by R. Boutruche; see *IXe Congrès International des sciences historiques: I, Rapports*, 445.

[148] Simon, *Gesta abbatum S. Bertiniani*, A. 1127, lib. II, c. 117, MGH, SS XIII, 658.

[149] *Securitas;* see Galbert, c. 1, n. 6 and F. L. Ganshof, *Qu'est-ce que la féodalité?* (3d ed. rev.; Brussels, 1957), pp. 115-16.

[150] Galbert, c. 20, 25.

[151] *Ibid.*, c. 54, 55, 66, 102, 103; see also c. 94 where homage is done by burghers to the pretender Arnold.

[152] The latter view is held by W. Kienast, *Untertaneneid und Treuvorbehalt in Frankreich und England* (Weimar, 1952), p. 23, n. 4. He believes that only the leaders among the burghers in Flanders actually took the oath.

[153] Galbert, c. 54.

[154] See Kienast, *Untertaneneid*, p. 23, n. 4, for other examples; and the comments

impression of a mobile society. It is noteworthy that in 1127-28
in Flanders this bond is no more honored than the feudal bond
between equals when interest conflicts with loyalty.

Even more striking in Galbert's account is the use of the oath,
without mention of homage or fealty,[155] to create binding agreements between all manner of men. The plotters, both kinsmen
and outsiders, solemnly form a sworn pact, sealed by their right
hands.[156] The burghers of Bruges enter into a bewildering succession of sworn agreements for specific purposes: with Gervaise
and his knights,[157] with the barons of the siege,[158] with the burghers of Ghent,[159] with representatives of the castellany,[160] with
maritime Flemings,[161] with individual knights who join their
side;[162] and similarly the burghers of Ghent form a compact with
the peers Ivan and Daniel.[163] At times it looks as if an order of
townsmen were emerging, but other elements are also involved.[164]
Similarly the barons form sworn associations among themselves[165]
and with burghers. And some form of sworn relationship is also
used to bind individuals, such as Walter the butler to the
provost[166] and William of Ypres to the traitors.[167]

The use of the oath is extended in remarkable ways after the
murder, by the barons to bind the king of France to respect his
pledges to them, and by the burghers to bind both king and count
to honor the privileges they had won from them, even in violation

---

of Marc Bloch, "Un Problème d'histoire comparée," RHDF, VII (1928), 56-57,
to the effect that "homage" long maintained "une signification extrêmement générale; il s'entendait de toute relation de dépendance...."

[155] The formula used above is generally triple—*fides, securitas, hominium*—with
considerable variation in order and occasional omission of one element. In the
following cases a great variety of mixed expressions is used, generally some form
of *conjurare*, or *jurare*, or *taxare* with or without *fides, compositio, juramentum,
amicitia, securitas*.

[156] Galbert, c. 11: *conjurare* and with *fides* and *taxatio*.
[157] *Ibid.*, c. 27, 28, 59, 98.
[158] *Ibid.*, c. 31.
[159] *Ibid.*, c. 33, 53.
[160] *Ibid.*, c. 51, 52, 53.
[161] *Ibid.*, c. 97; these may be the same as the above.
[162] *Ibid.*, c. 98.
[163] *Ibid.*, c. 95, 98.
[164] See the comments of J. Dhondt, *Les Origines des États*, pp. 16-17.
[165] Galbert, c. 34, 85.
[166] *Ibid.*, c. 21.
[167] *Ibid.*, c. 25.

of the rights of others.[168] It becomes clear to the student of
Galbert that the oath, "which makes Heaven and Hell guarantors
of one's loyalty,"[169] was, despite its frequent violation, the most
potent link in Flemish society at this time, and that in times of
need it could be adapted and extended in a variety of ways.

The plot against the count appears to be, as far as one can see,
a logical outcome of discontent and tension in Flemish society,
and the murder in which it culminated the desperate act of a
powerful clan whose position, challenged by the count, had become untenable. The prolonged crisis of 1127-28 laid bare the
desires of all groups and persons. Although it shook Flemish
society to its foundations, it led at the same time to the spontaneous development of new forms of cohesion in the social
order, the emergence of large groups, both homogeneous and
heterogeneous, bound by oath. At first separately and then in
shifting combinations, burghers and barons became self-consti-
tuted spokesmen, not only of class or local interests but of the
larger community of Flanders, claiming in theory and action the
right to be concerned with a matter vital to all, the choice of a
new count. And even more revolutionary claims were eventually
made by the burghers. But the new sense of community and
solidarity, so vigorously expressed, especially by the burghers,
was not strong enough to prevent the outbreak of civil war between rivals for the countship in which each received mixed
support from knights and townsmen. It is clear that Flemish
unity was still dependent upon loyalty to a generally accepted
ruler who could exert an effective control over all elements of
the population.

[168] *Ibid.*, c. 52, 55, 65, 106; see the comments of Ganshof, "Le Roi de France
en Flandre," RHDF, XXVII (1949), 213-14, 220-21.

[169] J. Dhondt, *Les Origines des États,* p. 19. In his latest penetrating analysis of
Flemish society at this moment of transition, based largely on Galbert's evidence,
Professor Dhondt finds the basis in self-conscious collectivities characterized by
relative permanence and cohesion, or *solidarités.* He identities five of these, noting
their similarities and distinctive qualities: the *potentia* or effective following of a
baron or powerful knight; the urban community, often including elements in addition to the burghers; the family or lineage; the heterogeneous regional solidarity;
and the more ephemeral league of the barons. He notes that each of these "solidarités" is bound together by oath, whether general and all-inclusive in nature, or
limited to a particular objective. See "Les Solidarités médiévales," *Annales,* XII
(1957), 529-60.

[IV] *How?*

> *"Oh what a frightful, savage death!*
> *Like Judas you betrayed your own Lord!*
> *The stars in heaven shudder at such an abominable crime!"*

To Galbert and his contemporaries the murder of the count seemed monstrous, not so much because it was an act of violence as because the victim was slain by his own vassals, and was killed in church during the holy time of Lent while prostrate in prayer and in the act of almsgiving. The murderers are not only "traitors" but "impious ones, full of the devil."[1] No known form of punishment was considered harsh enough for those guilty of such a crime; they must be reserved for a fate "heretofore unheard of,"[2] which proves to be precipitation from a high tower, a fall of symbolic meaning for Galbert.[3] This had probably been agreed upon in advance by the king, new count, and barons, and no form of trial was permitted those who finally surrendered, although certainly not all of them were guilty of murder.[4] The chief culprits, captured as they fled, suffered death by "lynch law," tortured and exterminated by mobs in the same spirit of brutality which they had shown in murdering the count and his friends.[5] The original murder thus unleashed as well as expressed the violence latent in Flemish society, and its aftermath throws light on the tenor of life in a period and place of accelerated change.

Life in Flanders was insecure at best, even under a strong and just prince. The unpredictable forces of nature as well as the ill-suppressed passions of men created an atmosphere of "perpetual precariousness,"[6] and an insensibility to human suffering. Great inundations of the sea had occurred four times in the

---

[1] In his day-by-day account Galbert usually calls them "traitors" (*traditores* or *perfidi*), or "wretches" (*pessimi*), or "serfs" (*servi*). Only in the introductory chapters, added later, does he call them "foul dogs, full of the devil." On the conception of treason at this time see Van Caenegem, *Geschiedenis van het strafrecht*, pp. 81-83.

[2] Galbert, c. 6, 52.

[3] *Ibid.*, c. 71, 81.

[4] *Ibid.*, c. 81; Walter, c. 50.

[5] Galbert, c. 57, 84.

[6] Bloch, *La Société féodale: la formation des liens de dépendance*, p. 117.

eleventh century,[7] despite progressive dessication of the maritime plain and intensified construction of dikes, and the threat was always present. More serious and disturbing for Flanders in the early twelfth century was the recurrence of spells of inclement weather, the worst falling in the period from 1124 to 1126, marked like most by a succession of hard, snowy winters and cold, rainy summers, bringing famine in its wake.[8] Few chroniclers connect this dreadful famine with its natural causes,[9] and several like Galbert interpret it as an act of divine wrath, coming after the celestial warning of an eclipse.[10] Only the extraordinary measures of control taken by Count Charles to check hoarding, inflation, and speculation, and his benevolence to the poor, saved the land from catastrophe.[11] There were still considerable crowds of beggars in Bruges in 1127.[12]

Fire was obviously another ever present danger, especially in the close quarters of the towns where, as at Bruges, the construction was still mostly of wood.[13] Victims of disease, as well as cripples, formed part of the crowd which sought the healing power of the count's blood immediately after the crime.[14] Neither the counts nor the clergy could deal adequately with the impact of natural disasters, although their joint and separate efforts could curb to some extent the violence of men towards each other.

The "great current towards peace"[15] in western Europe, initiated by the Church in the late tenth century and strongly supported by the counts of Flanders, was primarily an attempt to protect the defenseless members of society from their avowed

[7] *Annales Blandinienses,* A. 1003, 1013, 1042, 1094, MGH, SS V, 25-27; on the changing character of the maritime plain, see Blanchard, *La Flandre,* pp. 157-70, and Gottschalk, *Historische geografie,* pp. 212-14.

[8] See F. Curschmann, *Hungersnöte im Mittelalter* (Leipzig, 1900), especially pp. 82 ff., 132 ff.

[9] The most interesting exception is *Anselmi continuatio Sigeberti,* A. 1124, 1125, MGH, SS VI, 379.

[10] Galbert, c. 2.

[11] Walter, c. 11; Galbert, c. 3.

[12] Galbert, c. 22.

[13] Note the references to burning houses in Galbert, c. 28, 35.

[14] Galbert, c. 22; Walter, c. 31.

[15] J. Dhondt, "Petit-Dutaillis et les communes françaises," *Annales,* VII (1952), 383.

defenders, the military class. But even the peasants of maritime Flanders, toughened by their arduous existence and made more independent by their privileged agrarian status, were likened to "Scythians" by a contemporary.[16] In 1071 Robert the Frisian had found here supporters for his treachery, but they in turn proved to be traitors[17] and even he could not quell the anarchy in the Island of Walcheren.[18] Walter of Therouanne claims that Count Charles at last tamed this region,[19] but it is noteworthy that the Erembald clan were originally "men of Veurne,"[20] and that they still exercised great influence in this area.[21]

But lawlessness was widespread throughout Flanders, and the chief offenders were the knights whom Church and count strove jointly and separately to control. As early as 1030 Count Baldwin IV, at Oudenaarde, in the presence of bishops, abbots, and barons of the whole realm, "caused the peace to be sworn by all the people."[22] Far more explicit was the Truce of God proclaimed in 1063 by Baldwin V and Drogo, bishop of Therouanne, prescribing peace for all persons and places from Wednesday night to Monday dawn of each week.[23] Robert the Frisian in 1092 took an oath to respect a peace of God recently proclaimed at the Council of Soissons.[24] The intestine wars that broke out in his absence[25] must have led Robert II, on his return from the First Crusade, to join with Manasses II, archbishop of Rheims, and his suffragan bishops in proclaiming a new peace at Saint Omer in 1099.[26]

[16] Hariulf, *Vita Arnulfi*, c. 17, MGH, SS XV², p. 889. The brutal treatment of the Griselda-like Saint Godeliva by her husband and his household confirms this impression; see M. Coens, "La vie ancienne de Sainte Godelive de Ghistelles par Drogon de Bergues," *Analecta Bollandiana*, XLIV (1926), 102-37.

[17] Galbert, c. 69, 70.

[18] Theofrid, abbot of Echternach, was a more successful pacifier of the island, according to his own testimony in the *Vita S. Willibrordi*, c. 36, MGH, SS XXIII, 28.

[19] Walter, c. 12.

[20] Galbert, c. 71.

[21] *Ibid.*, c. 25, 108.

[22] *Auctarium Affligemense*, A. 1030, MGH, SS VI, 399.

[23] "Treuga Dei dioecesis Tervanensis," MGH, Leges Sectio IV, I, 599-601.

[24] M. Sdralek, *Wolfenbüttler Fragmente* (Münster, 1891), p. 140.

[25] See *Miraculi S. Donatiani*, A. 1096, MGH, SS XV², 858, concerning disorders in Bruges where the provost (Bertulf presumably) used the relics of the saint to pacify the people.

[26] G. D. Mansi, *Sacrorum conciliorum nova et amplissima collectio*, Vol. XX,

The repetition of these acts reveals the urgent need for more effective sanctions on the part of both Church and count. The Church in Flanders made good use of spectacular perambulations to inspire "pacifications" or "reconciliations" among the fighting class, such as the procession of the bones of Saint Ursmar in 1060, and the journey of the living Saint Arnulf in 1084. At Oostburg in Zeeland, for example, such a "tempest of enmities" prevailed among four hundred knights that "no one dared to leave his house," and they were paralyzed by their own "accumulation of vengeance" until the potent relics of Saint Ursmar induced them to throw away their arms and exchange the kiss of peace.[27] The nobles themselves begged Arnulf, "the man of God," to visit Flanders where daily homicide troubled the land.[28] At Bruges and Aardenburg he found such a "madness of killing" that a peaceful day was considered lost and shameful. Father did not spare son, or son his father, brother slew brother, and nephew his uncle. The success of Arnulf's tour in 1084 was evaluated in monetary terms by an inquest ordered by Robert the Frisian. It was computed, on the basis of the numbers murdered in and around Bruges, that more than ten thousand marks of silver would have been needed to achieve by "composition" what the saint had done by prayer![29] Solemn rites of "reconciliation" were enacted by the warrior class, including oath and kiss, often marked by the name and form of homage, sometimes in highly emotional scenes.[30] And woe to those who resisted the saintly efforts, such as a hardhearted rich widow at Veurne, whose house and person were suddenly destroyed by a great wind after she

cols. 969-71. In substance and character this was a renewal of the Peace of Saint Médard of Soissons (between 1083 and 1092), instituted by Raynaud, the previous archbishop of Rheims, which was designed primarily to protect the clergy and the property of the Church and was completely under episcopal control. Count Robert's acceptance of this kind of peace is explained in terms of his political needs by R. Bonnaud-Delamare, "La Paix en Flandre pendant la première croisade," RN, XXXIX (1957), 149.

[27] *Miraculi S. Ursmari*, c. 12, MGH, SS XV[2], 840.
[28] Hariulf, *Vita Arnulfi*, lib. II, c. 14, MGH, SS XV[2], 887-88.
[29] *Ibid.*, lib. II, c. 19, p. 890.
[30] See for example *Miraculi S. Ursmari*, c. 16, pp. 840-41. A full discussion of the institution of "reconciliation" is given by Van Caenegem, *Geschiedenis van het strafrecht*, pp. 280-307.

had scoffed at Saint Arnulf and refused him admission.[31] Sometimes the knights, finding their own anarchy intolerable, sought security in the shelter of a great abbey and its relics, such as Saint Trond,[32] or a more lasting peace in the monastic life. In 1083, for example, six knights sought out the scene of their former brigandage against "merchants and pilgrims" and founded the monastery of Affligem, where they were soon joined by others guilty of homicide.[33]

The counts meanwhile dealt with the problem of peace in their own autocratic and original ways by direct action against malefactors. Robert the Frisian intervened in person when a knight "whom he loved like a son" violated the peace of the fair at Torhout in 1084,[34] and Robert II recaptured the initiative from the Church by issuing his own "peace" for "his whole land" in 1111, prescribing that noble violators should purge themselves by the oath of twelve peers, and others similarly.[35] The most celebrated enforcer of the peace, however, was Charles's predecessor, Baldwin VII,[36] who despite his youth soon made his will felt by "boiling in a kettle" a knight, in full armor, who had robbed a poor woman of two cows,[37] and by arranging ingeniously to have nine of ten knights who had violated the peace of the fair at Torhout hang each other in succession; he himself assisted the last victim by kicking out the stool on which he stood.[38] A general peace was probably confirmed by oath at Saint Omer in 1114.[39] The concern of Count Charles for peace and his early success are attested by the sources,[40] but his more legalistic

[31] *Vita Arnulfi*, c. 19, pp. 889-90.

[32] Rudolf, *Gesta abbatum Trudonensium*, lib. I, c. 10, MGH, SS X, 234.

[33] *Chronicon Affligemense*, c. 2, 1083, MGH, SS IX, 408.

[34] *Vita Arnulfi*, lib. II, c. 16, MGH. SS XV², 888-89.

[35] *Actes*, no. 49, pp. 125-26. In contrast to the Peace of Saint Omer, this peace renewed not the ecclesiastical peace of Saint Médard, but the more secular peace of 1063 which was concerned with the protection of all inhabitants and was under the count's control. See Bonnaud-Delamare, "La Paix en Flandre," RN, XXXIX, 152.

[36] He may also have issued his own "peace" in 1111, soon after his accession; see *Actes*, no. 53 (suspect), pp. 133-34; see also Herman, c. 21.

[37] Herman, c. 22; see also c. 23.

[38] *Ibid.*, c. 24.

[39] *Actes*, "Actes supposés," no. 18, p. xxxviii.

[40] Galbert, c. 1; Walter, c. 12, 19.

approach was obviously less effective; the outburst of violence
in the murder itself and during its aftermath reveals the persistence of lawlessness.[41] The insistence of the burghers of Saint
Omer, and probably of Ghent, on the inclusion of a pledge of
peace in their charters in 1127 indicates the still urgent need.[42]

The whole text of Galbert is, in effect, a commentary on the
violence of the age and the insecurity of life. In the collapse of
the social order following the murder, no class of society is
guiltless of violence or immune to its effects, though the knights
are the worst offenders and the peasants the chief victims. During
the civil war, Count William set fire to a church where his
enemies had fled,[43] and either he[44] or Baldwin of Mons burned
the town at Oudenaarde, where as many as three hundred persons[45] were cremated in a church. His forces devastated a
monastic cell so completely that neither book nor chalice remained.[46] But fighting and pillaging were not the monopoly of
the knightly class. Communal forces of burghers and bands of
burghers and artisans participate in all warlike operations, sieges
and open battles,[47] and compete with knights for the spoils.[48]
The captors of the traitors, from the king down, torture the
leading culprits, Isaac, Bertulf, and Robert, to extort information
about the count's treasure.[49] As the traitors and their supporters
are seized they are killed summarily without trial, by burning,[50]
hanging,[51] decapitation,[52] breaking on the wheel,[53] drowning,[54]

---

[41] Even in 1142 Pope Innocent II was "stupified" by Herman of Tournai's report
on the number of homicides in the diocese of Noyon-Tournai; the figures were
doubtless exaggerated, however; see Herman, *Historiae Tornacenses*, lib. IV, c. 5,
MGH, SS XIV, 343-44.

[42] F. L. Ganshof, "Le Droit urbain," RHD, XIX (1951), 393-94.

[43] Galbert, c. 111; see also c. 97.

[44] *Ibid.*, c. 80.

[45] Herman, c. 33, says "more than a hundred."

[46] Galbert, c. 116.

[47] See for example, Galbert, c. 33, 59, 72, 98.

[48] For example, Galbert, c. 30, 41, 45, 120.

[49] *Ibid.*, c. 39, 57, 61.

[50] *Ibid.*, c. 56.

[51] *Ibid.*, c. 29, 57, 84. Death by hanging, inflicted on thieves and brigands, was
regarded as the most shameful punishment of all. See below, n. 54.

[52] *Ibid.*, c. 41, 84.

[53] *Ibid.*, c. 77, 80.

[54] *Ibid.*, c. 29, 41; Walter, c. 33. These recognized forms of punishment, mostly
Germanic in origin, could be legally carried out by popular action, however, because

or precipitation.[55] Only one of the accused is permitted to purge himself by the ordeal of hot iron.[56] In the period of defeatism in May, 1128, one "sorceress" is burned, another eviscerated.[57] The humane efforts of women to care for the wounded or dying are frustrated by men.[58]

Because of the very nature of his subject, Galbert pays little attention to those civilizing currents in Flemish society which were gradually creating "islands of peace" in this turbulent area and deflecting the energies of at least some men into peaceful channels. The self-assertion of the burghers and the creation of an urban way of life dependent upon peace were, of course, the most pacifying influences in the long run, but the events of 1127-28 plunged these communities into war and struggle. There is no evidence yet of the chivalric ideal or of the courtly way of life, with its cult of women and its softening effect upon the manners and customs of the knightly class. In fact, women hardly appear, and when they do they are nameless creatures, engaged in their perennial functions of caring for the dying[59] and mourning the dead[60] or used by their male relatives to advance their fortunes.[61] No women of the dynasty enter the scene, except the Countess of Holland in support of first one candidate and then another.[62] Charles's wife never appears. The

---

the victims had been proscribed, that is, placed outside the law (Galbert, c. 52). See the discussion of each form by Van Caenegem, *Geschiedenis van het strafrecht,* pp. 137 ff., and his interpretation of mass participation as partly a persistence of Germanic ritualistic elements, pp. 171-74.

[55] Galbert, c. 81. This, unlike the others, was not a recognized form of punishment in Flanders. Since it was known as a punishment for treachery in Normandy, however, and was imposed by the king and new count, William Clito of Normandy, it may have been derived from Norman usage, according to Van Caenegem, *Geschiedenis van het strafrecht,* p. 168, n. 3.

[56] Galbert, c. 87, 105.

[57] Burning (c. 110) was the standard punishment for witches and heretics; see Van Caenegem, pp. 162-63. This example of carrying entrails around (c. 112), an old Germanic custom, is a unique instance in Flemish penal law at this time, according to Van Caenegem, pp. 168-69.

[58] Galbert, c. 41, 81.

[59] *Ibid.,* c. 17, 41, 81.

[60] *Ibid.,* c. 21, 114.

[61] *Ibid.,* c. 7, 46, 54.

[62] *Ibid.,* c. 34, 99. But certain women of the dynasty had in the past been persons of influence, recently Clemence, the mother of Baldwin VII. See Introduction, II.

only female personality revealed is the sly wife of Walter the butler, who successfully deceived her husband.[63]

Nor does Galbert give his reader any sense of the growing intensity of religious feeling and its varied expression in his time. The continuing influence of the great Benedictine abbeys could hardly be grasped from the single appearance of the abbot of Saint Peter's at Ghent.[64] Nothing reveals the current of monastic reform inspired by Cluny, radiating from Saint Bertin in Flanders under the fervent leadership of Abbot Lambert (d. 1123), which was bringing about the widespread introduction of Cluniac customs, if not the incorporation of houses into the Cluniac system, a step which was firmly resisted by the counts.[65] There is no evidence here of the current reform of chapters of secular clergy by the saintly bishop of Therouanne, John of Warneton (d. 1130).[66] No reference is made to the travels of Saint Norbert, his effective preaching against the heretic followers of Tanchelm at Antwerp, and the foundation of new houses of Norbertines or Premonstratensians.[67] There is no echo of "the pestilential heresy" of Tanchelm[68] who was identified with Flanders by Abelard, and who may have been a notary of the counts of Flanders.[69]

The only aspects of religious life reflected by Galbert are naturally those manifested within the narrow confines of "our place," the castle and town of Bruges, as revealed in the life of the unreformed chapter of Saint Donatian, in the practices of the local clergy, and in demonstrations of popular piety. The most striking factor is the cult of saints, old and new, and the veneration of their relics. Clergy and burghers act as one in safeguarding the wonder-working body of Count Charles,[70] and when after seven weeks it is disinterred for solemn burial it is found

---

[63] *Ibid.,* c. 89. A whore was present in the church with the besieged, c. 35.

[64] *Ibid.,* c. 21, 22.

[65] See E. Sabbe, "La Réforme clunisienne dans le comté de Flandre au début du XIIe siècle," RB, IX (1930), 121-38; and Moreau, *Histoire de l'Église,* II, 177-93.

[66] Moreau, *Histoire de l'Église,* II, 110-14.

[67] *Ibid.,* III, 439-50.

[68] *Ibid.,* II, 415-25.

[69] Pirenne, "Tanchelin et le projet de démembrement du diocèse d'Utrecht vers 1110," *Bulletin de la classe des lettres de l'Académie royale de Belgique,* 5th ser., XIII (1927), 112-19.

[70] Galbert, c. 22, 43.

to be whole and sweet.[71] This spontaneous recognition of a new "saint" is not unique; Saint Godeliva in 1084 and Saint Arnulf in 1121 were officially recognized by the elevation of their relics.[72] The relics of the local patron saints at Bruges, Saints Donatian, Basil, and Maximus, were so precious that hostilities were suspended as they were reverently removed from the castle,[73] and they were present at all important public acts.[74]

Popular respect for established religious observances is shown in the general suspension of hostilities by both sides on Sunday,[75] by the importance attributed to penitence and confession before death both by the victims of the traitors[76] and by the traitors themselves,[77] by the observance of fasting in Lent and on Holy Days,[78] by acts of public penance by the whole community in the dark days of June and July, 1128,[79] and in many other ways. Even the impious traitors receive the Eucharist on Easter from an unknown priest[80] and place the customary four candles at the bier of the count whom they have just slain,[81] but as excommunicates they are denied holy burial.[82]

Belief in divine warnings is seen in the interpretation of unusual happenings as signs and portents, as, for example, the eclipse and famine of 1124.[83] Bloody water foretells bloodshed,[84] and falling timbers approaching doom.[85] The

---

[71] *Ibid.*, c. 77.

[72] Moreau, *Histoire de l'Église*, II, 394, 437.

[73] Galbert, c. 35.

[74] *Ibid.*, c. 55, 77, 103, 114. A list drawn up *ca.* 1300 reveals the extent and variety of the relics contained in Saint Donatian; see "Catalogue des reliques conservées à l'Église Saint-Donatien à Bruges au XIIIe siècle," *Le Beffroi*, IV (1872-1873), 199-202.

[75] Galbert, c. 33, 47.

[76] *Ibid.*, c. 16, 18.

[77] *Ibid.*, c. 57, 84.

[78] *Ibid.*, c. 2, 118.

[79] *Ibid.*, c. 114, 118.

[80] *Ibid.*, c. 54.

[81] *Ibid.*, c. 21.

[82] *Ibid.*, c. 84.

[83] *Ibid.*, c. 2. For a general discussion of this aspect of medieval mentality in the eleventh and twelfth centuries see P. Rousset, "Le Sens du merveilleux à l'époque féodale," *Le Moyen Âge*, LXII (1956), 25-38.

[84] Galbert, c. 14.

[85] *Ibid.*, c. 84, 102.

spontaneous elevation of a cross is interpreted as a warning.[86]

Galbert's focus upon Bruges, and upon the brief time-span of
the events he relates, probably accounts for his failure to reveal
either the major currents of the religious expression of his time
or its intellectual vitality. Being neither a monastic nor an
episcopal center, Bruges had no school renowned for its masters
to attract students from afar in this age of wandering scholars.
The school of the chapter, located next to the castral church,[87]
doubtless trained boys for the clerical life, perhaps to be canons.[88]
Its master was probably that "Master Ralph" who shared in the
count's treasure;[89] he may have been the author of the official
epitaph prepared for the new tomb of the count.[90]

The bright boys of Bruges could, however, find instruction
elsewhere, "far away in France," either in the liberal arts and
sacred learning at the celebrated cathedral school of Laon, under
the learned Anselm (d. 1117), so much maligned by Abelard, or
his brother Ralph (d. 1133),[91] or elsewhere in a useful acquisition of the French language.[92] Closer at hand the Flemish boys
could have gained the benefit of "Gallican studies" in the cathedral school of Tournai, from the teaching of Master Odo, native
of Orléans, who taught his eager disciples in the cloister or on
the steps of the church at night, pointing out the course of the
stars and the signs of the zodiac.[93] Perhaps Galbert's reference
to the increased use of rhetoric in the courts[94] reflects one aspect
of this intellectual ferment, but there is little evidence of intellectual activity in his narrative. The notary Fromold Junior,
however, seems to have been well educated in "grammar," to
judge by the poems or laments for his master's death attributed

[86] *Ibid.*, c. 115.
[87] *Ibid.*, c. 17, 42.
[88] Galbert speaks highly of the education of the canons; see c. 13.
[89] *Ibid.*, c. 85.
[90] According to De Smet, "Bij de latijnsche gedichten," in *Miscellanea ... de Meyer*, I, 434-35; the epitaph is included in the appendix to Pirenne's edition, p. 190.
[91] E. Lesne, *Les Écoles de la fin du VIIIe siècle à la fin du XIIe* (Lille, 1940), pp. 300 ff.
[92] Guibert de Nogent, *De vita sua*, lib. III, c. 5, ed. G. Bourgin (Paris, 1907), 146-47.
[93] Herman, c. 1.
[94] Galbert, c. 1.

to him, which reveal some mastery of classical verse forms.[95] If Galbert actually paraphrased one of the lost laments of his fellow notary,[96] he probably did it to embellish his own "arid style"[97] and meager learning in the arts.

Galbert's admiration for Saint Donatian, which, thanks to his description, is perhaps the best known church of its age in Flanders, gives no insight into the emergent Romanesque style of architecture and sculpture. It was a late Carolingian survival, a central-type church with polygonal core and massive west-work, built in imitation of Charlemagne's tomb-chapel at Aachen.[98] Not until after the damage caused by the siege of 1127 was it substantially rebuilt in the current Romanesque style which it retained until transformed into the Gothic church which was destroyed in 1799.[99] The only art object mentioned by Galbert is of foreign origin, the marvelous silver vessel purchased by the count from Lombard merchants.[100]

[V] *Where?*

> *"Did not Bruges rightly deserve all these misfortunes?"*
> GALBERT, C. 116

"Whom, why, when, where and how did you kill?" To contemporaries like Galbert and Walter the question "when" could be answered simply, in terms of the day and month and season, with special reference to their religious significance. March 2, 1127, fell "in the holy time of Lent,"[1] when bloodshed was

---

[95] De Smet, "Bij de latijnsche gedichten," in *Miscellanea . . . de Meyer*, I, 430-34, 440-43.

[96] Galbert in c. 64, according to De Smet, p. 440.

[97] Galbert, c. 1.

[98] The findings of Dr. J. Mertens have at last made possible the study of the monument itself. See the Appendix.

[99] See B. Firmin, *De romaansche kerkelijke bouwkunst in West-Vlaanderen* (Ghent, 1940), pp. 17-38; R. Lemaire, *De romaanse bouwkunst in de Nederlanden* (Brussels, 1952), p. 152.

[100] Galbert, c. 16.

[1] Galbert, c. 6; Walter, c. 43. This constituted an infraction of the special peace designed to protect holy places and seasons. See Van Caenegem, *Geschiedenis van het strafrecht*, pp. 62-63.

viewed with special horror, and to them this dreadful day should be identified by every possible chronological notation.[2] To the modern student the most significant factor is, of course, the year, 1127, and its place in that century of dynamic growth and change in all fields of human endeavor. "When" is implicit in any analysis of whom and why and how.

Similarly, "where" to Galbert and his contemporaries was answered in immediate and religious terms, "in a sacred place," "before the holy altar";[3] but to later generations the scene must be enlarged and must encompass the castle and town of Bruges. Here the discontents of Flemish society converged and exploded, and here close contact and interaction took place between the groups and persons most affected by the murder.

The stately city of Bruges today, quiet and serene in its late medieval beauty, bears little resemblance to "our town" or "our place"[4] as Galbert saw it in 1127. An agglomeration of small houses and shops, almost encircling the high stone wall of the castle, it must have looked like an excrescence unworthy of that imposing enclosure. Its flimsy dwellings, highly vulnerable to fire, are mentioned only incidentally by Galbert; and only one is referred to specifically.[5] But the ground on which they stood was highly important to the town dwellers, to judge by their demands and gains in the charter of 1127.[6] More substantial dwellings, some of stone and fortified, were located nearby but outside the town,[7] apparently. Doubtless, the churches of the two original urban parishes, Holy Savior and Holy Virgin,[8] were more im-

[2] Galbert, c. 15.

[3] *Ibid.,* c. 6.

[4] *Ibid.,* c. 55, *suburbium nostrum. Locus noster* is more commonly used, however; see for example, c. 22, 25, 55. In c. 98 town and castle are clearly differentiated, *locum et castrum.*

[5] For example, c. 9, 28, 35. The "house of Didier, brother of Isaac," is referred to in c. 28.

[6] The remission of ground-rent; see c. 55.

[7] The three tall houses "towards the east," c. 28; Isaac's "strong house" in c. 29; probably the house "next to the castle" which was burned in c. 113.

[8] Both these churches date from the ninth century, in the opinion of E. I. Strubbe, "De parochies te Brugge voor de XIIᵉ eeuw," *Album English,* 1952, pp. 377-78. The church of the Holy Savior was probably originally a chapel attached to the church of Saint Michael, serving the needs of an agrarian community, according to J. Noterdaeme, "Studiën over de vroegste kerkgeschiedenis van Brugge: II, De fiscus Weinebrugge en de herkomst van St-Salvatorskerk te Brugge," *Sacris Erudiri,*

pressive, although fire had recently injured the former.[9] Two "chapels," Saint Christopher "in the middle of the market"[10] and Saint Peter, both close by the castle gates, appear more frequently in Galbert's narrative,[11] perhaps simply because of their location. But judging by what is known of such early churches, they were all probably small, unadorned stone basilicas with wooden roofs.[12]

The earliest and still most distinctive feature of the town was the open space of the big market, its very *raison d'être,* lying at the entrance to the main castle gate and bridge.[13] Into this market led the main "streets"[14] of the town coming from the west through "the Sands," and from the south, the direction of Ghent. Here stood the gallows where some of the traitors were hanged "in the sight of all";[15] others were drowned in the marshy places of this unpaved area.[16] Here a brother of one of the traitors swore to be faithful to the burghers, in the presence of all.[17] Through this space poured most of the knights and citizens going into and out of the castle. At times it was so full of armed men that it looked to Galbert like a "dense forest of spears."[18]

For solemn meetings of "all the citizens" and their confederates, even the big market was apparently too small, since a larger

---

VII (1955), 131-39. But it is possible that it may not have been built until the eleventh century; see J. Dhondt, "De vroege topografie van Brugge," HMGG, XI (1957), 21-22, 30.

[9] Galbert, c. 78.

[10] *Ibid.,* c. 35. Galbert may mean here the original market of the urban agglomeration, now a small "fish market," and not the "big market" which developed in the eleventh century just to the south, according to Dhondt, "De vroege topografie," HMGG, XI, 25.

[11] Galbert, for example, c. 23, 35, 61, 77; Dhondt ("De vroege topografie," HMGG, XI, 25-30) suggests that these two "chapels" may have been built in the tenth century to meet the spiritual needs of the original urban community which had spread out on both sides of the Reie, and were thus the earliest town churches; and that as the town grew to the south and west it incorporated the already existing parish churches of the Holy Virgin and Holy Savior.

[12] Lemaire, *De romaanse bouwkunst,* pp. 160 ff.

[13] Galbert, c. 28.

[14] *Plateae: ibid.,* c. 28, 41, 109; implied in c. 16, 29.

[15] *Ibid.,* c. 29, 48.

[16] *Ibid.,* c. 29, 41.

[17] *Ibid.,* c. 98.

[18] *Ibid.,* c. 45.

field, "adjacent to the town" was used.[19] Here "in the usual place,"[20] the charters of April, 1127, were read and sworn, and homage to Count William was probably performed;[21] and here again, in 1128, the barons and people "elected" Count Thierry.[22]

Within "our town" lived the mercantile community of "citizens" or "burghers," distinct in their way of life from the country-dwellers and from the castle-dwellers. The very name Bruges, of Old Norse origin, meaning landing-place or quai, first mentioned in 892,[23] implies the economic importance of the site, which is confirmed by a reference to it as a *portus ca.* 1010.[24] By the middle of the eleventh century it was a flourishing port, full of merchants and goods of all kinds, able to load and unload ships at its quais along the left bank of the Reie.[25] It became a well-defined entity, however, only when it was set apart from the open country by an enclosure. The crisis of 1127 led to extensive, if hasty, fortifications,[26] first the construction of a wooden palisade with towers, lookouts, and gates, in imitation of the stone defenses of the castle, and later, in 1128, the addition of a system of ditches.[27] The area enclosed in 1127 has been reckoned at 70 hectares, 25 ares, including the castle and its advanced fortifications of 1 hectare, 50 ares,[28] or about 175 acres. The enclosed space was apparently not all built up,

---

[19] *Ibid.,* c. 51, 52. This field was "the Sands," probably partly enclosed by the town fortifications in 1127; see Dhondt, "De vroege topografie," HMGG, XI, 22-23, 27, and the Plan of Bruges.

[20] Galbert, c. 55.

[21] *Ibid.,* c. 56.

[22] *Ibid.,* c. 102, 103.

[23] See M. Gysseling, "Etymologie van Brugge," *Bulletin de la Commission royale de toponymie et dialectologie,* XVIII (1944), 77-78.

[24] Ganshof, "Iets over Brugge," NH, I, 282 and n. 11.

[25] *Encomium Reginae Emmae,* lib. III, c. 7, MGH, SS XIX, 524; see also Galbert, c. 20, and Ganshof, "Iets over Brugge," NH, I, 283.

[26] Galbert, c. 25. Ganshof ("Iets over Brugge," p. 286) believes that the burghers in 1127 were simply extending and strengthening earlier fortifications, dating at least from 1089. Dhondt suggests that in this age temporary fortifications were probably often constructed; see "De vroege topografie," HMGG, XI, 28.

[27] Galbert, c. 110.

[28] Ganshof, *Étude sur le développement des villes entre Loire et Rhin au moyen âge* (Paris and Brussels, 1943), pp. 45-46. The enclosed area at Ghent has been estimated at 80 hectares, *not* including the castle of about 3 hectares, 75 ares; see pp. 42-43. A hectare equals 100 ares or 10,000 square meters (2.471 acres).

but to Walter it seemed "like a city populous and ample."[29]

Were there hundreds or thousands of adult citizens, merchants and artisans with their families, dwelling within the town? Since no numbers of citizens are given by Galbert, and only two are named,[30] one can only speculate. Bruges had not yet acquired a marked industrial character; its predominantly commercial activities would not demand as many hands as more industrial towns like Ghent. Its four churches, presumably small, could hardly have cared for the spiritual needs of thousands. The concerted action of "all the citizens" in such restricted areas as the church, the court of the castle and the space just outside,[31] and of many citizens and knights in such joint efforts as the storming of the castle and the breaking into the church, again seems to imply hundreds of participants rather than thousands.[32] The same impression is given by such casual items of information as the fact that the mass of citizens could be so quickly informed by their leaders of the pact with Gervaise.[33]

Galbert sharply distinguishes between the dwellers in the town and those in "the castle,"[34] the original settlement on the spot. As early as the middle of the ninth century a stronghold, perhaps only a simple tower, existed at the site of Bruges[35] and also a chapel dedicated to the Virgin, which was soon enriched with the relics of Saint Donatian.[36] Here Baldwin II is known to have found refuge from the Normans in 892. At first only a point of defense and a domanial center, "the castle" grew steadily in size and importance. Stone was brought from Roman ruins at Oudenburg to strengthen its fortifications in the time of Count Arnold II (964-88).[37] The remarkable complex of buildings

[29] Walter, c. 28; Galbert, c. 33, speaks of the "space around the castle."
[30] Galbert, c. 48, names Gerbert, "one of our citizens"; also Lambert Benkin in c. 16.
[31] See, for example, c. 22.
[32] See, for example, c. 41, 45.
[33] *Ibid.*, c. 28.
[34] As, for example, in c. 24 and in c. 98.
[35] G. de Poerck, "Enceintes castrales et urbaines à Bruges," *Mémoires du 1er Congrès International de géographie historique*, II (1931), 83; Dhondt, "De vroege topografie," HMGG, XI, 15.
[36] P. Grierson, "The Translation of the Relics of St. Donatian to Bruges," *Revue Bénédictine*, XLIX (1937), 170-90.
[37] According to the *Tractatus de ecclesia S. Petri Aldenburgensis*, c. 20, MGH,

which Galbert describes probably took shape in the middle of the eleventh century. Under Count Baldwin V (1035-67) the castle at Bruges became the center of one of the new administrative units called castellanies and was endowed with a collegiate chapter of canons.[38] Here the exiled Anglo-Saxon queen, Emma, was entertained in regal style in 1037.[39] By the construction of artificial water courses connecting the Reie and the "Fuller's Stream," the castle enclosure and the adjacent land lying to the north and east had been transformed into a kind of vast "island,"[40] while the castle itself was surrounded by water only on the south and west sides.

By Galbert's time, therefore, "the castle" at Bruges had become a great walled enclosure within an "island," equipped with buildings and inhabited by persons necessary for the performance of its multiple functions as military stronghold, residence of the counts, seat of government, and fiscal as well as ecclesiastical center. Its general appearance[41] can best be gained from the imposing castle of the counts, built in the late twelfth century, which still stands in the heart of Ghent, but the life that animated it can be felt only in Galbert's narrative.

The account of the siege reveals the military strength of the castle, its strong walls[42] with towers[43] and gates so impregnable

SS XV, 872. The recent discovery of the ruins of a Roman fortress at Oudenburg by Dr. J. Mertens confirms this testimony; see the report in the New York *Times* for January 12, 1958.

[38] J. Dhondt, "Note sur les châtelains," in *Études ... Rodière*, p. 48; and "De vroege topografie," HMGG, XI, 16-17.

[39] *Encomium Emmae*, lib. III, c. 7, MGH, SS XIX, 524.

[40] This thesis of G. de Poerck ("Enceintes castrales"), is upheld, with some reinterpretation drawn from Galbert's evidence, by Dhondt, "De vroege topografie," HMGG, XI, 9-10. See the Plan of Bruges.

[41] The information supplied by Galbert serves as a basis for the description of the *castrum* at Bruges by P. Héliot, "Sur les résidences princières bâties en France du Xe au XIIe siècle," *Le Moyen Âge*, LXI (1955), 29-34, and 291-317 *passim*. See the Plan of the Castle.

[42] The height of "60 feet," attributed to the walls by Héliot (*ibid.*, p. 30 and n. 10), is applied by Galbert in c. 40 to the scaling ladders, not the walls. On the problem of the height of the walls which cannot definitely be established, see Dhondt, "De vroege topografie," HMGG, XI, 13-15.

[43] The word *propugnacula*, frequently used by Galbert (for example, c. 25, 29, 32, 37, 40, 43, 64, 81) and generally translated in this version as "towers" or "lookout towers" had varied meanings in the Middle Ages, according to Héliot, "Sur les résidences princières," *Le Moyen Âge*, LXI, 30, and n. 11; he prefers to

to direct attack that it could only be entered by ruse at night.[44] Well stocked with food and drink in its cellars,[45] it could have withstood a much longer siege than ten days (March 9-19) if its defenders had been more vigilant and less defeatist, especially since the castellan, Hacket himself, and knights of the castle were leaders of the defense.

The dominant buildings within the castle walls were "the count's house" and the collegiate church of Saint Donatian, connected with each other by a passage. Favored by the counts among several northern residences,[46] the count's great "hall" or "chamber," as it is sometimes called from its central feature,[47] was a two-storied stone structure[48] with a battlemented tower,[49] adorned with more than one balcony,[50] roofed with wood and equipped with lead gutters.[51] It was entered by stairs[52] from the castle courtyard, or "count's courtyard."[53] Its significance as a symbol of his authority can be seen in the bitter struggle among

interpret it here as "crénelage" or "des hourds en charpente" because Galbert once (c. 81) applies it to the tower of the count's house where the word seems to have one of these two meanings. It seems more likely, however, that Galbert uses this term loosely with reference to various defensive features, both crenellations or towers; he applies it not only to features of the castle walls and count's tower but also to the town fortifications (c. 25), and even to makeshift arrangements in the church (c. 43). In describing the town fortifications he speaks of *turres et propugnacula*. The *propugnacula* of the castle walls were probably "half-towers" which permitted "fighting outside" (see c. 37); such projecting towers, about half the height of the walls, and placed at intervals, are to be seen in the engraving of the walls of the castle at Bruges in Olivarius Vredius, *Historiae comitum Flandriae* (Bruges, 1650), Plate LIV.

[44] Galbert, c. 32, 37, 40, 41.
[45] *Ibid.*, c. 41.
[46] See Vercauteren, *Actes*, p. lxxxiv.
[47] Galbert uses *aula, camera* in c. 38, 74, 81.
[48] *Ibid.*, c. 44. This was the newer house built probably by Baldwin V, not the earlier "Steen" of the tenth century. According to Héliot, "Sur les résidences princières," *Le Moyen Âge*, LXI, 30, the house had recently been reconstructed for the count by Fromold. Galbert's statement (c. 19) seems to mean, rather, that the count had rebuilt the house of his favorite, Fromold.
[49] See Galbert, c. 81. Héliot, "Sur les résidences," p. 31 and n. 18, and p. 295, believes the tower was not a true "donjon" but rather an annex to the house.
[50] See Galbert, c. 29, 44. Héliot, "Sur les résidences," pp. 30-31, believes that *lobium*, here translated as gallery, may mean a *perron*, accessible by the outside wooden stair mentioned in c. 81. It seems doubtful, however, that a *perron* would have been high enough to permit those standing on it to see *over* the castle wall, as the traitors do in c. 29.
[51] Galbert, c. 41.
[52] *Ibid.*
[53] *Ibid.*, c. 37.

the attackers to plant their pennons on its summit,[54] and in Count William's solemn act of taking possession of it,[55] as well as in the decision to precipitate the traitors from its tower.[56]

Here in the great hall,[57] attended daily by his household of domestic officials, chamberlains, butlers,[58] seneschals, and the like, and by his chaplains and servants, the count conferred with his intimate counselors, dined ceremoniously, heard pleaders, received visitors, entertained his guests with wine in the evening.[59] Little privacy was possible.[60] Here on occasion he held his great court, as apparently Count Charles had planned to do at Easter, 1127,[61] for the discussion or determination or formal judgment of important matters.[62] Here he kept his treasure, including such objects as gold and silver goblets and vessels, locked in chests and strong boxes in care of his chamberlains or trusted officials.[63]

But the count's house was more than a residence, well-equipped for living, and a seat of government. Its cellars[64] served as storage place for quantities of basic foods such as grain, meat, wine, and beer,[65] and parts of it were used as a prison[66] and as a place of deposit for all the "iron implements of captivity."[67]

Connected with the count's house by a vaulted stone passage,[68]

[54] *Ibid.*, c. 44.

[55] *Ibid.*, c. 81.

[56] *Ibid.*

[57] On the "first" (upper) floor, above the *rez-de-chaussée*, according to Héliot, "Sur les résidences," p. 300, and of considerable size judging by other contemporary halls, that of Ghent being 22 by 8 meters. Héliot (pp. 305-6) considers this feature to be in the Carolingian tradition.

[58] The only two categories named by Galbert.

[59] See the "count's day" in c. 10.

[60] See Galbert, c. 81, where Count William has to resort to a ruse to empty the house.

[61] *Ibid.*, c. 19.

[62] See Monier, *Les Institutions centrales*, pp. 53-62.

[63] Galbert, c. 20, 41, 61, 83, 85.

[64] Whether the cellars were located in the *rez-de-chaussée* of the count's house or in a different building is uncertain, in the opinion of Héliot, "Sur les résidences," p. 32.

[65] Galbert, c. 41.

[66] *Ibid.*, c. 74, 81.

[67] *Ibid.*, c. 41.

[68] *Ibid.*, c. 41. Concerning the disputed location and character of this passage (*transitus*), see H. Mansion, "À propos de l'ancienne église Saint Donatien à Bruges," RBA, VIII (1938), 111-12; and Héliot, "Sur les résidences," p. 33, n. 23.

stood the collegiate church of Saint Donatian, also opening into
the courtyard, an imposing and venerable monument, "round
and high."[69] Somewhat smaller than its prototype at Aachen, its
octagonal core of black Tournai lime stone, over a meter thick,
was encased in a polygon of sixteen sides, made chiefly of local
stone.[70] Its massive "tower" or west-work, flanked by smaller
towers, was balanced by a rectangular double sanctuary at the
east, and the whole structure culminated in a tower roofed with
earthenware jars and bricks. Stairs in the turrets gave access to
the circular colonnaded gallery, lighted with windows, and led
on up to the ramparts of the great "tower." The gallery, besides
containing ecclesiastical equipment of all kinds, served as a place
of worship for the parishioners within the castle.[71] It opened at
the east end into a chapel dedicated to the Virgin, originally the
sole patron of the church, where the count was assassinated while
performing his private devotions. The central rotunda served as
a choir for the canons; it contained the relics of Saint Donatian,
whose cult had gradually overshadowed that of the Virgin and
relegated it to the upper eastern chapel.[72]

If the count's house was wholly identified with his functions
as a ruler, the castral church of Saint Donatian with its college
of canons under their provost was also in a sense his. Built by
his remote ancestors, its chapter had been installed and beneficed
by his more recent forebears and served his needs, both spiritual

---

The suggestion of L. Willems (referred to by Mansion, p. 112, n. 19) that the
transitus was shaped like a bridge, going up from the *rez-de-chaussée* of the count's
house and then down to the ground floor of the church seems to fit both the evidence
of Galbert and that of the later anonymous author of the *Passio Karoli*, c. 9, MGH,
SS XII, 622, who describes it as a "very high stairway, made of wood and stone,
suspended in air." If it had led into the *gallery* of the church, the besiegers would
not have had to breach the wall of the church in order to reach the traitors, as
Mansion points out (p. 112).

[69] Galbert, c. 37.

[70] See the plan of Dr. Mertens, and his description in the Appendix. For Galbert's
incidental description of the church, see esp. c. 37, 42, 43, 60, 63, 64.

[71] The enclosure of the castle was carved out of the older parish of Holy Savior
by 1089; see Strubbe, "De parochies te Brugge," *Album English*, 1952, pp. 378-79.

[72] Concerning this unusual development in a case of the "double cult," characteristic of many Carolingian churches, see P. Rolland, "La Première église Saint
Donatien à Bruges," RBA, XIV (1944), 102-3. The second center of worship in
such a church was more usually a chapel within the upper story of the west-work.
This two-story arrangement, serving both religious and practical purposes, was a
feature of many palatine chapels.

and administrative. Since 1089,[73] the provost, by virtue of his office, had been hereditary chancellor of all Flanders, receiver of the domanial revenues, and head of the notaries, chaplains, and "clerics of the court," that is, the personnel of the chancellery, as well as the elected head of the canons proper, the beneficed secular clergy, who performed the canonical offices and since 1089 had also exercised the cure of souls within the castle walls.[74] The church itself was the special preserve of the canons, and their common life was led in the adjacent buildings, the dormitory, refectory, and cloister, all well furnished and equipped.[75] The atrium served as a burial place both for themselves and for their parishioners.[76] Close by were the school of the canons and the provost's house.[77] Probably built of stone, all these structures, except the church, were covered with wooden roofs and vulnerable to fire.[78]

The provost's high position, derived from his triple role, was reflected in his lordly style of living, surrounded by his own household,[79] in his own house. Adorned with a balcony,[80] it was lavishly furnished within, and its cellars were stocked with supplies.[81] Here in a great beamed hall, seated on a raised chair, "in pride and arrogance," he received pleaders and guests.[82]

The castle-dwellers, whether domestic officials, knights, or clergy, were all identified with the count, supported by fiefs—offices, estates, or revenues—which they held from him or benefices endowed by his ancestors. Distinct from the town-dwellers by virtue of their functions and residence, they were nonetheless in close contact with them, separated only by a wall, and dependent upon the burghers for the satisfaction of their material

---

[73] *Actes,* no. 9, pp. 23 ff.
[74] See C. Callewaert, "Les Origines de la collégiale Saint-Donatien à Bruges," ASEB, LVI (1906), 395 ff.
[75] See Galbert, esp. c. 9, 37, 41, 60.
[76] Callewaert, "Les Origines," ASEB, LVI, 398-400.
[77] Galbert, c. 42.
[78] *Ibid.,* c. 37, 45.
[79] See references to his house by Galbert, c. 11, 19, 20, 41; to his chamberlain, c. 35, 85.
[80] *Ibid.,* c. 44.
[81] *Ibid.,* c. 41.
[82] *Ibid.,* c. 13, 84 (*potenter et imperiose*).

needs. The courtyard and church of the castle were obviously familiar ground to the burghers, as, apparently, was the count's house. Such close proximity of different social and economic groups must have acted as a spur to the discontent of the less privileged group. It also afforded opportunity for the growth of cliques and factions, the development of bonds of interest and loyalty between persons of different social strata.

That this inherently uneasy situation proved explosive at Bruges rather than at some other "castle and town" was the result of a curious combination of circumstances. The castle of Bruges was not only a favorite residence of the count, frequented by barons, castellans, knights, and clerics, but also the chief center of his domanial wealth and the seat of his treasure. In 1089 it had even been recognized as the permanent seat of the increasingly active chancellery, where the count's seal was affixed to various acts, generally at the request of beneficiaries. By chance, or design, in 1091, the office of chancellor and receiver had fallen into the hands of an ambitious prelate at Bruges, the provost Bertulf, whose family also included the castellan of Bruges, one of the count's chamberlains, and knights of the castle, as well as other substantial men in the castellany. Here in Bruges the provost could aggrandize his clan by spinning a network of bonds with the barons through his wealth and influence, with the knights by intermarriage, and with the townspeople by favors and attentions. The arrogance and power of this clan grew to such an extent that it became a threat to the count's role as strong and uncontested ruler of the land, to his position as preserver of peace and justice, and perhaps even to his control of the domanial revenues. When his efforts to counteract the power of the provost by creating an inner circle of trusted counselors proved insufficient, and his attempts to suppress the lawless ways of the nephews seemed vain, he tried to break them directly by challenging their free status, with the intention of degrading them socially and probably ousting the leaders from their posts of influence at Bruges. It was, therefore, natural that the conspiracy took shape in the castle of Bruges, with the provost at its center, that the pact was sworn in his house, that the crime was committed in his church, and that the monstrous deed was done by the hands of his nephews. It was here that the traitors took their stand and entrenched themselves, at first secure and hopeful in the expectation of wide support, in possession of the whole castle and unchallenged in the town. The constriction of their hopes is reflected symbolically in the constriction of the area they control as they withdraw successively into the castle, into the church, and finally into its great tower.[83]

And so Bruges became inevitably the focal point of the movement of vengeance which not only distorted the orderly relations of local groups by displacing the count's household and castral clergy, but utterly changed the composition of the town-dwellers by introducing a series of alien and intrusive elements, knights and barons, claimants of the crown, mercenaries and rabble, burghers from other towns, and even the king of France and his following. "Nothing remained in its proper place!"[84] What Galbert says of the church was true of the whole town and castle area. Thanks to this extraordinary situation created by the vengeance, the town of Bruges became also the chief center of that parallel course of events which was determining the broader issues of the crisis, the choice of a new count and the pacification of Flanders. Its burghers, in the midst of unprecedented confusion, pursued a consistent policy of local and class solidarity, reaching out to the men of the castellany and the burghers of Ghent and other towns and bargaining with king and new count. Even after the surrender of the traitors, Bruges remained the headquarters of the king, the point of departure and return in military campaigns, the scene of continued efforts to secure the count's lost treasure. And it became the seat of the new count, William. Count and court, canons and provost (new), castellan (new) and knights, then resumed their proper places in the castle, but the restoration of order did not lead to stability of relations. Bad feeling poisoned the attitude of both knights and townspeople to the count.

Although it was not the townspeople of Bruges who led the

---

[83] As Galbert himself points out, c. 75.
[84] *Ibid.*, c. 64.

revolt against Count William, and they were somewhat slow in shifting their allegiance to Thierry of Alsace,[85] it was finally at Bruges, at the civic meeting-place of the Sands, that Thierry was elected by burghers of Bruges and Ghent and homage was done to him.[86] And when the king of France made a final effort to influence the course of events in Flanders by summoning representatives of the Flemish towns to his court, it was the men of Bruges who answered him audaciously.[87]

They proved to be less effective, however, in military support of their new count than in big words.[88] Fear and demoralization set in. The fearful townsmen of July, 1128, their numbers swelled by refugees from the country, huddling within their newly dug ditches, bewailing their losses in men and money, and unwilling to listen to the truth,[89] were saved, not by their own efforts but by the death in battle of Count William, an act of divine intervention, according to Galbert.[90] Events had proved that townspeople, like castlepeople, still needed a strong and uncontested ruler of the whole land. After a period of unparalleled influence in the affairs of Flanders, the people and place of Bruges again became subordinate to the power of the count and did not come into political prominence again until the aggrandizement of the French crown under Philip Augustus forced the count into alliance with the "good towns" of Flanders, of which Bruges was only one.[91]

[VI] *Galbert the notary and his record*

> "*I, Galbert, the notary, recorded a summary of events on wax tablets.*"   GALBERT, C. 35

Early in his impersonal narration of events the writer abruptly reveals himself, "I, Galbert the notary,"[1] as if impelled to do so,

[85] *Ibid.*, c. 98.
[86] *Ibid.*, c. 102, 103.
[87] *Ibid.*, c. 106. Other towns may also have replied.
[88] *Ibid.*, c. 109, 111, 114, 116.
[89] *Ibid.*, c. 116, 118.
[90] *Ibid.*, c. 120.
[91] Dhondt, *Les Origines des États*, pp. 20-21.

[1] Galbert, c. 35.

though unwillingly, by the very difficulties of his self-imposed
task—that of setting down, in the midst of tumult and danger,
a strictly chronological account of events as they occurred. He
never again identifies himself, even in his prefatory words,[2]
although he occasionally slips into the first person, generally in
the singular.[3] His capacity to maintain on the whole a consistent
role as objective observer and recorder is remarkable in view of
his proximity to the events and his obvious identification with
the townsmen of Bruges. Not what he himself did in the stirring
days of 1127-28 matters to Galbert but what was actually happening on all fronts within his little world of Bruges, and in the
larger world of Flanders so far as he could learn it. For this
reason it seems proper to reserve for the last some consideration
of the author himself, who he was, how and why he wrote.

It was not until the end of May, 1127, when peace had been
restored to Flanders, temporarily as it proved, after nearly three
months of tumult, that Galbert was able to consider at leisure
what he had done. In this interval he filled in and rounded out
his account to some extent, shaping a "little work" in the obvious
belief his task was done.[4] But the revolt against Count William
which broke out, first in August, 1127, and then with greater
force in February, 1128, led him to resume his running account
of events until the final pacification of Flanders in July of that
year, when the death of Count William and the uncontested
succession of Thierry of Alsace brought an end to the "civil war."
This second part of the narrative was obviously never attached
properly to the first part; his introduction as it stands has reference only to the first part.

The composition of the work, therefore, can easily be divided
into three periods, as Pirenne points out.[5]

First: chapters 15-67 and 72-85, written during the months
of March, April, and May, 1127. These chapters form the

[2] That is, in his own introduction, added later, where he reiterates the difficulties
of his task.
[3] See for example c. 27, 41, 43, 54, 113; and the occasional use of the editorial
"we" in c. 6, 12, 61. "We" and "ours," however, generally refer to the townsmen
of Bruges, though "we" in c. 14 seems to mean the "inhabitants of Flanders."
[4] Galbert, introduction.
[5] Pirenne, *Histoire du meurtre de Charles le Bon*, p. x.

original day-to-day account of events occurring between March 2 and May 22, 1127.

Second: the introduction and chapters 1-14, a brief survey of Charles' reign; chapters 68-71, a genealogical interpolation; and chapters 86-92, an "epilogue," concerning certain events of September, October, and December, 1127. These additions to the running account were written in the period of peace following May 22, 1127, apparently to give some degree of unity and form to the original record.

Third: chapters 93-121, written during the period from February 3 to July 29, 1128. Like the first part, it is a running account of events as they happened (with the exception of chapter 93, which relates to an event of the previous August which Galbert now sees as relevant). These entries are less frequent, and in many cases briefer, than those of the first period, doubtless because the scene is greatly enlarged and Galbert's information is scantier. Chapter 122 was undoubtedly added later.

Nothing is known definitely about Galbert except what he himself states and reveals in this single work.[6] Only his name and function, Galbert, notary of Bruges, are certain. Whatever his age may have been, his writing is that of a man of vigor, not one enfeebled by old age.[7] As a notary[8] of the count of Flanders

---

[6] Vercauteren (*Actes*, p. li, n. 4) suggests identification with "Galbert," a witness to a charter of Baldwin VII in 1113 (*Actes*, no. 61, p. 147), named at the end in a group of "worthy clerics" without rank; and with a person named in a charter of the bishop of Utrecht in 1116; and possibly with a "Galbert the deacon" in a charter of Robert II in 1101 (*Actes*, no. 26, p. 82). In the last two cases he follows Pirenne (pp. ii-iii).

[7] The four bases of Pirenne's argument (pp. v-vi) that he was an old man do not seem valid to me. 1. Galbert's knowledge (c. 57) of Bertulf's "usurpation" of the office of provost in 1091 need not have been based on personal experience. 2. His reference (c. 6) to "rulers" in the plural does not necessarily imply that he had "lived under" many successive reigns. 3. His use of the Christmas era, not the Paschal era, in reckoning time was not anachronistic (see text, note 3 to c. 3). 4. There is no evidence that his failure to complete the work was due to his early death, presumably of old age.

[8] The notaries are named along with the chaplains and clerics of the court in the charter of 1089 (*Actes*, no. 9), where they are all put under the direction of the provost of Saint Donatian as chancellor and receiver-general. It has been argued from Galbert's evidence concerning Fromold's married state (c. 24) that the latter was a layman, and hence that some notaries were lay. But since marriage was not forbidden to clerics in *minor* orders, this argument is invalid. (Pirenne calls Fromold a layman in his pioneer study, "La Chancellerie et les notaires des comtes

he was probably a clerk in minor orders; there is no evidence
that he was a priest[9] or a canon.[10] But from a careful study of
how he wrote, and a consideration of why he wrote, perhaps
something can be learned about this remarkable recorder of
events.

A clue to the original motive and form of the account may lie
first of all in his profession as a notary, trained to record factual
data promptly and accurately and convinced of the importance
of written records. It seems to be the mention of his precious
archives being removed from the castle, along with the relics of
the saints, that goads Galbert into revealing himself and his new
activity on March 17.[11] A devoted and perhaps compulsive
functionary, deprived by circumstances of his normal work, might
well have begun without conscious motive to record what was
happening, and through such a substitute activity consoled himself by giving some kind of order to the appalling disorder which
suddenly engulfed his quiet and routine life. His very procedure
resembles that of a notary; day by day he sets down a summary

de Flandre avant le XIIIᵉ siècle," in *Mélanges Julien Havet* [Paris, 1895], p. 746;
De Smet believes both Galbert and Fromold were in minor orders, "Bij de latijnsche
gedichten," in *Miscellanea . . . de Meyer*, I, 432, n. 11.)

[9] Pirenne's only evidence (p. ii) that Galbert was a priest is the phrase in c. 114,
"*we* . . . were carrying on divine services and burying the dead. . . ." In the context,
however, "we" seems to imply rather "our priests" and the activities of the people
of Bruges as a collectivity.

[10] As a notary under the provost of Saint Donatian he was, of course, closely
associated with the clergy of Saint Donatian, but this does not prove that he was
a "member of the clergy of that church," as Pirennne suggests (p. iii). He was
certainly not one of the canons with whom he never identifies himself in his whole
account. (I agree here with Pirenne, who [p. iii] is emphatic on this point.)

[11] Galbert, c. 35. The heavy duties of receiving and recording the domanial
revenues at Bruges apparently necessitated the presence there of several notaries
of whom Galbert was one; among his colleagues were Fromold Junior and Basil
(c. 112). These are the only notaries whose names we know for the period of Count
Charles's reign, except a "Berengar of Aire" in a suspect document of 1123 (see
Vercauteren, *Actes*, pp. l-lii). Their functions were primarily fiscal rather than
secretarial. It is possible (as Pirenne suggests, p. v) that Galbert may have had
some duties in connection with the courts about which he seems well informed (c. 1);
certainly he is familiar with the findings of the inquest of September, 1127 (c. 87).
Whether the notaries were *personnages considerables* (Pirenne, "La Chancellerie,"
in *Mélanges Julien Havet*, pp. 746-47) seems debatable. Fromold's wealth and
influence at court seem to be attributes of his role as "favorite" rather than as
notary; there is no evidence that Galbert was intimate with the count. Galbert's
casual references (c. 6) to "emperors, kings, and rulers" can hardly be used to
prove that he was sent on foreign missions by the count (as Pirenne suggests, p. v).

of events on wax tablets, and then as soon as possible he trans-
cribes the information in more finished form.[12] The immediacy
of his recording is obvious not only from the internal evidence
of the items themselves but from the tone of the narrative as a
whole. In most cases only a few days seem to have elapsed
between the events (and the original notations) and the entry as
we now have it.[13]

This notarial impulse to record, despite all obstacles, was
probably strengthened by Galbert's sense of the personal tragedy
and drama enveloping the two figures who had dominated his
life: the good count, his prince, so foully murdered, and the
arrogant provost, his master, doomed by his own sin of pride
to fall into the depths and drag his whole family down. As he
continues to write Galbert obviously becomes greatly concerned
with the fate of "our place," so dear to him, and then with the
future of "our fatherland," which hangs on the solution of the
problem of succession. His interest in the persons involved, his
loyalties to Bruges and Flanders, and his proximity to the events
must have combined to keep him going, and as he continues his
powers as a writer develop and perhaps also his pleasure in this
new form of recording, but he still remains the notary, exact and
precise.

The sense of immediacy in Galbert's account is heightened by
the exactness of the chronological data with which he opens the
entry for each day. To the notation of the day of month and
week, always given, he often adds further identification, the feast
of the saint, the position within Lent, the opening of the Introit
of the Mass or the lesson for the day, and sometimes he notes
the time of day when events occurred, at dawn, or evening, or the
hour of the evening meal.[14] The time relations between events
are often indicated by such expressions as meanwhile, soon,
afterwards, at once, at the very moment, on the same day. Even

---

[12] Galbert, c. 35, and c. 14. Galbert's sense of the importance of recording
fiscal data promptly is evident in c. 112. In fact, Galbert is one of the chief sources
of information about the functions of notaries at this time.

[13] See the comments by Pirenne in his edition of Galbert, pp. vii-viii.

[14] Galbert, c. 28, 102. The other examples are too numerous to mention.

the seasonal weather is sometimes mentioned.[15] And although he names the year only once, in connection with the solar eclipse of August 11, 1124, he is highly conscious of "the revolution of the year," the anomalies of Leap Year, and the occurrence of anniversaries.[16]

Such a degree of chronological precision is unusual for the age, even in documents,[17] and displays an almost unparalleled "taste for exactitude"[18] which extends to other dimensions of Galbert's account. In his descriptions of movements and actions he shows an acute sense of direction and place and is able to make intelligible and graphic the complex maneuvers and simultaneous acts of individuals and groups.[19]

Something of the same zeal for exactness is seen in his use of figures, at least with reference to sums of money and numbers of people which he was in a position to know.[20] When he wishes to indicate large, uncertain numbers of men, he sometimes avoids figures and refers to "a great crowd" or "an infinite number,"[21] or lapses into the more conventional, loose use of "hundreds" and "thousands."[22] His enumeration of the varieties of loot seized in the castle is as specific as an inventory.[23]

Galbert's concern for the fullness and accuracy of his account leads him to include not only what he saw or heard firsthand or from eyewitnesses in Bruges, but to question all the bearers of news coming in from the outside—merchants, students, servants and messengers[24]—and to include the content of official documents, mandates from the king, and town charters, as well as

[15] *Ibid.*, c. 76, 80, 94.

[16] *Ibid.*, see c. 102, 104, 110.

[17] See Vercauteren, *Actes*, p. xl.

[18] See the remarks of Marc Bloch concerning "the vast indifference to time," and also to number, which prevailed in general: *La Société féodale: la formation des liens de dépendance,* pp. 118-20.

[19] Note, for example, his well-ordered and graphic account of the storming of the castle, c. 41-45. In contrast, consider the confused account of the storming of the castle at Amiens in 1115 written by his contemporary, Guibert de Nogent, in *De vita sua,* lib. IV, c. 14, ed. by Bourgin, pp. 194-205.

[20] Galbert, for example in c. 3, 81, 85, 87, 100.

[21] *Ibid.*, for example, c. 33, 51, 69.

[22] Such as the figures in c. 9, 10, 80; perhaps also in c. 108, 116, 118, though large numbers were undoubtedly involved here.

[23] Galbert, c. 41, 51.

[24] *Ibid.*, for example, c. 12, 39, 46, 80.

letters.[25] In his use of direct discourse many bits sound as if they were recorded verbatim;[26] others are doubtless based on hearsay.[27]

His role as a notary, however, does not explain his purpose when, after May 22, 1127, he made an effort to give greater form and unity to his chronological entries by adding certain kinds of information and by attempting to interpret the causes of the tragedy that befell Flanders. His impulse to give shape to his work at the cost of considerable literary and intellectual effort would seem to imply his expectation of an audience to whom this "little work" could be directed, and this impression is confirmed by his use of direct address in his "introduction," which sounds in part like a dedication, and at the end of his historical survey (c.14). Since he seems unclear in his own mind, however, about whom he is writing for, one person or many, listeners or readers,[28] it is obvious that at this moment he has not yet found a suitable audience or patron.

He could hardly have thought of dedicating it to Count William, whom he had pictured frankly as wholly subservient to the king of France and forced to buy his way into the countship. Perhaps when he addresses "you and all the faithful" he reveals the hope of offering it to a bishop, but was later discouraged in this intention by the enterprise of Walter of Therouanne, who was meanwhile writing his own account of the life and death of Count Charles for his bishop, John of Therouanne.[29] That he had a clerical audience in mind seems likely from the strong religious tone and Biblical language of the parts added, and his interpretation of the tragedy as God's punishment of evil men,[30] visiting the sins of the parents upon the children[31] and mani-

[25] *Ibid.*, c. 47, 52, 55, 99, 106.

[26] *Ibid.*, for example, c. 17, 18, 22, 38, 44, 59, 82, 100, 101; Galbert may have relied on eyewitnesses for some of these, however.

[27] *Ibid.*, c. 8, 11, 95, for example.

[28] Note Galbert's mixed use of words referring to reading and hearing in his introduction and in c. 14.

[29] Walter's account ends in early May, 1127; it was written after July, 1127, and obviously completed before the outbreak of the revolt against Count William which began in earnest in February, 1128.

[30] Galbert, introduction, c. 2, 7, 14.

[31] *Ibid.*, c. 69, 71 (in the interpolation).

festing the frightful consequences of disobedience to the powers that be.[32] Since he could apparently find no specific prelate as a patron, he may have thought it expedient to write in terms suitable to a wider public, the clergy in general, the only "readers" of his time, and to stress the theme of martyrdom[33] to enhance the appeal of his little work. It is even possible that the idea occurred to him of preparing the way for the beatification of Count Charles; after all, the virtue of the body had been demonstrated immediately in a miracle and was confirmed by its sound condition after seven weeks' entombment.[34] The clergy of Saint Donatian, guardians of the precious tomb, would presumably be responsive to such a project.

It was, perhaps, his failure at this time to find a suitable patron for his work that discouraged him and curtailed his editorial efforts. At any rate, it is clear that Galbert never went over his entries to eliminate repetitions and inconsistencies and to incorporate odds and ends of information that he had simply attached by *notandum*.[35]

What impelled him to resume his recording with the outbreak of the revolt against Count William in February, 1128, is not clear; perhaps it was a renewal of the original impulse and the obvious fact that the crisis, and his work in relation to it, was by no means over. In form he now reverts to the original pattern of simple, terse entries of events, but as the struggle becomes a civil war, desolating the land, his profound distress at the course of events breaks through the crust of the objective narrative. In fact the second part of his record, less epic and less sharply focused than the first, gradually acquires a quality of tension as the revelation of a dual conflict, an external struggle between two claimants for the countship, the legally established William

---

[32] *Ibid.,* introduction. This theme is resumed later, at the very end of the work, in c. 116, 118.

[33] *Ibid.,* c. 14, 15. Chapter 15, perhaps in its original form a simple account of the count's murder, like the entry which follows, was very probably rewritten at this time to develop the theme of the count's "passion," first suggested in c. 14; it is totally unlike the entries that follow.

[34] Galbert, c. 22, 77. If so, he was disappointed. The popular cult of Charles was not approved by the papacy until 1882.

[35] See Pirenne, pp. x-xi. Many of these elements are pointed out in the notes to the text.

Clito and his challenger, Thierry of Alsace, and an inner conflict in the mind of Galbert between habitual conformity to the opinions and attitudes of the people of Bruges and a growing impulse to question his environment and interpret the world of experience more independently and rationally. Up to this point Galbert has been able to view events dispassionately, because of his fundamental sympathy with the aims and actions of the burghers and the avenging forces which seem to him in harmony with his conception of the divine ordering of human affairs in bringing about the downfall and punishment of traitors, even unto the third and fourth generation.[36] (That his good Count Charles was an undeserving victim of this providential design does not trouble him, because he knows beatitude awaits the martyr.) But his strong belief in the reign of law and order on earth, secured by the rule of lawful, hereditary princes to whom God enjoins obedience, as well as his faith in the fulfillment of the plan of divine retribution, is rudely shaken by the events of 1128.

His confidence in the efficacy of the appeal to God's judgment in the proof by ordeal is undermined by the curious case of Lambert of Aardenburg, one of the Erembald clan, whose "innocence" was established by the ordeal of iron but whose "guilt" was proved soon after by his death in battle.[37] Far more shattering to his convictions is the fact that the legally accepted, though tyrannical, Count William is being seriously challenged by Thierry, who has a better hereditary right, to be sure, but who, like Count Charles, is a direct heir of the "traitor" Robert the Frisian, while the candidate with the best claim by right of kinship, Baldwin of Hainaut,[38] is losing ground. As the struggle becomes more bitter, moreover, and disaster threatens the supporters of Thierry—including Bruges—strange irrational elements emerge from the social depths. Galbert learns of two "sorceresses" who are destroyed, at least one because she cast a spell on Thierry.[39] Soon Bruges itself becomes a center in the

[36] Galbert, c. 69-71.
[37] *Ibid.*, c. 105, 108.
[38] *Ibid.*, c. 67.
[39] *Ibid.*, c. 110, 112.

war of anathemas waged by the clerical supporters of the two
major opponents, who are believed to be "casting spells on God
himself" in order to win victory.[40] To what extent Galbert shares
the popular belief in this kind of sorcery is not clear. (He is
obviously not free of superstition, though he interprets only one
event in the whole narrative as miraculous.[41]) But he is so
shocked by this gross credulity, this denial of his own rational
belief that "God rules all,"[42] that he even turns temporarily
against his people of Bruges, denouncing as senseless the austerities they perform at the behest of their stupid priests and their
open resistance to lawful authority, both ecclesiastical and
secular.[42]

His crisis of conscience grows as he sees his neatly conceived
scheme of retributive justice collapse with the resurgence of the
partisans of the traitors, who now become supporters of the
cause of Thierry in order to save themselves. Only the unexpected
death of Count William saves Flanders from further anarchy and
resolves Galbert's dilemma, actually if not ethically. His troubled
mind, in trying to explain to himself why God gave the victory
to one rather than the other, now follows a tortuous path to an
unconvincing answer.[43] But this should not obscure the fact that
during the course of events in 1128 Galbert had become a more
questioning and reasoning individual, and a wiser if more dis-
illusioned observer of his world. Perhaps it is not farfetched to
see in Galbert "les premiers balbutiements de la pensée rationelle
en lutte avec les traditions,"[44] even if at the end he finds it
expedient to slip back into the old pattern of loyalty and conformity and again uphold the policies of his townsmen.

Although some time elapsed between his notices of Count
William's death (c. 120) and Thierry's recognition as count by
the king of France (c. 122), it is obvious that Galbert neither
reworked his record of events from February, 1128, on, nor tried

[40] *Ibid.,* c. 113, 115.
[41] *Ibid.,* c. 22.
[42] *Ibid.,* c. 115, 116.
[43] *Ibid.,* c. 121.
[44] J. Dhondt, "Une Mentalité du douziéme siècle, Galbert de Bruges," RN,
XXXIX (1957), 102.

to connect this part with his account of the events of 1127 by revising and interpreting as a whole the narrative of the murder and its consequences. For one reason or another he was through with it. The events of 1128 may have seemed too painful to work over. Perhaps he had no more time because his duties as notary had to be resumed; and perhaps he had no further desire, since he had found no patron to receive it, and Walter's biography, with its strong emphasis on the miraculous, seemed to satisfy the needs of the reading public. At any rate, Galbert's account remained almost completely unknown[45] during the later centuries, probably less because of its imperfect form than because of changing tastes and widening interests. Charles took his place as only one of many able rulers in the succession of great Flemish "chronicles of the counts"[46] and his martyrdom became the subject of a "passion" written along the conventional lines of hagiography.[47] What is more puzzling is the failure of Galbert's narrative to become the basis of the local history of "our town," but that may be explained by the early popular distortion of the facts which soon attributed the murder to the family of Straten, loathed by the people of Bruges.[48]

But, in neglecting Galbert's honest account of the events of 1127-28, the burghers of Bruges ignored the true record of their birth as a recognized community and, moreover, rejected the product of a true son of Bruges. Whether a native or not, Galbert is heart and soul a "man of Bruges." In a thousand artless ways he displays his proprietary sense of place: "we men of Bruges" or simply "we," "our place," "our town," "our market," "our castle," "our priests," "our knights," "our students," and continuously "our burghers" and "our citizens."[49] And it is the actions of the citizens, in response to their dangers, their needs, and their

[45] Pirenne, pp. xviii-xix.

[46] See J. J. De Smet, *Corpus chronicorum Flandriae* (4 vols.; Brussels, 1837-65); *Genealogiae comitum Flandriae*, ed. by D. L. C. Bethmann, MGH, SS IX, 302 ff.

[47] *Passio Karoli comitis auctore anonymo*, ed. by Köpke, MGH, SS XII, 619-23, probably written in the late thirteenth century or early fourteenth century. This garbled account is derived in part from Galbert and Walter, especially from the latter.

[48] See the first echoes of this popular attitude in Galbert, c. 45, 113.

[49] Examples are too numerous to indicate.

desires, that he follows most closely, obviously proud of their enterprise and boldness—not concealing their greed and defeatism, forced to expose their disloyalty—but trying by ingenious logic to absolve them from blame for the death of Count William. The bitterness Galbert displays towards the priests of Bruges seems to spring from his sense that they have misled the burghers in the dark days of June-July, 1128, by deceiving and flattering their flock, by encouraging them to flout episcopal and secular authority, and pretending that they could even influence God himself![50] He reflects the burghers' hatred of mercenaries and all the evils of war,[51] and he shares their communal emotions, their love of Robert, their hatred of Thancmar, even their compassion for the captured traitors.[52] He consciously notes the "feeling of the crowd,"[53] for to him the burghers stand out not as individuals to be named and identified, like barons and knights, but as a collectivity and community acting as one in the pursuit of common ends. Perhaps he had future generations of burghers in mind when he once says that he commends his work to "our posterity."[54]

Of his qualities as a writer, the reader can best judge for himself. Evidence of training in the arts of grammar or rhetoric is slight: his sentence structure is clumsy, his locutions often obscure and incorrect, and his knowledge of the classics scanty.[55] His conscious efforts at style in the parts added at leisure are lamentable. His real gift as a writer lies elsewhere and is largely unconscious: the power to tell a swift-moving story with precision and vitality, to describe a complex scene vividly, and to lay bare the motives of men through their actions. The count's favorite Fromold, the opportunist Gervaise, the crowd's darling Robert the Young, the slayer Borsiard, and many others come alive as individuals. But his masterpiece of characterization is

[50] Galbert, c. 113-16, c. 118. Galbert's attitude throughout is certainly not anticlerical.
[51] *Ibid.*, for example, c. 33, 114.
[52] *Ibid.*, for example, c. 75, 81.
[53] *Ibid.*, c. 113 (*dico secundum sensum vulgi*).
[54] Galbert, introduction.
[55] His only classical quotation is from Ovid (c. 6), but there is a tag of Virgil (c. 81), and possibly of Horace (c. 63), and one mythological reference (c. 58).

the portrait of his master, the provost, in whom he sees good and evil so strangely compounded. The tragic theme of his fall and its symbolic meaning give unity to Galbert's narrative and a certain epic quality. His horror at Bertulf's treachery is accompanied by a growing compassion for this proud man, betrayed in turn by his own men and likened to a dog in his awful death.[56]

It is Galbert's compassion for the sufferings of men of all classes, from the peasants to the count, that makes endurable a tale of such violence and cruelty and impresses the reader quite as much as his transparent honesty, loyalty, and Christian piety. Galbert's good faith and humanity combine with his realism and accuracy to make his record a unique picture of Flemish society in the early twelfth century.

[56] Galbert, esp. c. 23, 46, 57.

THE RECORD OF
GALBERT OF BRUGES

THE RECORD OF
GALBERT OF BRUGES

Introduction

At a time when we saw the rulers of neighboring kingdoms displaying the greatest zeal in winning glory and praise for themselves by knightly exploits as well as a disposition for ruling well, Count Charles, marquis[1] of Flanders, exceeded in fame and power the emperor of the Romans, Henry,[2] who after reigning for many years died without heirs; he also surpassed in fame and strength the king of the English[3] who was ruling without heirs in his kingdom. As our natural[4] lord and prince, renowned for his knightly valor and royal blood,[5] he had presided over the county for seven years[6] like a father and protector of the churches of God, generous toward the poor, courteous and honorable among his barons,[7] cruel and wary toward his enemies, when he, also without heirs, fell dead in the cause of justice, betrayed and slain by his own, or, I should rather say, his most iniquitous serfs.

When I set out to describe the death of such a great prince,[8]

---

[1] This title, first used by Arnold I (918-65), had become archaic in Galbert's time; it no longer appears in the charters of the counts. See Introduction, p. 6.

[2] Henry V, d. 1125.

[3] Henry I, d. 1135; his only legitimate son, William, was drowned in 1120.

[4] In the sense of legitimate, ruling by hereditary right.

[5] As the son of Canute IV, king of Denmark, d. 1086. See Genealogy.

[6] From 1119 to 1127.

[7] His courtesy must have veiled his suspicion of a class which contained many elements hostile to him.

[8] *Tanti quidem principis mortem descripturus;* the metric quality of this phrase has led to the belief that Galbert drew it from one of the many mourning poems written soon after Charles' death. See J. M. De Smet, "Bij de latijnsche gedichten over den moord op den Glz. Karel den Goede Graaf van Vlaanderen," in *Miscellanea historica in honorem Alberti de Meyer* (2 vols.: Louvain and Brussels, 1946), I, 440.

I did not seek to embellish it with eloquence or to display the modes of different styles[9] but I related only the truth of things, and even if my style is dry I committed to writing for the memory of the faithful the strange outcome of his death. And, in fact, I did not have a favorable time or place when I turned my mind to this work, because our place[10] at that time was so disturbed by fear and anxiety that the clergy and people without exception were threatened continually with loss of life and property. It was, therefore, in the midst of many calamities and in the most constrained circumstances that I began to compose my mind, as unquiet as if it were tossed about in Euripus,[11] and to subdue it to the discipline of writing. In this distress of mind, a little spark of love, warmed and animated by its own fire, set aflame all the spiritual strength of my heart and consequently endowed my bodily self, which had been seized by fear, with the freedom to write. Now about this work of mine which I so carefully set down for you[12] and all the faithful to hear, despite the straits in which I was placed; if anyone tries to criticize and disparage it, I do not care very much. It reassures me to know that I speak the truth as it is known to all who suffered the same dangers with me, and I commit it to the memory of our posterity.

Therefore I ask and admonish anyone who happens upon this dry style and this little handful of a book not to make fun of it or condemn it but to read with fresh wonder what is written down and what came to pass by the ordinance of God only in our time. And let no one renounce or betray earthly rulers whom we are bound to believe were placed over us by the ordinance of God, as the apostle says:

"Let every soul be subject to every power, either to the king as supreme or to governors as sent by God."[13]

[9] Galbert's words here are drawn from the formal vocabulary of the arts of grammar and rhetoric.

[10] Galbert often uses this expression (*noster locus*) to indicate the town of Bruges.

[11] An illusion to the channel between Boeotia and Euboeia, now called Egribos, obviously drawn from classical sources.

[12] Concerning possible meanings of "you," see Introduction, pp. 69-70.

[13] I Peter 2.13. Galbert's version of the Scripture here is not exactly that of the Vulgate, and the same is true of many of his Biblical quotations. Perhaps he is using the language of the liturgical books, based on older Latin versions. His words, here and elsewhere, are translated literally.

(For "as" is not used figuratively but demonstratively; it is used in Holy Writ for that which is true, for example, "as or like a spouse" really means "a spouse.") Those murderers and drunkards and whoremongers and slaves of all vices in our land certainly did not deserve to have as ruler such a good prince, devout and strong, Catholic, the supporter of the poor, the protector, after God, of the churches of God, the defender of the fatherland, and one in whom the residue of earthly authority assumed the form of ruling well and the substance of serving God. When the Devil saw the progress of the Church and the Christian faith, as you are about to hear, he undermined the stability of the land, that is, of the Church of God, and threw it into confusion by guile and treachery and the shedding of innocent blood.[14]

[1] *Charles becomes count of Flanders in 1119; his concern for peace and justice, 1119-24*

Charles, son of Canute, king of Denmark, and born of a mother who was descended from the blood of the counts of the land of Flanders,[1] because of this relationship grew up from boyhood to manly strength of body and mind in our fatherland.[2] After

[14] The labored style of this introduction and of chapters 1-14, which were added to the running narrative of the events of March, April, and May, after May 22, 1127, when Galbert believed that peace had been restored to Flanders, is doubtless due to the fact that he had greater leisure in which to write. See Introduction, pp. 64-65, concerning the stages of composition.

[1] The marriage of Adele by her father, Robert the Frisian, count of Flanders (1071-93), to Canute IV of Denmark was intended to strengthen a Flemish-Danish alliance against William the Conqueror which crumbled in 1086 on Canute's assassination; following this event Adele fled to Flanders with her young son, Charles. See C. Verlinden, *Robert 1er le Frison, comte de Flandre* (Antwerp, 1935), pp.108-11. Neither the exact date of the marriage nor of Charles's birth has been established, but he must have been born between *ca.*1080 and 1086; see Vercauteren, *Actes*, p. xviii. He was still a "very small boy" (*parvulus*) on his arrival in Flanders, according to Walter of Therouanne's *Vita Karoli*, c. 2, MGH, SS XII, 540 (hereafter cited as Walter, giving only the chapter number). For fuller consideration of Charles's ancestry and youth, see Introduction, pp. 13-14.

[2] Galbert's frequent characterization of Flanders as "our fatherland" (*nostra patria*), and "our realm" (*nostrum regnum*) reveals the growing consciousness of Flanders as a true community, "un ensemble territorial et une collectivité humaine."

he was armed with the honors of knighthood[3] he fought with distinction against his enemies and gained a fine reputation and glory for his name among the rulers of the earth. Our barons had for many years shown a preference for him as prince if by chance such a possibility should occur.[4] Therefore when Count Baldwin, that extraordinarily brave youth, was dying, he, together with the barons,[5] handed the realm over to his cousin Charles and commended it to him under oath.[6] The pious

---

according to J. Dhondt, *Les Origines des États de Flandre* (Louvain, 1950), pp. 6-7 and n. 8.

[3] That is, after he had undergone the ceremony of induction into the knightly order, when the candidate was girded with the sword and "dubbed" by his knightly sponsor. On the changing significance of this ritual see M. Bloch, *La Société féodale: les classes et le gouvernement des hommes* (Paris, 1940), pp. 46-53.

[4] If, that is, his cousin Count Baldwin VII (1111-19) should die without heirs, as it so happened. Baldwin, born in 1093, was injured on the Norman border while serving in the host of his feudal lord, Louis VI of France, in September, 1118, and died on June 19, 1119; see Vercauteren, *Actes*, p. xviii. For the circumstances of his injury, long illness, and death see especially Walter, c. 6, and Herman of Tournai, *Liber de restauratione S. Martini Tornacensis*, c. 26, MGH, SS XIV, 284-85 (hereafter cited as Herman, giving only the chapter number).

[5] This was the normal procedure of succession in Flanders at the time, designation by the reigning count and confirmation by the barons. (See R. Monier, *Les Institutions centrales du comté de Flandre* [Paris, 1943], pp. 30-33.) That Baldwin had designated Charles as his successor during his last illness we know also from other sources, from Walter, c. 7, from Lambert of Saint Omer, *Genealogia comitum Flandriae*, c. 9, MGH, SS IX, 311, and from an act probably of 1119 (*Actes*, no. 92 ,p. 209) which Charles signed as "kinsman and successor of Count Baldwin, in his presence." For a fuller account of his relations with Baldwin see Introduction, pp. 14-15.

[6] It is difficult to interpret Galbert's phrase, *sub fidei securitate commendavit*. Here as in c. 48 it seems to mean simply "under oath." It should be noted that in characterizing the process by which binding relationships were established between men, Galbert usually employs three terms, in shifting combinations of two or three —*fides, securitas,* and *hominium.* His use of *securitas* in these cases indicates the persistence in Flanders of the original, negative notion of fealty or fidelity, the promise not to endanger or be harmful to one's lord, along with the later, positive pledge to fulfill certain obligations in good faith. (In the present translation *securitas* in this sense is always translated by "loyalty," although unfortunately this English word does not convey the specific meaning of this relationship.) This early conception of fealty is well expressed in the famous letter of Fulbert of Chartres to William V, duke of Aquitaine; see Bouquet, RHF, X, 463. Its persistence is seen also in the text of the secret Treaty of Dover in 1101 where Count Robert II of Flanders, on becoming vassal of King Henry I of England "fide et sacramento assecuravit regi Henrico vitam suam et membra que corpori suo pertinent, et capcionem corporis, ne rex eam habeat hanc ad dampnum suum..." (see *Actes*, no. 30, c. 1, p. 89). For an illuminating discussion of this point see F. L. Ganshof, "Les Relations féodo-vassaliques aux temps post-carolingiens," in *I Problemi comuni dell'Europa post-carolingia* (Spoleto, 1955), pp. 77-82, or the brief statement in his *Qu'est-ce que la féodalité?* (3d ed. rev.; Brussels, 1957), pp. 115-16. What

count,[7] acting with the prudence of his predecessor, now took such measures to strengthen the peace,[8] to reaffirm the laws and rights of the realm, that little by little public order was restored in all parts, and by the fourth year of his reign,[9] thanks to his efforts, everything was flourishing, everything was happy and joyful in the security of peace and justice. When he saw that such a great boon of peace made everyone happy, he gave orders that throughout the limits of the realm all who frequented markets or dwelt in towns[10] should live together in quiet and security without resort to arms; otherwise they would be punished by the very arms they bore. To enforce this, bows and arrows[11] and

---

makes Galbert's use of these terms of unusual interest is his application of them to the creation of bonds not merely between individuals of the noble class but also between groups of burghers and members of the noble class. (See, for example, in c. 20, 25, 27, 54, 55, 66, 94, 101, and 103.)

[7] This favorite epithet of Galbert's occurs throughout, often in the superlative.

[8] Galbert reveals here the evolution of a more advanced type of penal law which treated infractions as a matter of public concern, subject to public jurisdiction; it was gradually displacing the more primitive type which regarded violations of public order as a matter of private concern, to be settled directly and independently by the families affected through resort to arms or formal "reconciliations." From the early eleventh century the counts of Flanders had asserted their own authority in maintaining peace, both by recognition of the Peace of God, and by a positive guarantee of security to certain places (such as markets, fairs, towns) and persons (such as merchants) which became in time a general guarantee of public order known as "the count's peace." The counts also strove in various ways to suppress the persistent system of private vengeance. For a general account see R. C. Van Caenegem, *Geschiedenis van het strafrecht in Vlaanderen van de XIe tot de XIVe eeuw* (Brussels, 1954), especially pp. 61-74 and the French résumé, pp. 362-67. Count Charles was simply continuing the policies of his predecessors, of whom Baldwin VII was a notable enforcer of the peace. See Introduction, II, IV.

[9] Galbert's summary treatment of these years, 1119-22, omits entirely the revolt of 1119-20 immediately following Charles's succession, led by Baldwin VII's mother, Clemence, and involving some of the great lords of the land, especially Hugh of Saint Pol. Clemence had supported the candidacy of William of Ypres, an illegitimate grandson of Robert the Frisian (see Walter, c. 7, 8, and 9). This evidence of early disaffection, which Charles seems to have crushed easily, however, helps to explain the events of 1127-28.

[10] *Castra.* This is Galbert's first use of *castra*, by which he generally means "castles" or fortified places, especially the great "castral" centers of the count's domain; here, however, as in a few other cases, he seems to refer to the embryonic towns or mercantile agglomerations which had sprung up at the gates of the count's castles. (In some cases it is used by Galbert and his contemporaries to apply also to the complex of castle and town.) On the loose use of this and related words by Galbert and his contemporaries see J. F. Verbruggen, "Note sur le sens du mot castrum, castellum et quelques autres expressions qui désignent des fortifications," RB, XXVIII (1950), 147-55.

[11] Walter, c. 12, also mentions the prohibition of bows and arrows, along with other measures taken to subdue the wild folk of *maritime* Flanders. The count is

subsequently all arms were laid aside not only in those places already protected by the count's peace but in other places as well.[12]

Thanks to this boon of peace, men governed themselves in accordance with laws and justice, devising by skill and study every kind of argument for use in the courts, so that when anyone was attacked he could defend himself by the strength and eloquence of rhetoric,[13] or when he was attacking, he might ensnare his enemy, who would be deceived by the wealth of his oratory. Rhetoric was now used both by the educated and by those who were naturally talented, for there were many illiterate people, endowed by nature herself with the gift of eloquence and rational methods of inference and argument, whom those who were trained and skilled in the rhetorical art were not able to resist or refute. But, on the other hand, because these by their deceits brought action in the courts against the faithful and the lambs of God, who were less wary,[14] God, who sees all from on high, did not fail to chastise the deceivers so that He might reach by scourges those whom He had endowed with the gift of eloquence for their salvation because they had used this gift for their own perdition.

[2] *God desolates Flanders by famine, 1124-25*

Therefore God inflicted the scourge of famine and afterwards of death on all who lived in our realm, but first He deigned by the terror of omens to recall to penitence those whom He had

---

praised by Herman (c. 30) for having tamed such an ungovernable people as the Flemings and forced them to be "as quiet as cloistered monks."

[12] A free translation of *in forinsecis locis sicut et in pacificis;* that is, Charles must have extended as well as strengthened the peace regulations already enjoyed by markets, fairs, and towns. *Loci pacifici* is interpreted as referring to the special peace of towns and markets by Van Caenegem, *Geschiedenis van het strafrecht,* p. 68 and p. 245, n. 3.

[13] Galbert seems here to reflect an intensified interest in the study of rhetoric, one of the *trivium* (grammar, rhetoric, dialectic).

[14] In the Latin text *minus cautis* should be changed to *minus cautos,* according to the corrections made by P. Thomas, "Notes sur Galbert de Bruges," in *Mélanges d'histoire offerts à Henri Pirenne* (2 vols.; Brussels, 1926), I, 515-17. All these corrections are incorporated in the present translation and will be noted in sequence; the references will henceforth be simply to Thomas.

foreseen as prone to evil. In the year 1124 from the Incarnation of our Lord, in the month of August, there was visible to all the inhabitants of the lands an eclipse[1] on the body of the sun at about the ninth hour of the day,[2] and an unnatural failure of light so that the eastern part of the sun, darkened little by little, poured forth strange clouds on the other parts, not darkening the whole sun at the same time, however, but only partially. Nevertheless, the same cloud wandered over the whole circle of the sun, moving across from east to west, but only within the circle of the solar essence. Consequently, those who observed the condition of the peace and the wrongs in the courts, threatened everyone with the peril of famine and death. But when men were not corrected in this way, neither lords nor serfs, there came the hunger of sudden famine,[3] and subsequently the scourges of death attacked them. As it is said in the Psalms:[4] "He called for a famine upon the land, and broke the whole staff of bread."

During this time no one was able to sustain himself by eating and drinking in his usual way, but, contrary to habit, a person ate as much bread in one meal as he had been accustomed to consume in several days before this time of famine. So he was glutted by this unusual quantity, and since all the natural passages of the organs were distended by the excess of food and

---

[1] Scientific proof of this solar eclipse, visible in Europe at noon in the meridian of Paris on August 11, 1124, is given by T. von Oppolzer, *Canon der Finsternisse* (Vienna, 1887), pp. 222-23, and its course is charted on Blatt no. 111. It is puzzling that Galbert describes the obscuration as moving from east to west; actually in a solar eclipse the moon travels across the sun from west to east.

[2] Since the day was divided into two periods, each of twelve hours, beginning respectively at sunset and sunrise, the hours were variable. The ninth hour, or nones in the church offices, was originally reckoned in this way but later set back to midday, or "noon." See R. L. Poole, *Medieval Reckonings of Time* (London, 1918), pp. 11-12.

[3] This great famine is mentioned in many contemporary records, such as the *Annales Blandinienses*, A. 1125, MGH, SS V, 28: "Fames horrida invaluit" and A. 1126, "Iterum fames gravissima repetita per Flandriam"; *Sigeberti continuatio Praemonstratensis*, A. 1125, MGH, SS VI, 449: "Fames permaxima grassatur in Gallia . . .;" *Liber de restauratione S. Martini Tornacensis continuatio*, c. 13, MGH, SS XII, 323: "Eo tempore fames vehementissima totam provinciam oppressit. . . ." It is best explained in terms of a long, extremely cold and snowy winter in 1123-24, a late, cold, and rainy summer, followed by another bitter winter in 1124-25 and again in 1125-26; this interpretation is given in *Sigeberti continuatio Anselmi Gemblacensis*, A. 1124, 1125, 1126, MGH, SS VI, 379-80.

[4] Psalms 104.16, in the Vulgate, which Galbert follows here.

drink, he fell ill. Men were wasting away from repletion and indigestion and yet they suffered from hunger until they drew the last breath. Many swelled up, and food and drink were loathsome to them although they had plenty of both. In this time of famine, in the middle of Lent,[5] the men of our land living near Ghent and the Leie and Scheldt rivers ate meat because bread was completely lacking. Some who tried to make their way to the cities and towns[6] where they could buy bread[7] perished of hunger along the road, choking to death before they were halfway. Near the manors and farms[8] of the rich and the strongholds and castles, the poor, bent low in their misery as they came for alms, fell dead in the act of begging. Strange to say, no one in our land retained his natural color but all bore a pallor like that of death. Both the well and the ill languished because those who were sound in body became ill on seeing the misery of the dying.[9]

[5] That is, about March 4, 1125.

[6] In the expression *civitates et castra* (as also in c. 53), *castra* seems to mean "towns," but in *castra seu munitiones* in the next sentence the same word seems to refer to fortified places, probably rural (as in c. 67). Each use must be considered in its context.

[7] It is clear that grain was stored and could therefore be purchased not in the country but in the towns. The granaries of the counts, where the produce of the domain and payments in kind were assembled, were generally located in the "castles" (*castra*) of the counts, close to which mercantile settlements such as Bruges and Ghent had sprung up. A charter of Charles in 1123 refers to "my granary" at Veurne; see *Actes*, no. 114, p. 261. Concerning these granaries see R. Monier, *Les Institutions financières du comté de Flandre du XIe siècle à 1384* (Paris, 1948), pp. 39-40.

[8] By *villas et curtes* Galbert probably refers to larger and smaller units of agrarian exploitation. The older great domain or villa was now breaking up into smaller units, manors or farms of various sizes and kinds. On this complex process see F. L. Ganshof, "Medieval Agrarian Economy in its Prime: France, the Low Countries and Western Germany," in *The Cambridge Economic History*, Vol. I (Cambridge, 1941), pp. 290-302. In the area around Bruges and Ghent the domanial disintegration began early, probably in the tenth century; see J. Noterdaeme, "De graven van Vlaanderen en hun domeinen rond Brugge," HMGG, VIII (1954), 31-39, and A. Verhulst, "Différents types de structure domaniale et agraire en Basse et Moyenne Belgique pendant le haut moyen âge: un essai d'explication," *Annales*, XI (1956), 63.

[9] The distention described by Galbert sounds like a starvation edema rather than the consequence of overeating. The pallor could be attributed to "famine pigmentation," a peculiar splotchy appearance of the skin, resembling dirt, most frequently seen on the cheeks of starving men. See A. Keys, "Human Starvation and Its Consequences," *Journal of the American Dietetic Association*, XXII (1946), 583-85.

[3] *Count Charles takes steps to relieve the poor*

But the impious were not corrected in this way, for it is said that
at this very time they had plotted the death of the most pious
count Charles.[1] The count tried in every way possible to take
care of the poor, distributing alms in the towns[2] and throughout
his domain, both in person and by his officials. At the same time
he was feeding one hundred paupers in Bruges every day; and
he gave a sizable loaf of bread to each of them from before
Lent until the new harvests of the same year.[3] And likewise in
his other towns he had made the same provision.[4] In the same
year the lord count had decreed that whoever sowed two measures of land in the sowing time should sow another measure in
peas and beans,[5] because these legumes yield more quickly and
seasonably and therefore could nourish the poor more quickly
if the misery of famine and want should not end in that year.
He had also ordered this to be done throughout the whole
county, in this way making provision for the poor in the future

[1] Evidence that this chapter was written after the murder of Charles, March 2,
1127. It also reveals the current belief that a plot against the count had sprung up
earlier than his legal action (in 1126) against the Erembald clan, the villains of
Galbert's story. The complex motivation of the crime is discussed more fully below
and in the Introduction.

[2] In this case *castra*, here translated as "towns," may refer to the complex of
castrum and mercantile settlement close by, a usage not uncommon at this time.
See Verbruggen, "Note sur le sens du mot castrum," RB, XXVIII (1950), 147.

[3] Contrary to Pirenne's statement in his edition of Galbert (p. 6, n. 5), Galbert's
calculation of the yearly calendar, from Christmas, rather than from Easter, is not
unusual but is in accord with the general practice of the time in Flanders, where
the "Paschal style" did not appear until late in the twelfth century and then only
concurrently with the still predominant "Christmas style." See the conclusions of
C. Callewaert, "Les Origines du style pascal en Flandre," ASEB, LV (1905), 13-26,
121-43, and "Nouvelles recherches sur la chronologie médiévale en Flandre," *ibid.*,
LIX (1909), 41-62 and 153; also Vercauteren, *Actes*, p. lxxxix.

[4] Walter, c. 11, also speaks of Charles's order that a daily stipend be given to
the needy on every one of his many farms, and of his personal distribution of food,
money, and clothing wherever he was, in town, stronghold or manor (*urbe, oppido,
vel villa*). One day at Ypres he gave out 7,800 loaves of bread.

[5] Galbert obviously means measures of land sown with bread grains, probably
wheat. A "measure" probably refers to the Flemish *ghemet*; the *ghemet* of Bruges
contained 4,426.38 square meters, a little more than the English statute acre (4,047
square meters). See H. de Schrijver, *De oude landmaten in Vlaanderen* (Ghent,
1936), p. 18. Peas and beans were essential foods, used in a variety of ways. In
hard times flour ground from them was mixed with the usual bread cereals. See
R. Grand, *L'Agriculture au moyen âge* (Paris, 1950), pp. 329-32.

as well as he could.[6] He reprimanded those men of Ghent[7] who had allowed poor people whom they could have fed to die of hunger on their doorsteps.

He also prohibited the brewing of beer because the poor could be fed more easily and better if the townspeople[8] and country-people refrained from making beer in this time of famine. For he ordered bread to be made out of oats so that the poor could at least maintain life on bread and water.[9] He ordered a fourth of a measure[10] of wine to be sold for six pennies and not more dearly so that the merchants would stop hoarding and buying up wine[11] and would exchange their wares, in view of the urgency

[6] This seems to imply that the original order affected only those parts of the count's domain which he exploited directly as a landlord.

[7] The wealth of the Ghent "patricians," based on the textile industry as well as on trade, is exemplified in a charter of 1120 in which Charles deals with a contro-versy concerning 450 measures of land between a citizen of Ghent (oppidanus) named Everwacker and the Abbot of Saint Peter's at Ghent; see Actes, no. 95, pp. 213 ff. The last two witnesses to this charter are burghers of Ghent, according to Ganshof, "Iets over Brugge gedurende de preconstitutionelle periode van haar geschiedenis," NH, I (1938), n. 61, p. 301. "Gerard the Rich of Ghent" appears as a witness in an act of 1117 (Actes, no. 83, p. 188). See also F. Blockmans, Het gentsche stadspatriciaat tot omstreeks 1302 (Antwerp, 1938), p. 72.

[8] Galbert here uses cives, which, interchangeably with burgenses, always denotes townspeople as distinct from others in his account.

[9] This fact is confirmed by Walter, c. 11, who says he forbade the making of beer and "beverages," and by the Liber de restauratione S. Martini Tornacensis continuatio, c. 13, MGH, SS XIV, 323, according to which Charles said it was better for the rich to drink water than for the poor to perish of hunger. (It is clear that oats were not considered a normal bread grain.) Walter adds that Charles ordered the usual loaf of bread which sold for a penny to be halved in size so that a poor man with only an obole, or half a penny, could buy at least a small loaf.

[10] Quartam vini. It is difficult to determine exactly what amount Galbert refers to because of the various meanings of quarta in medieval Flanders. It might be the fourth part of a sextarius (zester), in which case it would be 16 pints (called in Bruges a schreve); or it might be the Flemish vierdeel of two 'pints (the pint of Bruges holds 0.5648 litres). For these and other possibilities see E. Gailliard, Inventaire des chartes de la ville de Bruges: Glossaire flamand (Bruges, 1882), under vierendeel, pp. 728-29; viertal, p. 729; and zester, p. 628.

[11] It seems obvious that speculation in wine as well as grain was going on at this time. Although the vine had been introduced into Flanders in the eleventh century, probably by Count Baldwin V (1035-67), it did not easily flourish there. (Archbishop Gervaise of Rheims praises Baldwin for bringing the "gifts of Bacchus" to the people in a letter prefatory to the Miracula S. Donatiani, MGH, SS XV, 854-56). Religious establishments, to which wine was essential, first met the problem by extending their domains into the nearby zones of viticulture in France, especially around Soissons and Laon, and in Germany in the Rhine and Moselle

of the famine, for other foodstuffs which they could acquire more quickly and which could be used more easily to nourish the poor.[12] From his own table he took daily enough food to sustain one hundred and thirteen paupers. In addition he provided daily for one of the poor a set of new garments, including a shirt, tunic, skins, cloak, breeches, hose, and shoes, from the beginning of that Lent and of his devout fasting (during which, betrayed, he fell asleep in the Lord) until the day when he died in Christ.[13] And after he had seen to these arrangements and completed such a merciful distribution to the poor, he was in the habit of going to church where, kneeling in prayer, he would sing psalms to the Lord, and according to his custom would distribute pennies to the poor while prostrate before God.[14]

---

valleys, but they gradually turned to the purchase and importation of foreign wine, brought generally by water routes. Commerce in wine is apparent from about the middle of the eleventh century; by *ca.*1100 Laon was a thriving center of export. See H. Van Werveke, "Comment les établissements religieux belges se procuraient-ils du vin au moyen âge?" RB, II (1923), 643-62, and R. Doehaerd, "Un Paradoxe géographique: Laon, capitale du vin au XIIe siècle," *Annales*, V (1950), 145-65. Those students at Laon who heard the news of Charles's murder on the second day may well have learned it from Flemish merchants; see Galbert, c. 12.

[12] This is one of the earliest known attempts at "price-fixing" by public authority since Carolingian times. Such a policy must have aroused antagonism against the count among the merchants, but there is no contemporary evidence to support the later tradition that the chief speculators were identical with the leading plotters against Charles, as stated in the *Chronicon comitum Flandrensium,* in *Corpus chronicorum Flandriae,* ed. by J. J. De Smet (4 vols.; Brussels, 1837-65), I, 81-85.

[13] Walter, c. 25, says that for a while before he died Charles had clothed and shod five of the poor daily. Even more striking is Walter's statement, c. 11, that in the two years before his death he mercifully remitted to the peasants (*agricolae*) a large part of the revenues from which he supported himself and his household. These were doubtless part of his domanial revenues, perhaps coming from maritime Flanders where the well-advanced work of reclamation had greatly enlarged the count's domain; the peasants may have been *hospites,* peasants of privileged status owing only small annual payments in money and kind. See especially Monier, *Les Institutions financières,* pp. 8-9, and F. L. Ganshof, "Medieval Agrarian Society in Its Prime," in *The Cambridge Economic History,* I, 280-81.

[14] The evidence of the use of money supports the theory that coins, especially in the form of silver pennies, were an indispensable instrument of daily life, even among the poor, at this time. See H. Van Werveke, "Monnaies, lingots ou marchandises? les instruments d'échange au XIe et XIIe siècle," AHES, IV (1932), 452-68. The penny was, in fact, the only real coin at this time, according to C. M. Cipolla, *Money, Prices and Civilization in the Mediterranean World* (Princeton, 1956), pp. 38-40.

[4] *Count Charles is offered and refuses the imperial crown,*
    1125

While the marquis Charles was reigning in his county of
Flanders in the splendor of peace and fame, Henry, the Roman
emperor,[1] died, and the realm of that empire was made desolate
and left without an heir to the throne. Therefore the leading
men among the clergy and the people of the realm of the Romans and Germans made a great effort to find someone for the
office of emperor who was noble both in ancestry and character.
After weighing the merits of rulers of various lands and kingdoms, those wise and powerful men of the realm decided, after
due consideration, that they would formally send suitable dele-
gates, namely, the chancellor of the archbishop of Cologne and
with him Count Godfrey, to the count of Flanders, Charles the
Pious, on behalf of the whole clergy and people of the kingdom
and empire of the Germans, to beg and entreat him by virtue of
his power and piety to assume the honors of empire and the
regal dignities with their appurtenances, if only for the sake of
charity.[2] For all the best men among both clergy and people
were hoping, ardently and rightly, that he would be elected so
that if, God willing, he deigned to come to them, they could

---

[1] Henry V, last of the Salian dynasty of the Empire, died May 23, 1125, without heirs.

[2] According to Otto of Freising, the German magnates assembled at Mainz (on
August 24, 1125) considered four candidates: Lothair, duke of Saxony; Frederick,
duke of Swabia; Leopold, margrave of Austria; and Charles, count of Flanders;
see *Chronica sive historia de duabus civitatibus*, lib. VII, c. 17, ed. by A. Hofmeister, MGH, SS *in usum scholarum* (1912), p. 333. But Charles is not mentioned
as a candidate in the *Narratio de electione Lotharii*, c. 2, MGH, SS XII, 510,
or in any other contemporary account except Galbert's. (C. C. Mierow in his
translation of Otto's chronicle, *The Two Cities* [New York, 1928], p. 424, n. 84,
apparently follows Hofmeister, p. 333, n. 4, in believing that Otto was mistaken
in including Charles.) Clerical opposition, led by the archbishops of Mainz and
Cologne, ruined the chances of Frederick, Henry's nephew, the most natural successor, and led to the election of Lothair, duke of Saxony, on August 30, 1125;
see Gebhardt's *Handbuch der deutschen geschichte* (7th ed.; 2 vols.; Stuttgart,
1930), II, 306. The presence of the chancellor of Frederick, archbishop of
Cologne (1099-1131), in the embassy to Charles suggests that he may have pro-
moted Charles's candidacy; see W. Bernhardi, *Lothar von Supplinburg* (Leipzig,
1879), p. 9. "Count Godfrey" was probably Godfrey of Namur (1105-39). On
the face of it, Charles's chances seem very slight, and the enthusiasm for him in
Germany is undoubtedly much exaggerated by Galbert.

elevate him unanimously by the imperial coronation and establish him as king by the law of the preceding Catholic emperors. When Count Charles had heard the embassy and their urgent request, he took counsel with the nobles and peers of his land[3] as to what he should do. But those who had rightly cherished and loved him, and who venerated him as a father, began to grieve and to lament his departure, predicting that it would prove the ruin of the fatherland if he should desert it. Those evil traitors, however, who were threatening his life, advised him to assume the German kingship and its dignities, pointing out to him how much glory and fame would be his as king of the Romans.[4] Those wretches were trying by this guile and trickery to get rid of him; later when they had been unable to remove him while he was alive, they betrayed him while he was contending with them on behalf of the law of God and men.

And so Count Charles remained in his county because of the insistence of those who loved him, seeking and establishing for all, so far as possible, the peace and well-being of the fatherland; he was a Catholic, good, and devout worshiper of God and a prudent ruler of men. When he wanted to perform deeds of knighthood, he had no enemies around his land, either in

[3] Galbert doubtless refers to a convoking of the count's *curia* or feudal court, a body of variable size, composed primarily of the great officials of his household, his more important direct vassals who came to fulfill one of their essential feudal functions, that of giving "counsel" to their lord, and other vassals who happened to be present. On the composition and competence of the feudal *curia*, see Monier, *Les Institutions centrales*, pp. 40 ff., and L. Génicot, "Le Premier siècle de la 'curia' de Hainaut (1060 env.-1195), *Le Moyen Âge*, LII (1947), 39-60. An effort is made in the Introduction, Part III, to clarify the distinctions that Galbert makes in referring to that heterogeneous mass of men, set apart by their military activities and their "noble way of life," which is often referred to by modern writers as though it were a homogeneous class of "nobles." The lowest and most numerous elements are simple "knights," called *milites* by Galbert; the highest are "peers" (*pares*), a very small select group. A larger group of important vassals seems to be implied in his use of the terms *nobiles, barones, principes, primates, optimates, proceres*, often in bewildering combinations, with and without *pares*. (The usage in the charters is almost as confusing; here *barones* is favored instead of *principes*, Galbert's most common term.) Since it is impossible to distinguish between these terms in English, they have all been arbitrarily translated here as "barons," in deference to English usage. On this subject see J. Dhondt, *Les Origines des États*, pp. 10-11, and P. Feuchère, "Pairs de principauté and pairs de château," RB, XLI (1953), 973 ff., *passim*, especially 977, 996-97.

[4] Clear evidence of the existence in 1125 of factions among the barons.

the marches or on the frontiers and borders, either because his neighbors feared him or because, united to him in the bond of peace and love, they preferred to exchange offerings and gifts with him.[5] So he undertook chivalric exploits for the honor of his land and the training of his knights in the lands of the counts or princes of Normandy or France, sometimes even beyond the kingdom of France;[6] and there with two hundred knights on horseback he engaged in tourneys,[7] in this way enhancing his own fame and the power and glory of his county. Whatever sin he committed by this worldliness he redeemed with God many times by almsgiving.[8]

[5] *Count Charles is offered but refuses the crown of the kingdom of Jerusalem, 1123*

During his lifetime it happened that the king of Jerusalem was taken captive by the Saracens, and the city of Jerusalem sat desolate without her king.[1] As we have learned, the Crusaders

[5] Concerning Charles's relations, generally good, with his feudal overlords, the king of France and the emperor, and with the king of England, see Introduction, II.

[6] Nothing specific is known of such exploits. Perhaps an enterprise of this kind is referred to in a charter of 1122 (*Actes,* no. 108, p. 249) where Charles speaks of returning to Arras "with military glory, after a conflict of arms with Godfrey of Valenciennes."

[7] The institution of the tourney, of ancient and popular origin, had become by the twelfth century a formal, regulated, fictitious battle, restricted to the knightly class, "un vrai plaisir de classe," which because of its realistic character was increasingly sought after as a training exercise. (See Bloch, *La Société féodale: les classes et le gouvernement des hommes,* pp. 33-35; and J. F. Verbruggen, *De krijgskunst in West-Europa in de middeleeuwen* [Brussels, 1954], pp. 84 ff.) The custom of tourneys spread rapidly in France and Flanders in the twelfth century, and thence to other lands. Perhaps Charles, like Baldwin VII, used the tourney to deflect his knights from private warfare.

[8] Tourneys were soon to be formally condemned by the Church as a "detestable form of amusement, deadly to men and animals," first in 1130 at the Council of Clermont by Innocent II and repeatedly thereafter until 1316, that is, throughout their functional period; those killed in them were refused ecclesiastical burial, though not the viaticum. See Hefele-Leclercq, *Histoire des conciles* (8 vols.; Paris, 1907-21), Vol. V, Part I, canon 9 of the Council of Clermont, p. 688.

[1] Baldwin II, king of Jerusalem (1118-31), was taken prisoner by Belek of Aleppo near Antioch in April, 1123, ransomed and released in August, 1124. See R. L. Nicholson, "The Growth of the Latin States, 1118-1144," in *A History of the Crusades,* Vol. I, ed. by M. W. Baldwin (Philadelphia, 1955), pp. 419-23.

who were pursuing the course of Christian knighthood there hated that captive king because he was grasping and penurious, and had not governed the people of God well.[2] Therefore they took counsel and by general consent sent a letter to Count Charles asking him to come to Jerusalem and receive the kingdom of Judaea, and in that place and in the holy city take possession of the crown of the Catholic realm and the royal dignity.[3] But he was unwilling, after consulting his vassals, to desert the fatherland of Flanders, which in his lifetime he was to govern well, and would have ruled even better if those evil traitors, full of the demon, had not slain their lord and father, who was imbued with the spirit of piety and wisdom and courage. Alas, what sorrow, that they should rob the Church of God of such a great man whom the church and the people of the Eastern Empire,[4] and the holy city of Jerusalem and its Christian population, had preferred and chosen, and even demanded to have as king!

[6] *In praise of Count Charles*

Strength of mind and memory and even reason, the greater virtue of the mind, fail me in praising the good Count Charles;[1] in

[2] Galbert's unfavorable opinion of him is not supported by William of Tyre's account of Baldwin's character and reign in his *Historia rerum in partibus transmarinis gestarum*, RHC, Occ. I; perhaps the very qualities praised by William (especially in lib. XII, c. 4, 7, 14, 15), his piety, strength, and vigor as a ruler, liberality to the citizens of Jerusalem and to the Knights Templars, made him less acceptable to the restless barons of the realm. Is it possible that Galbert's impression came from Flemish sources in contact with Eustace of Grenier, lord of Sidon and constable of the kingdom, supposedly a native of Therouanne, who was chosen as regent by the barons during the king's captivity? Or that the candidacy of Charles was suggested by Eustace? Little is known about Eustace; see the note of A. C. Krey to the English translation of William of Tyre, *A History of Deeds Done Beyond the Sea* (2 vols.; New York, 1943), I, 541, n. 57, and J. L. La Monte, "The Lords of Sidon in the Twelfth and Thirteenth Centuries," *Byzantion*, XVII (1944-45), 185-88.

[3] No other source, so far as I know, confirms Galbert's mention of the invitation to Charles. In view of his reliability in general, it seems unlikely that Galbert would have fabricated such an incident; it is possible that during the king's captivity there was some kind of an approach to Charles which Galbert expands in order to glorify Charles.

[4] That is, the "Roman" empire; "eastern" probably refers to the fact that its nucleus was the former kingdom of the "East Franks" which had emerged in 843.

[1] This is Galbert's first use of the epithet, "the good Count Charles." The

comparison with him all you earthly princes are less worthy and less powerful, lacking experience and judgment, and disorderly in habits.[2] For Count Charles held such a place among the devout sons of the Church that in his merits he excelled the leaders and many philosophers of the Christian faith; and although he had once been a sinner and guilty,[3] at the end of his good life, from the fruit of penance, all things worked together for his good and for the eternal salvation of his soul. As it is said,[4]

> And none be counted happy till his death,
> Till his last funeral rites are paid.

And, according to the Apostle,[5] "We know that to them who love God all things work together for good, even to them that are called according to his purpose." For in a holy place and in holy prayer, and in holy devoutness of heart, and in the holy time of Lent, and in the holy act of almsgiving, and before the sacred altar and the sacred relics of Saint Donatian, archbishop of Rheims,[6] and Saint Basil the Great,[7] and Saint Maximus, the one

---

title "consul" used here and occasionally throughout will be translated as "count," Galbert's more usual term.

[2] Galbert's treatment of Henry I of England, Louis VI of France, the Emperor Lothair, and others is rather cavalier!

[3] If Galbert refers to any specific sins of Charles nothing is known about them.

[4] Ovid, *Metamorphoses*, III.136-37.

[5] Romans 8.28. Galbert's Latin here follows the Vulgate.

[6] It is not clear how the relics of Saint Donatian, seventh archbishop of Rheims who lived in the fourth century, reached Bruges. They may have been installed first at Torhout and later moved to Bruges for safekeeping by Count Baldwin I at the time of the Danish attack in 864. The clerics who accompanied the relics were established along with them in the church of Saint Mary within the castle at Bruges. From this settlement of clerics the collegiate church and chapter of "Saint Donatian" were to develop in the later eleventh century. The earliest documents refer to the church as "Saint Mary and Saint Donatian," thus revealing its dual character as parish church and church of the college of canons, but after 1104 the first name was dropped. The relics were moved to a new shrine in Saint Donatian in 1096 (see AASS, Oct. VI, p. 488, n. 6). For the early history of the church see C. Callewaert, "Les Origines de la collégiale Saint-Donatien à Bruges," ASEB, LVI (1906), 395-408; P. Grierson, "The Translation of the Relics of St. Donatian to Bruges," *Revue Bénédictine*, XLIX (1937), 170-90; É. de Moreau, *Histoire de l'Église en Belgique*, Vol. I (2d ed., Brussels, 1945), p. 289, and also his "Bruges," in *Dictionnaire d'histoire et de géographie ecclésiastique*, Vol. IX (1938), cols. 890-95; and H. Sproemberg, in Wattenbach-Holtzmann, *Deutschlands Geschichtsquellen*, I (Tübingen, 1948), 697.

[7] Saint Basil the Great, bishop of Caesaria (d. 379). His relics are not mentioned before the twelfth century, according to the Bollandists, who say that parts of

who raised three dead,[8] those foul dogs, full of the demon, those serfs, murdered their lord! Certainly there is no one so senseless, so stupid and obtuse, as not to sentence those traitors to the vilest and most unheard-of punishments,[9] those serfs who by unheard-of treachery[10] did away with their lord, the very one whom they should most have protected.

It is certainly a marvelous and memorable fact that among the many emperors, kings, dukes, and counts whom we have seen, we have never yet seen or heard of any one whom it so well became to be lord and father, and advocate[11] of the churches of God. That he knew how to be lord, father, advocate, to be pious,

---

his body and other extraordinary relics were reputedly brought to Bruges by a returning crusader; see AASS, June III, p. 929.

[8] Saint Maximus (d. 460), abbot of Lerins and bishop of Riez, whose feast day fell on November 27; see L. Duchesne, *Fastes épiscopaux de l'ancienne Gaule* (3 vols.; Paris, 1894), I, 283-84. The three miracles of resurrection attributed to him in his lifetime are related in the *Vita Maximi* by the patrician Dynamius (Migne, PL, Vol. 80, col. 36-38, 8-10) and are referred to in the praise of the saint by Ado (*Martyrologium*, Migne, PL, Vol. 123, col. 405) whose phrase "qui tres mortuos ... suscitavit" is apparently echoed by Galbert. (It is quoted in the Auctaria to the *Martyrologium* of Usuardus in Migne, PL, Vol. 124, col. 741). Saint Maximus was honored not only in the south of France but also at Therouanne, whence his cult radiated to Bruges, Tournai, Arras, and Amiens. See E. Van Drival, "Mémoire liturgique et historique sur S. Maxim," *Mémoires de l'Académie d'Arras*, sér. 2, XIV (1883), 312-34. Mention of the relics of these three saints is made in the "Catalogue des reliques conservées à l'Église Saint-Donatien à Bruges au XIIIᵉ siècle," *Le Beffroi*, IV (1872-73), 201: "Corpus Sancti Donatiani qui fuit VII Remorum archiepiscopus. Magna pars corporis Sancti Basilii.... De Sancto Maximo due coste."

[9] This suggests that Galbert wrote after May 5, 1127, the date of the punishment of the traitors.

[10] Galbert errs in calling this an "unheard-of" act of treachery. Charles's own father was slain by his men in Saint Alban's church at Odense, on July 10, 1086; see *De martyrizatione Sancti Kanuti regis*, MGH, SS XXIX, 5. And it is reported that William, count of Burgundy, was slain in church while praying before the altar on March 2, 1127, the same day on which Charles was killed; see *Sigeberti continuatio Anselmi*, A. 1127, MGH, SS VI, 380. On the violent tenor of life in general, see M. Bloch, *La Société féodale: les classes et le gouvernement des hommes*, pp. 198-201; on the "paradox of vassalage" see *La Société féodale: la formation des liens de dépendance*, pp. 354-61.

[11] "Advocate" may be used here in the general sense of "protector" (as it seems to be in Galbert's Introduction and in c. 6) but it also possesses a specific meaning since the counts of Flanders were the "superior-advocates" of almost all the abbeys in their realm. This function of military protection and limited judicial authority, which they exercised at the expense of the abbots and their officials, as well as of the lesser lay advocates, gave them a substantial control over these great and rich religious establishments. See C. Pergameni, *L'Avouerie ecclésiastique belge* (Ghent, 1907), pp. 115 ff.; Monier, *Les Institutions centrales*, pp. 16-17, and Moreau, *Histoire de l'Église en Belgique*, II (2d ed.; Brussels, 1945), 222-28.

gentle, compassionate, an honor to God and an ornament to the Church, cannot be doubted, for after the death of such a great man, everyone bore witness to his merits. Friends and enemies, foreigners and neighbors, nobles and common people, and the inhabitants of every land whatsoever, even if they had only heard of his extraordinary reputation, were convinced that he would be held worthy of great merit by God and men, because he died like a Christian ruler, seeking the justice of God and the welfare of those over whom he ruled. But the men whom he trusted tripped him up and betrayed him, as it is said in the Psalm: "Why, my own intimate friend, who shared my bread, has lifted his heel to trip me up." [12]

[7] *The discovery of the servile origin of the Erembald clan, 1126*

Now after the clemency of God had withdrawn the scourges[1] and completely removed the troubles of the time, He began in His mercy to bestow plenty on the land, and He ordered the granaries to be filled with the produce of the fields and the earth to abound in wine and other foodstuffs, and by divine order the whole land flourished again in the loveliness of the seasons. The pious count, wishing to reestablish proper order in his realm, sought to find out who belonged to him, who were servile and who were free men in the realm.[2] When cases were being heard in the courts,[3] the count was often present, and he

---

[12] Psalms 40.10 in the Vulgate, which Galbert follows here.

[1] "The scourges" doubtless refer to the famine of chapters 2 and 3. What follows seems to be a direct continuation of those chapters and therefore it is likely that chapters 4, 5, and 6 were a later interpolation.

[2] Was this a conscious effort of the count to preserve the *status quo* by checking the current upward push of various elements in the population who already enjoyed a considerable degree of social liberty *de facto* but whose legal status was not clearly determined? (A discussion of this changing society will be found in the Introduction, III.) See R. Van Caenegem, *Geschiedenis van het strafprocesrecht in Vlaanderen van de XIe tot de XIVe eeuw* (Brussels, 1956), pp. 91 ff. concerning *placita generalia*.

[3] Galbert is probably referring to the count's local tribunals or judicial assemblies exercising common law jurisdiction within most of the great territorial

learned from the judgments concerning secular liberty and the status of serfs that in important cases and general pleas[4] free men scorned to answer charges made by servile ones. Those whom the count had been able to identify as belonging to him, he now set about trying to claim for himself. A certain provost, that Bertulf of Bruges,[5] and his brother the castellan of Bruges,[6]

---

units of the domain, the castellanies, and hence called in French *tribuneaux de châtellenie*. They were presided over by the count's key local official and vassal, the castellan, and were composed of a variable number of *scabini* (*échevins*) or "judges," named by the count, free men of standing in the area, probably often knights of the petty nobility; they are often referred to as *échevinages*. These tribunals possessed a broad competence, both civil and penal, over free men, but none in cases of a strictly feudal nature or over the persons of vassals of the count. They met regularly, thrice yearly in certain castellanies, and also held special sessions at certain times. The classic account of this institution is found in the work of F. L. Ganshof, especially in his *Recherches sur les tribuneaux de châtellenie en Flandre avant le milieu du XIIIe siècle* (Antwerp and Paris, 1932), and in the synthesis of all his previous work on judicial institutions, "Les Transformations de l'organisation judiciaire dans le comté de Flandre jusqu'à l'avènement de la maison de Bourgogne," RB, XVIII (1939), 43-61. On the *scabini*, see especially A. M. Feytmans, "Scabini terrae," RB, X (1931), 170-74.

[4] These phrases are difficult to interpret. Professor Ganshof in a letter to the translator agrees with Pirenne, in his edition of Galbert (p. 12, n. 5), that "important cases" (*magna negotia*) here refers to cases involving *la haute justice;* he suggests that "general pleas" (*generalia causa*) refers to those matters normally treated in these judicial assemblies, the scope of whose jurisdiction was probably derived ultimately from the Carolingian tradition of the *plaids generaux*.

[5] Galbert's first mention of the leading member of the family descended from Erembald, former castellan of Bruges, whose career he relates in c. 71. Bertulf, son of Erembald, appears frequently as a signatory or witness in the charters of the counts, first as "canon" in 1089 (*Actes*, no. 9, p. 32) and frequently as "provost" from 1093 to 1124. According to Galbert's reckoning in c. 57, he must have become provost of the collegiate church of Saint Donatian at Bruges in 1091, two years after the important charter of 1089, in which Count Robert II made that official *ex officio* chancellor of Flanders, receiver of the count's domanial revenues and head of the notaries, chaplains and clerics of the count's court. (*Actes*, no. 9, pp. 23 ff.) Walter, c. 14, gives Bertulf the full title of "provost, arch-chaplain and chancellor." This triple position, thanks to its close proximity to the count, gave him a unique place of influence and eminence in the realm which he had used for the aggrandizement of his whole family. His character and role will be revealed in the account of the treason and fall of the family by Galbert, who as a notary of Bruges must have known him well in a subordinate position. See the Introduction, pp. 60-62.

[6] Desiderius or Didier Hacket, who also appears frequently as witness in the charters, for the first time as castellan of Bruges in 1115 (*Actes*, no. 73, p. 169). In this capacity he held a key position in the realm, exercising military and judicial, and certain administrative powers, over one of the count's most important castellanies. He held his office, but not the castle or territory, as a fief from the count. Since members of his immediate family, from Erembald *ca.*1067, had succeeded each other in this post, it had become practically hereditary. (There is evidence that other members of the family were or had been castellans, Gilbert at

with their nephews Borsiard,[7] Robert,[8] Albert,[9] and other leading
members of that clan, were striving by every device of craft and
guile to find a way by which they could slip out of servitude
and cease belonging to the count; for they belonged to him, being
of servile status.[10] Finally, after due consideration, the provost

---

Bergues according to Galbert, c. 49, and Baldwin at Saint Omer according to
Walter, c. 37; see Genealogy.) Hacket's role in the events of 1127, however, is
subordinate to that of his brother. (His name Hacket was a common surname in
Flanders at this time, meaning *brochet* or pike.) The basic account of the office
of castellan is that by W. Blommaert, *Les Châtelains de Flandre: étude d'histoire
constitutionelle* (Ghent, 1915), which has been modified by more recent works
to be mentioned in due course. F. L. Ganshof deals with the Erembalds as
castellans in his *Étude sur les ministeriales en France et en Lotharingie* (Brussels,
1926), pp. 365 ff., in which he suggests that most of the early castellans may
have been of lowly origin, but this theory is challenged by P. Rolland, "L'Origine
des châtelains de Flandre," RB, VI (1927), 699-708, and more recently by
J. Dhondt, "Note sur les châtelains," in *Études historiques dédiées à la mémoire
de M. Roger Rodière* (Calais, 1947), pp. 49-52.

[7] Borsiard or Burchard (as he is called in Walter's account) was the son of
Lambert Nappin, another son of Erembald, according to Galbert, c. 71. Along
with Bertulf, he is a prime actor in the events of 1127.

[8] Robert the Young, or "Junior," was the son of Robert II, castellan of Bruges
(*ca.*1087-*ca.*1109 from the evidence of the count's charters, *Actes*, pp. 21, 175),
another of the five sons of Erembald named by Galbert, c. 71. As the darling of
the people of Bruges he occupies a curiously romantic role in the story.

[9] Albert, presumably the brother of Robert the Young, never again appears in
Galbert's account.

[10] The legal status of the Erembald clan is not clear. Pirenne (ed. of Galbert,
p. 12, n. 4) states that Galbert's use of the phrase *de pertinentia sua* or *de
pertinentia comitis* (here translated as "belonging to him") implies that they were
his "ministerials." But were the Erembalds actually "ministerials" or *chevalier-
serfs* as Ganshof (in his *Étude sur les ministeriales*, p. 343) and others, following
Pirenne, have asserted? As Ganshof clearly shows (pp. 336-38), the word *ministeriales* is never used in twelfth-century Flanders except in the general sense of
servants or functionaries, not, as in Germany, in the specific sense of a recognized
juridical class of officials, of servile origin, but elevated socially by their duties
and way of life, especially if their functions were aulic or military. If, as Ganshof
says (*Étude*, pp. 358-59) such lowborn though important functionaries, called by
a variety of names in Flanders, never constituted in Flanders a juridical or even
a distinct social class, and if, as is clear from Galbert's account, the low origin
of a family like the Erembalds could be almost completely forgotten, it may be
better not to call them "ministerials." The extraordinary social position they had
achieved may reveal, not so much the existence of high-placed "ministerials" in
Flanders as the character of a society in flux, not yet a hierarchy of well-defined
classes, but rather "une agglomération, un enchevêtrement, si l'on veut, de groupe-
ments personnels, serfs ou vassaux, dépendants de seigneurs qui à leur tour se
rattachaient à d'autres groupes analogues," as Marc Bloch describes it. ("Un Problème d'histoire comparée: la ministérialité en France et en Allemagne," RHDF,
VII [1928], 79-80.) In such a mobile society it was apparently possible for an
able family, regardless of origin, to slip imperceptibly into the class of those
"who lived nobly" and become merged in it successfully unless by chance they
aroused the hostility of the older *lignages vassaliques*, as Bloch suggests (pp. 81-

gave his marriageable nieces, whom he had reared in his home, in wedlock to free knights, resorting to this policy of intermarriage as a means by which he and his kin might gain a certain measure of secular liberty.[11]

But it happened that a knight who had married a niece of the provost[12] challenged to single combat in the presence of the count another knight, who was free according to the descent of his family;[13] and the latter replied vigorously with an indignant refusal, asserting that by birth he was not of servile status but rather of free rank, according to his family lineage, and for this reason he would not contend as an equal in single combat with his challenger. For, according to the law of the count,[14] a free

---

83), or of a powerful ruler like Count Charles. Since Galbert gives the impression that the Erembalds had long been considered "free men," perhaps they should be treated as successful "climbers," possibly *fraudeurs* in the opinion of E. Champeaux, in his review of Ganshof's work, RHDF, VI (1927), 755-56. The dangers of generalizing in this matter from single instances such as that of the Erembalds are pointed out by K. Bosl, *Die Reichsministerialität der Salier und Staufer* (Stuttgart, 1950), pp. 109-10. Perhaps an analogous case is that of Henry of Lorraine, counselor to King Louis VI of France, who in 1112 was charged with being of servile descent through his father; when he appeared before the king's court to answer the charge, and his accuser failed to appear, he was permitted to clear himself by his own oath to the effect that like himself, his father and grandfather had been born free and had remained free. The identity of the accuser is not revealed. See A. Luchaire, *Histoire des institutions monarchiques de la France sous les premiers Capétiens* (2d ed. 2 vols.; Paris, 1891), Vol. II, App. no. 19, pp. 341-42.

[11] Galbert reveals four such cases in the course of his narrative, Robert of Creques (c. 25), Walter Crommelin (c. 54), Guy of Steenvoorde (c. 58), and the "son" of Walter of Vladslo (c. 89). See the Genealogy.

[12] Robert of Crecques by name; see c. 25. He was charged in the court of the count with violation of the peace, according to Walter, c. 15. He appears as witness to charters several times between 1107 and 1117; see *Actes*, Index. The lords of Crecques, in the castellany of Saint Omer, were among the chief vassals of the bishop of Therouanne, holding in fief from him extensive rights of jurisdiction and certain fiscal rights in the diocese. See H. Van Werveke, *Het bisdom Terwaan* (Ghent, 1924), p. 82, and a French analysis of this work by H. Nowé, "Une étude récente sur l'évêché de Térouanne," RN, XIII (1927), pp. 52-53.

[13] The validity of proof of free status by "line of origin" was clearly affirmed by Count Charles in an act of 1122 (*Actes*, no. 108, p. 250); proof "by oath" is there explicitly condemned. The case in question, however, is entirely different from this one.

[14] Was this simply the common law of Flanders concerning serfs, or was it a recent measure of the count, a part of his general attempt to recover lost rights by clarifying the status of persons, which he was now using as a device for undermining the Erembalds? In c. 25 the same law is called that of the *counts*.

man who had taken to wife a female serf was no longer free after he had held her for a year, but had come to be of the same status as his wife. And so that knight mourned who had lost his liberty on account of his wife, through whom he had believed he could become freer[15] when he married her; and the provost and his kin mourned, and for that reason kept on trying in every way possible to free themselves from servitude to the count.[16] Therefore when the count had learned from the judgment of the courts[17] and the report of the elders of the realm that they—the Erembald clan—belonged to him beyond doubt, he set about trying to claim them as his serfs. Nevertheless, because the provost and his kin had not heretofore been molested or accused of servile status by the predecessors of the count, this would have been consigned to oblivion, having been laid to rest, as it were, and disregarded for so long, if it had not been brought to the attention of the courts by the challenge to combat.[18]

[15] "Freer" here probably means more "noble."

[16] What happened after the open challenge must be filled out from other sources. After some delay, the Erembalds were summoned to the count's court at Kassel to prove that they were not his serfs, according to the judgment of the *optimates* (Herman, c. 29). The proof was to take the form of an oath by the wife of Robert of Crecques, sworn with twelve noble co-jurors (Walter, c. 15), but on the appointed day Bertulf with "3,000" supporters appeared at Kassel, and the count, fearing a tumult, postponed the hearing (Herman, c. 29); the number is obviously exaggerated. Walter and Herman say nothing about the inquiry in the lower court, and Galbert says nothing about the abortive hearing at the count's court at Kassel.

[17] This inquiry (*veritas*) probably refers to the same process mentioned earlier by Galbert. The sequence of events is not entirely clear, nor is their relationship; some questions arise. Did the count suspect the origin of the Erembalds and hope to expose them as servile when he set the inquiry on foot in the lower courts? Did he act in collusion with the knight, who had made the challenge "in his presence" in order to reveal publicly this apparently well-hidden secret? Having failed to secure a judgment against the Erembalds in his court at Kassel, did he next turn back to the inquiry, presumably going on in the territorial courts, as a means of attacking them?

[18] Walter, c. 15, considers this "calumny of servitude" as the first reason for the slaying of the count because it was the source of such hatred against him on the part of the Erembalds. (It is not clear whether Walter accepts the charge as valid or not.) Herman, c. 28, seems to agree, saying that the Erembalds denied that they were his serfs and conspired against him because of "the justice he was doing," that is, his measures against them. Suger, c. 30, implies the same in his *Vie de Louis VI le gros*, ed. and trans. by H. Waquet (Paris, 1929), p. 242.

[8] *Bertulf and his nephews become desperate, 1127*

But the provost, who with the whole line of his nephews[1] was more powerful than anyone in the realm except the count and more eminent in reputation and in religion,[2] asserted that he himself was free, as were both his predecessors and successors in the clan, and he insisted that this was so with a certain irrationality and arrogance. And so he endeavored by laying plans and using influence to extract himself and his family from the possession and ownership of the count, and he often attacked the count in these terms:

"That Charles of Denmark[3] would never have succeeded to the countship if I had not been willing. But now, although he became count by my efforts, he does not remember how much I did for him but instead seeks to cast me and all my line back into serfdom, trying to find out from the elders whether we are his serfs.

"But let him try as much as he wants, we shall be free and we are free, and there is no man on earth who can make us into serfs!"[4] He talked so boastfully in vain, however, for the count, on his guard, had found out that they were slandering him and had heard of their deceit and also of their treachery.[5] And when the provost and his kin realized that they could not succeed in defending themselves but were, on the contrary, about to be

[1] "Ceterum prepositus cum tota nepotum successione...." Although Galbert occasionally uses *nepos* in the sense of "kinsman" (for example in c. 1, referring to Charles in relation to Count Baldwin), in this case there seems little doubt that he means "nephews"; his future use of the word in relation to Bertulf seems always to bear that meaning.

[2] Walter, c. 14, stresses above all the wealth of Bertulf as a source of his power and pride. "Religion" here probably refers to Bertulf's ecclesiastical position rather than to his piety.

[3] Obviously derogatory, stressing the fact that Charles in his eyes was a foreigner, and perhaps implying some weakness in Charles's right to the succession. Bertulf's claim to have supported Charles when his succession was challenged by Clemence, the mother of Baldwin VII, is not sustained by any other evidence in the sources.

[4] This speech, like several others in Galbert's narrative, was probably based on hearsay, though Galbert's position as notary must have afforded him sources of information close to the provost. Its powerful content reveals the profound impression that the plight of the Erembalds made on their contemporaries.

[5] It seems unlikely that Charles was aware of any definite plot to kill him.

deprived of their usurped liberty, he preferred to perish together
with the whole line of his nephews rather than be handed over
in servitude to the count.[6] At last, in the guile of abominable
deliberation, they began secretly to plot the death of the most
pious count, and finally to fix on a place and an opportunity for
killing him.[7]

[9] *Private war breaks out between Borsiard and Thancmar,*
1127

When strife and conflict broke out between his nephews and
those of Thancmar,[1] whose side the count justly favored, the

[6] The count's exact intentions with respect to the Erembalds are never made
clear because he was killed before he carried them out. Ganshof (*Étude sur les
ministeriales,* p. 348) believes Charles intended to exercise his rights, especially
fiscal, over them as *chevaliers-serfs* but did not intend to debase them to the
social condition of serfs or to deprive them of their offices or fiefs. It is possible,
however, that Charles did intend to take from them the offices of castellan and
provost which were the real bases of their wealth and power. This may be implied
in the provost's speech to Fromold in Galbert, c. 19, and is suggested by Rolland
("L'Origine des châtelains," RB, VI, 704-5) as a better explanation of the terrible
rage and desperation of the family.
[7] Although the other chief sources (Walter, c. 15, Herman, c. 28, Suger, c. 30)
agree with Galbert that the prime cause of the murder was Charles's attempt to
establish his rights over the Erembalds, Galbert's own narrative gradually reveals
a more complex and deepseated opposition to the count and a widespread complicity in the plot against him.

[1] The head of the family of Straten, neighbors and inveterate enemies of the
Erembalds, who were detested by the people of Bruges, as Galbert's narrative
will reveal (see c. 45, 101, 113). The names of several members appear occasionally in lists of signers or witnesses to charters of the count, close to those
of their bitter enemies, for example, that of Athelard of Straten, perhaps the
father of Thancmar, coming after that of Erembald and his son Robert (*Actes,*
no. 9, 1089, p. 32); and Thancmar and Berenvold of Straten in the same list as
the brothers Bertulf, Didier Hacket, and Lambert (*Actes,* no. 94, 1119, p. 213).
Both Galbert, c. 113, and Walter, c. 16, also mention "Walter, nephew of
Thancmar." By a curious distortion of fact, the beginnings of which can be seen
even in Galbert, c. 45, this family came to be held responsible for the murder of
Count Charles, though it is clear in c. 9 and c. 10 that the count favored them;
moreover, Walter, c. 16, pictures Thancmar as a pious man. Borsiard, the actual
murderer of Charles is erroneously called "of Straten" in the anonymous *Passio
Karoli comitis,* c. 5, MGH, SS XII, 621, a source of the later thirteenth or early
fourteenth century, and the legend reaches full development in the later and unreliable *Chronicon comitum Flandrensium,* ed. by De Smet, in *Corpus chronicorum
Flandriae,* I, 80. As the name suggests, the stronghold of the Straten, at the
present site of Saint-André lez Bruges, probably dominated the road from Bruges
to Ypres and hence threatened the commercial activities of the burghers.

provost was delighted because it gave him an opportunity to betray the count, for he had called to the aid of his nephews all the knights of our region,[2] using money, influence, and persuasion.[3] They besieged Thancmar on all sides in the place where he had entrenched himself, and finally with a considerable force strongly attacked those within.[4] Breaking the bolts of the gates, they cut down the orchards and hedges of their enemies. Though the provost did not take part and acted as if he had done nothing, he actually did everything by direction and deception. He pretended in public that he was full of good will and told his enemies that he grieved to see his nephews engaged in so much strife and killing, although he himself had incited them to all these crimes. In that conflict many on both sides fell on that day wounded or dead. When the provost had learned that this fight was going on, he himself went to the carpenters who were working in the cloister of the brothers[5] and ordered that their tools, that is, their axes, should be taken to that place for use in cutting down the tower and orchards and houses of his enemies.[6]

[2] Galbert is doubtless referring to the coastal region north and west of Bruges which he elsewhere treats as an entity; it was roughly identical with the early *pagus Flandrensis*. This "maritime Flanders" was notorious for its turbulent population. The influence of the Erembald clan here was doubtless strengthened by the fact that Bertulf, as chancellor, administered the count's domain which was very extensive in the area.

[3] The persistence of private war, even under a strong feudal ruler like the counts of Flanders, is abundantly proved by the Flemish sources of the eleventh and twelfth centuries. The strength of the kinship bond in such feuds (called *faida* in early Germanic law) is discussed by Marc Bloch in *La Société féodale: la formation des liens de dépendance*, pp. 195-207; the legal aspects are analyzed at length by Van Caenegem, *Geschiedenis van het strafrecht*, pp. 230-322. Often the result of slight causes, as Walter (c. 16) says of this one, they continued for years. See the Introduction, IV, concerning the scourge of private war in Flanders.

[4] According to Walter, c. 17, the count had forced the unwilling adversaries to accept a truce (*treuga*) and thus halted their feud; the Erembalds now violate this peace and thus catch Thancmar off guard. Concerning the institution of the truce see Van Caenegem, *Geschiedenis van het strafrecht*, pp. 248-63.

[5] That is, of the canons of the church of Saint Donatian, within the enclosure of the castle at Bruges, over whom Bertulf was provost. The location of the various structures within the castle is shown in the Plans.

[6] Adding Walter's account, c. 17, a clearer picture of Thancmar's country stronghold emerges. An enclosure, probably of wood, which his enemies break into through gates, contains orchards and hedges, forming an outer or lower courtyard, where everything is cut down or demolished in the first assault. Thancmar is driven into his upper or inner defense, a tower, probably wooden, since axes were to be used against it. Just where the "houses" were located is not clear.

Then he sent around to various houses in the town[7] to collect axes which were quickly taken to that place. And when in the night his nephews had returned with five hundred knights and squires[8] and innumerable footsoldiers, he took them into the cloister and refectory of the brothers where he entertained them all with various kinds of food and drink and was very happy and boastful about the outcome.

And while he was harassing his enemies in this way, spending a great deal in support of those who were helping his nephews, first the squires and then the knights began to plunder the peasants,[9] even seizing and devouring the flocks and cattle of the country people.[10] The nephews of the provost were forcibly seizing the belongings of the peasants and appropriating them for their own use.[11] But none of the counts from the beginning of the realm had allowed such pillaging to go on in the realm, because great slaughter and conflict come to pass in this way.[12]

[7] This is Galbert's first use of the word *suburbium* for which no exact English equivalent can be found. It refers to the mercantile settlement which had grown up outside and around the count's castle, whose inhabitants he calls citizens (*cives*) or burghers (*burgenses*) or *suburbani*. There is evidence of the existence of a *portus* or *suburbium* at Bruges at least as early as the first decade of the eleventh century. For a fuller discussion of various aspects of the *suburbium* of Bruges, see the Introduction, pp. 52-55; consult also the Plan of Bruges.

[8] Galbert, who is an accurate observer in so many respects, and who as a notary might be expected to be careful in the use of numbers, here follows a common medieval habit of inaccuracy in dealing with large numbers. On this curious trait see Bloch, *La Société féodale: la formation des liens de dépendance*, pp. 118-20 and the Introduction, p. 68. It would have been difficult to feed more than five hundred men in the quarters of the canons!

[9] Galbert uses *rustici*, rural folk, not *servi*, the word for serfs.

[10] Galbert does not mention an incident which seems to have occurred between the attack on Thancmar's stronghold and the ravaging of the country-side by Bertulf's nephews. Walter, c. 18, says that when Thancmar sought justice from the count, Charles summoned the Erembalds but they did not even deign to answer him; that Charles then personally reproved the provost who promised satisfaction but did nothing; and that the patience of the count only increased their arrogance.

[11] The opportunity for this ravaging, which according to Walter, c. 19, was marked by destruction of houses, seizure of furniture, and maltreatment of the poor, even to the point of killing, was afforded by Charles's absence in *Francia*, where he had gone to lend aid to his suzerain, King Louis VI of France, in the latter's second expedition against the count of Auvergne for the protection of the bishop of Clermont. Suger, c. 29 (ed. by Waquet, p. 236) speaks of this participation of the "very powerful count of Flanders."

[12] Walter, c. 19, speaks even more strongly, saying that this violence was the more intolerable because it was not customary, that the counts had long decreed, and it had been observed "almost like a law," that no one in Flanders should

[10] *The count takes measures against the nephews of Bertulf,
February 27-28, 1127, and returns to Bruges*

When the country people heard that the count had come to
Ypres,[1] about two hundred of them went to him secretly and at
night, and kneeling at his feet[2] begged him for his customary
paternal help. They entreated him to order their goods to be
returned to them, that is, their flocks and herds, clothes and
silver, and all the other furniture of their houses which the
nephews of the provost had seized together with those who had
fought with them continuously in that attack and siege. After
listening solemnly to the complaints of those appealing to him,[3]
the count summoned his counselors, and even many who were
related to the provost, asking them by what punishment and with
what degree of severity justice should deal with this crime.[4] They
advised him to burn down Borsiard's house without delay because he had plundered the peasants of the count;[5] and therefore
strongly urged him to destroy that house because as long as it
stood, so long would Borsiard indulge in fighting and pillaging

---

presume to pillage or seize or despoil any one. There is evidence of peace efforts
on the part of the counts from at least the time of Baldwin IV, in 1030; see the
Introduction, II and IV. According to Walter, the very presence of Charles was
"a burden and intolerable restraint on all evil-doers."

　[1] Where, on his return from *Francia,* he called his barons to meet on February
27, 1127, according to Walter, c. 20, who says he, Walter, was present on this
occasion "on other business"; he is therefore a more reliable witness here than
Galbert. Walter does not mention specifically the plea of the peasants but speaks
of the count's grief and horror at these outrages, especially because they took
place during Lent.
　[2] Thomas, "Notes sur Galbert de Bruges," here corrects *convoluti* to *provoluti.*
　[3] Thomas also corrects *proclamorum* to *proclamatorum.*
　[4] Walter, c. 20, says that "men from Bruges" were also present, demanding
justice for the injuries and pillaging they had suffered. Are these citizens of the
town (*suburbium*) or persons of the environs? They may be the country people
mentioned by Galbert.
　[5] Could this mean that the pillaging had extended beyond the estate of Thancmar
and affected even some parts of the count's own domain and hence "his" peasants?
Or does it mean that the peasants in general, being under the special protection
of the count's peace, are in a sense "his"? The latter seems likely in view of the
plea of the delegation of two hundred "rustics" mentioned above. It is, however,
quite possible that the ravaging went beyond Thancmar's estate; Walter, c. 19, says
"almost the whole region" was affected, and Galbert implies the same in this
sentence.

and even killing, and would continue to lay waste the region.[6]
And so the count, acting on this advice, went and burned the
house and destroyed the place to its foundations.[7] Then that
Borsiard and the provost and their accomplices were beside themselves with anxiety both because in this act the count had clearly
lent aid and comfort to their enemies and because the count was
daily disquieting them about their servile status and trying in
every way to establish his rights over them.

After burning the house the count went on to Bruges.[8] When
he had settled down in his house, his close advisers[9] came to him
and warned him, saying that the nephews of the provost would
betray him because now they could claim as pretext the burning
of the house, although even if the count had not done this they
were going to betray him anyway. After the count had eaten,
mediators came[10] and appealed to him on behalf of the provost
and his nephews, begging the count to turn his wrath from them
and to receive them mercifully back into his friendship. But the
count replied that he would act justly and mercifully toward

  [6] Walter, c. 20, reveals some difference of opinion among the barons, who
finally agreed, however, that Charles should go and see for himself and let the
nature of the crime determine the punishment.
  [7] When the count went the next day, February 28, to inspect the scene, according
to Walter, c. 21, he was moved to tears by the wrongs done to the poor and at once
burned the stronghold (*munitionem*) of Borsiard (probably a wooden tower like
Thancmar's), "the root and seed of so much evil." Destruction of houses was one
of the punishments characteristic of "peace" legislation in Flanders. See A. Delcourt,
La Vengeance de la commune: l'arsin et l'abattis de maison en Flandre et en Hainaut
(Lille, 1930), *passim*, and Van Caenegem, *Geschiedenis van het strafrecht*, pp. 179-
180.
  [8] On the same day, February 28, according to Walter, c. 21. But the count's
day at Bruges, described below, is obviously that of March 1, as Walter indicates,
c. 21, 22.
  [9] Galbert uses *familiares* here, a word difficult to translate exactly; it could
mean "members of his household," that is domestic officials, or more likely, his
intimate circle of counselors, those who were close to him and in his confidence.
The term is employed by Galbert only with reference to a small number of lesser
individuals, forming an inner circle of "new men," whom the count trusted more
than he trusted the barons, and who were more likely to be loyal because they owed
everything to him.
  [10] Walter, c. 22, says the provost sent Guy of Steenvoorde and "a few others
who seemed to be intimates of the count (*familiares*)." Guy of Steenvoorde, who
had married a niece of the provost, proves to be one of the traitors (Galbert, c. 58);
he appears frequently as signer or as witness to charters of Baldwin VII and Charles
from 1111 on (see *Actes*, no. 52, p. 132, and *passim*). Galbert calls him "a strong
and famous knight, prominent in the council of the counts," c. 58.

them if they would henceforth give up their fighting and pillaging; and he assured them, moreover, that he would certainly
compensate Borsiard with a house that was even better. He
swore, however, that as long as he was count, Borsiard should
never again have any property in that place where the house had
been burned up, because as long as he lived there near Thancmar
he would never do anything but fight and feud with his enemies,
and pillage and slaughter the people.[11]

The mediators, some of whom were aware of the treachery,[12]
did not bother the count very much about the reconciliation, and
since the servants were going about offering wine they asked
the count to have better wine brought in. When they had drunk
this, they kept on asking to be served again still more abundantly,
as drinkers usually do, so that when they had finally received the
very last grant from the count they could go off as if to bed.
And by the order of the count everyone present was abundantly
served with wine until, after receiving the final grant, they departed.[13]

[11] Walter, c. 22, gives a more dramatic account of this interview by using direct
discourse and by stressing the arrogance of the pleaders and the indignation of the
count (whom he calls *heros*) at their effrontery. Charles insisted that Borsiard
should restore what he had seized and "recognize the status of his family" before
seeking pardon.
[12] This could hardly refer to a definite plot since that had not yet been sworn;
see c. 11.
[13] Galbert gives here a revealing picture of the count's "day," his conference
with his intimates while eating, his audience to others later, his hospitality to all
in the evening. The importance of wine in the social life of the time is clear;
mass drinking was probably the chief indoor diversion of the fighting class. Some
formalities in the drinking ceremony seem to be observed.

[11] *The Erembalds seal the plot against the count, during the night of March 1, 1127*

Then Isaac[1] and Borsiard, William of Wervik,[2] Ingran,[3] and their accomplices, after receiving the assent of the provost,[4] made haste to carry out what they were about to do,[5] by the necessity of divine ordination, through free will. For immediately those who had been mediators and intercessors between the count and the kinsmen of the provost went to the provost's house and made known the count's response, that is, that they had not been able to secure any mercy either for the nephews or their supporters, and that the count would treat them only as the opinion of

[1] Isaac was a chamberlain of the count; see Galbert, c. 17, 28, and a charter of 1115 (*Actes,* no. 76, p. 174). Called a "kinsman" of the provost by Walter, c. 24, he is associated with his brother Didier by Galbert, c. 28, 29, and in a charter of 1122 (*Actes,* no. 107, p. 246). There is no doubt that Isaac and Didier, brothers, were nephews of the provost, since Isaac's sister is clearly a niece of the provost (Galbert, c. 58 and Walter, c. 34). But it is curious that Galbert never calls Isaac a *nepos* of Bertulf or seems to include him among those called *nepotes* (see, for example, c. 7, where even the obscure Albert is so included); and the same is true of Didier whom Galbert always designates simply as "brother of Isaac" (c. 28, 29, 44, 92). Pirenne's assumption that Isaac was the son of Didier Hacket because Isaac's brother was also called "Didier" does not seem tenable. As Professor Dhondt suggests, it seems more likely from the evidence that Galbert reserves the name *nepotes* for sons of *brothers* of the provost, and that Isaac, Didier and their sister were children of a *sister* of Bertulf. (See the family genealogy.) The reference to the provost "and his brothers," "and their sons" in c. 55 seems to support this supposition. And so does the fact that Isaac is never identified as the "son of a brother" of the provost as is Borsiard (c. 55, 71), and Walter (c. 20, 42, 81) and Robert (by Walter of Therouanne, c. 24).

[2] An important member of the conspiracy, though apparently not related to the Erembald clan, he appears only twice as witness, in charters of 1125 (*Actes,* no. 118, p. 271, and no. 119, p. 275). See Galbert, c. 25, 39.

[3] Ingran of Esen, also not a kinsman of the Erembalds, does not appear in the charters; he was a nephew of Thierry, castellan of Dixmude, according to Walter, c. 51. See Galbert, c. 39.

[4] Walter, c. 23, attributes more initiative to the provost, saying it was he who stimulated his kinsmen to action, enraged by the report of the intercessors who, deliberately exaggerating the intransigeance of the count, reported to the Erembalds that they could expect no mercy unless they all admitted openly that they were serfs of the count; he also says that the provost and pleaders now began to plot the death of the count.

[5] It is difficult to explain this precipitate action solely in terms of the count's attitude toward the Erembald-Straten feud, which Galbert pictures as stern but not vindictive. It seems possible that Isaac, as one of Charles's household, had learned during the morning consultation of some imminent and drastic action to be taken against the provost, perhaps the confiscation of his office; see Galbert, c. 19.

the leading men of the land had determined in strict justice.[6]

Then the provost and his nephews withdrew into an inner room and summoned those whom they wanted. While the provost guarded the door, they gave their right hands to each other as a pledge that they would betray the count, and they summoned the young Robert[7] to join in the crime, urging him to pledge by his hand that he would share with them what they were about to do and what they had pledged by their hands.[8] But the noble young man, forewarned by the virtue of his soul and perceiving the gravity of what they were urging upon him, resisted them, not wishing to be drawn unwittingly into their compact until he could find out what it was they had bound themselves to do; and while they were pressing him, he turned away and hurried toward the door. But Isaac and William and the others[9] called out to the provost guarding the door not to let Robert leave until by the pressure of his authority Robert should do what they had demanded. The young man, quickly influenced by the flattery and threats of the provost, came back and gave his hand on their terms, not knowing what he was supposed to do with them, and, as soon as he was pledged to the traitors he inquired what he had done. They said:

"We have now sworn to betray that Count Charles who is working for our ruin in every way and is hastening to claim us as his serfs, and you must carry out this treachery with us, both in word and in deed."

Then the young man, struck with terror and dissolved in tears, cried out:

[6] Galbert is referring to the judgment of the count's court at Ypres.

[7] Robert the Young, another nephew of the provost; see Galbert, c. 7. The following episode, which portrays him as an innocent and also, inadvertently, as a rather stupid member of his clan, hardly squares with Walter's unequivocal inclusion of him in the plot, c. 24 and c. 50. The only possible source of such a story is Robert himself who may have spread the tale among his ardent admirers, the people of Bruges, whose attitude Galbert obviously shares; see c. 41, 44, 60, 65, 74, 75, 82. His epithet *puer* does not imply adolescence; it may simply mean "junior" since his father was also named Robert, or it may be a popular term of endearment.

[8] The conspiracy is apparently sealed with considerable formality. Walter, c. 24, speaks of a sworn compact.

[9] Walter, c. 24, includes Wulfric, brother of the provost, among the "six leaders

"God forbid that we should betray one who is our lord and the count of the fatherland. Believe me, if you do not give this up, I shall go and openly reveal your treachery to the count and to everyone, and, God willing, I shall never lend aid and counsel to this pact!"

But they forcibly detained him as he tried to flee from them, saying:

"Listen, friend, we were only pretending to you that we were in earnest about that treachery so that we could try out whether you want to stay by us in a certain serious matter; for there is something we have concealed from you up to this point, in which you are bound to us by faith and compact, which we shall tell you about in good time."

And so turning it off as a joke, they concealed their treachery.

Now each one of them left the room and went off to his own place. When Isaac had finally reached home,[10] he pretended to go to bed, for he was awaiting the silence of the night, but soon he remounted his horse and returned to the castle.[11] After stopping at Borsiard's lodgings[12] and summoning him and the others whom he wanted, they went secretly to another lodging, that of the knight, Walter.[13] As soon as they had entered, they put out the fire that was burning in the house so that those who had been awakened in the house should not find out from the light of the fire who they were and what sort of business they were carrying on at that time of night, contrary to custom. Then, safe in the darkness, they took counsel about the act of treason to be

---

of their faction"; he is first mentioned by Galbert in c. 27, where he is characterized as "one who had sworn the death of the count."

[10] Isaac's house, probably a fortified stone house, stood just outside the *suburbium* or "town," as we learn from Galbert, c. 29; it was reached by a bridge near the church of the Holy Virgin. In the Inquest of September, 1127, he is referred to as "Isaac of Saint Mary's bridge." The text of this Inquest is preserved in French translation in the *Chronicon Hanoniense quod dicitur Balduini Avennensis*, MGH, SS XXV, 441-43, hereafter cited as the Inquest.

[11] That is, the fortified enclosure of the "castle" which contained numerous buildings besides the count's house proper. See the Plans.

[12] This sentence seems to indicate the existence of a special place within the castle enclosure which afforded quarters to the "knights of the castle," among whom were probably Borsiard and Walter. Borsiard also had a country house or stronghold, recently destroyed by the count.

[13] Probably Walter, son of Lambert, and hence cousin of Borsiard. See Genealogy.

done as soon as dawn came, choosing for this crime the boldest
and rashest members of Borsiard's household,[14] and they promised them rich rewards. To the knights who would kill the
count they offered four marks[15] and to the servingmen who
would do the same, two marks, and they bound themselves by
this most iniquitous compact. Then Isaac returned to his home
about daybreak, after he had put heart into them by his counsel
and made them ready for such a great crime.[16]

[12] *Borsiard and his accomplices slay the count on March 2,
1127; the news spreads*

Therefore when day had dawned, so dark and foggy that you
could not distinguish anything a spear's length away, Borsiard
secretly sent several serfs out into courtyard of the count[1] to
watch for his entrance into the church.[2] The count had arisen
very early and had made offerings to the poor in his own house,
as he was accustomed to do,[3] and so was on his way to church.
But as his chaplains reported, the night before, when he had
settled down in bed to go to sleep, he was troubled by a kind of
anxious wakefulness; perplexed and disturbed in mind, he was
so disquieted by the many things on his mind that he seemed

[14] Clear evidence of the social prestige of the Erembalds: Borsiard, only a knight,
has a "household" including both knights and servingmen (*servientes*). It is not
surprising that the castellan, Hacket, had the same, c. 29, and the provost also, c. 35.

[15] Probably marks of silver, not coins but a certain weight of silver, payable in
lingots or in a fixed number of pennies, sometimes 144, according to Van Werveke,
"Monnaies, lingots ou marchandises?," AHES, IV (1932), 463-64. Such "money
of account" is called "ghost money" by Cipolla, *Money, Prices and Civilization*,
pp. 38-42.

[16] Isaac here appears as the brains of the plot, as Galbert later suggests, c. 28.

[1] That is, the courtyard of the count's house within the castle.

[2] From the court they could observe his progress through the passage which
connected his house with Saint Donatian, the "castral" church, an essential part of
the castle at Bruges, as at Ghent, Lille and other important centers of the count's
administration. The passageway was constructed of stone and arched, according to
Galbert, c. 41. Herman, c. 28, says the count went from the *solium* (upper story)
of his palace to the *solium* of the church. Concerning this passage see the Introduction, V, and c. 41, n. 3.

[3] Walter, c. 25, adds that Charles, barefooted in his piety, administered alms to
to the poor with his own hands, offering food to each and kissing the hand of
everyone.

quite exhausted, even to himself, now lying on one side, now sitting up again on the bed.[4] And when he had set out on his way toward the church of Saint Donatian, the serfs who had been watching for his exit ran back and told the traitors that the count had gone up into the gallery[5] of the church with a few companions. Then that raging Borsiard and his knights and servants, all with drawn swords beneath their cloaks, followed the count into the same gallery, dividing into two groups so that not one of those whom they wished to kill could escape from the gallery by either way, and behold! they saw the count prostrate before the altar,[6] on a low stool, where he was chanting psalms to God and at the same time devoutly offering prayers and giving out pennies to the poor.

Now it should be known what a noble man and distinguished ruler those impious and inhuman serfs betrayed! His ancestors were among the best and most powerful rulers who from the beginning of the Holy Church had flourished in France, or Flanders, or Denmark, or under the Roman Empire.[7] From their stock the pious count was born in our time and grew up from boyhood to perfect manhood, never departing from the noble habits of his royal ancestors or their natural integrity of life. And before he became count, after performing many notable

---

   [4] Doubtless the count was disturbed by the rumors of a plot against him; see c. 10. According to Herman, c. 28, he had received a warning at Ypres, but disregarded it, being ready to die "for justice," if God so wished; Walter, c. 24, reports that he was warned during the night at Bruges but did not credit the rumor because his conscience was clear.

   [5] The *solarium* (*solium lapideum,* according to Herman, c. 29) was probably an open colonnaded gallery encircling the hexagonal core or "choir" of the church as in the tomb-chapel of Charlemagne at Aachen. From the narrative which follows, it seems to have been accessible only from the stairs in the two smaller towers which flanked the great "tower" or west-work. To the east it opened out into a chapel, directly over the apse or sanctuary, and to the west probably into another chapel over the "porch."

   [6] "The altar to Saint Mary which is in the upper part of the church," says Walter, c. 25; that is, in the upper eastern chapel, "over the apse," according to *Continuatio Tornacensis Sigeberti,* A. 1127, MGH, SS VI, 444.

   [7] Pirenne (ed. Galbert, p. 21, n. 2) suggests that Galbert here refers to his great-grandmother Adele, daughter of Robert II, king of France, who married Baldwin V of Flanders; to his maternal grandmother, Gertrude of Saxony, widow of Florent I, count of Holland, and hence a princess of the Empire, who married his grandfather, Robert the Frisian; and to his father, Canute, king of Denmark, who married Adele, daughter of Robert the Frisian.

and distinguished deeds, he took the road of holy pilgrimage to Jerusalem.[8] After crossing the depths of the sea and suffering many perils and wounds for the love of Christ, he at last fulfilled his vow and with great joy reached Jerusalem. Here he also fought strenuously against the enemies of the Christian faith. And so, after reverently adoring the sepulcher of the Lord, he returned home. In the hardship and want of this pilgrimage the pious servant of the Lord learned, as he often related when he was count, in what extreme poverty the poor labor, and with what pride the rich are exalted, and finally with what misery the whole world is affected. And so he made it his habit to stoop to the needy, and to be strong in adversity, not puffed up in prosperity; and as the Psalmist teaches,[9] "The king's strength loves judgment," he ruled the county according to the judgment of the barons and responsible men.

When the life of such a glorious prince had undergone martyrdom, the people of all lands mourned him greatly, shocked by the infamy of his betrayal. Marvelous to tell, although the count was killed in the castle of Bruges on the morning of one day, that is, the fourth day of the week, the news of this impious death shocked the citizens of London, which is in England, on the second day afterwards[10] about the first hour; and towards

[8] Walter, c. 2, also says that Charles went to Jerusalem to visit the Lord's sepulcher when he had grown up and "received the belt of knighthood," and that he stayed "for some time" fighting against the enemies of the faith, but there is no evidence of his activity as a pilgrim or crusader in the sources relating to the crusading movement. Since Charles was born *ca.*1080-86, and probably reached maturity at fifteen or sixteen years, this journey must have taken place in the early years of the twelfth century. It is possible but not probable that Charles accompanied his uncle, Robert II, on the First Crusade; Robert left Flanders in the fall of 1096 and returned in the spring of 1100. Perhaps Charles went in 1107-8 with the great fleet of English, Danes, and Flemings mentioned by Albert of Aachen, *Liber Christianae expeditionis* . . . lib. x, RHC, Occ. IV, 631. He must certainly have returned before 1111 when Robert II died, for his uncle welcomed him home, Walter reports, c. 2. Charles is not mentioned in either of the two most recent authoritative works on the crusades, S. Runciman, *History of the Crusades,* Vol. I (Cambridge, 1951), and *A History of the Crusades,* Vol. I, ed. by M. W. Baldwin (Philadelphia, 1955). It is notable that Galbert pictures Charles primarily as a pilgrim, rather than a fighter.

[9] Psalms 98.4 in the Vulgate, here not quoted exactly.

[10] That is, from Wednesday to Friday. Is it possible that a ship could sail from Bruges to London in this time? Galbert does not think so, but Bloch estimates that from 100 to 150 kilometers a day was not an exceptional record for a ship,

evening of the same second day it disturbed the people of Laon who live far away from us in France.[11] We learned this through our students who at that time were studying in Laon,[12] as we also learned it from our merchants who were busy carrying on their business on that very day in London.[13] For no one could have spanned these intervals of time or space so quickly either by horse or by ship!

[13] *Bertulf's past: his ambition, pride, and simony*

It was ordained by God that bold and arrogant descendants of Bertulf's ancestors should be left behind to carry out the crime

---

granted that the winds were not too unfavorable; see *La Société féodale: la formation des liens de dépendance,* p. 100.

[11] Galbert uses *Francia* here in the more restricted sense of the royal domain or Isle de France; the county of Flanders was, of course, a fief of the French crown and therefore part of "France" in the larger sense. If a courier with urgent news could double the average rate of 30 to 40 kilometers a day by land, as Bloch believes, p. 100, it is not impossible that the word could reach Laon, about 200 kilometers away as the crow flies, on the second day.

[12] Perhaps at the cathedral school of Saint Mary of Laon, the reputation of which, founded by the learned Anselm (d. 1117) and continued by his brother Ralph (d. 1133), attracted students from all parts; see É. Lesne, *Les Écoles de la fin du VIIIe siècle à la fin du XIIe* (Lille, 1940), pp. 299 ff.

Two young Flemings sent to Barizis in the diocese of Laon to learn French are mentioned by Guibert de Nogent, *De vita sua,* lib. III, c. 5, ed. by G. Bourgin (Paris, 1907), p. 147. Perhaps the students heard the news from Flemish merchants buying wine in Laon; see c. 3, n. 11.

[13] In this period of rapid economic expansion, the late eleventh and early twelfth century, Flanders was in the "active" phase of commerce (*ca.*1000-1300) when her merchants went in person to seek and to sell goods. England was the earliest and still the most important market, especially from *ca.*1100 as a source of the indispensable commodity, wool, needed in the growing textile industry of the Flemish towns, and of other necessary materials, such as hides and metals, which the Flemings exchanged for their own luxury cloths or paid for in money or in wine fetched from Germany. We hear, for example, of a group of Flemish merchants who went to England to buy wool, sometime between 1123 and 1136, carrying 300 marks in silver in their purses, who spent it all as they traversed England and finally assembled their purchases at Dover for shipment to Flanders; see Herman, *De miraculis S. Mariae Laudunensis,* lib. II, c. 4 (Migne, PL, Vol. 156, cols. 975-977). Galbert is probably referring to Flemish merchants in general, not merely to those of Bruges. See especially G. G. Dept, "Les Marchands flamands et le roi d'Angleterre (1154-1216)," RN, XII (1926), 303-304; P. Grierson, "The Relations between England and Flanders before the Norman Conquest," *Transactions of the Royal Historical Society,* 4th ser., XXIII (1941), 104-6; R. Doehaerd, *L'Expansion économique belge au moyen âge* (Brussels, 1946), pp. 47-59; and the numerous works on this subject of H. Van Werveke, among others *Bruges et Anvers: huit siècles de commerce flamand* (Brussels, 1944).

of treachery.[1] The others, prevented by death, were influential men in the fatherland in their lifetime, persons of eminence and of great wealth, but the provost passed his life among the clergy, extremely severe and not a little proud. For it was his habit when someone whom he knew perfectly well came into his presence, to dissemble, in his pride, and to ask disdainfully of those sitting near him, who that could be, and then only, if it pleased him, would he greet the newcomer.[2] When he had sold a canonical prebend to someone he would invest him with it not by canonical election but rather by force, for not one of his canons dared to oppose him either openly or secretly.[3] In the house of the brothers in the church of Saint Donatian the canons had formerly been deeply religious men and perfectly educated, that is, at the beginning of the provostship of this most arrogant prelate.[4] Restraining his pride, they had held him in check by

[1] Almost nothing is known about his forebears except what Galbert tells us concerning his father, Erembald, in c. 71; see notes to that chapter.

[2] Galbert, as a notary of Bruges, and hence a subordinate of the provost, could speak from personal experience. Perhaps Bertulf was simply near-sighted.

[3] Galbert accuses him more specifically of the "heresy of simony" in c. 57, with reference to his trafficking in the prebends, the ecclesiastical benefices held by the canons. The impulse of the Gregorian reform had slackened in the last decade of the eleventh century; see A. Fliche, *La Réforme grégorienne* (Paris, 1946), pp. 214-15.

[4] The colleges or chapters of canons within the castral churches, such as that of Saint Donatian, had been established by the counts to serve their administrative even more than their spiritual needs, and hence were not exclusively religious establishments although their members lived under a degree of clerical discipline. The word chapter (*capitulum*), never used by Galbert, was just beginning to come into common use at this time; see P. Torquebiau, "Chapitres de chanoines," in *Dictionnaire de droit canonique*, Vol. III, cols. 530 ff. There was as yet no sharp distinction between "secular" and "regular" canons, and these expressions are rarely found at the time; efforts at canonical reform from 1059 on had resulted in a great diversity of "religious life" among the chapters in Flanders. See Moreau, *Histoire de l'Église*, II, 115-21, and III, 423-26, 438-39. The "religious life" of the canons at Saint Donatian probably conformed to that moderate degree of observance of the "common life" embodied in the Carolingian "Rule of Aix," 816, with emphasis on regularity, rather than austerity; it was substantially reaffirmed in the fourth canon of the Council of 1059, which insisted on chastity and a common life in refectory and dormitory, but did not specifically require the renunciation of all private property demanded by Hildebrand, the future Gregory VII, at the time. See C. Dereine, "Vie commune, règle de S. Augustin et chanoines réguliers au XIᵉ siècle," *Revue d'histoire ecclésiastique*, XLI (1946), 365-406, especially 385 ff., and Hefele-Leclercq, *Histoire des conciles*, Vol. II, Part II, pp. 1167-68. Such, at any rate, seems to have been the ideal of the religious life prescribed by Robert the Frisian in his charter establishing a church and chapter of twenty canons at Kassel in 1085 (*Actes*, no. 6, pp. 16 ff.) rather than the more stringent

advice and by Catholic doctrine so that he could not undertake anything unseemly in the church. But after they went to sleep in the Lord, the provost, left to himself, set in motion anything that pleased him and toward which the force of his pride impelled him.[5] And so when he became head of his family, he tried to advance beyond everyone in the fatherland his nephews who were well brought up and finally girded with the sword of knighthood.[6] Trying to make their reputation known everywhere, he armed his kinsmen for strife and discord; and he found enemies for them to fight in order to make it known to everyone that he and his nephews were so powerful and strong that no one in the realm could resist them or prevail against them. Finally, accused in the presence of the count of servile status, and affronted by the efforts of the count himself to prove that he and all his lineage were servile, he tried, as we have said, to resist servitude by every course and device and to preserve his usurped liberty with all his might. And when, steadfast in his determination, he could not succeed otherwise, he himself, with his kinsmen, carried through the treachery, which he had long refused to consider, with frightful consequences involving both his own kinsmen and the peers of the realm.[7]

---

discipline called for by the so-called "Rule of Augustine" which became the new ideal of canonical reform in the twelfth century, with its insistence on the absolute poverty of the *vita apostolica*. The efforts at canonical reform of John of Warneton, bishop of Therouanne, 1099-1130, do not seem to have extended beyond his diocese.

[5] We have no other account of Bertulf's relation with his canons. According to Galbert, c. 57, Bertulf had, in 1091, "usurped" the office of provost though, according to canon law, reaffirmed by Robert II in 1089 (*Actes,* no. 9, p. 30), the canons had the right of free election. The count had, however, reserved to himself and his successors the right to confirm the election of the provost.

[6] Walter, c. 14, pictures Bertulf as a *paterfamilias,* supporting a whole entourage of relatives and servants, and in his wealth receiving the obedience of a "great crowd" of friends, relatives and vassals.

[7] In the midst of unnecessary repetition here Galbert introduces one new and important note, the complicity of the peers of the realm in what now appears to be a widespread and long-considered plot against the count, rather than simply a violent act of treason by the Erembald clan to avenge their own wrongs.

[14] *Omens and predictions of the crime; the character of Galbert's work*

But the most pious Lord thought fit to recall His own by the terror of omens, for in our vicinity bloody water appeared in the ditches, as a sign of future bloodshed.[1] They could have been called back from their crime by this if their hardened hearts had not already entered into a conspiracy for betraying the count. They often asked themselves, if they killed the count, who would avenge him?[2] But they did not know what they were saying, for "who," an infinite word, meant an infinite number of persons, who cannot be reckoned in a definite figure; the fact is that the king of France with a numerous army and also the barons of our land with an infinite multitude came to avenge the death of the most pious count! Not even yet has the unhappy consequence of this utterance reached an end, for as time goes on they do not cease to avenge the death of the count upon all the suspect and the guilty and those who have fled in all directions and gone into exile.[3] And so we, the inhabitants of the land of Flanders, who mourn the death of such a great count and prince, ever mindful of his life, beg, admonish, and beseech you, after hearing the true and reliable account of his life and death (that is, whoever shall have heard it), to pray earnestly for the eternal glory of the life of his soul and his everlasting blessedness with the saints. In this account of his passion, the reader will find the subject divided by days and the events of those days,[4] up to the vengeance, related at the end of this little work,[5]

[1] This omen of bloody water is mentioned in several other sources, for example, *Annales Blandinienses*, A. 1127, MGH, SS V, 28; and Simon, *Gesta abbatum S. Bertini*, c. 117, A. 1127, MGH, SS XIII, 658, who notes the accompanying stench and equates it with that of treachery.

[2] According to Walter, c. 20, Borsiard was charged with having asked this question, which seems to have been known by the count at Ypres on February 28 before he set out for Bruges.

[3] It is clear that Galbert is writing or completing these first fourteen introductory chapters after the punishment of the leaders and during the reestablishment of peace in Flanders, that is after the events recounted in c. 85, the last of which took place on May 22, 1127. (He also added at this time chapters 86-92 as a kind of epilogue, and interpolated chapters 68-71.)

[4] Galbert uses here *distinctiones*, a rhetorical expression meaning divisions or parts.

which God alone wrought against those barons of the land whom
He has exterminated from this world by the punishment of death,
those by whose aid and counsel the treachery was begun and
carried through to the end.

[15] *The murder of Count Charles, Tuesday, March 2, 1127*

In the year one thousand one hundred and twenty-seven, on the
sixth day before the Nones of March,[1] on the second day, that
is, after the beginning of the same month, when two days of the
second week of Lent had elapsed, and the fourth day was subsequently to dawn,[2] on the fifth Concurrent,[3] and the sixth
Epact,[4] about dawn,[5] the count at Bruges was kneeling in prayer[6]
in order to hear the early Mass in the church of Saint Donatian,
the former archbishop of Rheims. Following his pious custom
he was giving out alms to the poor, with his eyes fixed on
reading the psalms, and his right hand outstretched to bestow
alms; for his chaplain who attended to this duty had placed near
the count many pennies which he was distributing to the poor
while in the position of prayer.[7]

---

[5] Galbert obviously believed that his work was now completed and did not anti-
cipate the renewal of conflict in February, 1128, which led him to resume his work
in chapters 93 to 122, until the final settlement of July, 1128. See Introduction,
pp. 63-65, for a fuller account of the way in which the work was constructed.

[1] The Nones fell on the seventh day of the month in March, as in May, July,
and October, not on the ninth as in the other months.

[2] The days of the week were counted from Sunday as the first day, and so
Tuesday, the day of the murder, was the "third" day.

[3] The Concurrents were a series of numbers used in determining the date of
Easter, using March 24 and Friday as key days. "If March 24 . . . falls on a Sunday,
the Concurrent of that year is 1 and the Sunday letter F." See Poole, *Medieval
Reckonings of Time*, p. 36.

[4] The Epacts are a feature of the Lunar Year, the calculation of which was
essential in the determination of Easter. "The age of the Moon on January 1 is
called the Epacts (*adiectiones lunae*); if the number is 1 in a given year, it is 12 in
the next and 23 in the third. The year was reckoned for this purpose as beginning
on September 1 preceding the current year." *Ibid.*, pp. 34-35.

[5] This elaborate calculation of time is justified by the fact that it is the date
of the actual murder of the count. All the contemporary accounts agree on the
date of the murder.

[6] Walter, c. 25, says that after praying long on his knees he went prone on the
pavement; Herman, c. 28, merely says he was prostrate in prayer.

[7] Walter, c. 25, mentions his almsgiving only incidentally in connection with

The office of the first hour was completed and also the response of the third hour,[8] when "Our Father" is said, and when the count, according to custom, was praying, reading aloud obligingly;[9] then at last, after so many plans and oaths and pacts among themselves, those wretched traitors, already murderers at heart, slew the count, who was struck down with swords and run through again and again, while he was praying devoutly and giving alms, humbly kneeling before the Divine Majesty.[10] And so God gave the palm of the martyrs to the count, the course of whose good life was washed clean in the rivulets of his blood and brought to an end in good works. In the final moment of life and at the onset of death, he had most nobly lifted his countenance and his royal hands to heaven, as well as he could amid so many blows and thrusts of the swordsmen; and so he surrendered his spirit to the Lord of all and offered himself as a morning sacrifice to God. But the bloody body of such a great man and prince lay there alone, without the veneration of his people and the due reverence of his servants. Whosoever has heard the circumstances of his death has mourned in tears his pitiable death and has commended to God such a great and lamented prince, brought to an end by the fate of the martyrs.[11]

---

the severing of his right arm but Herman, c. 28, speaks of thirteen pennies which the count had placed on his psalter.

[8] That is, Prime and Tierce, the canonical hours or offices which the clergy ("his chaplains," Walter, c. 25, says) were chanting before the celebration of the Mass. Herman, c. 28, does not mention the offices but says Charles ordered the Mass to be sung.

[9] The count was reading the fourth of the seven penitential psalms (Psalm 50) and the clergy were simultaneously chanting the prayers of Tierce, according to Walter, c. 25. Herman, c. 28, says the prayer of Hester was being read in the epistle. The count was reading aloud as usual, so that those nearby could hear him, says Walter, c. 25.

[10] Walter, c. 25, far more precise, says that Borsiard, with his six swordsmen, approached the count suddenly, from the rear and to the side, and touched the count's head lightly with his sword; when Charles lifted his head and turned at this touch, Borsiard smote him on the brow, casting his brains out on the pavement, and the accomplices joined in, striking his head and almost severing his right arm. Herman, c. 28, attributes the count's raising of his head to the warning cry, "Lord count, watch out!" uttered by a poor woman to whom Charles had just given a penny. Walter merely mentions the woman as a recipient of alms at this moment.

[11] The three major accounts of the murder, by Galbert, Walter, and Herman, differ somewhat in tone and detail but they are complementary and not contradictory. Galbert's is the least factual and most subjective, primarily concerned with the religious significance of the event. None of the three was an eyewitness, but

[16] *The murders continue; the flight of the count's friends and the panic of the merchants, March 2, 1127*

They also killed the castellan of Bourbourg.[1] First wounding him mortally, they afterward dragged him ignobly by his feet from the gallery into which he had gone up with the count, to the doors of the church and dismembered him outside with their swords. This castellan, however, after making confession of his sins to the priests of that very church, received the body and

---

each derived his account directly or indirectly from eyewitnesses, probably from among the clergy chanting the offices, to judge by the precision of the liturgical information. Galbert, at Bruges, was in the best position to secure the facts; he seems, however, to be more interested in the count's piety at the moment of his death than in the brutal details of his murder; his informant may well have been the "alms-chaplain," the only cleric he singles out. Walter, c. 25, names as his witnesses to Charles's "death and miracles" Helias, deacon of Bruges, Fromold, provost of Veurne, and "other clerics and laymen"; his informant from the scene of the murder must have had his eye on Borsiard, whose actions he follows closely. Herman's source was probably Abbot Gilbert of Eename, a close friend of the count, who questioned one of the attending clergy; see Dom Nicolas Huyghebaert's "Abt Giselbrecht van Eename en de Gelukzalige Karel de Goede: nota over Herman van Doornik," *Sacris Erudiri,* I (1948), 225-31. Perhaps the special points noted in each case can be attributed to the different positions occupied by the clerical witnesses in the chapel and their range of vision. It is curious that Galbert does not name Borsiard as the actual murderer here, as both Walter and Herman do, but he has already pictured Borsiard and his men pursuing Charles into the church in c. 12. Herman's "old woman" is mentioned by Walter but not her warning cry, and she is omitted completely by Galbert; perhaps Herman's usual strong sense of drama added this touch. Walter is the most outspoken in his denunciation of Borsiard, whom he calls "master of deception, leader of crime," c. 25. Other briefer contemporary accounts are in substantial agreement with the major ones and add nothing new; for example, *Translatio S. Jonati,* ed. in part by E. Sackur, in *Neues Archiv,* XV (1890), 448-52; Suger, *Vie de Louis VI le gros,* c. 30, ed. by Waquet, p. 243; and *Chronicon S. Andreae Castri Cameracesii,* lib. III, c. 34, MGH, SS VII, 547. The most vivid and lively is that of Suger, who also mentions Bertulf's "light touch" on the neck of the count.

[1] Themard, the first known castellan of Bourbourg, appears frequently as witness in the charters of the counts from 1093 to 1125 and was obviously a person of some consequence. See F. Vercauteren, "Études sur les châtelains comtaux de Flandre du XIe au début du XIIIe siècle," in *Études d'histoire dédiées à la mémoire de Henri Pirenne* (Brussels, 1937), pp. 434-35, and *Actes,* especially no. 120, pp. 276 ff. The object of the conspirators is now apparently to do away with as many as possible of the count's inner circle, those whom they had "marked for death" earlier, beginning with Themard, who "by chance was close at hand," according to Walter, c. 28. His presence at the count's private Mass is proof of his intimacy with the count; probably the only others present besides the clergy were the count's favorites, Walter of Loker and Fromold Junior. Sixteen persons are charged with the death of Themard in the Inquest, MGH, SS XXV, 441.

blood of Christ according to Christian custom.² For immediately after killing the count, the swordsmen, leaving the corpse of the count and the castellan at the point of death in the gallery, went out to attack those of their enemies who happened to be present at the court of the count, so that they could slay them at will as they moved about in the castle.³ They pursued into the count's house a certain knight named Henry whom Borsiard suspected of the death of his brother Robert.⁴ He threw himself at the feet of the castellan, Hacket, who had just gone into the house with his men to take possession of it and who now took Henry and the brother of Walter of Loker⁵ under his protection and saved them from their attackers.

At the same moment, there fell into the hands of the traitors two sons of the castellan of Bourbourg who meanwhile was confessing⁶ his sins to the priests in the gallery of the church; these sons of his were praised by everyone for their knighthood and also for their character. Walter and Gilbert they were called,⁷ brothers in blood, peers in knighthood, handsome in appearance, worthy to be loved by all who knew them. As soon as they had heard of the murder of the count and their father they tried to flee,⁸ but the wretched traitors, going after them on horseback, pursued them to the Sands at the exit of the town. A wicked knight named Eric, one of those who had betrayed the count,

---

² After being wounded, but before being dragged brutally down the steps from the gallery by the murderers on their return to the church; see Galbert, c. 17 and Walter, c. 28. Thus Themard, unlike Charles, was able to receive the viaticum, thanks to this interval.

³ Walter, c. 28, says they searched "the whole town (*villam*) which, like a city, was populous and wide," and even beyond.

⁴ Nothing more is known about this Henry or Borsiard's dead brother, Robert. Note the evidence of blood-feud.

⁵ Concerning Walter, see Galbert, c. 17; his brother was Eustace, c. 18. Hacket's role here is not clear.

⁶ *Confitentes,* nominative plural, here must be an error since it was the father who was confessing, not the sons. It should probably be genitive singular, *confitentis.*

⁷ With another brother, Henry, they are mentioned with their father as witnesses to charters of the count; see *Actes,* nos. 105 and 120, pp. 240, 278-79.

⁸ Where were these young men at the time of the murder? Probably moving about in the castle or in the town. Both Galbert's and Walter's accounts sound as if both sons were killed in the town, one (Walter) as he resisted at his lodgings and the other (Gilbert) on horseback near the exit of the town, at or near the *Harenae,* or Sands, an open space west of the town, crossed by a road leading to the town, which later became known as the *Sablon* or Friday market.

pulled one of the brothers off the horse on which he was fleeing and then together with the pursuers slew him. The other brother, who was rushing in flight to the threshold of his lodgings, they came upon face to face and pierced him through with their swords. As he fell, one of our citizens named Lambert Benkin[9] cut him down as if he were a piece of wood. And so they sent those slaughtered brothers to the holy beatitude of the celestial life.

They also pursued for a mile Richard of Woumen,[10] the mighty master of that stronghold whose daughter had married a nephew of Thancmar, against whom the provost and his nephews formerly stirred up strife and conflict. He with his vassals had gone up to the court of the count, like many of the barons who on the same day were getting ready to go to court.[11]

The traitors, frustrated in their pursuit, returned to the castle[12] where the clergy and people of our place had poured in and were wandering around, stunned by what had happened. Those who were known to have been friends of the count as long as he lived, were now, without doubt, in a state of fear, and, lying low for the time, they were avoiding being seen by the traitors; while those in the count's court who depended on his friendship quickly took flight and got away while the people were in a state of confusion.[13] Gervaise, a chamberlain of the count,[14] whom the

---

[9] It is noteworthy that a townsman is aiding the conspirators.

[10] He is named only once as a witness in the charters of the count; see *Actes*, no. 42, 1110, p. 118. He appears infrequently in Galbert's account (c. 31, 114) but his alliance with Thancmar and his close relation to Thierry of Dixmude made him a marked man.

[11] The count had apparently summoned his Easter court for that day or the next. It seems likely that he was planning some immediate action against the Erembalds; see c. 19.

[12] Walter, c. 28, says to seek Walter, "the seneschal," that is, Walter of Loker. A crowd has gathered in the open courtyard of the castle. Galbert uses "clergy and people" frequently to indicate the whole population.

[13] The distinction between these groups is not entirely clear but the second seems to refer to the count's aulic or domestic officials and servants.

[14] Gervaise, a knight, not mentioned in the counts' charters until later in 1127, after Charles's death (see *Actes*, pp. 299, 302), was one of several chamberlains of the count, who together with the seneschals, constables, butlers, and marshals, directed the count's household from the later eleventh century on. From *ca.*1100 an almost complete list is available, and it is clear that one office often had several title-holders. See Monier, *Les Institutions centrales*, pp. 45-46 and Vercauteren, *Actes*, pp. lxxx-lxxxiii. Since he did not rise up to avenge the count until

hand of God armed first to avenge the death of his lord, fled on horseback toward those Flemings who were his kinsmen. A certain John, a servant of the count who looked after his room,[15] and whom the count had loved most among his serving men, fled at dawn on horseback, riding by side paths until noon, and at noon reached Ypres where he broke the news of the death of the count and his men. At this time merchants from all the kingdoms around Flanders had come together at Ypres,[16] on the feast of Saint Peter's Chair,[17] where the market and all the fairs were going on; they were in the habit of carrying on their business safely under the peace and protection of the most pious count.[18] At the same time merchants from the kingdom of the

---

March 7 (c. 26) it is clear this chapter was written after that date. "Flemings" here probably refers to the maritime people, residents of the former *pagus Flandrensis*.

[15] Galbert calls him "serviens comitis ... quem prae servis dilexerat comes." Ganshof, *Étude sur les ministeriales*, p. 364, suggests that John was a "ministerial," serving as one of the count's "chamberlains," in support of his thesis that there were still some ministerials among the aulic officials at this time, although most were now noble.

[16] One of several Flemish fairs, international, long-term, as distinguished from local, weekly markets, which seem to date from the late eleventh century. Their appearance was probably due to the initiative of the counts, and was one of several measures undertaken to create a powerful economic bond across Flanders, from the Scheldt to the sea, and thus unify their lands; see Dhondt, "Développement urbain et initiative comtale en Flandre," RN, XXX (1948), 145 ff., 155-56. Galbert's is the first mention of the already flourishing fair at Ypres, first named as an urban agglomeration in 1102 (Dhondt, p. 148). He notes the presence there of "merchants from all the lands around Flanders" (c. 16); he speaks of merchants going to the fair at Ypres (c. 20), and of Flemish merchants at the fair from all parts (c. 25). It became a major center of Flemish textile exportation, especially to England and the Baltic, by 1200 opening the annual cycle of "the five great fairs" on Ash Wednesday for a monthly session, and again on the Saturday before Ascension. See H. Laurent, *Un Grand commerce d'exportation au moyen âge: la draperie des Pays-Bas en France et dans les pays méditerranéens* (Paris, 1935), pp. 39 ff; J.-A. Van Houtte, "Les Foires dans la Belgique ancienne," in *La Foire* (Brussels, 1953), pp. 180-83.

[17] The feast of Saint Peter's Chair was celebrated on February 22 in the Vatican basilica in honor of the day when the Apostle supposedly assumed the episcopal office at Rome. (The same feast was also celebrated on January 18 in the Via Salaria, outside the city; it is clear, however, that February 22 is meant here.)

[18] The rigorous enforcement by the counts of the peace of the fair, essential to its functioning, is illustrated by incidents in contemporary sources, one in 1084, at Torhout (Hariulf, *Vita Arnulfi*, lib. ii, c. 16, MGH, SS XV, pp. 888-89) and another at Torhout in the reign of Baldwin VII (Herman, *Liber de restauratione S. Martini*, c. 24, MGH, SS XIV, 283-84.) See the Introduction, p. 45, and Van Caenegem, *Geschiedenis van het strafrecht*, pp. 67-68.

Lombards[19] had come to the same fair;[20] the count had bought from them for twenty-one marks a silver vessel which was marvelously made so that the liquid which it held disappeared as one looked at it.[21] When the news reached all these people from various places who had come together at the fair, they packed up their goods and fled by day and by night, bearing with them word of the disgrace of our land and spreading it everywhere.

[17] *The murder of Walter of Loker and the death of the castellan of Bourbourg, March 2, 1127*

And so every man of peace and honor who had heard of the fame of this count now mourned him. But in our castle[1] where our lord and most pious father was lying slain, no one dared openly to weep for his death.[2] Looking at their lord as if he were unknown to them, and acting as if their father were a stranger, they repressed their sorrow and sighs and did not weep. They felt their sorrow all the more grievously, however, because they did not dare relieve it outwardly by tears and lamentations.

---

[19] A geographical expression only: that is, from the valley of the Po, formerly the center of the Lombard kingdom.

[20] The commercial expansion of the north Italian merchants (coming probably from the smaller cities such as Asti and Piacenza rather than Genoa) was even more precocious than that of the Flemish. By the late eleventh century they had reached Flanders en route to England but Galbert's reference is the first sure evidence of their presence at the Flemish fairs. Their fear and flight at the mere news of the murder reveal the precariousness of their position and the relatively slight influence of this commercial current at the moment; they can be compared to modern "colonial" merchants who have overreached themselves, according to Laurent, *Un Grand commerce*, p. 46. Flemish commerce was still largely "active," and oriented toward the north more than the south, though it is likely that the merchants "from beyond the mountains" who sold woolen and linen cloth in Genoa in 1128 were Flemings; see R. Doehaerd, *Les Relations commerciales entre Gênes, la Belgique et l'Outremont* (3 vols.; Brussels and Rome, 1941-1952) I, 82, 89. The commercial currents by land from the north and south were soon to find their most satisfactory meeting-place at a midway point, that of the Champagne fairs. For a general account see R. S. Lopez, "The Trade of Medieval Europe, the South," in *The Cambridge Economic History*, II (Cambridge, 1952), 315 ff.

[21] Probably a false bottom!

[1] On Galbert's proprietary attitude toward the castle and town of Bruges, see the Introduction, pp. 73-74.

[2] Walter, c. 29, confirms this.

For when the nephews of the provost and that most criminal of men, Borsiard,[3] with their accomplices, returned to the castle immediately after the flight of their enemies, he and his knights hunted for Walter of Loker whom they had hated most of all. For he was a counselor of the count and harmful to them in every way; it was he who had urged the count to reduce to servitude the whole family of the provost.[4] But that Walter, in desperate fear of death, had been hiding in the organ-case,[5] that is, in a kind of container of the church organs[6] in the very gallery where the count was lying dead, from the time of the count's murder until the return of those wretches to the castle, that is, when they came back about noon after their enemies had fled. Now they rushed through the doors into the church, and running around with their swords bare and still dripping, with great noise and clash of arms, they searched among the chests and benches of the brothers of the church, calling Walter by name, and they found the castellan of Bourbourg, whom they had mortally wounded in the gallery, still breathing. Then they finally killed him, after dragging him by the feet to the doors

[3] Galbert uses *sceleratissimus*; Walter, c. 26, also uses the superlative, addressing Borsiard as *nefandissime*.

[4] Walter of Loker, whom Galbert first names in c. 16, is denoted by Walter of Therouanne as "seneschal" (*dapifer*), and is so called by Pirenne, ed. Galbert, p. 27, n. 2. "Walter the seneschal" appears as witness in four charters of 1121, all concerned with donations to the Abbey of Bourbourg (see *Actes*, pp. 231, 232, 233, 235). "Walter of Loker" appears as a witness once under Baldwin VII and six times under Charles, from 1120 to 23 (*Actes*, pp. 146, 216, 225, 240, 247, 252, 265). Galbert reveals him as one of an inner circle of "new men" who had the count's ear and confidence. This clique, jealous of the power of the Erembalds, seems to have stimulated Charles's hostility toward them. They are probably the ones referred to in c. 16, as being "dependent on the friendship" of the count. (The seneschal exercised important administrative and judicial functions in the name of the count; the only other official designated as such in the charters of Charles is "Baldwin" who appears many times as witness from 1122 to 1126. See *Actes*, pp. lxxxii-lxxxiii.)

[5] Walter of Therouanne, c. 28, says he ran from his hiding place in the church to the altar and tried to conceal himself under the altar cloth.

[6] *Organistrum* probably refers to some kind of storage place for the organs which were rather small portable instruments at this time. This chapter amplifies the picture of the gallery which was large enough to contain an organ-case, benches and stools for the "brothers" or canons, an alcove for the school. See G. Kinsky, ed., *A History of Music in Pictures* (London, 1930), p. 45. Galbert obviously does not refer to the small stringed instrument known as *organistrum* at this time, probably so called because a sustained organ-like tone was produced from it by means of a crank-driven plucker.

of the church.[7] While he was dying in the gallery he had given his ring to the abbess of Origny[8] to bear to his wife as a sign of his death and as a token of the requests which he had made, through the abbess, to his wife and sons, whose death he did not know about until after his own death.

Meanwhile Walter of Loker was being hunted everywhere, inside and outside the church, for one of the custodians of the church had hidden him and even given up his robe to him. But when in his hiding place he heard the noise of arms and himself called by name, he became confused in the peril of death and came out, thinking he could be saved more easily in the church proper.[9] Jumping down from the high alcove[10] of the school into the midst of his enemies he fled as far as the choir of the church,[11] calling on God and his saints with a great and piteous cry. He was pursued at close quarters by that wretch Borsiard and by Isaac, serf and chamberlain and likewise vassal[12] of Count Charles, maddened with rage in that holy place, their swords drawn and horribly bloodstained. They were indeed furious and ferocious in countenance, tall and savage in stature, inspiring terror in everyone who saw them. After Borsiard had seized Walter by the hair of his head, brandishing his sword, he reached back to strike him, and was in no mood to delay for even a moment because he now held in his hand such a long-sought

---

[7] This careless repetition of the first sentence of c. 16, as well as the discrepancy noted above, shows that Galbert did not rework these chapters.

[8] The abbess of the nunnery of Origny in the diocese of Laon. She, too, may have been present at the count's private Mass.

[9] Walter, c. 28, says his hiding place was revealed by a boy.

[10] Galbert's word is *testudine;* in the architectural language of the time it means roof or covering, but here it may refer to an alcove or stalls used as a school. See V. Mortet, *Recueil de textes relatifs à l'histoire de l'architecture en France* (Paris, 1911), glossary.

[11] That is, the central core of the church which served as the choir of the canons.

[12] The enormity of Isaac's crime is here, and also later, in c. 28, stressed by Galbert. His triple relationship to the count as serf (because he belonged to the Erembald clan), as chamberlain (and hence as official of the count's household), and as vassal enhances his treachery. Of all the Erembalds he was closest to the count, and yet he was the "head of the conspiracy," according to Galbert, c. 28. It may have been he, with a foot in both camps, who warned the provost of some impending action against the clan after conferring with the count on February 28, and thus precipitated the murder. (The chamberlains, of whom three are named by Galbert, were entrusted with the care of the count's treasure, as appears in c. 18.)

enemy. On the intervention of the clergy,[13] however, he put off
Walter's death, since he had already seized him, until he could
lead him out of the church. Walter, now captive and sure of
death, went along crying, "Have pity on me, oh Lord!"[14] They
answered him, saying: "We must repay you with the kind of
pity you have deserved from us!" And when they had led him
out into the court of the castle, pushing him from them, they
threw him to their serfs to be killed. How quickly the serfs put
him to death, beating him down with swords and sticks, clubs
and stones!

[18] *The murderers find Fromold Junior and other adherents
of the count, March 2, 1127*

Running back to the sanctuary they searched around the altar to
see if anyone whom they had decided to kill was in hiding, and
they sent servants inside to see who was there.[1] In the first

[13] These clerics may have been chaplains of the count, or "clerics serving at his
court," or canons of Saint Donatian (who when serving at court had the rank of
chaplains); these categories are distinguished in the charter of 1089 (*Actes*, no. 9,
p. 30). Since the chaplains and "clerics" were more closely identified with the
count, it was probably only the canons who dared to intervene, probably with the
aim of saving their church from further desecration.

[14] Walter, c. 28, says only that he begged in vain to be allowed to confess his sins.

[1] Most of the individuals hiding in the sanctuary, which seems to have been
double, were petty bureaucrats, members of the count's administrative system, and
in their several capacities as notaries, chaplains and "clerics of the count," were
subject to the authority of the provost, according to the act of 1089 (*Actes*, no. 9,
p. 30). (Arnold, as chamberlain, was one of the count's aulic officials and does
not belong in this category.) The functions of the notaries, as revealed in c. 112,
were primarily fiscal, while those of the "clerics" were largely secretarial in character; the chaplains, among whom some were priests, e.g. Baldwin, performed the
offices of the count's private chapel, as for example in the gallery of Saint Donatian
on March 2. The relation of these officials to the canons of Saint Donatian, whom
Galbert generally refers to as "brothers" or "canons" is not entirely clear. It is
complicated by the fact that these canons had the right to the rank of chaplains
when serving at the count's court, according to the charter of 1089 (*Actes*, no. 9,
p. 30). There were several notaries attached to the domanial circumscription of
Bruges where the revenues of the count were notably large. It is clear from these
chapters that the count's entourage of clergy and petty officials, probably mostly
clerics, is sharply divided; those loyal to the count are in terror while others,
perhaps adherents of the provost, move among the traitors with impunity, hearing
confessions (e.g., of Themard and Fromold), and persuading the murderers to
remove their intended victims from the church. A struggle for control of the

sanctuary, hiding next to the altar, were Baldwin,[2] a chaplain and priest, and Godbert,[3] a cleric of the count, who remained sitting there by the altar, huddled together in fear. Into the second sanctuary Odger,[4] a cleric, had fled and also Fromold Junior,[5] a notary, more intimate with Count Charles than others of the court and for this reason more suspect in the eyes of the provost and his nephews; and Arnold,[6] chamberlain of the count, was also hiding with them. Now Odger and Arnold had covered themselves up with a tapestry and Fromold had made a hiding place for himself under bundles of palms, and so they were awaiting death. Then the serfs who had come in, searching through and turning over all the vessels, vestments, books, tapestries, and palms, which the brothers carried annually on Palm Sunday, first found Odger and Arnold. They had also previously found a brother of Walter of Loker, Eustace,[7] a cleric, who was sitting with Baldwin and Godbert, but did not know who he was. Those who were found had promised the serfs who discovered them to give them money afterwards if they would conceal them.

When those who had gone to the sanctuary had finally returned to Borsiard and Isaac and the others, the latter adjured them to tell whom they had found. When the truth was revealed, Isaac was seized with such a sudden and violent rage against Fromold Junior that he swore by God and the saints that Fromold's life could not be redeemed even by a pile of gold as big as the church itself. He also turned the rage of them all against that

---

chancellery between the provost and the count was apparently going on. For a fuller discussion of the inhabitants of the castle, see the Introduction, pp. 55 ff.

[2] Baldwin, called "chaplain" or "priest and chaplain," is named several times as witness to charters, from 1116 to 1119-27; see *Actes*, p. lii.

[3] Godbert, "cleric," is named twice as witness in charters of 1123(?) and 1124; see *Actes*, pp. 265, 267.

[4] Odger or Oger, perhaps the "Otger, cleric," who signed an act of 1111-15 (*Actes*, no. 75, p. 172); or the more important Oger, "notary" and "chancellor," according to Vercauteren, *Actes*, pp. li, lv.

[5] Fromold Junior, notary, does not appear in the charters. As a brother-in-law of Isaac, he may have been the count's spy in the provost's camp, as Isaac was the provost's spy in the count's circle, but he had learned less than Isaac, as his faith in Isaac reveals.

[6] Arnold, the third "chamberlain" named (the others being Gervaise and Isaac) does not appear as such in the charters.

[7] See Galbert, c. 16; this Eustace does not appear in the charters.

Fromold, shouting that no one had done more to slander the provost and his nephews to the count.[8] Then bursting through the doors, Isaac rushed in at once and seized Fromold in person and started to lead him out. When Fromold saw him he thought Isaac was going to save him from death, not take him captive, and he said: "Isaac, my friend, I beg you, by the friendship which has so far existed between us, save my life, and take care of my sons, who are your nephews, by saving me, for if I am killed they will be without a protector." But Isaac replied: "You are going to receive the mercy you deserve for having slandered us to the count!" Meanwhile one of the priests approached Fromold quietly and advised him to make confession of his sins to himself and to God. When he had done this, despairing of his life, he took a gold ring[9] from his finger and sent it by the priest to his daughter. Meanwhile Isaac was discussing with Borsiard what it was better to do, whether he should kill Fromold on the spot or save his life until they could extort the whole treasure[10] of the count from him and also from the chamberlain, Arnold, whom they had taken captive in the same place.

[8] A similar charge is made against Walter of Loker in c. 17. Perhaps Isaac had been the source of this accusation also.

[9] Fromold's wealth as a favorite of the count becomes clear in c. 19. The count's confidence in him is indicated by the fact that he held the keys of the treasure (and of other chests and receptacles of the count; see c. 20). The great size and varied contents of the count's treasure become apparent as all parties try to get hold of it; see esp. c. 41, 43, 49, 61, 83, 85.

[10] Galbert's account of these events is so lively and vivid that it sounds like that of an eyewitness. Could he have been one of the "clergy," mentioned in c. 17, who intervened?

[19] *The provost saves Fromold Junior, March 2, 1127*

Meanwhile the canons[1] of that place ran to the uncle[2] of Fromold Junior advising him to intercede with the provost for the life of his nephew whom they had seen placed in mortal danger, for Isaac had sworn his death. Then the older man, hastening to the provost, entered his house[3] with the brothers of the church, and kneeling at his feet, begged and beseeched him to protect the life of his nephew. Finally the provost sent a messenger to forbid his nephews to injure Fromold. But they sent back word that this could not be done even if he himself were present. On hearing this, the older man again fell prostrate at the knees of the provost, exhorting him to go in person to save Fromold; and the provost went, not with a quick step, however, but very slowly, inasmuch as he was little concerned about Fromold, whom actually he held in great suspicion.[4] Finally he reached the sanctuary, where indeed nothing sacred but everything evil was going on. At the demand of the clergy[5] he took all the captives there into his custody, on condition, however, that when Isaac and his nephews should ask for those entrusted to him, he, the provost, would hand over the captives. Then the provost went back and led those under his charge into the hall of his house, and he looked at them very warily and said to Fromold

[1] That is, members of the chapter of canons, also called "brothers" by Galbert, attached to the church of Saint Donatian, who lived as a community within the castle; see above, c. 13. This seems to be their first intervention (unless they are the "clergy" referred to in c. 17 who persuaded Borsiard to postpone Walter of Loker's death), and their fearless approach to the provost on behalf of Fromold seems to indicate they were not deeply committed to either side. Had they been in their own quarters until this time?

[2] The canons' intervention can be explained partly in terms of loyalty to a member of their group if the uncle of Fromold Junior is Fromold, named successively in the charters as "notary" (*Actes*, no. 37, 1107, p. 104), "canon of Bruges" (no. 38, 1109, p. 106; no. 40, 1110, p. 109), and finally, "provost of Veurne" many times from 1111 to 1124, once as "our provost and notary" (no. 61, 1113, p. 147).

[3] Also within the castle; see Plan.

[4] Galbert seems to impugn Bertulf's intentions here although actually Bertulf saves Fromold. Bertulf's slow pace may have been due to his age or more likely to his dilemma as to what course to take on this, his first appearance since the murder; his nephews seem to be defying him. Galbert's attitude toward Bertulf undergoes an interesting development in the course of events.

[5] Galbert probably means the canons.

whom he had led away captive: "You must know by now, Fromold, that you are not going to get possession of my provostship by next Easter, as you were hoping to do. I have not deserved your undermining me in this way."[6] But Fromold swore that he had done him no harm. Yet it was true that no one in the court was so intimate with the count in his lifetime, or so dear to him as this Fromold.[7] For after his house, a splendid structure, had been completely destroyed by fire, the count rebuilt it for him even better and finer than it had been before; in comparison to it, no house in the world could be considered finer or more desirable.[8]

Now when they were held in captivity, shut up and locked in, at any rate they had time and place to mourn the pious count, who in his intimacy with them had been like an equal, a father rather than a lord, and toward the rich and poor of the realm had been merciful, humble, gentle, and benevolent. In their sorrow the captives could not speak to each other except with sighs and sobs, which came from the profound sadness of their hearts. What a deplorable crime, when servants[9] cannot die with their lord and father, but must live on in greater misery after him! They might have done better to pass from the world with him in a death which was noble and honorable toward God and men rather than live on with the sorrow of their lord's death and, God forbid!, to see the traitors flourish under the rule of another count.[10] And while they were in this state of dismay and lassitude, none of their friends dared even secretly to approach

[6] This cryptic remark may help to explain the immediate cause of the murder, some imminent action contemplated by the count against the Erembalds, perhaps the removal of Bertulf from the office which gave him such great power and influence, and the elevation of his rival, the favorite Fromold, to this position. The great court held annually at Easter by the count would be a dramatic moment for this action.

[7] Perhaps a touch of jealousy is here apparent, on the part of one notary, Galbert, toward another, so favored by the count.

[8] We learn more about this house in c. 24, when Fromold goes into exile. See also c. 107, n. 4.

[9] Galbert uses *servi* (serfs) here, but it probably means "servants," in the sense of those devoted to the count, rather than "serfs" in the usual sense.

[10] Does this imply that Galbert was writing after the election of William Clito on March 30? Probably not, for the traitors did not "flourish" then.

them to offer words of consolation, for if anyone did, he was
deprived of life.[11]

[20] *Other events of March 2, 1127*

Meanwhile the bodies of the slain, that is, of the castellan and
of Walter of Loker, were carried out of the castle and immediately put on board ships, the castellan with his beloved sons,
and they were conveyed to their respective houses and castles.[1]
The provost was now walking up and down in his house with
his canons, absolving himself as well as he could in words, on
the grounds that he had known nothing about the treachery in
advance.[2]

And on the same day the traitors made an attack against their
enemies, that is, against Thancmar and his men at Straten, but
they found their strongholds empty and their farms deserted.
For when they had heard of the crime committed in the death
of the count, they were very much afraid for themselves because
they had lost their protector; and if, by chance, they should be
besieged by the traitors, there would be no one to help them, for
they had finally learned that all the peers of the realm had approved of the treachery.[3] Convinced that much more serious
dangers would threaten them as well as the whole realm in the
future, they took no care for their possessions, and thought it
important only to save their lives and flee to safer places.

[11] There is no evidence of such an occurrence but Galbert's statement reveals
the state of terror which prevailed.

[1] Transport by water was easier in both cases. Walter's home in Loker near
Ypres could be reached most easily by the Zwin and the Yperleet, and Themard's
castle at Bourbourg, the center of his castellany, by the Zwin and the sea, since
Bourbourg was then still a port.
[2] Bertulf had planned and plotted, but he had not apparently taken an active part
in the murder itself. While his nephews continue to act, he is confronting the
dilemma of his and their situation. Walter, c. 26, makes this distinction: "Oh most
evil Borsiard, what have you done! Oh most insane Bertulf, what have you agreed
to!"
[3] This statement is an exaggeration, as Galbert's own narrative will prove, but
it is significant that he himself seems to believe it at this stage of events or at any
rate thought that Thancmar believed it.

The traitors then overran Thancmar's stronghold as well as his farm, seizing all the arms and equipment within, and also carrying off a great booty of flocks and clothes of the peasants of that manor;[4] and they ravaged in this way the whole day through, not returning until evening. And not only did these men pillage our vicinity but many others, who had known about the treachery in advance,[5] ran at once to the crossroads of the merchants who were on their way to hold the fair at Ypres, and plundered them and their bundles. William of Ypres, hearing of the treacherous murder,[6] believed that he could now obtain the countship for himself, and he forced all the merchants whom he had been able to seize in the market, no matter where they came from, to swear loyalty and fidelity to him; moreover, he would not let them go but held them captive until they had done homage[7] and promised loyalty to him;[8] and he did all this on the

[4] This "stronghold" is probably the "tower" referred to in c. 9. The manor or estate consisted of the fortified house, the court or "home-farm," and the tenures of the peasants.

[5] This seems to indicate widespread knowledge of the plot, or at least Galbert's belief to that effect. Perhaps the plundering is simply early evidence of the collapse of the social order on the count's death which is revealed by Walter, c. 43. The author of the *Translatio S. Jonati* gives a vivid picture of the count's enemies now crawling like wild beasts out of their holes; see fragment in *Neues Archiv*, XV (1890), 448-51.

[6] Perhaps from John, servant of the count, who had fled to Ypres on horseback early on March 2; see c. 16.

[7] Thomas corrects *omnia et securitates* to read *hominia et securitates*, the forms used in c. 25 and elsewhere.

[8] This is the first of numerous interesting cases of the performance of "non-noble" homage by free men in Galbert, which demonstrate the extremely general significance of that term and its possible application to almost any form of personal dependance at this time. (See Bloch, "Un Problème d'histoire comparée," RHDF, VII, 57-58). It is here marked by the same basic elements of "faith and security" (the positive and negative aspects of fidelity or fealty) and "homage" that characterized the act by which a "noble" became "vassal" of the count (see Galbert, c. 56) but it apparently lacks the preliminary ceremony of the hands and the kiss, and the concluding oath and investiture with a fief. See Ganshof, *Qu'est-ce que la féodalité?*, pp. 115-16, concerning the meaning of *securitas*. Whether the non-noble persons, "merchants" here, who performed this act can be termed "vassals" is not clear; Professor Ganshof in a letter to the translator interprets this as a case of William's forcing "vassalage" on individuals to bind them to him as closely as possible. These cases are, however, interpreted somewhat differently by W. Kienast, who sees in them primarily a form of emergent "territorial allegiance" on the part of free subjects to a territorial ruler, which in Flanders was simply strengthened by the ceremony of homage. See *Untertaneneid und Treuvorbehalt in Frankreich und England* (Weimar, 1952), pp. 23, 24 and n. 4. William's eagerness to secure such pledges from merchants can perhaps be explained by the traditional

advice of the provost and his traitorous nephews.[9] Now late on the same day, toward evening, by common agreement of the provost and his nephews and their accomplices, they demanded the keys of the count's treasure from Fromold Junior, whom they were holding captive, and also seized by force all the keys of the house and of the strong boxes and chests in the house. Borsiard and the castellan, Hacket, and Walter,[10] son of Lambert of Aardenburg, took charge of these.

[21] *Bertulf tries to establish control, March 2, 3, 6*

Nothing had been done in the meantime about the body of the count, so it was still lying bloody and alone, just as it had been left by the murderers; but his soul had been commended to God, secretly however, by the priests at the time when they had administered the last sacrament to the castellan. Therefore the brothers[1] of the church were considering anxiously what they should now do and what obsequies they could prepare for him since no one dared, even secretly, to perform divine offices in the same church where it was evident that so much slaughter and crime had been committed.[2] Finally, having received permission

---

role of the count as the protector of merchants in his realm; to receive their "homage" was tantamount to being acknowledged by them as count of Flanders.

[9] William of Ypres, or "of Loo," was by descent the best qualified candidate for the succession in 1119, and is again in 1127, being the son of Philip, second son of Robert the Frisian, but he was passed over on both occasions apparently because of his illegitimacy (see Galbert, c. 47). He had been supported in 1119 by Clemence, mother of Baldwin VII, whose niece he had married, according to Walter, c. 7; and now, 1127, proceeded to seize Aire, whose inhabitants he forced to swear fidelity to him, and other important centers such as Ypres, Kassel, Bergues, and Veurne, and to impose peace, according to Walter, c. 43. Galbert's statement here, among other events of March 2, that William was already acting in league with the traitors, is not supported by his fuller account of William's approach to Bertulf on March 6, c. 25. A much more favorable impression of William is gained from Walter, c. 43, 48.

[10] Lambert, mentioned here for the first time, was another son of Erembald, hence a brother of Bertulf; he is named as witness along with his brothers in numerous charters from 1109 to 1119 (see *Actes*, pp. 106, 118, 152, 172, 174, 175, 213).

[1] That is, the canons.

[2] The church, having been defiled by murder, had to be liturgically purified before being used again for divine services. This purification did not take place until April 25; see c. 78.

from the provost and with the approval of the brothers, Fromold Senior with due veneration laid to rest the noble body, wrapped in linen and placed on a bier in the middle of the choir, and after setting four candles around it, as is our custom, he carefully looked after other matters. Only women kept vigilant watch over the body throughout that day and the following night, sitting around it in pious lamentation. Meanwhile the traitors discussed with the provost and his castellan[3] by what device the body of the count could be removed so that it would not bring eternal opprobrium upon them by the fact of being buried in their presence.[4] Having reached a clever decision they sent word to the abbot in Ghent[5] to come and bear away the body of the count, and when he had taken it to Ghent, to bury it there.[6]

And so closed that day, full of sorrow and misery, which had already given rise to so much evil and created disturbance in the lands around us, and would cause more in the future. When night came on the provost ordered the church to be protected on all sides with arms and guards, especially the gallery and the tower into which he and his men could retreat, if by any chance an attack should be made by the citizens.[7] And that very night armed knights, on the order of the provost, entered the gallery of the church, guarding the tower and its exits by continuous watches, fearful of an assault and attack by the citizens on the following day or later.

On Sunday after the death of the count,[8] the provost sent

[3] That is, Didier Hacket, his brother, who was castellan of Bruges.

[4] Is this folk tradition? Walter, c. 29, says the traitors did not want the count buried there lest his monument be an opprobrium to them in the eyes of posterity.

[5] Walter, c. 29, identifies him as Arnulf, abbot of Saint Peter's at Ghent (1117-1132), one of the great Benedictine abbeys of Flanders; founded by Saint Amand in the seventh century, reformed in the tenth century, it was undergoing a new reform inspired by Cluny in the early twelfth century. See Moreau, *Histoire de l'Église,* esp. II, 183-85. An assembly of clergy and lay nobles had been held there in 1117 on the command of Baldwin VII, to "correct or emend the monastic observance"; see *Actes,* no. 83, pp. 187 ff. Arnulf, together with "the castellan of Ghent" (Wenemar II) had been sent to Aachen by Charles in 1127 to do homage in his name to the new emperor, Lothair; see *Anselmi continuatio Sigeberti,* A. 1127, MGH, SS VI, 380.

[6] Saint Peter's contained the tombs of many of the early counts of Flanders.

[7] Galbert's first reference to the citizens of Bruges as a "collectivity" or community.

[8] That is, March 6.

greetings to our bishop, Simon, of the see of Noyon[9]. Now Ralph, a monk of Saint Trond,[10] was the bearer of the letter in which he implored the bishop to purify the church in which the count lay, betrayed, asserting that he knew nothing about it. He also offered evidence in his own behalf by which he could prove his innocence canonically in the presence of all the clergy and people. But the bearer, captured and hurled from his mount, did not reach the bishop; and when the provost heard this he feared very much for himself. On Wednesday and Thursday[11] the provost sent word through a certain squire to Walter of Vladslo[12] that by the faith he had sworn to him and his nephews he, Walter, should hasten to aid him with his following; and he sent him forty marks of silver. But Walter kept the money, pretending that he would come, though he never came except to injure him and his nephews. Bishop Simon, who was a brother of the wife of Count Charles, took measures against the church

[9] Simon of Vermandois, bishop of the dual diocese of Noyon-Tournai (1123-1146), although under the canonical age, had been elected bishop in 1123 through the influence of Louis VI of France, his cousin, and Charles, the husband of his sister; he was an unhappy pawn in the struggle of Tournai, carried to the papal court, to recover its ancient independence, which was finally successful in 1146. See Herman, *Liber de restauratione S. Martini Tornacensis, continuatio*, c. 10, MGH, SS XIV, 322, and *Historiae Tornacenses*, lib. IV, c. 3, pp. 342-43, concerning the election, and the latter, lib. IV, c. 4-6, concerning the struggle. Simon, on the division of the diocese, went off on the Second Crusade in 1147 and died in Seleucia, 1148; see Moreau, *Histoire*, III, 28.

[10] Pirenne (ed. Galbert, p. 37, n. 3) believes he was probably a monk of the lesser monastery of Saint Trond d'Oedegem near Bruges, rather than the former abbot of the Merovingian foundation of Saint Trond in the diocese of Liège, although the latter identification is not impossible since the abbot of the great abbey was now in exile, at Saint Peter's at Ghent, according to É. de Moreau, *Histoire de l'Église*, II, 213. Saint Trond d'Oedegem was a priory of canons regular of S int Augustine, founded at an unknown date and destroyed in 1128, according to Moreau in *Histoire de l'Église*; see "Circonscriptions ecclésiastiques: chapitres, abbayes, couvents en Belgique avant 1559," in the *Tome complémentaire I: texte*, p. 502.

[11] That is, Wednesday and Thursday, March 2 and 3.

[12] Walter "of Vladslo," generally called "the butler" by Galbert, and also a "peer" (c. 89), is named "butler" in a charter of 1119 (*Actes*, no. 94, pp. 211-13), where he and his brother, Cono, both appear as parties and signers. He should be identified with Walter, son of Alard of Eine, one of the baronies of eastern Flanders, named in three charters of Charles, *Actes*, no. 107, 115 (suspect), 120. His equivocal attitude toward the provost, to whom he was bound by oath for some reason not disclosed, may indicate that he was an *attentiste*. Although Galbert finally brands him as a traitor in c. 89, the degree of his complicity is not clear; his sworn relationship to Bertulf does not necessarily imply treasonable intent.

of the castle of Bruges and struck with the sword of anathema[13] those guilty of sacrilege and treachery. He absolutely forbade any of the faithful to deviate from the right path by conspiring with them or lending them aid in the future; if this should happen, he would damn with anathema all who helped them in their evil.

[22] *The struggle over the count's body, March 3, 1127*

On March 3, Thursday,[1] the abbot for whom they had sent to Ghent, after riding all night,[2] reached the castle at dawn and went to the provost and his nephews, asking for the count's body, which they had promised him. Then the provost went out and, summoning the castellan and his nephews, who had betrayed the count, he discussed with them how the abbot could carry off the body without creating an uproar. For the poor, who were waiting for the provost to distribute alms for the count's soul, began at once to spread the rumor that the abbot had come craftily, and on the advice of the traitors, to carry away the corpse. They had quickly found out about the decision because except for them none of the citizens wanted to approach or be seen any more in the company of the traitors.[3] The abbot had already ordered a litter to

13 That is, excommunicated.

1 Beginning with chapter 15, his original starting-point, Galbert divides his narrative into "days" and gives the successive events of almost every day, in regular sequence for the most part (as he explains in c. 14 at the end of his "introduction") though with occasional references to earlier events which he had since learned. The events of March 2, however, required so much space that this fact is obscured until Galbert reaches March 3. The opening sentence for each day gives its number in the month and week according to the normal medieval reckoning; for example, this heading reads "on the fifth day before the Nones of March, on the fifth day of the week." This and all other such entries have been put into modern form for the convenience of the reader.
2 It is not clear whether the abbot was afraid of disobeying Bertulf, or whether his haste was due to his impatience to get hold of the body. According to Walter, c. 29, the abbot came spontaneously on hearing the news.
3 Galbert gives the impression that there was a considerable crowd of "the poor." It is not true that they alone dared to approach the traitors; "one of our citizens," Lambert Benkin, had aided them in c. 16, and other cases will appear in the future. It is difficult to tell from their speech, below, whether "the poor" suspect Bertulf of complicity in the crime or not.

be made on which the body was to be placed and carried away on horseback. Meanwhile the paupers were following the provost around wherever he went, crying out:

"Oh, lord, don't ever let it happen that the body of our father and of such a glorious martyr[4] should be taken away from our place, because, if it does happen, the place and its buildings will be destroyed in the future without mercy. For the enemies and pursuers who come to this castle will have enough pity and mercy not to destroy completely the church in which the body of the blessed count has been reverently buried."

And a great rumor about the body's being carried off spread among the citizens.

But the provost and abbot were working fast before the rumor should arouse the town, and they had the new litter, the one just made for carrying off the corpse, brought to the door of the church. And the knights had come in who were to lift up the bier on which the count lay, in the middle of the choir,[5] and carry it over to the new litter at the door. Then the canons of the place rushed up and forcibly replaced the bier in the choir, saying they would first hear from the provost why he had ordered this done. And they went out into the court of the castle where the provost and his nephews were standing, together with a great crowd of citizens who had heard the rumor about carrying off the body, and one of the older ones[6] spoke out in front of all the people:

"Lord provost, if you had wished to act justly, you would not have given away without the consent and advice of the brothers such a precious martyr, such a great ruler, a great treasure of our church whom divine mercy and dispensation have granted to us as a martyr. There is no reason at all why he should be taken

---

[4] This is the first note of a new and significant theme, the count as a "martyr," a concept of vague meaning at this time but approximating "saint" or miracle-worker. (See Introduction, pp. 48-49.) Walter, c. 27, affirms that the count had revealed to him at Ypres on February 27 both his expectation of imminent death and his longing for the glorious role of "a martyr."

[5] Probably the central core or nave of the polygonal church which Galbert sometimes refers to as "choir," for example in c. 17, but possibly the choir proper at the east end of the church.

[6] That is, of the canons.

away from us, in whose midst he grew up and spent most of his life, and among whom, by God's ordinance, he was betrayed in the cause of justice; on the contrary if he is taken away, we may well fear the destruction both of the place and of the church. For by means of his intervention God may spare us and have pity on our place, but if by chance he is taken from us, God may avenge without any mercy at all this treachery which has been committed among us."

But the provost and traitors, who were growing indignant, had ordered the body to be carried off. Therefore the brothers of the church rushed to the doors of the church, shouting that they would not give up the body of the most pious Charles, count and martyr, as long as they lived, and that they would rather die on the spot than permit it. Then you could have seen the clergy armed with benches and stools and candleholders and any kind of church utensil which they could use as a weapon! In place of the trumpet they rang the bells,[7] and so called out all the citizens of the place who came running with arms as soon as they had heard the news, and with drawn swords surrounded the bier of the count, ready to resist if anyone should try to take it away.[8] And while the tumult was going on both inside and outside the church, divine mercy acted to calm her sons and call them from madness and the clash of arms. For while the sick and crippled were lying under the bier in the midst of the tumult, a lame man, who was born with his foot attached to his buttocks, began to cry out and bless God who, through the merits of the pious

---

[7] This is a very early mention of church bells which were apparently not the signal regularly used to summon the people. Bells of large size were not cast until the thirteenth century, according to G. Sarton, *Introduction to the History of Science* (3 vols. in 5; Baltimore, 1927-48), Vol. III, Part I, p. 728.

[8] Townspeople and canons are united in their determination to keep the body of the count for very practical reasons: its presence may save from destruction "our place," meaning here both town and castle, when the avengers come, and it is a potential source of honor and profit to both town and clergy if the tomb should become a miracle-working shrine. The enormous and varied tangible benefits to the clergy guarding such a shrine are enumerated in the *Gesta abbatum Trudonensium*, lib. I, c. 10, MGH, SS X, 234-235, and incidentally to the merchants, who could scarcely supply the needs of the throngs of pilgrims who camped outside the abbey in tents. Walter, c. 29, says both clergy and people valued the martyred count as a heavenly intercessor.

count,[9] had restored his natural capacity to move, in the sight of all the bystanders. And so the news of this miracle quieted everyone.

But the provost and castellan and those traitors had gone up into the count's house, afraid of the tumult; they sent word to the citizens that they would do nothing about removing the body against their will. The abbot went back, happy to have escaped. The provost kept coming and going, talking things over with the traitors and considering what they should do in view of the turn of events.[10] And the brothers of the church set about finding artisans and workmen who would know how, in this critical moment, to construct a tomb in which to bury the count in the very place where he had assumed the martyr's palm.[11] They did this with all haste and care so that the body should not be stolen away from them by some trickery while it was still unburied and therefore more easily removable. And so ended that day full of disorder and of deceit in connection with the attempt to carry off the remains of one so pitiably slain.

[9] Fuller accounts of this first miracle, based on the testimony of eyewitnesses, are given by Walter, c. 30, 31, and Herman, c. 29. Walter says the cripple was a boy who had lived eight years on the generosity of the monks of Saint André of Bruges (a Benedictine priory since 1100), whose prior had made him a "kind of instrument" on which he could crawl around. Herman learned from the abbot of Saint Peter's that the cripple, whom the count had often aided, crawled up to his bier, and out of gratitude smeared the count's blood on his legs; suddenly finding himself cured, he leapt down the steps like a goat! A great crowd of men and women then went after the count's blood and scattered hairs (and not in vain, says Walter, c. 31, for his cap brought health to many suffering from fever) but the provost, skeptical and scornful, ordered the church doors closed. On the cult of relics, see Moreau, *Histoire,* II, 401-10.

[10] They seem to be without any definite plans for the future. Had they been too precipitate in murdering the count?

[11] Walter, c. 29, says the body was carried back to the "upper part" of the church to be buried, and, c. 32, that a few of his "vassals and clients" came and buried him in the place where he was killed, in a sarcophagus of stones and cement on the pavement (that is, of the gallery). It was the provost, according to Herman, c. 30, who, in order to exonerate himself, had a fine sepulcher with marble columns made in the "upper story" where the count had been killed, and where his body was to lie for "almost sixty days"; Herman, c. 35, says he saw this sepulcher when he was sent to the formal burial of the count on April 22 (Galbert, c. 77).

[23] *The burial of the count, March 4, 1127*

On March 4, Friday, after the sepulcher had been made ready, the canons and provost assembled in the church of Saint Peter outside the walls,[1] to perform the customary funeral rites, and here the Mass of the Dead was celebrated for the soul of the pious count.[2] Only a few besides the canons were there to participate in the ceremonies,[3] for no one came from the court except Baldwin, the chaplain, and Odger the younger, and Godbert, clerics of the count.[4] Afterwards the provost and the brothers returned to the church of Saint Donatian where the corpse was lying; admitting the poor to the church, Fromold Senior distributed pennies, but by the hand of the provost, to all the needy who wanted to receive them, for the salvation of the soul of the pious count, Charles. Fromold Senior wept as he did this, actually pouring forth more pious tears than pennies. In fact a big crowd of paupers had come to receive alms.[5] When the distribution of alms was over, the noble body was transported to the gallery, and the provost, now standing next to the sepulcher, at last wept for the count whom he acknowledged by the dictates of reason as having been the father of the whole region of Flanders. And he mourned him as such even though he could not bear to recognize the count as a father in his obstinate mind.[6]

[1] That is, outside the walls of the castle but inside the town. Little is known about Saint Peter's; it was close to the castle, and a chapel, like Saint Christopher's (c. 35), not one of the two parish churches, Holy Savior and Holy Virgin. See B. Firmin, *De romaansche kerkelijke bouwkunst in West-Vlaanderen* (Ghent, 1940), pp. 64-66. These chapels may have been the original churches of the urban community, built as early as the tenth century, according to J. Dhondt, "De vroege topografie van Brugge," HMGG, XI (1957), 25-30. See also Ganshof, "Iets over Brugge," NH, I (1938), 285-86 and n .34. Saint Peter's did not become a parish church until *ca.* 1200, according to E. I. Strubbe, "De parochies te Brugge voor de XIIᵉ eeuw," *Album English,* 1952, p. 379, n. 2.

[2] Bishop Simon had forbidden divine services in the polluted church of Saint Donatian, and it was contrary to ecclesiastical usage for the body to be transferred to another church, according to Herman, c. 30.

[3] Galbert uses the word *offerebant,* referring to the ceremonies of the burial Mass, kissing, giving out money, and the like. Only fear could have kept the people away, because this was an important social occasion.

[4] These clerics, hiding in c. 18, were taken into custody by the provost in c. 19, and now seem to be at large. No household officials are present.

[5] The count had fed one hundred a day at Bruges during the famine, c. 3.

[6] Does Galbert's attitude toward Bertulf begin to soften here?

Now the body was shut up within the sepulcher which had been constructed hastily in this critical time and was therefore hardly suitable; it was, however, a work of decent craftsmanship.[7] Undoubtedly his soul, purged by the pains of martyrdom, is enjoying the rewards of his merits in the presence of him who ordained that he should die to this earthly order and live in celestial company with that God and Lord to whom is due all power, praise, honor and glory through infinite ages to come.

[24] *Fromold Junior goes into exile, March 5, 1127*

On March 5, Saturday, toward evening of that day, Fromold Junior was released from captivity, and this was brought about by the greatest effort on the part of those interceding for him with the provost and his nephews.[1] They finally let him go on this condition, that within eight days after leaving captivity he should either become reconciled[2] with the evil men into whose hands he had fallen or go into exile, renouncing his fatherland for the future.[3] So he went out to his home with his friends and household who were exhausted beyond words by sorrow and fear of death, both for him and for themselves. For after he was seized, his servants never dared to emerge for fear they would be immediately pursued just because they belonged to his household. He dined with his friends and household, taking it for granted that he would renounce his fatherland rather than go back into the hands of the traitors who had betrayed his lord, one who had loved him more than all others, and whom he had loved almost more than himself. He would have chosen perpetual exile for himself

[7] See c. 22, n. 11.

[1] Was the price of his release the surrender of the keys to the treasure? See c. 20.
[2] This probably means to agree to cooperate with them or to serve them as notary.
[3] Exile or banishment as a form of punishment, although appearing sporadically in Frankish law, was a creation of Flemish urban law, according to Van Caenegem, *Geschiedenis van het strafrecht*, pp. 147-56. (It should not be confused with proscription which implies death and confiscation of goods.) Galbert's words, "patriam abjuratus deinceps exularet," may echo a juridical formula of exile (Van Caenegem, p. 152, n. 6).

before ever joining them in friendship. For it is a most grievous thing for a man to be in accord with his enemy, and against nature, for every creature flees what is inimical to itself, if it can. And so when he had eaten, he made arrangements concerning his house and goods, and with the agreement of everyone, he distributed grain, cheese, and meat[4] to his servants to support them for the time being, hoping, by God's dispensation, that he would again possess in happiness and security all that he was now giving up out of necessity and out of love for the most pious count. With his father-in-law he departed from the castle and from the town[5] in which they had lived until now. Commending him to God with groans and tears, his friends followed him as far as they could.

At the same time those traitors, obstinate in every kind of crime, were making an attack on their enemies, Thancmar and his men.[6] After suffering a most humiliating defeat, they returned to the castle in fear and shame.

[25] *The provost tries to secure support, March 6, 1127*

On March 6, Sunday, Godescalc Thailhals,[1] a messenger from Ypres, brought these words to the provost at Bruges: "My lord, and your intimate friend, William of Ypres, openly sends you and yours greetings and friendship and will help you at once in every way possible."[2] After they had all applauded him and taken him into the hall, he revealed to the provost and William of Wervik[3] and Borsiard, and a few others whom they had

---

[4] These were the three basic foods.

[5] This seems to imply that Fromold's splendid house, referred to in c. 19, was located within the castle enclosure, but in c. 107 Galbert speaks of Fromold's fortified house at Beernem, near Bruges.

[6] Just where is not clear; according to c. 20 they had fled from their nearby strongholds and lands to "safer places."

[1] "Godescaus Tahyaus" is named as a guilty vassal of the count (Charles) in the inquest held in September, 1127, by Count William; see MGH, SS XXV, 442.

[2] Perhaps Galbert heard these words himself or learned them from an ear-witness since they were apparently spoken publicly.

[3] Named as one of the chief conspirators in c. 11. Walter, c. 52, reports that immediately after the death of the count and the seizure of the treasure he returned to Wervik with a considerable part of it.

admitted, other matters which it would have been shameful to report publicly. And the whole house joyfully gave assurances, one after the other, that they would call him count and accept him as such. Those who were aware of the secret aspect of the mission, and drew the proper conclusions,[4] put the stigma of treachery on the name of William, who had greeted the traitors of our place in the fullness of their crime and had offered them the promptest aid with all his following by his faith and in writing and with the pledge of loyalty. Therefore when the messenger returned, the merchants of Flanders were seized, no matter from what place they had come to the fair in Ypres, and they were forced to swear faith and loyalty and do homage to William, and so to recognize him as count. Now this was done on the advice of the provost and his men, who hoped that in this way they could escape the consequences of having betrayed the pious Count Charles.[5] And certainly William would have been raised to the countship at this time if he had gone at once to Bruges to avenge his lord and cousin, the betrayed count;[6] but because it was not so disposed by God it was necessary for others, both the barons and the people of the land, to follow the divine ordinance and become of one mind in avenging the death of the most pious count.

Now for the first time the townsmen of our place openly entered into the councils of their lords,[7] that is, the provost and

---

    [4] Perhaps Galbert was one of these shrewd observers.

    [5] This account expands and clarifies what Galbert reported out of place and probably in a spirit of prejudice in c. 20, and shifts the onus of responsibility from Bertulf to William. It seems likely that William began to assert himself at once on hearing of the count's death (see Walter, c. 43), that he took the initiative in approaching Bertulf, now in apparent control at Bruges and in possession of the treasure (Walter, c. 32), and that the provost responded because he saw in him a potential partner or tool. By guiding and supporting William's actions and helping him to secure recognition from the merchants, the provost doubtless hoped to further the ultimate election of one who, being indebted to his family, would favor their cause, both by clearing them of the crime and by helping them maintain control of the administrative system. See c. 20, n. 9.

    [6] This is pure hypothesis on Galbert's part. The coming struggle over the succession shows that no claimant could have had an easy road to the countship.

    [7] In c. 16, Galbert reveals the participation of one of the citizens in the murders, but in c. 22 he says they would have nothing to do with the murderers. Is he now trying to justify their more friendly attitude on the grounds of self-preservation? The townsmen (called *suburbani* here) may be *attentistes* but they are also bound to the traitors as their "lords" by virtue of the fact that the castellan is a member

castellan and their wicked nephews, and tried to find out their secret decisions so that they might be more wary in the future, having so cleverly learned their designs and machinations. Meantime the provost and his kinsmen never ceased trying to persuade and to induce everyone to support them, making gifts and promises on all sides. He sent word to William that the countship would be given to him, and therefore he urged him to secure homage and loyalty from all the men of Flanders[8] whom he could coerce by force or persuade by bribe. The provost sent word to the men of Veurne, who were allied to him in friendship,[9] that they should bind themselves to William in loyalty and homage. He also sent a letter to the bishop of Noyon, offering as his defense that he had not been accessory to the betrayal of the count in word or in deed; he even urged the bishop to show his great love for the sons of the Church, that is, himself and his canons, by advising them and by purifying the places of the church, and to come quickly in person to celebrate the divine offices by his pontifical authority.[10] In the same vein he addressed John, bishop of Therouanne.[11] He sent word to Robert

---

of the Erembald clan. They seem to form part of the mixed group composing the castellan's *potentia* or effective supporters. This strong bond between the castellan and the burghers is evident also in c. 25, 45, 59, 100, 103. See the analysis of J. Dhondt, "Les Solidarités médiévales: une société en transition, la Flandre en 1127-1128," *Annales*, XII (1957), 538, n. 5.

[8] Walter, c. 43, says that William at once seized Aire and forced its citizens to swear fidelity to him, and then subjugated a number of other towns in the same way.

[9] Veurne was the native home of the Erembald clan; see Galbert, c. 71. *Amicitia* undoubtedly implies a stronger relationship than "friendship"; it probably indicates a bond of alliance or even of *solidarité*, regional in this case, in the sense developed by J. Dhondt, "Les Solidarités," *Annales*, XII (1957), 545.

[10] This letter of March 6 was mentioned earlier, in c. 21, and hence c. 21 must either have been written on or after March 6, or been added to after that date. In both chapters Galbert seems to be trying to assemble all evidence of the provost's initiative.

[11] John of Warneton, bishop of Therouanne, 1099-1130, famous for his reforming efforts, appears frequently as a witness in the count's charters among the great ecclesiastics of the land. Bertulf is here appealing not only to the bishop of his own diocese, Noyon-Tournai, his ecclesiastical superior, but also to the bishop of the adjacent diocese. (Concerning John, see Moreau, *Histoire*, II, 110-14.) It was John who ordered Walter, archdeacon of Therouanne in 1127, to write the life of Charles. Walter also wrote the life of John in 1130, *Vita Iohannis episcopi Teruanensis*, MGH, SS XV[2], 1136 ff.; he says little there about the death of Charles except that the bishop suffered from the tribulations of his three last years, c. 13, p. 1147.

of Crecques, who had married one of his nieces, to fortify his house and place very strongly until he had established William of Ypres as count. (Robert was that knight who was free before he had taken to wife the provost's niece but who, after he had kept her for a year, belonged to the count in servile status according to the law of the counts of Flanders; and from this source sprang that most ruinous conflict over servitude and liberty between the pious count Charles and the provost and his kinsmen.[12]) He also sent word to those Flemings who were his neighbors by the sea[13] to come with their forces to help him and his nephews in case anyone should rise up in vengeance in the realm and the county.

He strongly urged our citizens to encircle the area of the town with ditches and palisades so that they could defend themselves against anyone.[14] At that very time the citizens had in fact enclosed the town, but for reasons utterly different from those for which they had been advised and ordered, as was later made clear.[15] For the citizens, led by the castellan,[16] were seizing the hedges and timber of the dead count and of Fromold Junior[17] (who, because of the confiscation of his goods, was expecting

---

[12] See c. 7.

[13] That is, the residents of maritime Flanders lying north and west of Bruges, adjacent to the region of Veurne.

[14] Whether this work of fortification of "the town" was the first to be undertaken is not clear. Professor Ganshof believes the citizens were only strengthening and enlarging earlier defences, dating from at least 1089; Professor Dhondt suggests that temporary fortifications may have been thrown up earlier to meet some danger and then abandoned. If earlier fortifications existed they were obviously not in condition to meet the emergency of 1127. The fortifications of the castle had, of course, existed for centuries. See F. L. Ganshof, "Iets over Brugge," NH, I (1938), 286 and notes 37-39; and J. Dhondt, "De vroege topografie van Brugge," HMGG, XI (1957), 27-28.

[15] Does Galbert imply that their real motive is not merely protection of themselves and their property against all comers but rather greater strength in relation to the traitors and for the purpose of avenging the count? The former seems more likely and is supported by their attitude toward Gervaise in c. 28.

[16] The castellan, Hacket, is here extending his military function of directing the defense of the castle proper to the adjacent town; see Blommaert, *Les Châtelains de Flandre*, p. 19. Both Bertulf and Hacket apparently hope to increase their own security within the castle by these measures.

[17] This work must then have started before March 5, the day on which Fromold went into exile, see c. 24. Where the materials came from is not clear; Galbert in c. 107 says Fromold possessed a fortified house at Beernem (13 kilometers from Bruges).

exile) outside the town, and also everything that seemed useful for the work of enclosure, and they were constructing towers and ramparts and gates for the common defense against the enemy.[18] Everybody, clergy and people, made haste to accomplish this. And so there was no respite from watching at night and working by day until, after the work of enclosing the town was completed, they could place guards at every gate and tower and rampart, so that no one could go out unless he was known and no one would be admitted except the citizens.

[26] *Gervaise of Praat takes up arms, March 7, 1127*

On March 7, Monday, God unsheathed the swords of divine punishment against the enemies of His Church, and He moved the heart of a certain knight Gervaise[1] to undertake vengeance more forcefully and quickly than was thought possible at that time. And so gathering his wrath, with the whole strength of his following, he vented his rage against those criminals, who had slain the best of all princes, pious and just in the service of God, when he was humbly kneeling in veneration of Him and His

---

[18] The citizens are constructing the most primitive kind of defense-work, a ditch from which the earth was thrown up on the inner side to form a mound, surmounted by a wooden barrier or palisade. "The towers and ramparts" are probably a crude imitation of the stone defenses of the castle. The ditch was not completed until 1128, see c. 110.

[1] Gervaise had fled to his relatives on March 2, according to Galbert, c. 16, who calls him "the first to avenge his lord." His attack on Raverschoot is not mentioned by Walter, c. 33, who does not introduce this "honest and upright man" until his arrival at Bruges on March 9 (Galbert, c. 28); and his role is completely omitted by Herman, c. 31, who gives the barons and especially Baldwin of Aalst the initial part. There is no reason, however, to doubt Galbert's account, based on his own observation of affairs in and near Bruges, despite his obvious bias in favor of Gervaise. It is striking that the first action against the traitors should be taken, not by the barons and peers of the realm, but by a "little man," a knight who, as an aulic official, seemed to have lost everything by his lord's death, but who was willing to gamble, successfully, as it proved, on the future turn of events. The passivity of the barons until March 9 may have been due to the complicity of some, the satisfaction of others at the removal of a strong ruler and perhaps also to some fear of the murderers whose position at first seemed so secure that no one but the bishop of Noyon-Tournai had openly defied them (c. 21). (Note the compliant or equivocal attitude of the abbot of Saint Peter's, c. 22; of William of Ypres, c. 25; of Walter of Vladslo, c. 21; and of the citizens of Bruges, c. 25.)

saints, in the holy time of Lent, and in a holy place and in holy prayer—those wretched serfs, among whom he had believed he would always be safe![2] Now Gervaise, who was intimate with and faithful to his lord, the most pious Charles, inasmuch as he had been his chamberlain and had clearly been a party to his counsels and secret affairs, was both sorrowful and wrathful at the death of his beloved lord. Supported by a fierce army of footsoldiers, a circle of knights,[3] and a great supply of arms, he prepared himself against the enemies of God, and hastened to lay siege to a stronghold named Raverschoot, which was well fortified by the traitors for their defense. It proved both invincible and inaccessible because of the difficulty of the terrain and the nature of the fortifications, and he took a great booty in the flocks of that castle and of others nearby.

At this time all who belonged to[4] those criminals went about securely, believing that no one in the whole world either could or would rise up against their lords because those wretches had carried out a crime of such great audacity against their lord the count. For God had so blinded them that they no longer possessed any reason or prudence, but, cast down into every kind of evil and drunk with wrath and rage, they went astray in fear and dread, both those who had betrayed the count, and those who were lending them aid. Since they had believed themselves safe and thought that everyone in the realm was either weaker than they or friendly to them,[5] they were not on guard against attack,

[2] This is doubtful in view of what Galbert said earlier about the count's suspicions. These first two sentences in theme and language echo the introductory chapters (especially c. 6) which were composed later; they may have been added to c. 26 at that time.

[3] The forces of Gervaise must have been largely footsoldiers, here named first; a "circle" (*coronam*) of knights does not sound impressive. (Walter, c. 33, says he had "about thirty horsemen" when he attacked the castle on March 9.) Galbert refers to the following of Gervaise here and elsewhere, and that of the castellan of Ghent in c. 30, as a *potentia*. This word is used to characterize the peculiar feudal *solidarité* of this society by J. Dhondt in his "Les Solidarités médiévales," *Annales*, XII (1957), 538-40.

[4] This expression (*qui ... pertinuissent*) was formerly used by Galbert, c. 7 and elsewhere, to indicate the count's relationship to his "serfs" (the Erembald clan) but here it probably means both vassals and serfs.

[5] Walter, c. 32, also stresses their sense of power and security. Bertulf's control of the administrative system as provost and chancellor doubtless contributed to this short-lived illusion, as did the seizure of the treasure, but the breakdown

and therefore when Gervaise made his attack on Raverschoot, he
carried off a great amount of plunder. Now those who were
besieged, being cut off by the unexpected assault, were struck
with terror because they, who were so few in numbers, were
trying to defend themselves against so many thousands;[6] despairing of their lives, they surrendered at once to Gervaise on condition
that they could come forth safe in life and limb. And when they
had put them out, the knights and footsoldiers who had besieged
the stronghold rushed in, and set about plundering whatever they
found inside. But those who had surrendered in the siege, that is,
the men of the traitors, escaping by night, fled to us, reporting
to the provost and his supporters on the course of events. From
now on they suffered from an unremitting fear, undergoing a
change of heart from that state of pride and arrogance in which
they had gone about up to this time, cruel and without moderation or humility.

Robert the Young, whose stronghold had been destroyed by
fire and sword in a short time, tried to make a sortie with a few
men against the besiegers, but when he had heard there was such
a great multitude he gave up the attack.[7] It would take too long
to tell with what sorrow and fear those traitors were afflicted
and, on the other hand, with what joy all the others exulted
because now both sides knew that God himself had begun his
vengeance impartially.

[27] *Gervaise and the citizens of Bruges reach an agreement,
March 8, 1127*

On March 8, Tuesday, the stronghold of Raverschoot was burned
and destroyed by fire and arms, and near Bruges the house of

---

of the social order is apparent in the panic of the merchants (Galbert, c. 16), in
the emergence of all the lawless elements in society (Walter, c. 43) and the
general anarchy as portrayed by the author of the *Translatio S. Jonati*, in *Neues
Archiv*, XV (1890), 448 ff.

[6] Certainly an exaggeration, although Gervaise's footsoldiers may have been
very numerous.

[7] Another attempt of Galbert to present Robert in a favorable light—at least
his intentions were courageous!

Wulfric Cnop,[1] a brother of the provost, who had sworn the death of the count, was burned up.[2] Gervaise with his following also made an approach toward the castle in which the traitors had fortified themselves, preventing them from coming out by surrounding the stronghold and not allowing them to move around in the neighborhood of the castle.[3] Our burghers, on hearing that God had begun the vengeance so quickly, rejoiced in this knowledge but did not dare to congratulate the avengers openly on account of the traitors who were still going and coming among them, exercising their power in safety. In their hearts they gave thanks to God who with merciful eyes had deigned to look again upon His faithful in this place of horror and confusion, and was hastening to exterminate the wicked murderers who had scourged the people of God with pillage, fires, wounds, and every kind of disorder. Now they secretly sent messengers to Gervaise and his men, promising mutual faith and friendship and pledging the most faithful loyalty.[4] In addition they swore to avenge their count and, on the following day, to admit the army of Gervaise inside the town and receive them like brothers[5] within their defenses. I cannot tell you how joyfully Gervaise and his men, on hearing this embassy, received the words of the messengers, and rightly so, knowing that whatever they did in carrying out the vengeance had been ordained by God. And Gervaise and his men did in fact swear an oath with the messengers of our citizens, and they bound themselves by this same oath of faith and loyalty to avenge their lord, the most just count of our land. All this lay completely hidden from those traitors and from most of our citizens except for a few of the leading

[1] He is named by Walter, c. 24, as one of the six leaders of the conspiracy. His name appears only twice as witness to charters of the counts, in 1115 and 1122 (*Actes*, pp. 174, 247).

[2] Presumably both were destroyed by Gervaise's troops.

[3] Gervaise is at this moment still outside the newly fortified town (*suburbium*), which practically envelops the castle, intercepting communications between the traitors and their supporters outside, and apparently not yet engaged in an attack on the castle, which could best be reached by passing through the town.

[4] These words ("componentes de fide et amicitia et fidissima securitate") seem to denote a strong binding agreement between two parties, marked by a declaration and oath of fidelity.

[5] Since Gervaise's "men" were at least partly knights, this is an interesting case of negotiations between townsmen and knights on a basis of equality.

men[6] of the place who secretly, at night, arranged this agreement which was so advantageous to all concerned.

[28] *Gervaise and the citizens begin the siege of the castle, March 9, 1127*

On March 9, Wednesday, when the octave had dawned of that blessed count (who had passed from earth to the true octave[1]), Gervaise, according to the agreement with the citizens, was admitted within the town at the Sands, west of the castle, and this was to prove the greatest misfortune for the traitors.[2] But before this, on the same day, by setting some houses on fire he had alarmed Borsiard and Robert the Young and their accomplices who, on seeing the conflagration of the houses, had come out of the castle on all sides to keep an eye on the incendiaries, in case they should attack. Now to the east of the castle three tall houses, set on fire, were burning, the flames fanned by the winds; on seeing this the citizens, at the same time as Borsiard and his knights, and not knowing about the pact which had been formed between the burghers and Gervaise, came rushing forth,[3] most of them in an armed band with those evil men. And Isaac, who during the lifetime of the pious count Charles had, as chamberlain, shared his counsels and been on familiar terms with him,[4] and who was the head of the treachery, made a sortie on

[6] Galbert's earlier implication that *all* the citizens were involved is now corrected. These "leading men" (*sapientiores*) are never named. Earlier the citizens were united with the clergy in keeping the count's body; now some make an alliance with the knights. The impact of the crisis is drawing different social groups together.

[1] The chief feasts of the Church had a subsidiary observance a week, or "eight days," later, called "the octave"; the eighth day after the count's death as a "martyr" would then constitute his true or heavenly octave in Galbert's eyes.

[2] This may be meant as a pun in Latin since west (*occidens*) and misfortune (*occasus*) are derived from the same root. The sentence is awkward in this place, anticipating Gervaise's later entry into the town and the beginning of the siege which was to last from March 9 to April 19.

[3] A fire in this area, adjacent to the castle and close by the town, was doubtless a source of alarm to the citizens as well, anxious to safeguard their own quarters.

[4] Galbert uses some form of this expression denoting intimacy with the count only in reference to three persons, Fromold Junior (c. 18), Gervaise (c. 16), and Isaac. He has already indicated his horror at Isaac's dual role of intimate

horseback with his knights. When the knights on both sides approached each other, the traitors saw they could not stand up against such a great army because they were so few in numbers and turned in flight; their pursuers, following them in hot haste, chased them back into the castle. When they had finally come into the town,[5] Borsiard and his men paused for a few minutes in front of the house of Didier,[6] Isaac's brother, trying to decide what they should do now. Meanwhile Gervaise, violently pursuing them, went toward the west to the gate of the town, and there, after exchanging pledges of fidelity with the citizens, rushed in with a very strong band.[7]

Up to this point the citizens had remained quietly at home according to their custom, for it was about evening and most of the citizens had sat down to eat, not knowing about this event.[8] Then while the traitors were standing there,[9] disturbed about their flight and trying to decide what to do, they saw their pursuers at a distance rushing through the streets, coming after them with spears and lances, arrows and all kinds of arms. Now a great

---

counselor and arch-villain, c. 17. Walter (who in c. 24 calls him a "kinsman" of Bertulf) says Isaac was "rich and powerful," c. 34.

[5] Borsiard and his men, coming from the area east of the castle, have apparently passed through the castle into the town, west of the castle, which as yet is undisturbed and where they still feel secure.

[6] He should be distinguished from Didier Hacket, brother of Bertulf; see c. 11, n. 1. Galbert changes his opinion of Didier, calling him ignorant of the plot in c. 29, but implicating him indirectly in c. 44 and directly in c. 92. Walter portrays him without hesitation as a partner of Gervaise, c. 34 and 36, and praises him as one whose horror at the crime prevailed over his fraternal feeling.

[7] Gervaise, having succeeded in his diversionary tactics east of the castle, now returns to the west where he is assured of entry to the town by virtue of his earlier pact with the citizens. Once inside the town he has direct access to the two bridges of the castle lying across the river to the west of the castle, while the troops he left on the southeast already have access to the bridge over the canal on that side. See the Plan.

[8] How can one reconcile Galbert's earlier statement that a great part of the citizens (pars plurima) rushed out with the traitors towards the burning houses, with this statement, that most of them (cives plurimi) had been staying quietly in their houses? Only if the two groups are the same, a majority concerned only with self-defense, who had been active earlier and had now returned home, ignorant of the pact and of its consequence, the entry of Gervaise, which now occurs. It is clear, at any rate, that only the small group of his supporters admits Gervaise.

[9] It seems likely that Didier's house, as well as Isaac's (see c. 11), was close to the church of the Holy Virgin in the southern part of the town, at first undisturbed by the entrance of Gervaise who probably rushed directly toward the castle gates through the northern part of the town.

tumult and clash of arms and thunder of shouts disturbed all the citizens who ran to arms and got ready; some who knew absolutely nothing about the pact prepared to defend the place and the town against Gervaise, while others, who did know about it, rushed to Gervaise with all their forces and chased the fleeing traitors back into the castle. When the citizens learned about the pact with Gervaise, sealed by his faith and oath, then for the first time they acted in unison,[10] rushing over the castle-bridge against those who, on behalf of the traitors, were continuing to resist from the castle. At another bridge, which led toward the house of the provost, a great conflict took place in which they fought at close range with lances and swords. On a third bridge,[11] which lay on the eastern side of the castle and led up to the very gates of the castle, such a fierce combat was going on that those who were inside, not able to bear the violence of the attack, broke the bridge and closed the gates on themselves. And wherever the citizens had access to the men in the castle, the fight went on very fiercely until the latter could not keep it up because they were intercepted and taken captive by the citizens. Whether they liked it or not the wretches inside the castle were full of anxiety; a great part of them were wounded and at the same time dispirited by fear and sorrow, and faint from the weariness of fighting.

[29] *The siege of the castle begins, March 9, 1127*

Meanwhile, at the moment when Gervaise entered the town, Isaac fled from the place where they had been talking things over

---

[10] It is surprising that unity was achieved so quickly, in the midst of the tumult. Walter, c. 33, says God moved their hearts so that they turned against "their lords" and aided Gervaise. Perhaps this is an evidence of strong urban solidarity.

[11] A study of the Plan of the castle will show that only two sides of the castle were enclosed directly by water, the west side by the Reie and the southeast side by a canal. Galbert here mentions three of four bridges which led to the castle, two on the west (marked 4 and 5 on the Plan) and one on the southeast (3 on the Plan). In c. 45 he names the other (Saint Peter's bridge, 6 on the Plan). For a full discussion of the location of these bridges see J. Dhondt, "De vroege topografie van Brugge," HMGG, XI (1957), 5-13. The fighting becomes more intelligible if one notes that there is a narrow strip of land on the west *between* the wall and the river so that the bridges over the water here are not in direct

and took refuge in his house, which was fairly strong.[1] And when he had crossed the bridge which led from the town to his house he tore it down and broke it into pieces so that no one could pursue him as he fled. At this time George, the most powerful knight among the traitors, was intercepted; it was he who with Borsiard had killed the count. The knight Didier, brother of Isaac the traitor, hurled him from his horse and cut off both his hands. (This Didier, although he was the brother of the traitor, was not, however, an accessory to the plot.) That most wretched George, his hands cut off, fled to a place where he hoped to hide but he was immediately denounced to a certain Walter, a knight of Gervaise, and dragged out. The knight, sitting on his horse, ordered a fierce young swordsman to kill him. The latter rushed at George, struck him with his sword and knocked him to the ground; then, dragging him by his feet into the sewer, he saw to it that he drowned for his evil deserts. Robert, a messenger and servant of the castellan, Hacket, who came from his manor, was also intercepted; after being slain in the middle of the market,[2] he was dragged off to the swamps. Another one[3] taken was the most evil of Borsiard's serfs, Fromold by name, who in his flight had hidden between two mattresses, dressed in a woman's cloak as disguise. Pulled out, he was taken to the middle of the market and, in the sight of all, hanged with a stick thrust through his shanks and shins, and his head bent down so that his shameful parts, his behind and buttocks, were turned toward the castle to the disgrace and ignominy of the traitors who were standing attentively on the balcony of the

---

connection with the castle gates, whereas, as Galbert says, on the east (actually southeast) "the bridge led up to the gate."

[1] It seems likely that his "strong house" was built partly of stone, a *domus lapidea* or *steen* as such houses were called in Flanders; it was also partly of wood (c. 30). Walter states, c. 34, that Isaac was at this time in the Church of the Holy Virgin, and, caring nothing for his house, fled at once. See Galbert, c. 11, n. 10.

[2] The chief market, as in most Flemish towns, was located outside the main gate of the castle.

[3] According to Walter, c. 33, "two of those who cooperated in the murder" were taken and slain, meaning probably George and the serf, Fromold; the latter seems to have been a common name at the time. In the Inquest, six more living persons are charged with the death of the count; MGH, SS XXV, 441-42.

count's house and on the towers[4] watching this done to dishonor
them. Meanwhile both sides kept on shooting arrows at each
other, and throwing stones and hurling spears from the walls.
Finally day closed and by night alarms and vigils prevailed on
both sides; and they lay in wait for each other so that no one
could steal out to escape from the besieged nor could anyone
secretly slip over the walls to aid the besieged.

In the same way, throughout the whole course of the siege,[5]
both sides stationed watches and laid ambushes. In general, the
besieged made an attack on the besiegers every night with the
strongest possible forces; and they fought more bitterly at night
than by day because the besieged did not dare to show themselves
by day, in view of the shamefulness of the crime, but hoped
somehow to conceal themselves and escape, if possible, so that
if by chance they did get away, no one would suspect them of the
crime of treachery. And they fought so much the more fiercely
by night, because they had believed they could perhaps come out
later and easily be purged of the crime through the influence of
the barons of the siege[6] who had looked with favor on their
undertaking. But the barons did not care what they promised
to the besieged or how many oaths they swore but were concerned
only with extorting from them the money and treasure of the
good count. And they acted rightly in accepting from the besieged the treasure of the count[7] and also many gifts, since they

---

[4] The outside balcony (*lobium*) was sufficiently high to enable them to look
over the walls of the castle; small lookout towers placed at intervals in the castle
wall surrounding the castle are probably meant by *propugnacula*. Concerning
these architectural features, see the Introduction, pp. 56-58.

[5] This second part of the chapter seems to have been added later since it refers
to the "whole course of the siege"; the castle was stormed on March 19 but the
traitors did not surrender until April 19.

[6] This first mention of the "barons of the siege" (*principes obsidionis*) is
confusing because the barons as leaders in the action against the traitors did not
arrive until March 10 and 11. Again Galbert implies that some at least among
them had been in close contact with the Erembald clan; whether simply out of
hostility to the count's strong rule or as accessories to the plot against him, is not
made clear. Galbert's interpretation of their present motives and curious justifi-
cation of their bad faith, in purely mercenary terms, may not be entirely correct.
Perhaps the leaders were at the moment sincere in their promises to the traitors but
were waiting to see what would happen before committing themselves too far. The
intervention of the king of France on March 20 clarified the situation.

[7] The large number of persons who received part of the count's treasure is

were under no obligation to keep faith or to honor their oaths toward those serfs who had betrayed their lawful and natural lord. And yet those who had slain their lord, the father of the whole county, tried to get their enemies to respect to their advantage the faith and oaths which they in no way deserved! Certainly it was more just for those who loved the count[8] even in death, and who came to avenge him and there endured alarms and vigils, wounds, attacks, and all the hardships that must be suffered in a siege—more just for them, I say—to have obtained the castle and treasure and rights of the count after the death of their lord than those wretched traitors who destroyed both the place and its riches. In this vein the besiegers and the besieged often talked back and forth to each other, but the besieged only made excuses for their treachery.

[30] *The first barons arrive; the flight of Isaac, March 10, 1127*

On March 10, Thursday, the castellan of Ghent[1] with his following hastened to the siege of the betrayers of Charles, and also Ivan,[2] brother of Baldwin of Aalst. On the night before that

---

revealed in the Inquest of September 16, 1127, which Galbert mentions in c. 87, 88; see MGH, SS XXV, 441-43.

[8] Perhaps Galbert is referring here more specifically to loyal men like Gervaise whose conduct was unequivocal rather than to the barons or leaders of the siege in general.

[1] Wenemar II was castellan of Ghent from 1122 to 1135; his tenure of the office was not interrupted in 1127 (as Blommaert believed, *Les Châtelains*, p. 46), according to Vercauteren, *Actes*, p. 299, note a. He appears as witness to two charters of Charles in 1122 (*Actes*, pp, 243, 247). As military commander of the castellany he could summon the knights of the castellany or even order a *levée en masse* of all able men in the area; see Blommaert, pp. 18-21.

[2] Ivan and Baldwin II were the sons of Baldwin I of Aalst or "of Ghent"; their names appear frequently as witnesses to charters of the counts, especially those of Baldwin VII, from 1114 to 1127. Of particular interest is one of 1122 in which Charles checked the abusive practices of Baldwin as advocate of Saint Peter's of Ghent for its lands in Brabant (*Actes*, no. 106, 1122, pp. 240 ff.). The family held in fief from the count the most important of several baronies, the barony of Aalst, in eastern Flanders on the right bank of the Scheldt; these were parts of "Imperial Flanders" which the great counts of the eleventh century, Baldwin IV and Baldwin V, had wrung from the emperor and held in fief from him. The power and wealth of these barons were based on the extensive property in allods which they possessed in the region and also on their function as advocates of the lands

Thursday, Isaac, because he knew that he was accessory to the crime and damned himself for it, and was driven by fear of death, took to flight with only his squire, and so did his wife and serfs, men and women, and all his household; and wherever they happened to find themselves in that difficult flight by night, there they hid.[3] The house and manor and more valuable equipment, and other things they had once held in freedom and power, they now abandoned heedlessly and left as plunder for the enemy.[4] On hearing this, at early dawn, the castellan of Ghent and Ivan rushed out from the siege with a crowd, seizing everything useful they found that could be carried off.[5] Finally, by placing burning torches under the roofs they set fire to the house and farm buildings, and whatever they found there that could be destroyed by fire. Everyone who saw it marveled at how exceedingly quickly everything was destroyed by the fanning and fomenting of the winds and the mad fury of the fire, for such a big building and such a large amount of wood had never before been so quickly consumed.

[31] *The barons form a sworn league, March 11, 1127*

On March 11, Friday, Daniel,[1] one of the peers of the realm, who before the betrayal of the count had been allied in strong

---

of Saint Peter's of Ghent in this area. See Ganshof, "Les Origines de la Flandre impériale," *Annales de la Société royale d'archéologie de Bruxelles*, XLVI (1942-1943), 99-137, and L. Dhondt-Sevens, "Les premiers seigneurs d'Alost, de Bornem et de Termonde," *ibid.*, appendix III, pp. 161-65.

[3] Galbert must have written this before March 17, the date on which he found out what had become of Isaac (c. 39). Walter, who is very much concerned with the flight and fate of the traitors, gives a full account of Isaac's end in c. 34, 35.

[4] Galbert is always moved by the drama of those who fall suddenly from wealth and power, even if they are traitors. His tone here is reminiscent of his account of Fromold's exile (c. 24) and anticipates his treatment of other cases.

[5] Walter, c. 34, says that Didier, Isaac's brother, destroyed the house and would probably have killed Isaac if he had found him. Here it sounds as if Isaac's house was made at least partly of wood; cf. Galbert, c. 29, where it sounds like a stone house.

[1] Another of the great lords of "Imperial Flanders" whose fief, Dendermonde, lay astride the Scheldt and who enjoyed the office of advocate of Saint Bavon of Ghent. His name appears several times in charters of the counts, especially in one concerned with Count Charles's efforts to check the abuses suffered at his hands

friendship with the provost and his nephews, hastened to the siege together with Richard of Woumen,[2] Thierry, castellan of the fortress of Dixmude,[3] and Walter, butler of the count.[4] And so each one of these barons had come with his whole following to avenge the death of his count and lord.[5] Now after meeting with our citizens,[6] and also summoning all the leaders of the siege,[7] they all took an oath, before they were permitted to enter the town, to respect as inviolate the area and property of the town out of consideration for the safety and welfare of our citizens. And they swore that they would then proceed against their enemies with one mind, and would attack, storm, and, God willing, conquer those most impious murderers; and that they would not spare the life of any of the guilty or lead out and save the guilty by any trickery but would destroy them utterly, and they would act in accordance with the common judgment of the barons for the honor of the realm and for the welfare of all its inhabitants.[8] And at the same time they bound themselves to

---

by Saint Bavon (*Actes,* no. 107, 1122, pp. 243 ff.). He is the first to be identified as a "peer" by Galbert, though Baldwin of Aalst, Ivan, and several others are later so called.

[2] See c. 16 concerning Richard's flight from the count's court immediately after the murder.

[3] Thierry, the first known castellan of Dixmude, appears several times as witness to charters of the counts, in 1110, 1119, and 1127 (*Actes,* pp. 122, 213, 302, 303); see Vercauteren, "Étude sur les châtelains," in *Études . . . Pirenne,* p. 443. See c. 41, 96.

[4] Walter of Vladslo, first named in c. 21, whom Galbert also identifies as a "peer" in c. 89 and denounces as a traitor in the same chapter.

[5] Walter, c. 36, says that Baldwin and Ivan came "from the east," and Walter, Richard, and Thierry "from the west." The arrival of these great vassals of the count alters the whole scene; they now assume control; and the leadership of Gervaise (and Didier, according to Walter) ends. Herman, c. 31, names only Baldwin among the barons who came, he says, in order that the crime, unavenged, should not be an eternal opprobrium to them.

[6] According to Herman, c. 31, Baldwin addressed the "good men" (*viri boni*) among a motley crowd of the murderers, their knights and followers, and won "the people" over to the side of the barons. It is noteworthy that the citizens feel strong enough, or bold enough, to enforce respect for their persons and goods even on the part of the great barons of the land.

[7] This may refer to such leaders as Gervaise and Didier.

[8] The formation of this "sworn league" of barons to act together for a common purpose, and thus fill the vacuum created by the count's death, marks their first emergence as an organized collectivity or embryonic "order." The binding character of this agreement is emphasized by both Walter (c. 36) and Herman (c. 31). Circumstances will strengthen their self-consciousness and enlarge the sphere of their common action. See especially Dhondt, *Les Origines des États de Flandre,*

avenge the death of the count without violating the property of the citizens and their people or that of anyone who was taking part in the siege.

[32] *The first assault on the castle fails, March 12, 1127*

On March 12, Saturday, the barons ordered all those who had settled down for the siege to attack the castle at every point where they had access to it. And so about noon the knights armed themselves together with the citizens and they made the circuit, setting fire to the gates of the castle; in this enterprise they burned a postern[1] which stood near the house of the provost. But when they were attacking the main gates of the castle, where they had piled up dry hay and straw and summoned a knight to set fire to it, those who were advancing were overwhelmed by stones, sticks, lances, and arrows from within the castle. A great number were wounded by stones as large as millstones hurled from the battlements, and their helmets and shields were crushed so that they could scarcely flee in safety from the shelter of the gates[2] under cover of which they were setting the fires. Therefore when anyone was hit by a stone hurled from above, he suffered most grievous injury, regardless of his courage or strength, so that he fell prostrate and broken, dying or dead. In this conflict one squire outside expired, his heart pierced by an arrow. There was tumult and clamor on both sides, and heavy fighting, and the clash and clank of arms reverberated in the high vault of heaven. The fight was still going on at evening, and when those outside had gained nothing but death and de-

---

pp. 14-19, and "Les Solidarités médiévales," *Annales,* XII (1957), 549-51. It is clear, however, that they do not entirely trust each other with regard to the treatment of the traitors. Are the barons formulating here for the first time the "law of the siege" which Galbert refers to more explicitly in c. 59 and c. 88?

[1] A postern (*posticum*) was usually a small unfortified door in the less visible and less exposed parts of the fortifications, used for sorties and other minor actions. See C. Enlart, *Manuel d'archéologie,* IIeme partie, tome II (Paris, 1932), pp. 536-37.

[2] *A portarum testudine.* The main gates were probably protected by crenelated towers between which there ran a vaulted passage, similar to the main gate of the castle of the counts at Ghent, still standing.

struction, they drew back from the walls and towers of the castle, and assembled part of their forces to take thought for the perils of the night. The besieged were more and more encouraged by this conflict because they had seen their attackers repelled from the walls, undone by so many disasters[3] and wounds.

[33] *The men of Ghent arrive, March 14-15, 1127*

On March 13, the Lord's day was observed on both sides, under the guise of peace.

On March 14 and 15, Monday and Tuesday, burghers from Ghent[1] arrived to take part in the siege, together with a greedy band of plunderers[2] from the villages round about. For their castellan[3] had sent word to them to assemble their communal forces and come, armed and girded for fighting, to make an attack of their own on the castle, by themselves, inasmuch as they were men with a name for conflict and battle who knew how to demolish defenses in sieges.[4] And when they heard that they could make their own attack in the siege, they assembled all the bowmen and skilful makers of military equipment, and also bold plunderers, murderers, thieves, and anyone ready to take advantage of the evils of war,[5] and they loaded thirty wagons with arms. They came in haste, on foot and on horse, hoping to obtain a great deal of money if by chance the besieged sur-

---

[3] Literally "fallings" (*ruinis*).

[1] The burghers of Ghent were subject to call by the castellan of Ghent, who had arrived on March 10 with other local forces, probably knights of the castellany. The use of the word *communio* (translated as "communal" here) in the next sentence is a rare example in Flemish sources; it also appears in the charter granted in 1127 to Saint Omer (*Actes*, no. 127, c. 12, p. 296 and also at the end), apparently in the sense of a legally recognized community.

[2] These doubtless comprise the "thieves and murderers" mentioned below. Whether they were true "mercenaries" as Pirenne suggests (ed. Galbert, p. 55, n. 4) or merely a greedy rabble, is not clear; Galbert generally uses specific professional words with reference to this class (*solidarii* in c. 49, 120; *coterelli* in c. 75, 77) which was of growing military importance in the twelfth century. See J. Boussard, "Les Mercénaires au XIIe siècle," *Bibliothèque de l'École des chartes*, CVI (1945-1946), 189-224.

[3] Wenemar II, see c. 30.

[4] That is, they come as technical experts.

[5] Galbert here reflects the burgher hatred of war.

rendered to them. There was certainly a strong and enormous army of them. When they had reached the gates of the town, they dared to enter forcibly, but all the men of the siege, who ran up from the inside, resisted them face to face, and there would have been a general struggle if the wiser ones in both ranks had not come to terms. For, after giving and receiving hands, the men of Ghent pledged themselves by faith and swore an oath that they would join them in the siege and share fully their efforts and arms and counsels, while respecting the place and the property of our citizens, and that they would keep with them only their own men and those who were expert in fighting, and send the others away. Then the men of Ghent came in with a great crowd and filled up the area around the castle. At that time Razo the butler[6] returned from Saint Gilles[7] and came with his following, rightly mourning the death of his lord, the count.

[34] *The barons consider the problem of succession, March 16, 1127*

On March 16, Wednesday, "cum sanctificatus,"[1] on the night of Saint Gertrude, the countess of Holland[2] came to the siege with her son, and a big crowd came with her. Now she was hoping that all the barons of the siege would elect her son[3] as count, because our citizens[4] and many of the barons had sug-

---

[6] Razo of Gavere appears frequently as a witness to charters of Count Charles from 1120 to 1125 (see *Actes,* nos. 95, 97, 106, 108, 120). He was one of two known butlers in Charles's household, the other being Walter of Vladslo.
[7] In Provence.

[1] From this point on Galbert occasionally identifies the day also by the opening words of the Introit of the Mass for that day, especially if they bear some relation, even merely verbal, to his account.
[2] Gertrude (or Petronilla), the widow of Florent II, count of Holland, and regent for her son; see the Genealogy.
[3] Thierry VI, whose hereditary claims to the countship were tenuous, being based on the second marriage of his paternal great-grandmother, Gertrude, to Robert the Frisian, count of Flanders (1071-93).
[4] His candidacy was probably favored by the people of Bruges because as count of Holland he controlled the mouth of the Scheldt, the navigation of which was

gested it to him. The countess expressed her thanks for this, and she tried hard to secure the friendship of all the barons, bestowing gifts and making many promises.

On this day the knights Froolf and Baldwin of Zomergem[5] pretended that they had come from William of Ypres, announcing to the barons of the siege that the king of France had given the countship to the same William, and they created anxiety about this among all who had promised the countess that her son would be elected. These knights cleverly and deceitfully announced this lie as the truth in order to prevent the barons of the siege from making any concession in the matter of receiving the countess's son as count. On hearing this news, the barons were very indignant, if it should indeed prove true that William of Ypres had been given the countship by the king.[6] Therefore they swore an oath and pledged themselves by their faith never to serve as vassals under him as count of Flanders, for he was suspected by all and under the stigma of treachery to the lord count.[7]

[35] *The canons remove the relics from Saint Donatian; Galbert*
identifies himself, March 17, 1127

On March 17, Thursday, the canons of Saint Donatian by means of ladders scaled the walls of the castle[1] on the south side. Here they brought out the reliquaries and biers of the saints and their relics, and with the consent and approval of the barons,

---

essential to their trade. It is clear here, and becomes clearer later, that considerations of hereditary right weigh less with the people of Bruges than their own interests.

[5] Baldwin appears twice as witness to charters of Charles, both times in 1122 (see *Actes*, pp. 243, 247), together with his brother Walter, whom Galbert mentions in c. 113. Froolf cannot be identified.

[6] Two conceptions of the method of succession have now appeared, election by the barons or choice by the king.

[7] The barons are now extending their collective action under oath from direction of the siege to consideration of the election of a count, weighing the candidacy of Thierry and rejecting that of William of Ypres. It is hard to tell whether their absolute rejection of William springs from his failure to make offers to them or from the earlier barrier to his succession, his illegitimacy (see c. 47).

[1] It seems clear that the canons had already abandoned their church and the castle and are returning from the town to perform this mission.

they transferred them to the church of Saint Christopher[2] which is located in the middle of the market; they also carried off vessels, tapestries and hangings, woolen and silken cowls, sacred vestments, and a pile of books and church utensils and other things belonging to the church. The provost, on the intervention of Fromold Senior, permitted the accounts and records of the revenues of the count,[3] which he had saved for himself and for his William of Ypres, to be carried away because he saw a complete change in his fortune,[4] just as he allowed, though unwillingly, all the reliquaries of the saints and equipment of the church to be taken out.

And so the church of Saint Donatian stood alone and deserted, finally abandoned to the traitors who kept a whore in it, and had latrines, stoves, and ovens, and there, foul in themselves, they did all sorts of foul things. And the servant of God, the most pious Count Charles, was also still lying alone in that place where he had received martyrdom, abandoned to his betrayers. Then after everything was carried out which they were permitted to remove, the canons in tears and without the usual formalities bore out the relics of the saints, in sorrow and with sighs and lamentation. No one except the clergy and a few bearers of the holy objects was allowed to approach the walls, for on both sides they were standing armed and watching each other; nevertheless, in the midst of arms they venerated the saints by offering peace and safe passage[5] to their bearers. This was certainly a strange and unusual procession in which Alger, chamberlain of the provost,[6] wearing a cowl like a cleric, was

---

[2] Probably a chapel, like Saint Peter's, not a parish church. See c. 23, n. 1.

[3] The provost as ex officio chancellor of Flanders was receiver of the revenues from the count's private domain and hence in charge of the accounts (*brevia et notationes*) prepared by the notaries under him, of whom Galbert was one. These records of receipts and expenditures were essential to the sound administration of the realm and were probably guarded carefully, perhaps with the count's treasure. See Monier, *Les Institutions financières*, pp. 41, 51, and Vercauteren, *Actes*, pp. xlix-lii.

[4] It appears that Bertulf has abandoned hope of future control of the administration in partnership with William despite the early military success of the traitors on March 12.

[5] *Pacem et viamen* is corrected by Thomas to read *pacem et tutamen*.

[6] Alger later reveals the whereabouts of the treasure; see c. 85. It is clear that the provost had a considerable household.

carrying the cross, for since he despaired of his life he escaped in this disguise. Then all good men and all the citizens mourned at this turn of events, though they were happy that they had obtained the relics of the saints which would have fallen prey to the enemies and to looters of the place if they had remained in the church, as it became clear later at the time of the storming of the castle and the invasion of the church.[7]

And it should be known that I, Galbert,[8] a notary, though I had no suitable place for writing, set down on tablets a summary of events; I did this in the midst of such a great tumult and the burning of so many houses, set on fire by lighted arrows shot onto the roofs of the town from within the castle (and also by brigands from the outside in the hope of looting) and in the midst of so much danger by night and conflict by day. I had to wait for moments of peace during the night or day to set in order the present account of events as they happened, and in this way, though in great straits, I transcribed for the faithful what you see and read. I have not set down individual deeds because they were so numerous and so intermingled but only noted carefully what was decreed and done by common action throughout the siege, and the reasons for it; and this I have forced myself, almost unwillingly, to commit to writing.

Now[9] the ladders were made in this way: at first a wider ladder with rungs was constructed according to the height of the castle walls; to the left and right, green branches, woven tightly together, formed a kind of "wall," and in front of the ladder a similar "wall" was woven. On this ladder another ladder, longer and narrower, and made in a similar way, was superimposed, lying on its side, so that after the erection of the bigger ladder, the smaller ladder could be slid over the wall of

[7] Since these events took place on March 19 (see c. 41, 43), Galbert must have written this chapter, or added to it, on or following that date.

[8] This unique autobiographical note in the chronicle is of immense interest in revealing Galbert's procedure and the journalistic character of his narrative. (A discussion of his possible motives for writing and of his status, whether clerical or lay, is included in the Introduction, pp. 65 ff.) At the end of introductory chapters 1-14, which were added later, Galbert also addresses his reader directly and refers to his arrangement of material as being "by days and their events"; see c. 14, end.

[9] Galbert now abruptly resumes the thread of the military narrative, abandoned in c. 33.

the castle and the woven "walls" to right and left and in front would protect the climbers on all sides.[10]

[36] *Who the besieged were, and what some of them were doing*

It should not be forgotten that there were many confined within the castle who were not guilty of the death of the count in deed or in word but had been intercepted with the guilty on the day when the latter had first been shut up within the walls. There were also many who had gone in voluntarily with the criminals and who, though they had not taken part in the deed and actual slaying, were, nevertheless, in sympathy with the guilty.[1] And there were many others who on the first and subsequent days of the siege had gone in for the sake of gain and money; among these was a fiery young fighter named Benkin,[2] expert and swift in shooting arrows. He kept going around the walls in the fighting, running here and there, and though he was only one he seemed like more because from inside the walls he inflicted so many wounds and never stopped. And when he was aiming at the besiegers, his drawing on the bow was identified by everyone because he would either cause grave injury to the unarmed or put to flight those who were armed,[3] whom his shots stupefied and stunned, even if they did not wound. There was also present with the guilty a knight, Weriot, who from the time of his youth had lived as a thief and brigand; he had caused great slaughter among those making the attack outside the walls by

[10] This description of scaling ladders, completed with dimensions in c. 40, is a classic account; see Enlart, *Manuel d'archéologie*, IIeme partie, tome II, pp. 484-86. The artisans of Ghent were no doubt responsible for this construction.

[1] More evidence of the extent of opposition to the count. Who were these men? Probably mostly knights, vassals of the Erembalds who were loyal to them, as well as other independent and restless elements in society who were hostile to the firm peace measures of the count. See the Introduction, pp. 31-34.

[2] Galbert refers to Benkin again in c. 75, and in c. 77, where he identifies him as a mercenary (*coterellus*).

[3] Galbert is distinguishing between those unprotected by coats of mail, probably citizens, and those wearing such armor, probably knights.

rolling down and hurling stones⁴ which he could do using only his left hand.

There was indeed an infinite number of the guilty and their accomplices within the walls ready for these evil deeds, day and night; they were engaged in vigils, fights, attacks, and also every kind of exhausting labor, for they had blocked up the gates of the castle on the inside from bottom to top with loads of dirt and stones and dung so that they could not be reached from the outside even if by chance the gates should be destroyed by fire and conflagration. And certainly on the eastern side where fires had been set, the big gates had been almost completely burnt up so that an enormous opening would have appeared if they had not blocked it up with a mound of stuff. Finally, while on the inside they had blocked the exits of the gates with piles of stones and earth, on the outside, at the two ends, both the besieged and besiegers had destroyed the bridges which had formerly led to the castle⁵ so that no means of getting in was left to the attackers and no way of getting out to the besieged.

[37] *The besieged prepare for further assaults; many assert their innocence and come out, March 17, 1127*

When the besieged had made themselves secure at the exits they set about blocking up the doors of the church on the south¹ and the doors of the count's house that opened out into the castle, and the doors that led into the castle from the cloister, so that if by some misfortune they should lose the courtyard of the count, they could retreat into the count's house and the provost's

---

⁴ Through holes in the ramparts made for this purpose?

⁵ Galbert does not mean the main bridges, those over the Reie, now in possession of the besiegers, but lesser bridges across the ditch immediately around the castle, its original defensework, and thus in direct contact with the gates of the castle. A narrow strip of land lay between the river and the ditch. See the Plan and Dhondt, "De vroege topografie," HMGG, XI, 10-13.

¹ There must have been side doors in the nave.

house, and also into the refectory and cloister of the brothers as well as into the church.[2]

There stood the church of Saint Donatian,[3] built round[4] and high, roofed over with earthenware material, its peak vaulted with hollow jars and bricks,[5] for the original roofing of the church had been made of wood but when the structure of the bell-tower[6] was erected, the basilica itself had been covered with this man-made material. From this place it dominated the scene in the splendor of its beauty like the throne of the realm; in the midst of the fatherland it called for safety and justice everywhere in the land through security and peace, right and laws. For, in fact, all the wooden material had formerly been consumed

[2] They are blocking up all the doors that opened from these buildings out into the open "court of the castle"; see the Plan of the castle.

[3] The following description of the original Saint Donatian has been studied and analyzed by several Belgian scholars whose work was summarized and expanded by P. Rolland, "La Première église Saint Donatien à Bruges," RBA, XIV (1944), 101-11. His conclusions, based primarily on literary evidence, especially on Galbert's comments and implications, have been substantiated, and further evidence has been added, by a series of excavations made on the site in 1955 by Dr. J. Mertens. A description of the foundations of the church by Dr. Mertens is given in the Appendix; the notes here and following will include only what is essential to an understanding of the text.

[4] It was actually polygonal, a central-type church, modeled on Charlemagne's tomb-chapel at Aachen, an octagon within a polygon of sixteen sides; the octagonal core may have culminated in a pyramidal tower, perhaps similar to that of the surviving eleventh-century church of Ottmarsheim in Alsace, a faithful reproduction of the church at Aachen except for the fact that both polygons are octagonal. See E. Mâle, "L'Église d'Aix-la-Chapelle et son influence dans la vallée du Rhin," *Mémoires de la Société nationale des antiquaires de France*, LXXXIII (1954), 129. Saint Donatian is considered by Hans van Agt to be the first known imitation of Aachen, built around 900. "Die Nikolauskapelle auf dem Valkhof zu Nymwegen," in *Karolingische und ottonische Kunst: Werden-Wesen-Wirkung* (Wiesbaden, 1957), p. 191.

[5] *Ollis et lateribus: ollis* undoubtedly means whole hollow jars, which were set at intervals in mortar, along with bricks, probably with the aim of forming a light as well as fire-proof vaulting for a structure whose walls had not been designed to carry a heavy dome such as that at Aachen. The accoustical value of such hollow jars, suggested by Vitruvius, was obviously ineffective when they were completely imbedded in mortar. The architectural use of hollow pots in walls and vaulting throughout Europe from antiquity down to the seventeenth century is proved with a wealth of archaeological evidence by Professor Jean de Sturler, "Note sur l'emploi de poteries creuses dans les édifices du moyen âge. À propos de la première église de Saint-Donatien à Bruges," *Le Moyen Âge*, LXIII (1957), 240-65. His conclusion that Galbert's words refer to such an architectural practice seems incontestable and at last clears up a much-disputed point.

[6] *Materia campanarii:* Galbert may be referring to the central tower or possibly to one of the two flanking west towers which are called *gemellis campanaribus* in the eleventh-century *Gesta episcoporum Tullensium*, c. 47, MGH, SS VIII, 647.

by fire, and therefore as protection against the danger of fire they had fabricated this "stony" material out of hollow pots and bricks which fire could not destroy. In the western part of the church a very powerful tower stood out, part of the structure of the church itself but greater in height, dividing at the top into two more slender towers.[7] The wall encircled the house of the provost and the dormitory of the brothers and the cloister and likewise the whole castle; and that wall, which they expected to hold on to until the end, stood high and strong, with lookout towers and a circular walk for fighting outside.[8]

And although the wall was strong in itself and the ascending stairs were firm, they labored day and night to make themselves safer inside because they had now learned that they would have to fight against the whole world. Then finally they could remember their own saying, "If we kill Charles, who will come to avenge him?" But, in fact, those coming to avenge him were infinite and the number of men was unknown, except to God; and therefore the word "who," interrogative and infinite in their saying, achieved its just and full meaning.[9] And it should be known that there were some restless knights inside with the guilty whose minds were bent on getting out by falling or slipping from the wall, if by chance they should have an opportunity, because whoever was besieged with the guilty was marked with the stigma of the traitors. Knowing this, the barons of the siege,

---

[7] The great "tower" was a massive tower-like façade, variously called *tour-porche*, *église-porche* or *Westwerk* by European scholars, and now generally called "west-work" in English. At the two extremities of the west-work were slender towers or turrets containing the stairs that furnished the only access to the gallery. The west-work must have been similar to the original façade of Charlemagne's octagonal tomb-chapel at Aachen, the model of Saint Donatian. In appearance it may have resembled the massive façade of the basilican church of Saint Mary at Maestricht; see R. Lemaire, *De romaanse bouwkunst in de Nederlanden* (Brussels, 1952), plate 10. The origins and meaning of this remarkable architectural feature have been much debated. It should be sharply distinguished from the two-tower façade, in the opinion of H. Schaeffer, "The Origin of the Two-Tower Façade in Romanesque Architecture," *The Art Bulletin*, XXVII (1945), 105-8. For summaries of recent controversy see P. Francastel, "À propos des églises-porches: du carolingien au roman," in *Mélanges d'histoire du moyen âge dédiés à la mémoire de Louis Halphen* (Paris, 1951), 247-57; and E. B. Smith, *Architectural Symbolism of Imperial Rome and the Middle Ages* (Princeton, 1956), 79-95.

[8] A *chemin de ronde*.

[9] See c. 14.

assembling their advisers and men of good judgment, approached the walls and held a parley with all the besieged. They ordered that those among the besieged who were not guilty should be summoned to the ramparts of the walls, and they offered them liberty and the opportunity of leaving the besieged, if they wished, promising to save the life and limbs of those whose innocence should be clear. If any others except the guilty wished to come out and to prove their innocence according to the judgment of the barons, they could leave with the same freedom, but no consideration of any kind would be granted to the guilty who had committed such a great and unheard-of crime; on the contrary, they should suffer such destruction and experience such bitterness of dying as no one had ever before heard of. Then, following this edict and agreement, a good many came out either because their innocence was clear, or because they were prepared to prove their innocence to those who did not believe it.

[38] *The castellan Hacket pleads for mercy, March 17, 1127*

Finally the provost, sad in countenance and no longer stern and proud in his dignity, came out to the parley dismayed in mind, and he and his brother, the castellan Hacket, expressed themselves humbly in these words. The actual spokesman for the provost and all the besieged, however, was the castellan Hacket who alone spoke for all and answered the barons:

"Our lords and friends, on whom we should have taken pity[1] if things had turned out differently, you ought, out of some vestige of former love, to show as much gratitude to us as you can, with due regard to your honor and position. We beg and beseech you, barons of this land—and don't forget how many good things you secured thanks to our favor!—have mercy upon us, for we deplore and mourn the death of the count along with you; we condemn the guilty and would cast them out from us forthwith if we did not, though unwillingly, pay heed to our

---

[1] *Miserentur* is changed to *misererentur* by Thomas.

blood-kinship with them.[2] Nevertheless, we beg your authority, hear our plea on behalf of our nephews whom you call guilty; let them now receive from you permission to come out of the castle and later, after their punishment for such an inhuman crime has been determined by the bishop and magistrates,[3] let them go into perpetual exile,[4] so that they may deserve somehow, in haircloth and penance, to be reconciled to God whom they have so gravely offended. Now we, I and the provost and Robert the Young, together with our vassals, are prepared, according to judgment of every kind,[5] to give satisfaction to everyone that we are innocent of the deed of treachery and of consent to it, and to this end we are prepared to prove our innocence in every way, if anyone on earth will deign to receive the evidence of our proof. My lord the provost offers to make proof of his innocence, no matter how severe,[6] in the presence of all the clergy, because he attests that his conscience is clear. We beg you again to permit our nephews who are guilty and marked with the stigma of the treachery to have permission to go forth into exile, safe in life and limb; and to allow us to be purged by the process of true proof, the knights to be examined according to the secular law, the clerics according to canon law. But if you reject this offer as abominable, we prefer to stay with the guilty, besieged as we are, than to come out to you and die shamefully."

And when the castellan Hacket had completed his speech, a certain knight of the siege named Walter stepped out to reply to the foregoing words:

"We are no longer under any obligation to be mindful of your favors nor should we in justice show any trace of former love towards you, who forcibly shut the lord count off from us after he was slain and prevented us from burying and mourning him properly, and who have also shared the treasure of the realm

---

[2] Evidence of the persistent strength of the kinship bond.

[3] The word "magistrates" (*magistratibus*) probably refers to the members of the local courts, the *scabini* of the tribunals of the castellany. The bishop would presumably determine the penance, not the punishment.

[4] For the punishment of exile see R. Van Caenegem, *Geschiedenis van het strafrecht*, pp. 147-56.

[5] That is, by lay or clerical courts.

[6] This probably refers to proof by ordeal.

with the guilty, and hold his royal hall unjustly, you most impious traitors of your lord, who now possess nothing in the realm
and county! For you possess nothing justly, neither your own
life nor your goods, seeing that you have acted without faith
and without law; and therefore you have armed against your-
selves all those who profess the name of Christian, because you
betrayed the prince of this land, who died on behalf of the
justice of God and men, in holy Lent, in a holy place, while he
was prostrate in holy prayer to God. And so henceforth we
throw away, reject and cast from us the faith and homage which
we have heretofore observed towards you."[7]

The whole crowd of the siege was present at this parley, and
immediately after this reply, they seized rods and cast away their
homage, breaking their faith and loyalty to the besieged; and
now the two groups separated, talking among themselves angrily
and stubbornly, some to take the offensive, the others to resist.

[39] *The news of Isaac's flight, capture, and confession,
March 17, 1127*

On the same day we heard from the squires of the abbess of
Origny[1] about the fate of Isaac, who on the very night of his
flight[2] reached the vicinity of Ypres, though he thought he had
arrived at Ghent. From there he fled to Steenvoorde, to the
manor of his brother-in-law, Guy,[3] and on his advice, went by

---

[7] What follows is the formal rite of *exfestucatio,* the solemn rejection of the
festuca (stalk or rod), an act which symbolized the renunciation of the bond of
vassalage and was as essential to the legal validity of this act as the solemn statement to that effect. Like the rite of *inmixtio manuum* (the vassal's placing of his
clasped hands between those of his lord), which was essential to the creation of
the bond of vassalage, it reveals the "medieval taste for the concrete and actual."
See Ganshof, *La féodalité,* p. 134. Whether this act was performed only by those
among the besiegers who were knights, and who were vassals of the provost and
his relatives, is not clear. Could it also have been performed by non-noble free
persons, such as citizens? A clear case of purely "feudal" *exfestucatio* is given by
Galbert in c. 95.

[1] See c. 17.
[2] That is, March 10; see c. 30.
[3] Walter of Therouanne gives fuller details about this matter in c. 34. Guy,

night to Therouanne where he secretly and privately assumed the habit of a monk. But he could not escape the rumor that he had fled or the numerous inquiries about himself, so that he was never actually concealed but was found out at once. For the son of the advocate of Therouanne,[4] as soon as he heard about Isaac, rushed into the cloister of the brothers and found him hiding in the church, in a cowl, acting as if he were muttering psalms. When he had led Isaac out captive, he beat him with sticks and bound him with chains and so forced him to reveal the names of those guilty of betraying the count. Isaac yielded, naming as guilty himself and some others, and adding, over and above, the names of more who had been accessories to the crime and accomplices of the guilty, that is, of the ones who had actually slain the count with their swords. Concerning the swearing of the plot, he added to the names of Borsiard and William of Wervik and Ingran of Esen[5] and Robert the Young, that of Wulfric,[6] brother of the provost, and also a few other wretched murderers. And some reported that Isaac said he had dug a deep hole at the roots of an oak tree in the orchard adjoining his house and hidden money there, but the knights of our place searched for it in vain, though they hunted everywhere and dug down into the very bowels of the earth.

[40] *The first assault with the ladders, March 18, 1127*

On March 18, Friday, the ladders were brought out to the walls, and both sides attacked with arrows and stones. Those who

---

who had married Isaac's sister, took him to the monastery of Saint John "near our city."

 [4] Eustace, the advocate, and his son, Arnold, are named as witnesses in a charter of April, 1127 (*Actes*, no. 127, p. 298). According to Walter, c. 35, Arnold and his men surrounded the monastery, seized Isaac, stripped off his monastic garb, and dragged him nude to the city where a mob of citizens demanded that he be hanged or burned at once.

 [5] These are the three named, in addition to Isaac, by Galbert in c. 11. William and Ingran are named first in the list of the guilty found in the Inquest, MGH, SS XXV, 441.

 [6] Galbert includes Wulfric in the sworn conspiracy in c. 27, and so does Walter, c. 24.

brought out the ladders now advanced defended by shields and wearing coats of mail. Many followed, to see how they could set the ladders up against the walls, because they were very burdensome owing to the fact that the wood was green and damp, and very heavy, being about sixty feet in height; the lower ladder was twelve feet wide while the upper ladder was much narrower but a little longer.[1] And while the ladders were being dragged along, the cries and shouts of the pullers aided their hands,[2] and the noise resounded in the high heavens.

The men of Ghent, in an armed band, were protecting with their shields those who were dragging the ladders, for the besieged, having heard and seen the dragging, mounted the walls and appeared on the lookout towers, hurling an infinite number of stones and a cloud of arrows against the bearers of the ladders. But notwithstanding, audacious young men, who wished to outstrip the assault of the bigger ladders, set up small ladders such as ten men are accustomed to carry, and climbed the walls one after the other. But when anyone of them reached out to grasp the summit and go over the wall, those hiding inside and lying in wait for the climbers, hurled him back with spears and pikes and javelins as he clung to the ladder so that no one, no matter how bold or swift, any longer dared to approach the besieged by the smaller ladders. Meanwhile, others were trying to drive holes in the walls with the mallets of masons and all kinds of iron instruments, and though they tore away a great part of the wall they had to retire, frustrated. But when the crowd of pullers

[1] See the description in c. 35; the "upper ladder," to be used in descending once the wall is scaled, is affixed horizontally to the "lower ladder," to be used in ascending. Since Galbert says in c. 35 that the ladders were made "in accordance with the height of the wall," and now says they were sixty feet long, it is possible to speculate about the height of the castle wall. Pirenne (ed. Galbert, p. 65, n. 1) states that 60 feet, by the measurement of Bruges, would be the equivalent of 16 meters 38 millimeters and concludes that the wall must have been about 15 meters high; he apparently estimated an angle of emplacement of about 20 degrees. A wall of considerable height also seems to be implied by the fact that ten men were needed to carry the "small ladders" mentioned below. The "ladders or lattices" successfully used by the citizens to scale the wall (c. 41) must have been short units joined together in some way; they could hardly have been as long as the other ladders since "one man could carry them." See the discussion of the walls in the Introduction, pp. 56-57.

[2] Thomas removes the comma after *manus* (hands) in the text, and thus makes possible the present translation.

had come close to the walls, and the fighting grew more bitter on both sides as the overwhelming mass of stones came from inside, the dense shade of night put an end to the fighting on both sides; and the men of Ghent, suffering from many wounds, had to wait for the next day when, with the help of all the besiegers, they hoped to erect the bigger ladders by force and so gain access to the besieged.

[41] *The storming of the castle, March 19, 1127*

On March 19, Saturday, when day dawned, the besieged, stationed in various parts of the castle after the day's fighting, had lain down to rest, thinking they would be safer for a little while since they had fought so well the day before against the men of Ghent outside. With this sense of security after the day's success, the guards of the walls had even gone into the count's house to warm themselves because of the bitterness of the cold and wind, leaving the court of the castle empty. Then our citizens, on the southern side where the relics of the saints had been carried out, climbed over the walls by means of slender ladders and lattices which a single man could carry.[1] Once inside, without sound or noise, they assembled in battle-line, ready to fight, and at once ordered the lower ranks among them to go to the big gates and remove the mass of earth and stones from the gates in order to make an entrance for all those still outside who as yet knew nothing about what was going on. They had also found one gate of the castle on the west firmly closed with key and iron bolt, but not obstructed by a pile of earth or stones, which the traitors had kept free so that they could by this means admit or send out anyone they wished. Taking possession of this, our burghers had immediately forced it open with swords and axes, and the ensuing noise and clamor of arms inside threw into

---

[1] "Our citizens" accomplish what neither the knights nor the men of Ghent had been able to do; Galbert's pride in them is obvious.

[2] Galbert may be making an invidious distinction between the citizens, who have proved themselves so resourceful, and the rest of the besiegers, a mixed lot with various motives.

tumult and motion the army around the castle. Then a great crowd from the siege[2] rushed into the castle, some to fight, some to plunder whatever they could find inside, others so that once they got inside the church they could seize the body of blessed Count Charles and carry it off to Ghent.

Now the traitors, who were lying sunk in deep sleep in the count's house, were aroused by the great noise, and alarmed, not knowing what had happened; they ran here and there trying to find out what was the cause of the noise. And when they had learned what dangers threatened them, rushing to arms, they took their stand at the doors of the church, awaiting the attack. Some of them were intercepted at one of the gates during the advance of our citizens into the castle; in fact, many knights, to whom the custody of those gates on the east had been entrusted, on suffering the impact of the invading citizens, surrendered to the pity and mercy of their captors when they could do no more. Some of them, despairing of their lives if they were taken by the citizens, slipped over the walls; one of these, a knight, Gilbert, fell in sliding over and died. When some women had dragged him into a house and were caring for his remains, the castellan Thierry and his men, discovering the dead man, dragged him, tied to the tail of a horse, through all the streets of the town and finally threw him into the sewer in the middle of the market and decapitated him.

When the citizens realized that they intended to resist at the doors of the count's house, they climbed the steps leading up to those doors and cut them down with their axes and swords; rushing in on the besieged they pursued them through the middle of the house as far as the passageway by which the count had been accustomed to go across from his house to the church of Saint Donatian.[3] In this passageway, which was vaulted and made of stone, the clash was fiercest; here the citizens were fighting only with swords, face to face, because the besieged scorned to flee further. Putting their strength and courage to

---

[3] See Galbert, c. 12, n. 2. The exact form and location of this passageway have not been determined. It is described as a "high stairway, made of wood and stone suspended in the air" in the later *Passio Karoli comitis*, c. 9, MGH, SS XII, 622. See Introduction, pp. 58 f.

the test, on both sides they stood firm like a wall, until the citizens, gathering their forces, put them to flight not so much by fighting as by rushing upon the besieged. Among them was Borsiard, huge and wrathful, ferocious and undaunted, mighty in bodily strength, who resisted the citizens steadily face to face, wounding many, prostrating and hurling down more who were stunned by the hammer-like blow of his sword.[4] They also put to flight Robert the Young, on whom no one wished to lay a hand because they had heard that he was said to be innocent of the treachery and, even more, because he was so much beloved by all in the realm both before and after the betrayal. That noble one had not troubled to flee but at the request of his friends followed those fleeing; and if this had not been the case, they could have captured Borsiard and his knights on the spot and also all who were guilty of the treachery.[5]

And when the traitors had retreated into the church, the citizens did not pursue them further but turned back to plunder and loot, running through the count's house, and the provost's house, and the dormitory and cloister of the brothers. All who had taken part in the siege did the same, hoping to lay hands on the treasure of the count and the equipment of the houses located within the walls.[6] And in fact, believing they could loot without any sense of guilt, they set about seizing in the count's house a great many mattresses, tapestries, linens, cups, vessels, chains, iron bolts, bonds, shackles, fetters, collars, manacles, in other words, the iron instruments of captivity in general,[7] the iron doors of the count's treasure, and the lead gutters which had carried the water off the roofs.[8] In the provost's house also they seized beds, chests, benches, clothes, vessels, and all his furniture. In the cellars of the count and provost, and also in the cellar of

[4] Galbert conveys a similar impression of Borsiard in c. 17.

[5] This seems unlikely.

[6] Despite his pride in their bravery, Galbert does not conceal the fact that the citizens as well as the "crowd from the siege" engage in looting.

[7] A collection of these instruments can be seen today in the museum of the castle of the counts at Ghent. The iron was useful for many purposes.

[8] This is a rare example of one of the uses to which lead, probably brought from England, was put at this time; the actual commerce in lead seems to have been slight, however. See H. Van Werveke, "Note sur le commerce du plomb au moyen âge," in *Mélanges ... Pirenne*, I, 653-62, esp. 657.

the brothers, I cannot tell how much grain and meat and wine and beer they seized! In the dormitory of the brothers which was spread with precious and expensive coverings[9] they did so much looting that they kept on going and coming for that purpose from the time they entered the castle until far into the night.

[42] *The besieged try to defend the church, March 19, 1127*

Therefore nothing but the church was left to the besieged except for the foodstuffs they had carried into the church, that is, wine and meat, flour, cheese, legumes, and the other necessities of life. The names of those who were the leaders among the besieged should be told: the castellan Hacket, Borsiard, Robert the Young, Walter, son of Lambert of Aardenburg, Wulfric Cnop.[1] For the provost Bertulf on the third night, that is, Thursday night, before the storming of the castle,[2] after giving a sum of as much as forty marks to Walter the butler[3] was swung down by ropes from beneath his balcony and escaped alone. He trusted Walter more than any man on earth but nevertheless, Walter, after leading him to a wasteland called Mor,[4] abandoned him, exposed to his enemies and forsaken in his flight since in that unfamiliar place he did not know where he should flee or to whom.

Then the besieged ascended the tower[5] of the church and rolled down mill stones on those who were moving about in the castle, and they inflicted serious injuries on those who were carrying

---

[9] Bed or wall coverings? The canons must have lived in good style.

[1] Note there are now left two Erembald brothers, Hacket and Wulfric, and three nephews, including two sons of Lambert, Borsiard and Walter, and one son, Robert, of another brother (also named Robert). Isaac has already escaped (c. 39).

[2] That is, March 17, which was three days before March 19, according to medieval computation, which counted both end dates of any given period.

[3] That is, Walter of Vladslo, formerly bound to Bertulf by oath but now one of the leaders of the siege outside; see c. 21 and 31. How the provost could now trust Walter is baffling. Walter of Therouanne, c. 37, says Bertulf escaped either through the negligence of the besiegers or thanks to their aid, since many were corrupted by money.

[4] *Mor* means marshland.

[5] That is, to the ramparts of the west-work.

out all the furniture as loot; many of these, fatally crushed, perished on the spot. The victors of the castle at once shot arrows against the windows of the tower[6] so that no one in the tower could put his head out the windows without having a thousand arrows and a thousand missiles aimed at him. The whole tower looked bristly with so many arrows sticking into it! But since nothing was accomplished in this way on either side, the besieged hurled fire onto the roof of the school, adjacent to the church, trying in this way to set fire to the provost's house which was next to it.[7] But, frustrated in this, they ran hither and thither on the floor of the church, both in the choir[8] and in the inner sanctuary, armed and watchful, trying to prevent anyone from getting in through the windows or forcibly breaking open the doors of the church.

[43] *The storming of the church, March 19, 1127*

At early dawn, a young man, one of the crowd[1] from Ghent, climbed by ladder up to the chief window of the sanctuary of the church, and breaking the glass and iron work with his sword and pike, boldly slipped in and opened one of the chests of the sanctuary, hunting for booty. Leaning over, he had begun to go through the contents, moving his hand here and there, when the lid of the chest, which was heavy and inclined to fall, struck that thief and looter and threw him back dead; and he lay there dead for a long time, covered up by a pile of feathers, for an enormous pile of feathers was lying in the sanctuary.[2] Mean-

---

[6] The great tower or west-work was flanked by two slender towers or turrets (see c. 37) which were apparently pierced by narrow windows on the stairs (see c. 74). There were also windows in the central part, above the doors (see c. 74).
[7] The roofs of all the buildings except the church seem to have been made of wood. See Plan for the relationship of structures.
[8] By "choir" Galbert here probably means the central part of the church, used as a choir by the chapter. In c. 43 he explicitly identifies "choir" and "church."

[1] Galbert probably means to disparage the men of Ghent by referring to them as a "crowd" or mob. In c. 33 he distinguishes between the burghers from Ghent and the rabble.
[2] To what use were these feathers put?

while, when the boy did not return, the men of Ghent, who had
been waiting for him for a long time, wanted to force their way
through the window, for they had sent him ahead, as the boldest,
to try and open a way for them into the church; they had hoped
in this way to secure the body of the count. But our citizens
resisted them with arms and they have never allowed the men
of Ghent even to speak of carrying off the count's body in their
presence.[3]

Our citizens were very indignant, even more than anyone
would believe, that any of the men should attempt to carry the
body away from our place. When the men of Ghent tried to go
ahead, both sides drew their swords, and a tumult broke out, and
everybody ran to the fight. The besieged, moreover, seized the
moment to attack the victors as strongly as they could. The men
of Ghent contended that they had the right to carry off the
count's body with them to Ghent because it was their equipment
of ladders that had struck terror into the besieged and forced
them to flee from the castle,[4] whereas our citizens asserted, on
the contrary, that their equipment had proved to be no good,
that they had done nothing in the siege but steal and impose a
great burden on our place. The more sensible men among the
victors, hearing the uproar and finding out about the victory[5]
and the strife, halted the fight and quieted the tumult, saying:

"Do not fight over this! Let us wait rather until God has
bestowed on us and the realm a good and legitimate count. Then
a decision about the body will be reached by his counsel and that
of the barons of the realm and our bishop[6] and all the clergy."

And so, having restored peace in this way, they appointed men
who were armed and audacious for the assault on the church.

When the best troops were assembled, they broke in by force

---

[3] Examples of attempts to steal the bodies of those who were reputed saints are
numerous; see Hariulf's *Vita Arnulfi*, lib. III, c. 3, MGH, SS XV[2], 900-1, where
three monks of Saint Médard, Arnulf's original monastery, were authorized by
their abbot to steal his body from the monastery of Oudenburg, where he had died,
but were thwarted three times by divine intervention.

[4] Galbert means "into the church."

[5] That is, of "our citizens" in preventing the men of Ghent from breaking into
the church.

[6] The bishop of Noyon-Tournai.

and rushed through the door of the church that opens into the cloister and chased the besieged from the floor below up into the gallery. And here those serfs, who had impiously and fraudulently betrayed the most worthy count of the land, were now shut in with their lord although it was through no desire of theirs that they were confined with their lord the count. Then at last the men of Ghent, having entered the sanctuary, hunted for the young man whom at dawn they sent ahead through the main window of the sanctuary, and they found him among the feathers, crushed and dead. Some said falsely that he had been killed by Borsiard when he was heedlessly sliding down into the church. There is not time to tell how many stones were hurled from the gallery at the victors on the floor of the church, and how many were struck down, crushed and wounded by spears and arrows, so that the whole choir of the church was covered with piles of stones and no pavement could be seen. The walls and glass windows round about and also the stalls and seats of the brothers were thrown down,[7] and so complete was the ruin and confusion that nothing in the church retained its holy and untouched appearance but everything looked defiled and deformed, more horrible than if it were a prison. For in the gallery the besieged had made defense posts for themselves out of chests and altar tables and choir seats and stools and other furniture of the church, and had tied them together with the ropes of the bells. They broke into pieces the bells and the lead[8] which had formerly covered the roof of the church, using them to crush those below. Within the church, that is, the choir,[9] the fight raged most fiercely, but from the tower and the doors of the tower[10] such slaughter went on that I cannot describe or consider further the multitude of those who were struck down and wounded.

[7] This and the previous sentence confirm the impression of a circular gallery.

[8] Apparently the original wooden roof had been covered with lead but it had been replaced by an earthenware, fireproof covering; see c. 37. This is another rare example of the use of lead; see Van Werveke, "Note sur le commerce du plomb," in *Mélanges . . . Pirenne,* p. 656.

[9] Galbert here equates "church" and "choir" for the first time.

[10] Apparently not all the besieged were able to reach the shelter of the gallery above. These doors may be those which opened into the stairs leading to the gallery.

[44] *The besiegers plant their banners in the castle, March 19,
1127*

Then Gervaise, knight, chamberlain, and counselor of the counts
of the realm,[1] took possession of the upper part of the count's
house with a strong force and he ordered his banners[2] affixed to
the summit of the house. This was done out of jealousy of the
besieged who had immediately, on the first day of the siege and
even on the very day when the impious serfs had betrayed their
lord, raised their standards against their enemies. Whereupon that
William of Ypres, as if he were lord and count of the land,
raised his standards against some who had refused to pay him
revenues due the count,[3] because they scorned the idea that he
would ever become count. On the first day of the siege those
traitors, showing no humility at all because they believed the
barons of the realm were their accomplices in crime and bound
to them in faith and friendship, had arrogantly set up their
banners on the highest point of the count's hall[4] and on the
summit of the tower of the church and on the three lesser ones,[5]
and on the balcony of the provost as well as at the exit of the
gates. They wished in this way to make it appear that they
themselves were lords, awaiting the great men of the realm, their
friends and accomplices, with whose support they would break
the siege, and so the count, whom they had betrayed, would
remain unavenged. Didier, brother of Isaac, got hold of the
lower part of the count's house along with our citizens and fixed
his banner on the bigger balcony[6] of the count. When Robert the

[1] Only of Charles, so far as we know. Gervaise was last mentioned as entering
the town on March 9; see c. 28 and 29.
[2] What were the banners or standards of this period like? Perhaps small rectangular pennons like those represented in the Bayeux Tapestry, with three-pronged
ends.
[3] These could be revenues of many different kinds, perhaps tolls in this case or
feudal dues; see Monier, *Les Institutions financières*, pp. 7 ff.
[4] That is, the count's house, of which the principal feature was a great hall.
[5] Meaning probably the tower in the center and the two smaller towers or turrets
flanking the great tower or west-work.
[6] There must have been two balconies on the count's house; see c. 42 where another is mentioned.

Young from the tower saw him crossing the castle he attacked him in these words:

"Oh Didier, don't you remember that you once advised us to betray the lord count? You have betrayed your faith and loyalty in this and now, seeing our misfortune, you are glad and persecute us. Oh, if I could only get out, I would challenge you to single combat! God be my witness that you are more of a traitor than we because formerly you betrayed your lord and now you betray us."[7]

This taunt was not made without everyone's noticing it.

[45] *The citizens turn against Thancmar, March 19, 1127*

Now Thancmar's nephews, who were partly responsible for the treachery,[1] so they say, had fixed their standards on the provost's house arrogantly and proudly, as a sign of their power. Everyone took this very ill, and our citizens were very much aggrieved because before the time of the treachery the provost and his kin were religious men, friendly in their attitude towards them, and they had treated honorably everyone who lived in our place and in the realm.[2] For those nephews, once they had gained the houses and planted their banners, took possession of whatever they found inside as if it belonged to them. Then the hearts of our citizens swelled with anger against Thancmar's nephews, and they tried to find an opportunity for fighting and killing them. On Saturday evening, therefore, when Thancmar's nephews were carrying out to their country place the grain and wine they had seized in the provost's house,[3] our citizens attacked

---

[7] This charge by Robert, his favorite, must have convinced Galbert that Didier, whom he called innocent on March 9 (c. 29), was guilty; see c. 92.

[1] See c. 9 concerning the conflict between the nephews of Bertulf and those of Thancmar whose cause the count had favored.

[2] This curious defense of the Erembald clan may be due partly to the hatred of Thancmar's clan felt by the citizens of Bruges, whose attitudes Galbert often reflects; it does not seem consistent with his picture of Bertulf in c. 13 or of Borsiard and Isaac throughout. It is also likely that the provost may have favored the citizens in various ways and created a nucleus of support among them; they did not turn against him until Gervaise appeared with his forces.

[3] Just as the citizens and others had done earlier, and without any sense of guilt!

them in the cloister, and drawing their swords, slashed open a cask of wine. A great tumult broke out, and the citizens closed the gates of the town so that none of the nephews could escape. Moreover, the besieged called out to the citizens, their former friends, begging them to destroy those enemies on whose account they had perpetrated such a grievous crime. When Thancmar's nephews found they could not resist the citizens in the provost's house, they tried to escape. Thancmar himself got as far as the exit of one of the gates in flight; finding it closed he falsely told those who asked him what was creating such a great uproar that a conflict between the besieged and the besiegers was going on. Finally he hid in a little house until he could see what would happen to his nephews.

And when the citizens in an armed band were crossing over the bridge of Saint Peter and the castle bridge[4] they were met by Walter the butler and other barons of the siege, who were making a great effort to calm the uproar. So many men with lances were standing in the market that the tops of the spears seemed like a very dense forest! And it was not surprising, for everybody in the whole realm[5] had poured into the town that day, some for loot, some for vengeance, others to steal the count's body, some out of sheer wonder at everything that was going on there. And they were all crying out that Thancmar and his nephews ought by right to be hanged because they were responsible for the fact that the count had been killed, and the provost and his nephews besieged, and many from their own families either killed or condemned to a most shameful death.[6] And therefore they

---

(see c. 41). They had already carried off a great deal from the provost's house and cellar; competition for the rest of the loot seems to be another cause of antagonism against Thancmar.

[4] From what follows it seems that the citizens are going out of the castle into the town; their aim is not clear, perhaps pursuit of Thancmar. The bridge of Saint Peter lay across the river just north of the castle wall, connecting the two agglomerations of the town centered around Saint Peter's and Saint Christopher's. See Plan.

[5] A great exaggeration no doubt! But it gives the impression of a crowd enormous in Galbert's eyes; he sees clearly their mixed motives.

[6] Concern for the fate of their relatives among the besieged is beginning seriously to affect the citizens although the nature of the punishment of those ultimately captured is probably not yet determined. The seed of the later legend of Thancmar's responsibility appears here.

could not bear to have the barons spare Thancmar and his nephews; they ought rather to condemn to shameful and cruel death those who by deceit, discord, and influence had prejudiced the count[7] against their own lords,[8] that is, the provost and his brothers and also his nephews, who were very powerful and noble men in the county. The barons could hardly restrain the aroused citizens because the castellan Hacket and Robert the Young with the friends and relatives of those very citizens were standing on the higher tower, signaling to them with their arms and hands that they should make an attack on Thancmar's nephews who had so arrogantly gone into the provost's house and set up their banners in victory as if they had stormed the castle by their own strength, when actually at the time when the citizens had forced their way into the castle the nephews of Thancmar were sleeping at home in the country.[9] The tumult was quieted finally on condition that they should evacuate the house, take down, to their shame, the banners they had set up and get out. Then they withdrew under escort of the barons but they were in such danger among the distrustful citizens that each nephew of Thancmar went out with his escort mounted on the same horse.

So the house was left in charge of the knights and citizens of our place, and the grain and wine were divided between the barons of the siege and the citizens by whose courage victory was won on that day. And finally that day came to an end; it had made them very anxious about the watches to be kept during the night, both in the court of the castle and in the cloister of the brothers, and in the provost's house and the refectory and dormitory of the brothers. For the besieged had formed the plan of destroying by fire the roofs of the cloister and of the houses around the church so that the besiegers would have no way of

[7] The same charge was brought by the Erembalds against Fromold (c. 18, 19) and Walter of Loker (c. 17). The provost himself was accused of stirring up trouble against Thancmar in c. 16.

[8] The Erembalds are "lords" of the citizens because they are the family of the castellans of Bruges. See c. 25, n. 7.

[9] Another element in the citizens' hatred of Thancmar's nephews now appears. Thancmar's country place had supposedly been sacked on the day of the murder, March 2; see c. 20.

access to them. Therefore the night watches stood guard throughout the whole night, stupefied with anxiety and fear. Often the besieged, coming out secretly during the nocturnal hours, struck fear into the guards. Even in such a confined space as the tower of the church the traitors had ordered their watches to sound the trumpets, both the straight and crooked ones, and to blow the horn every night during the siege,[10] still hoping to escape because the barons of the realm were offering them friendship and aid by means of messages shot into the tower by arrows.

[46] *Bertulf's flight, March 17, 1127*

Now on Thursday night, on the order of Walter the butler, the provost, under escort of a crafty knight,[1] the brother of Fulco, canon of Bruges, was taken on horseback to Keiem, the native village of the same Walter and of Borsiard. When he had lain hidden there for a short time and had been found out, he fled with one companion by night to his wife[2] at Veurne; and then because he could not hide there safely, on the night of Holy Preparation[3] he crossed over to Warneton.[4] Continuing his flight on the same night, as we have heard, he went on his way with bare feet, suffering voluntarily punishment for his sins so that

[10] Perhaps both to keep up their courage and to harass their enemies.

[1] See c. 42. The Inquest of September 1127 names several persons as Bertulf's guides; see MGH, SS XXV, 441.

[2] It is not made clear whose wife she was. Pirenne (ed. Galbert, p. 75, n. 2) states that she was Walter's, but the text seems rather to imply Bertulf's wife or even the wife of his companion. Bertulf, as provost, was not necessarily in holy orders, and, if in minor orders, could be lawfully married and retain his benefice. His "heir presumptive," Fromold Junior, was married (see c. 18). But special rules against the marriage of canons were being formulated at this time in French and English councils. See T. P. McLaughlin, "The Prohibition of Marriage against Canons in the Early Twelfth Century," *Mediaeval Studies*, III (1941), 94-100.

[3] Pirenne (ed. Galbert, p. 75, n. 3) identifies this as the eve of Good Friday and therefore March 31, 1127.

[4] Walter, c. 37, 38, says he went to the house of Alard of Warneton, husband of his niece Aganitrude, formerly wife of the castellan of Saint Omer, where he stayed about three weeks and was then shunted about until his capture on April 11. Alard is charged in the Inquest (p. 441) with harboring Bertulf. See c. 49, n. 6.

God might forgive such a great sinner the crime he had committed against the pious count. And this is very probable, because immediately after he was captured, the soles of his feet looked as if the skin had been torn off, because on his journey by night he had injured his feet so badly that the blood was flowing from them. He must have been in a state of profound grief, that man who had recently lorded it over everyone, who had abounded in wealth and worldly honors, and who was so given to luxury that he feared the prick of a louse as much as a javelin! Consider him now, as he wandered alone, a solitary exile within his own boundaries!

Now we must return from this digression[5] to the watches of the night mentioned above; since both besiegers and besieged aroused nightly fears in each other, and both sides were so exhausted and worn out, they had exchanged day for night so far as sleeping was concerned.

[47] *The king of France summons the barons to Arras, and they set out, March 20-22, 1127*

On March 20, Sunday, on the eve of Benedict the abbot,[1] King Louis of France[2] sent from Arras[3] to the princes and barons of

---

[5] This chapter was obviously written after his capture on April 11 and inserted here then or later.

[1] Saint Benedict (480-543), abbot of Montecassino, whose monastic rule became the basis of ascetic life in the west.
[2] The intervention of Louis VI, suzerain of the now vacant fief of Flanders, opens an entirely new phase in the course of events. Its implications and effects are analysed by F. L. Ganshof in a masterly article based primarily on the accounts of Galbert, Walter of Therouanne, and Herman of Tournai, "Le roi de France en Flandre en 1127 et 1128," RHDF, XXVII (1949), 204-28, supplemented by "Trois mandements perdus du Roi de France Louis VI intéressant la Flandre," ASEB, LXXXVII (1950), 117-33. Professor Ganshof's conclusions have been incorporated into this translation and its notes; his argument will not be repeated except in special cases. His analysis corrects at some points the chronology of A. Luchaire, *Louis VI le gros* (Paris, 1890), pp. 175 ff.
[3] Arras, situated in the south of Flanders and the seat of a bishopric closely related to the crown, was a safe and convenient spot from which to act; the king had arrived there about March 13 (Ganshof, "Le roi de France en Flandre," RHDF, XXVII, 207); he stayed there fifteen days before the election, hearing the messengers from various claimants, says Walter, c. 44.

the siege his greetings, faith, and aid, and in addition all his thanks for avenging Charles, his kinsman[4] and the most just count of Flanders, who was more worthy to be a king than the count of wretched traitors.

"I do not at present have a favorable opportunity of joining you because I came here hastily with only a few men on hearing and learning about the crime and the siege. For it did not seem wise to me to fall into the hands of the traitors of the land, since, as we have learned, there are still many who mourn over the besieged and defend their crimes and work for their escape in every way. Therefore, because the land has been thrown into disorder and sworn support has been given to the person of William[5] so that he may gain the realm by force, and in opposition almost all the cities[6] have sworn that they will under no circumstances accept that William as count because he is illegitimate, born of a noble father[7] and an ignoble mother who continued to card wool as long as she lived,[8] therefore I wish and I order you to come to my presence without delay[9] and by common agreement elect as count someone who seems suitable to you and whom you will agree to accept as ruler over the land and its inhabitants. The land cannot continue long without a count without being threatened by even graver dangers than at present."

And when the letter[10] was read in the presence of all, and

[4] Charles and Louis were cousins by marriage; the king had married Adelaide, niece of the countess Clemence, the wife of Charles's uncle, Robert II.

[5] A reference to William of Ypres, undoubtedly.

[6] This description of William's support does not seem to reflect the facts. William had forced various merchants (Galbert, c. 25) and the inhabitants of several towns (Aire, Ypres, Bergues, Veurne, Kassel, Bailleul, and Saint Venant) to swear fealty to him (Walter, c. 43); only the barons of the siege had sworn not to accept him, and for the reason that he was suspected of complicity in the murder, according to Galbert, c. 34. Does the king refer to the traitors' support of William?

[7] Philip of Loo, second son of Robert the Frisian.

[8] A sign of low social status, not necessarily servile. William is never accused of being servile as he might have been if his mother had been a serf.

[9] The king has the feudal right to summon the vassals of the count of Flanders to his own court because he is temporarily their direct feudal lord; the fief of Flanders has reverted to the crown on the death of the count without an undisputed successor and become theoretically a part of the royal domain; see Ganshof, "Le Roi de France en Flandre," RHDF, XXVII (1949), 211.

[10] In "Trois mandements perdus," ASEB, LXXXVII (1950), 119-25, Ganshof states that this "letter," undoubtedly heard and probably read by Galbert, had the

before they had even replied to it saying whether they were coming or not, who should appear but another messenger from a kinsman of Count Charles, sending his greetings to the barons of the siege and his natural sentiment of good will towards all the inhabitants of the land:

"You all know for a certainty that the realm of Flanders pertains to my lot and power by right of kinship after the death of my lord the count.[11] Therefore, I want you to take thought and proceed carefully concerning the election of my person, and I warn and urge you not to estrange me from the realm. If, out of respect for right and kinship, you send back a favorable reply to me, I shall hasten to become your count, and I shall be just, peaceful, tractable, and concerned for the common good and welfare."

But the barons and everyone else who had heard the letter sent from Alsace by the count's cousin, asserting that it was not genuine,[12] did not take the trouble to reply because the common welfare was in danger, and the king was making haste to call an assembly nearby, and they did not see how they could manage to elect that kinsman without a great deal of effort. Therefore, anticipating a most advantageous meeting they made ready, on the order of the king, to set out on Monday and Tuesday.[13] By

---

form of a *mandement* or official order of the king, various elements of which Galbert incorporates, mostly in his own words. Elements of the protocol, both of the address and greeting, are apparent in the narrative section (the first sentence of the chapter). Vestiges of the text appear in the direct discourse which follows, of the *exposé* (from the beginning down to "I wish") and the *dispositif* (from "I wish" to the end). There is no sign of validation.

[11] Thierry of Alsace, like Charles, was a grandson, through his mother, of Robert the Frisian; see the Genealogy. He is the third candidate to emerge in Galbert's account; after William of Ypres, Thierry of Holland had appeared in person at Bruges as a claimant on March 16 (c. 34). Galbert does not mention until much later (c. 67) another candidate, Baldwin IV, count of Mons or Hainaut, who had, as he later says, the best hereditary claim, being in the direct male line and representing the older branch of the dynasty, which had been dispossessed of Flanders in 1071 by Robert the Frisian. Baldwin's efforts at Arras to secure the countship are discussed by Herman, c. 35; after his overtures had been first encouraged then rejected by the king, he left in a rage and took up arms against the king. Another and insignificant candidate named by Walter, c. 44, is Arnold, nephew of Charles by one of his Danish sisters; he is not mentioned by Galbert until c. 94.

[12] Why Thierry's letter was rejected as "false" is not clear. Was there some deep-seated opposition to him or were the barons simply confused by the situation, as Galbert implies?

[13] That is, on March 21 and 22.

remarkable effort and determination, however, the barons, after summoning the citizens, took up arms on that very Sunday and attacked the besieged in the tower. They did this to discourage the terrified besieged even more and to make them so fearful that they would not dare to come out of the tower or try to escape on the sudden departure of the barons to meet the king. It was a bitter fight on both sides, and yet the besieged did not know why they were being attacked on Sunday when all the preceding Sundays had been observed in peace. Then they set out for Arras on Monday and Tuesday to confer with the king, after arranging for armed guards to watch the tower night and day, faithfully and carefully, so that none of the besieged could escape.

[48] *The death of Isaac, March 23, 1127; the escape and capture of Lambert Archei*

On March 23, Wednesday, Isaac was captured and hanged,[1] "Liberator meus,"[2] three weeks after the slaying of the count, before the annunciation of the Virgin Mary. And before Palm Sunday[3] Lambert Archei[4] slid down from the tower and got away, fleeing to the village of Michem by boat. He was a counselor of Borsiard and always up to some evil in his words and deeds, urging his lords on to all kinds of crime, and therefore he was hateful to everyone who had heard of his tricks in the siege. For from the beginning of the siege when he was shut up within the castle up to the time he took to flight, he was active in every enterprise going on inside; most expert with the bow, and very strong in hurling spears and all kinds of missiles, he had been responsible for great slaughter among the enemy.

[1] Isaac had fled on March 10; see c. 30. He was seized at Therouanne by William of Ypres, taken off to Aire and hanged there on March 20, says Walter, c. 35. Galbert describes his death in c. 84.
[2] The beginning of the Introit of the Mass for Wednesday after the fifth Sunday of Lent, that is, in 1127, March 23
[3] March 27 in 1127.
[4] He is named in the Inquest as one of the vassals of the count who voluntarily joined the traitors in the castle; MGH, SS XXV, 442.

While he was fleeing he was hunted by the citizens from day-break throughout the whole day of his flight, for, as he was stealing out of the tower, Borsiard called out to the besiegers of the tower, telling them when and where his counselor, who had been so intimate with him, had fled. Finally the citizens closed in on the village where the fugitive lay hidden and dragging him from his hiding place led him away captive; and they would have killed him by hanging in our marketplace if the leaders of the siege had been present at the time but they were in Arras conferring about the realm. Finally he was entrusted under oath to Gerbert, one of our citizens, his kinsman,[5] who was to keep him bound in chains until the return of the leading men of the county so that it should be determined by their judgment what was to be done with him.[6]

[49] *William of Ypres claims he has received English support, March 24, 1127*

On March 24, Thursday, Woltra Cruval reported to us that the king of the English[1] had approved peace with William of Ypres and had lent him an enormous sum of money and three hundred knights[2] to aid him in securing the county of Flanders. Although this was false, the lie seemed credible as he spread it abroad. For the fact was that William of Ypres had received five hundred pounds of English money[3] from the treasure of Count

[5] It is noteworthy that a knight and a burgher were kinsmen; for another case see c. 59.

[6] Lambert, a vassal of the count, must have been a knight and as such he is subject to the jurisdiction of the barons on the spot who, in this emergency, have formulated rules which become known as the "law of the siege" (see Galbert, c. 31, 88).

[1] Henry I, 1106-35.

[2] This is a very large number in medieval military terms. The minimum military service owed by the count of Flanders to the king of France at this time was that of only forty-two knights, according to F. Lot, *L'Art militaire et les armées au moyen âge* (2 vols.; Paris, 1946), I, 121. For a discussion of effective forces see Verbruggen, *De krijgskunst*, pp. 31-40.

[3] This was only part of the count's treasure, of enormous size for its time; see c. 85. The presence of English pounds can be explained by the Treaty of Dover (now dated 1101; see Introduction, II, n. 34) renewed in 1110, between the

Charles through the hands of the nephews of the provost Bertulf. Those most impious traitors had tried to set up over themselves and the realm that same William who had indeed secured money, aid, and counsel from them, and in daily letters sent back and forth they were making clear to each other their mutual desires and secret aims. That knight[4] falsely said that William had received gifts of money from the king of the English because he wished to cover up the complicity of William who had in fact received money sent to him by the traitors to hire mercenaries with; and so when he should have obtained the county by force, the traitors would have consequently gained their ends through him. In fact, no one hoping to secure primacy in the realm wished openly to receive any word or messenger from the traitors because, if they did, they were immediately marked with the stigma of the treachery. Therefore that William was concealing what he knew and falsely said the money had been sent to him by the king as if he had nothing in common with the traitors and shared no secrets with them, although before the time of the siege he had clearly sent greetings and aid in signed letters to the provost and his kin.[5]

At this time Gilbert,[6] a kinsman of the traitors, the castellan of Bergues, who was under the stigma of the treachery, had fled to the castellan of Saint Omer,[7] trying to clear himself and

---

count of Flanders and Henry I; it provided for an annual money-fief of 500 pounds to Count Robert II in return for the promise of certain military services (see *Actes*, no. 30, pp. 88 ff. and no. 41, pp. 109 ff.). That Charles had renewed this bond seems to be implied by Galbert, c 122. Such a large amount may have been paid in lingots rather than coined money, which was largely confined to silver pennies at the time; see Van Werveke, "Monnaies, lingots ou marchandises?" AHES, IV (1932), 454-55, 461-64. A "pound" was originally the weight of silver from which 240 pennies were struck; in time it came to be considered equivalent to 240 pennies, regardless of weight. See Cipolla, *Money, Prices and Civilization*, pp. 40-42.

[4] Woltra Cuval, about whom nothing is known.

[5] See c. 25.

[6] Gilbert, castellan of Bergues, *ca.* 1125-53, was a grandson of Baldwin, castellan of Saint Omer, *ca.*1092-*ca.*1097, who had married Aganitrude, a niece of Bertulf; see Vercauteren, "Étude sur les châtelains," in *Études . . . Pirenne*, p. 432. He must have exonerated himself for he continued as castellan under Charles's successors. See Galbert, c. 46, n. 4, concerning Aganitrude as the wife of Alard of Warneton, and the Genealogy of the Erembald clan.

[7] Probably his uncle, William I, castellan of Saint Omer *ca.* 1097-*ca.* 1127; see *Actes*, especially no. 104 (1121), p. 236, and Blommaert, *Les Châtelains*, pp. 170-72.

saying he was ready to prove his innocence in the presence of the king and the peers of the realm.

[50] *The men of Ghent try to steal the count's body, March 26, 1127*

On March 25, Friday, the feast of the Annunciation of the Lord was celebrated, which was the same day as the Lord's Passion.[1]

On March 26, Saturday of the Palms, by guile and trickery the men of Ghent made arrangements to get into the castle when that night was ended, with the guidance of the chief officer of justice[2] and Ansbold, a knight, and with the approval of some of our citizens[3] and also the consent of the traitors. The brothers from the monastery of Ghent[4] were to receive the body, which was to be let down from the windows of the gallery by the hands of the traitors, and carry it off, done up in bags and sacks. Two monks, in fact, had waited that whole time for the chance of stealing the body. Now when those who had escorted the monks were going around the tower[5] in arms, the guards, taking fright, sounded the horns on all sides, and the aroused citizens and guards of the tower attacked the chief officer and the knight, Ansbold, and their accomplices, putting some to flight and wounding others who were overcome by fear of death. The fact was that the monks had promised their helpers a hundred marks of silver if by chance they could obtain the body of the count

---

[1] This unusual doubling of feast days occurred in 1127.

[2] *Magnus praeco; praeco* doubtless refers to one of the inferior officers of justice (later called *amman*), subordinate to the castellan, to be found in every castellany; another *praeco* is mentioned in c. 111. See Ganshof, "Les Transformations de l'organisation judiciaire," RB, XVIII (1939), 46. An urban tribunal with its own officials probably did not exist in Bruges until after the town received a charter in April, 1127, according to Ganshof, p. 51; see also "Le Droit urbain en Flandre au début de la première phase de son histoire (1127)," RHD, XIX (1951), 395.

[3] Evidence that the citizens are by no means unanimous as Galbert suggests earlier.

[4] The abbot of Saint Peter's, Arnulf, who had departed (c. 22), had evidently left some monks behind.

[5] The striking appearances of the west-work led to the occasional use of the word "tower" as synonymous with "church." See H. Reinhardt and E. Fels, "Étude sur les églises-porches carolingiennes," *Bulletin monumental*, XCII (1933), 364, n. 1.

through their aid. After learning that the monks would use theft and bribery and any means whatsoever to carry off the count's body, the citizens, now forewarned, devoted themselves to watching more carefully, with a vigilant band.

[51] *The chief citizens of Bruges and the leading men of the castellany form a sworn association, March 27, 1127*

On March 27, Palm Sunday, our burghers assembled in the field that lies next to the town within the enclosure,[1] after summoning the Flemings from the region all around us, and they swore together on the relics of the saints as follows:

"I, Folpert, judge,[2] swear that I will elect as count of this land one who will rule the realm of his predecessors, the counts, beneficently, who will be able to maintain by force the rights of the fatherland against its enemies, who will prove himself to be kind and generous toward the poor and reverent before God, who will tread the narrow path of rectitude, and who will be willing and able to serve the common interests of the land."

Then following him all the leading citizens swore.[3] From Ijzendijke, Adalard, the *échevin*, with his following; from Oost-

---

[1] This probably means the *Harenae* or Sands. Part of it may have been enclosed by the defenses constructed on March 6 but the Sands seem to have lain largely outside the fortification; see c. 16 and the Plan.

[2] *Judex* here must not be interpreted literally as "judge"; it doubtless means *échevin*, a member or "assessor" of the territorial court or *échevinage* of the castellany of Bruges, more commonly called *scabinus* in the texts of the period. (Galbert calls Adalard *scabinus* just below, which seems to confirm this identification. He does not repeat *scabinus* after the subsequent names of men and places, but it is reasonable to suppose that he refers to *scabini*.) These *scabini*, coming from different parts of the castellany, were named for life by the count, probably from among the members of the petty nobility; Adalard with his armed following seems to be a man of substance, and Haiolus and Hugo also have followers, whether armed or not is not clear. Their number, perhaps twelve in theory, was variable in practice. See especially Ganshof, *Recherches sur les tribuneaux de châtellenie*, pp. 68-73.

[3] Pirenne's edition puts a colon, not period, at this point, but certainly "citizens" (*cives*) here must refer to the "burghers" of Bruges mentioned in the first sentence, and not to the following list of *scabini*, indicated by name or place. (Galbert uses "citizens" as synonymous with burghers throughout, and always to indicate inhabitants of towns.) That the oath of Folpert, "judge," is given as a model may be out of deference to his social position.

burg, Haiolus with the leading men of that place; from Aardenburg, Hugo Berlensis and the strong men of that place; and
from Lapscheure, Oostkerke, Uitkerke, Lissewege, Slijpe, Gistel,
Oudenburg, Lichtervelde, and Jabbeke,[4] all the strong and influential men swore by a similar oath, and there was a great
crowd of swearers to this effect.

[52] *The barons return from Arras and announce the election
of William Clito as count, March 30, 1127*

On March 30, Wednesday, when the bells were silenced,[1] our
barons who had gone to take counsel with the king concerning
the welfare of the realm and the choice of a count, returned
from Arras[2] after designation of the count by King Louis, em-

[4] The existence of the first two places, in Zeeland, reveals the growth of communities in the coastal plain made habitable by dike building in the eleventh
century; see M. K. E. Gottschalk, *Historische geografie van Westelijk Zeeuws-
Vlaanderen* (Assen, 1955), p. 26. All the other places are located from 9 to 31
kilometers from Bruges, according to Pirenne's estimates (ed. Galbert, p. 81, n. 2-12).
This extraordinary assembly is due to the initiative of the citizens of Bruges and
perhaps represents in a remote sense the birth of an "urban order" asserting itself
in a sworn association in reaction to the sworn association of the barons (see c. 34)
who have assumed the direction of affairs, but it transcends the normal social
structure of the time. By drawing in the *scabini*, from the petty nobility of the
region, it lines up burghers and knights against the great barons and assumes
temporarily a regional character. The significance of this assembly is discussed by
J. Dhondt, *Les Origines des États de Flandre*, pp. 16-17, who notes the emergence
here of a new *puissance*, that of the towns which, parallel to the recently organized
puissance of the barons, now attempts to fill the vacuum of power created by the
elimination of the count and dynasty, the original and fundamental *puissance* in
Flanders.
    The initiative of the citizens of Bruges in claiming a share in the election of the
new count here and again, even more emphatically in c. 106, has few parallels.
The citizens of London, however, had exercised influence in the election of their
kings from the early eleventh century to 1066; after a period of quiescence, on the
death of Henry I in 1135 they asserted that it was "their own right and peculiar
privilege, that if their king died from any cause, a successor should immediately
be appointed by their own choice." This incident, recorded in the *Gesta Stephani*,
lib. I, c. 2, tr. by K. R. Potter (London, 1955), pp. 3-4, is analyzed by M. McKisack,
"London and the Succession to the Crown during the Middle Ages," in *Studies in
Medieval History Presented to F. M. Powicke*, ed. by R. W. Hunt and others
(Oxford, 1948), pp. 76-89.

[1] That is, during the period before Easter when the bells are not rung.
[2] Where they had gone on March 21 and 22; see c. 47.

peror of France,[3] and election[4] by all his barons and those of our land, and due consideration of what was likely to be of advantage to the fatherland. Happy and glad to bear such a report, they brought greetings and an assurance of fidelity on the part of the king and barons to us and to all the inhabitants of the land, and especially to those who had labored unremittingly in the siege to avenge the death of their lord, Count Charles:

"Louis, king of France, to all the good sons of the realm, greetings and thanks, and the invincible support of his presence with royal forces strong with the might of God and the courage of arms! Because we have been troubled, foreseeing that grievous ruin of the fatherland would follow the murder of the count, we have come to carry out vengeance with inflexible severity and with punishment unheard-of before this time; and in order that the land may be restored to order and peace under the count recently chosen by us, you should obey and carry out whatever you hear in what follows the text of this letter."[5]

Then Walter the butler produced the sealed letter[6] of the king in the presence of all the citizens who had poured into the field to hear the king's mandate, and now he spoke out loud, confirming the substance of the letter:

"Now let our citizens[7] hear what matters were carefully con-

[3] A title sometimes applied to the kings of France and other feudal monarchs to imply their complete independence of any superior such as the emperor of the Holy Roman Empire; see G. Post, "Two Notes on Nationalism in the Middle Ages," *Traditio*, IX (1953), 296 ff., esp. pp. 303 ff.

[4] "Designation" (*consilium*) and "election" (*electio*) are probably used here in a technical sense to indicate the two essential steps in the choice of a prince at this time, designation by his feudal suzerain and confirmation by his vassals, the barons. In this case the procedure took place in the court of King Louis VI at Arras, attended not only by his normal direct vassals but also by the leading barons of Flanders who have temporarily become his direct vassals on the decease without heirs of their immediate feudal lord, the count, and the consequent reversion of the fief of Flanders to the crown. See Ganshof, "Le roi de France en Flandre," RHDF, XXVII (1949), 210-11.

[5] The king here, as in c. 47, makes use of a *mandement* or royal order to announce the election of the new count. Galbert reveals the structure of the order but little of its content, perhaps to avoid repetition of what follows, a commentary on the order by Walter the butler; his phraseology seems to include only a few phrases of the original, now lost. See Ganshof, "Trois mandements perdus," ASEB, LXXXVII (1950), 125-30.

[6] Royal orders of this kind were always sealed, on a simple parchment attachment, according to Ganshof, p. 130.

[7] It seems likely that the same or a similar "letter" was sent by the king to other

sidered and what was actually done by the king and his barons.[8] The barons of France and the leading men of the land of Flanders, on the order and advice of the king, have elected as your count and the count of this land the young William,[9] born in Normandy, and noble by birth, who formerly grew up among you from infancy to boyhood and then to strong young manhood. It is well known that he has always had good habits and you will be able to direct him so that he will observe good customs and be gentle and docile, as you see fit. In fact, I[10] have chosen him; and Robert of Bethune,[11] Baldwin of Aalst[12] and Ivan, his brother, the castellan of Lille,[13] and other barons have raised

Flemish towns, especially Ghent where Baldwin and Ivan of Aalst may have played the rôle of Walter at Bruges, according to Ganshof, p. 125, n. 21.

[8] That is, at Arras. Galbert here, as in other places, is not as well informed about events which transpired outside Bruges as Walter of Therouanne and Herman of Tournai. Before the arrival of the barons from Bruges (the summons arrived March 20, and they departed on March 21 and 22), the king had wisely turned down the suggestion of some Flemish barons that he name one of his own young sons as count (Herman, c. 32), had also rejected the urgent claims made in person by Baldwin of Hainaut (Herman, c. 35) and had apparently already decided on William Clito, whose cause was ably supported by the queen, his sister-in-law (Walter, c. 44). If, as Walter says, the king designated William as count on March 23, the barons from Bruges could have had little or no share in these deliberations, probably arriving only in time to confirm the king's choice. See Ganshof, "Le roi de France en Flandre," RHDF, XXVII (1949), 209, n. 3.

[9] William of Normandy, surnamed "Clito," born 1101, was the son of Robert Curthose, duke of Normandy, who had been defrauded of his duchy and imprisoned by his brother, Henry I of England, in 1106. The child William took refuge on the continent among the enemies of his uncle and became the pawn of their anti- English policies. Count Baldwin VII received him in Flanders as a boy of ten and knighted him at fourteen (Herman, c. 25). His tragic history is given in detail by the English and Norman chroniclers, especially by Ordericus Vitalis, *Historia ecclesiastica, passim*, esp. lib. XII, c. 45, ed. by A. le Prévost, Vol. IV (Paris, 1852). The king's choice of William, whose hereditary claim to Flanders was slight, immediately aroused the hostility of Henry I, who asserted his own remote claim in order to weaken that of his nephew and formed a coalition against him which included the disgruntled Baldwin of Hainaut and William of Ypres, as well as the duke of Louvain, Thomas of Coucy, and Stephen of Blois; see Walter, c. 45.

[10] That is, Walter the butler, last mentioned in c. 46 as aiding Bertulf's escape; perhaps he had led the barons in the ceremony of "election" at Arras, as Ganshof suggests, "Le Roi de France en Flandre," RHDF, XXVII (1949), 210.

[11] Robert IV, lord of Bethune, one of the baronies of southern Flanders, also advocate of the church of Arras, whose name appears frequently among witnesses to charters of the counts from *ca.*1100 to 1127; see *Actes*, Index.

[12] This is the first appearance of Baldwin, mentioned in c. 30. His role is a matter of dispute: Herman, c. 31, names him as the leader of the opposition to the traitors, but Galbert, later, c. 91, gives a different picture.

[13] Roger II, named frequently as witness in the charters from 1096 to 1127; see *Actes*, Index.

him up to the countship; we have promised faith and loyalty and done homage to him according to the custom of the counts of Flanders, his predecessors. And as a reward for our efforts he has given us the lands and estates of the traitors who, according to the judgment of all the barons, have been condemned by proscription and who, now irrevocably deprived of their goods, and without hope of mercy, can expect only the most terrible and unheard-of punishment of death.[14] Therefore I order and wish and advise you people of the town,[15] as well as all others who are present, to receive as your lord and count, William, recently elected as count and invested with the county by the king.[16] And what is more, if there is anything which he can give you by right of his authority, such as toll and ground rent,[17] he will freely remit it to you without any guile or trickery, if you wish the toll to be remitted and likewise the ground rent of your houses inside the town; and I declare this on the part of the king and the new count."

When the citizens had heard the letter and the speech of its bearer, they put off deciding whether they would agree to accept and elect the new count until they could summon those Flemings[18] with whom they had taken an oath concerning the election and could take joint action with them in approving or opposing

[14] The royal court at Arras had not only settled the problem of succession by choosing William Clito, but had also exercised its judicial authority by proscribing the traitors, that is, putting them beyond the protection of the law, a sentence which implied death and confiscation of goods. (See Van Caenegem, *Geschiedenis van het strafrecht*, pp. 140-47, 206). The Flemish barons assured themselves of the undisputed possession of these goods by forcing the king to swear an oath that he would pardon none of the condemned without their consent, as Galbert reveals in c. 65. Ganshof considers this an infringement of the royal authority, not only in fact but in law; see "Le Roi de France," RHDF, XXVII (1949), 213-14.

[15] *Suburbani* here probably means simply "townspeople," as it does in c. 25, not the inhabitants of the whole castellany, as Pirenne here suggests (ed. Galbert, p. 83, n. 4) in contradiction to an earlier note (p. 43, n. 5).

[16] In "Le Roi de France en Flandre," RHDF, XXVII (1949), 210-11, Ganshof suggests that these words imply formal investiture of William with the fief, perhaps following his performance of homage and fealty to the king. The latter is not mentioned, however, and may have been omitted as unnecessary since William had doubtless performed this ceremony on receiving the fief of Pontoise and other lands at the time of his marriage to Jeanne, the queen's sister, in January, 1127.

[17] The king and count are now attempting to buy the support of the townsmen by material concessions. For an explanation of "toll" and "ground-rent" see c. 55.

[18] See c. 51.

the content of the royal message. And because they had used up the day with so much tedious talking, the citizens went home from the place where the speeches were made and by common agreement sent word throughout the night to the men of Flanders that they should come to approve or reject the election of the new count which had already been carried out.[19]

[53] *The men of Bruges and Ghent decide to accept William, March 31-April 2, 1127*

On March 31, Thursday, after the citizens had met with the men of Flanders, they decided by common agreement that on Holy Saturday[1] twenty knights[2] and twelve of the older and wiser citizens should go to meet messengers of the king for a conference at the stronghold of Raverschoot,[3] and there the men of Ghent were to await the arrival of our men. For the burghers of the cities and towns[4] of Flanders were pledged to each other in loyalty and friendship so that they would neither accept nor reject anything in the matter of the election except in common. In this matter our burghers would take no action without the counsel of the men of Ghent who lived in their vicinity.[5] And

---

[19] The concern of the citizens of Bruges about the choice of William Clito was doubtless due in part to fear that their commerce with England would suffer from Henry I's hostility. Is it possible that some knowledge of the king's support to Clito had led to the assembly on March 27 (see c. 51)? Their self-interest leads them to assert here a revolutionary principle, the right of burghers to a kind of veto over the choice made by king and barons; later their claims become more explicit and extensive.

[1] That is, April 2.

[2] Some of these are probably the *scabini* referred to in c. 51, where twelve are indicated by name or place.

[3] This former stronghold of the traitors was destroyed on March 8, according to c. 27.

[4] By "cities and towns" *(civitates et castra)* Galbert here, as in c. 2, probably means only urban centers in general. He rarely uses *civitates,* which, strictly speaking, should be applied only to episcopal centers, and there were no episcopal cities in the part of Flanders to which Galbert seems to be referring, the castellany of Bruges. Certainly Bruges and Aardenburg are implied here; see c. 55.

[5] It is not clear when or how this understanding with the men of Ghent had been reached, perhaps through those who had joined the seige, as seems to be implied below. But relations between the burghers of Bruges and the men of Ghent *at* Bruges seem far from cordial in c. 50!

so they went, as they had decided, on that same Holy Saturday. The king, as he had decided at Arras, went to Lille with the newly elected count, and here, as in Arras, homages[6] were done to the count, and from there he went to the village of Deinze on the road he was to take to Ghent. In the same place the king waited for the men of Ghent who were to accept the new count according to his order and the election of the barons of the land. Then an agreement was reached[7] between our men and the men of Ghent concerning the acceptance of the newly elected count to the effect that they would receive him as count and advocate of the whole land.

[54] *Gervaise is named castellan of Bruges, April 2, 1127*

On April 1, Friday, the day of preparation, the castellan Hacket escaped alone from the tower and went to Lissewege where he hid with his daughter whom a knight[1] of that place, belonging to an important family and very rich, had formerly married. The fugitive was waiting to see what would happen.

On April 2, Holy Saturday, certain of our citizens and those of Ghent who had returned from the conference[2] elected William

---

[6] By whom is not clear, whether knights or burghers or both.

[7] Where and when did this agreement take place? If at Raverschoot, between Bruges and Ghent, as seems likely from the first sentence of the chapter, it could have been no earlier than April 2, on which date the chosen representatives actually went to that place to meet messengers of the king, and not on April 1, as Ganshof states in "Les Origines du concept de souveraineté nationale en Flandre," RHD, XVIII (1950), 142. If at Deinze near Ghent, as Ganshof suggests in "Le Roi de France," RHDF, XXVII (1949), 214, and the latter part of the chapter seems to imply, it must have been *on* April 2, because the agreement must have preceded the "election" which also occurred on that day (c. 54). How did the representatives cover so much ground in one day (April 2), presumably from Bruges and the environs, to Raverschoot, to Deinze?

[1] Walter Crommelin or "of Lissewege." "Walter of Lissewege" is named in a charter of 1127; see *Actes*, no. 128, p. 302. He appears later in Galbert, c. 98 and 103.

[2] From Raverschoot, the place of the conference, presumably, but why does Galbert say "returned"? Where did this "election" of April 2 take place? Ganshof interprets Galbert's text to mean at Deinze, "in the presence of the king"; see "Les Origines du concept de souveraineté," RHD, XVIII (1950), 142, also "Le Roi de France en Flandre," RHDF, XXVII (1949), 214. Luchaire, however, also interpreting Galbert, believes it was at Ghent; see *Louis VI le gros: annales de sa vie et*

as their count and count of the fatherland, doing homage and pledging faith and loyalty[3] to the count according to the custom of the counts, his predecessors.[4] On the same day Gervaise was installed as castellan of our castle at Bruges by the king and the new count, although his merits were not yet fully rewarded by this act in view of the number and greatness of his deeds in the siege which I carefully call to the attention of the readers. For in that very hour when Count Charles was betrayed, he ran through the castle weeping, tearing his hair and clothes, wringing his hands, and he cried out: "Alas, alas, that by myself I cannot avenge my lord and the most just prince of our land, whom not even one of his vassals dares to defend and avenge!" And in that place Gervaise by himself set the vengeance on foot and afterwards, with God fighting beside him, brought it to a happy conclusion.[5]

On April 3, Easter Sunday, the feast of Theodosia the virgin, Sunday (or Dominical) Letter B,[6] the clergy and people were in a state of suspense about the arrival of the king and count among us. On that day the wretched traitors received the body and blood of Christ in Holy Communion though it is not known by what priest this could have been administered. On the same day those moving around in the castle were attacked with arrows by

---

de son règne (Paris, 1890), no. 381. It seems clear that the king went to Ghent before coming to Bruges on April 5 (c. 55): Galbert (c. 53) says he was en route to Ghent at Deinze, and Walter (c. 45) says he went to Lille, then to Ghent and Bruges. Galbert's reference to the men of Ghent who "returned" from the conference would make better sense if the "election" had taken place at Ghent. Ganshof ("Les Origines du concept," p. 143, n. 1) believes that the king's sojourn in Ghent "on April 3 and 4" can be deduced from Galbert, c. 54.

[3] Another clear example of "non-noble" homage, similar to that done by the merchants to William of Ypres in c. 20, except that this seems to be "collective and voluntary," rather than "individual and compulsory," as Professor Ganshof has kindly pointed out to me in a letter.

[4] To strengthen the cause of the burghers, Galbert claims for them the most binding sanction of his time, custom, though there is no evidence to support his assertion.

[5] Gervaise of Praat, Galbert's hero (whose initiative is not recognized by Herman, c. 31) is now rewarded with the office of Hacket. In c. 16 Galbert states that Gervaise's first act on March 2 was flight, but that he returned to Bruges with his forces on March 7, three days before the great barons arrived.

[6] The "Day Letters" were used chiefly to note the place occupied by Sunday in the first week of the year. If the first day is Friday, the Dominical or Sunday Letter is A, and so on. See Poole, *Medieval Reckonings of Time*, p. 18.

the besieged, those wretched traitors with no faith or reverence,[7] who were continuing life with the expectation of nothing but the most shameful death.

[55] *The count grants charters to the chapter of Saint Donatian and the citizens of Bruges and Aardenburg, April 5 and 6, 1127*

On April 5, Tuesday, "Aqua sapientiae,"[1] at twilight, the king with the newly elected Count William, marquis of Flanders, came into our town at Bruges.[2] The canons of Saint Donatian had come forth to meet them, bearing relics of the saints, and welcoming the king and new count joyfully in a solemn procession worthy of a king.

On April 6, Wednesday, the king and count assembled with their knights and ours, with the citizens and many Flemings in the usual field[3] where reliquaries and relics of the saints had been collected. And when silence had been called for, the charter of liberty[4] of the church and of the privileges of Saint

[7] Their "faith" would seem to be proved, contrary to Galbert, by their taking communion; they show no "reverence" because they fight on Easter Sunday. The priest may have been the "priest and sacristan" Robert, who had access to them throughout the seige, according to Galbert in c. 85.

[1] The beginning of the Introit of the Mass for the day.

[2] Galbert's first use of "our town," although he frequently speaks of "our castle" and even more often of "our place." See Introduction, pp. 73-74.

[3] The *Harenae* or Sands.

[4] This charter, known only from Galbert's text, is analyzed by Ganshof, "Le Roi de France," RHDF, XXVII (1949), 216-19. Probably drawn up by the canons themselves, after negotiations, perhaps at Arras, it had the form of a royal diploma, *un précepte royal*, to which the king and the canons were parties; it was not simply a charter of the count, confirmed by the king. In content it seems to have been largely a reaffirmation of earlier privileges either well-established or claimed. No authentic foundation charter of the chapter exists, as P. Grierson has shown, "The Translation of the Relics of St. Donatian to Bruges," *Revue Bénédictine*, XLIX (1937), 173. The earliest charter of the counts relating to the chapter of Saint Donatian is that of 1089 (see *Actes,* no. 9, pp. 23 ff.), in which Robert, son of Robert I, frees it from all public exactions and confirms it in certain possessions; he elevates the provost to the role of chancellor of Flanders, and provides that he shall be freely and canonically elected by the canons, subject to the approval of the counts; he grants the canons the rights of "chaplains" when serving at his court, and the same liberties with reference to their prebends as those enjoyed by the canons at Lille. In two charters Bishop Radbod II of Tournai granted privileges to the

Donatian was read aloud before all, in the presence of the king and count, in order that neither the king in his person, nor the count, should ever arrogantly violate what had been written down in the pages of the privileges and sanctioned by the Roman Catholic pontiffs, and what had never been impaired by any of the Catholic kings and counts; he should rather honor what had been sanctioned by the prerogative of his royal dignity and confirm it by the authority of his office. The brothers of the same church asserted that they had the liberty of electing the provost canonically and without simony by grant of the lord pope, as was affirmed in the text of his privilege.[5] After the provost had been elected canonically and without simony, the king, if he was present, by virtue of his own authority, should confirm the provost in the office and dignity of the prelacy, and install him in the seat of the prelacy; but if the king should not be present, the count, exercising by delegation the latter's authority, should perform the investiture[6] of the canonically elected provost and install him personally in his place according to the custom of his predecessors, the Catholic princes.[7]

---

chapter; in 1086 certain rights of sepulture within the castle, and in 1089 the complete cure of souls over the "parish of Saint Mary" lying within the castle, privileges springing naturally from the original status of Saint Donatian as a parish church; see Callewaert, "Les Origines de la collégiale Saint-Donatien," ASEB, LVI (1906), 395 ff. In 1101, Count Robert II, on his return from the Crusade, gave the church a "better status" by clarifying its privileges (*Actes*, no. 26, pp. 77 ff.); he reaffirmed its possession of certain fiscal and judicial rights over its lands and tenants, and guaranteed its possession of certain buildings within the castle (the provost's house, and others) against the claims of Everard of Tournai.

[5] They do not seem to produce the actual text of this papal grant, otherwise unknown, but merely reaffirm its content within their charter.

[6] Galbert probably draws his word (*concessio*) from the text of the charter itself; it has the technical meaning of investiture with the temporalities pertaining to the office, and is distinct from, although often confused with, the act of "confirmation" of the preceding election. See Ganshof, "Le Roi de France," RHDF, XXVII (1949), 218, n.l.

[7] The king's arrogation to himself of this right, formerly the count's, to confirm and invest the povost, as he did the French "royal bishops", marks an early stage of his progressive attempt to exercise direct authority within one of the great fiefs of France, even after he had fulfilled his original feudal duty, that of providing Flanders with its own feudal suzerain. This process is carefully analyzed by Professor Ganshof who points out the great potential advantage gained by the king in this step, that of acquiring the right to confirm the election of a high ecclesiastical official who, as chancellor of Flanders, exerted great influence throughout the land ("Le Roi de France"' RHDF, XXVII, p. 216). The king was to make use of this right on April 25; see c. 78.

There was also read the little charter of agreement[8] reached between the count and our citizens about the remission of the toll[9] and the ground rent on their houses.[10] As the price of their election and acceptance of the person of the new count, they were to receive from the count this liberty, that neither they nor their successors in our place should pay toll or rent henceforth to the count or his successors. And having been granted this liberty in perpetuity, as it was written in the charter of agreement, they should receive confirmation of this same liberty by an oath which they demanded of both king and count, to the effect that neither king nor count, either in person or through their agents, would any longer disturb our citizens, or their successors in our place, about paying the toll and rent but would respect inviolably the privileges of the canons as well as the

---

[8] In this modest phrase Galbert refers to an event of great, even revolutionary, significance in the social evolution of Flanders, the self-assertion of one of several urban communities who now seize the opportunity afforded by the insecure position of the new count to extract from him charters which incorporate liberties far in excess of the limited privileges enjoyed by a few of the lesser Flemish towns before that time. We owe to Galbert the brief analysis of the charters gained by Bruges and Aardenburg, and references to those gained by Ghent (c. 95) and Saint Omer (c. 66). The only extant contemporary text of a complete charter is that of Saint Omer, edited by Vercauteren in *Actes,* no. 127, pp. 293 ff, and more recently in a revised version by G. Espinas, "Le Privilège de Saint-Omer de 1127," RN, XXIX (1947), 43-49. The charter of Aire-sur-Lys is known only from a confirmation of 1188. For a thorough analysis of these charters see Ganshof, "Le Droit urbain en Flandre au début de la première phase de son histoire (1127)," RHD, XIX (1951), 387-416; see also F. Blockmans, "De oudste privileges der groote vlaamsche steden," NH, I (1938), 421-46.

[9] The *teloneum* (*tonlieu*) or toll was a direct tax levied by the count on the sale of merchandise within his realm; in this case the remission did not cancel the toll collected at Bruges but simply relieved the citizens of Bruges from paying it in their own port. (This concession was to become a subject of controversy; see c. 88). That the citizens of Ghent gained a similar privilege is implied in their protest of February 16, 1128; see c. 95. It seems probable that the burghers of Ghent and Bruges gained a reduction of toll in each other's towns; see Ganshof, "Le Droit urbain," RHD, XIX, 407-8. The case of Saint Omer is more complex; see pp. 408-9.

[10] The *census mansionum* was a fixed annual rent which the burgher as tenant paid to the proprietor of the piece of land which he used as a site for his house and shop or for other purposes. At Bruges the direct proprietor of the soil (except for the limited domain of Saint Donatian) was the count himself whose concession here transforms the tenures or *censives* of all the burghers into allods or freeholds. The allodiation of the soil at Ghent had already been accomplished in the late eleventh century. There, a small number of the richer burghers had "redeemed" the tax by purchasing it from the local proprietors of the soil, the abbeys of Saint Peter and Saint Bavon, to their own advantage; and the common lands had been redeemed for the benefit of the town as a community. See Ganshof, "Le Droit urbain," RHD, XIX, 400-2. No allodiation took place at Saint Omer, only a moderation of the rent.

remission of tolls and rent, honestly and fairly, without reservation. Binding themselves to accept this condition, the king and count took an oath on the relics of the saints in the hearing of the clergy and the people. Subsequently the citizens swore fidelity to the count, according to custom, and did homage and pledged loyalty to him, as they had done formerly to his predecessors, the lawful princes and lords of the land.[11] In order to make our citizens well disposed towards himself, the count granted to them in addition the right freely to correct their customary laws from day to day and to change them for the better as circumstances of time and place demanded.[12]

Finally when everything had been confirmed by the oath of the swearers, the king and the count returned to their quarters where there was produced in the hearing of all the following letter from the leading men of Aardenburg[13] who had taken part in the siege.

"We, who have also shared in the siege, will proceed on our part to elect the newly chosen count of Flanders, but on this condition, that you will condemn and completely free us and the inhabitants of our vicinity from expeditions[14] about which we have not been consulted, and do away with the evil exactions[15] of the barons

[11] This voluntary and collective act of non-noble homage on the part of the citizens of Bruges acting as a *universitas* or community is probably the first occurrence of the sort, and was by no means "customary" as Galbert claims, obviously in order to strengthen the position of the burghers whose cause he supports. See Ganshof, "Iets over Brugge," NH, I (1938), 292; and "Le Roi de France," RHDF, XXVII (1949) 216, n. 2.

[12] This concession, according to Ganshof ("Le Droit urbain," RHD, XIX [1951], 395-96), implies the creation, perhaps by word of mouth, of an urban tribunal (*échevinage*) authorized to enforce this law, which was distinct from the tribunal of the castellany. Such a tribunal seems to be implied also in the action of the burghers on April 11; see c. 59 and also c. 88. A similar tribunal may already have existed in Ghent; see c. 95. The only explicit grant of this essential urban privilege is found in c. 1 of the charter of Saint Omer (*Actes*, p. 295).

[13] At this time Aardenburg was a small port, northeast of Bruges, linked to the Zwin by the Elde, where the growth of trade had created an agglomeration around the count's castle. For an analysis of its charter see Ganshof, "Le Droit urbain," RHD, XIX (1951), 387-416, *passim*.

[14] Certain limitations, not clearly defined, are here placed on the count's right to summon the inhabitants to his host. The military privileges gained by the burghers of Saint Omer are more explicit, their service being limited to the case of a hostile invasion of Flanders; see charter, c. 4, *Actes*, p. 295.

[15] The "evil exactions" probably refer to seigneurial dues, tallage, and the like, which were specifically forbidden in the charter of Saint Omer, c. 13, and

and the new tolls[16] which were levied recently and contrary to the customary law of the land on the crafty advice of Lambert of Aardenburg; and also on condition that our farmers secure the liberty of going out and pasturing their flocks on the land which is called 'Mor' without the evil payment levied by Lambert.[17] Moreover, concerning the very burdensome payment on the houses in Aardenburg, we want to propose to the king and count that each of those pennies which sons, on the death of their fathers, formerly redeemed for sixteen pennies by reason of the location of the houses, should henceforth be redeemed by only twelve pennies.[18] We have also enacted a law for ourselves, that if an expedition on the count's part is announced to us, anyone who does not have a legitimate excuse shall pay to the count twenty shillings.[19] Concerning all these things, we beg your approval, lord king, and concession and confirmation from the new count, so that he may confirm by oath all those things that we have written down in this charter and that have been

---

probably also at Ghent (see Galbert, c. 95). Nothing similar is implied at Bruges, perhaps because the citizens of Bruges trusted their new castellan, Gervaise of Praat; it was the function of the castellan to collect such exactions (see Galbert, c. 94, 95). See Ganshof, "Le Droit urbain," RHD, XIX (1951), 411.

[16] The citizens of Aardenburg do not gain a remission of the toll but merely a restoration to their former levels of tariffs recently raised by the local lord who perhaps held them in fief or hoped to secure them, according to Ganshof, "Le Droit urbain," p. 408.

[17] The brother of Bertulf and father of Borsiard, mentioned in c. 20. The free use of commons for pasturage was essential to communities which though "urban" still largely supplied their own foodstuffs. Explicit provisions for right of common are made in c. 17 of the charter of Saint Omer, *Actes,* p. 297 (c. 18 in Espinas' revision, RN, XXIX, 43-49). See Ganshof, "Le Droit urbain," p. 412.

[18] The various interpretations of this difficult passage have been critically analyzed by Ganshof, "Coemptio gravissima mansionum," *Archivium Latinitatis Medii Aevi (Bulletin du Cange),* XVII (1942), 149-61. The exaction in dispute was not the annual ground-rent (such as that remitted to the burghers of Bruges), or the customary relief paid to the proprietor of the soil by the heir of a deceased tenant in order to secure occupancy, but rather the *payment necessary to redeem the relief* which the burghers now wish to be reduced by one-fourth. The relief was generally equivalent to the annual rent or lower; it could now be redeemed for twelve times its value rather than sixteen, as formerly. By facilitating the redemption of the relief, a very burdensome payment, the count, proprietor of the soil here as at Bruges, improves the conditions of tenure for the burghers but does not grant allodiation of the soil.

[19] This provision for a heavy fine, equivalent to one pound, is one of the rare instances of penal law included in the charters of 1127; it is the counterpart of the count's promises to limit his calls to arms. See Ganshof, "Le Droit urbain," RHD, XIX (1951), 404.

announced in the hearing of all. And we warn and beseech the person and authority both of king and count never again to permit the provost Bertulf and his brothers, Wulfric Cnop, the castellan Hacket, Robert the Young,[20] Lambert of Aardenburg together with their sons, Borsiard and the other traitors, to become owners of property in the county of Flanders."[21]

And when the charter had been read through in the sight of all, the new count took an oath to confirm it and to grant honestly and fairly and without reservation everything they had demanded from him.[22] And then throughout all the rest of the day those who had formerly been enfeoffed by the most pious Count Charles did homage to the count, receiving now in the same way their fiefs and offices[23] and whatever they had held before rightfully and lawfully.

[56] *The new count receives homages, April 7-10, 1127*

On April 7, Thursday, homages to the count were again performed; they were carried out in this order in expression of faith and loyalty. First they[1] did homage in this way. The count asked each one if he wished to become wholly his man, and the latter replied, "I so wish," and with his hands clasped and enclosed by those of the count, they were bound together by a kiss. Secondly, he who had done homage pledged his faith to the count's spokesman[2] in these words: "I promise on my faith that

---

[20] Robert was a nephew, not a brother, of Bertulf.

[21] That is, their goods were to be confiscated, as the court of the king at Arras had already determined (c. 52); this was to the advantage of the barons of the siege, however, not of the burghers.

[22] In this case the king apparently did not take an oath as he did above.

[23] Many offices or functions, as well as lands, were held in fief, such as those of the aulic officials, great and small, of the castellans and advocates. Other categories of fiefs included rights to certain tolls (see c. 88) and market dues; also revenues of an ecclesiastical character, particularly tithes, parish churches (see c. 107), and the like. See Ganshof, *La féodalité*, pp. 148 ff.

[1] There is no doubt that Galbert is here referring not to citizens but to men of the "noble" class, knights and barons, who were holders of fiefs of various kinds from the former count, Charles.

[2] A *prolocutor* or spokesman was necessary to speak the formal words for the count because the ceremony was doubtless conducted in Flemish and William of

I will henceforth be faithful to Count William and that I will maintain my homage toward him completely against everyone, in good faith and without guile." And in the third place he swore an oath to this effect on the relics of the saints. Then the count, with a wand which he held in his hand, gave investiture to all those who by this compact had promised loyalty and done homage and likewise had taken an oath.[3]

On the same day, Eustace of Steenvoorde,[4] seized earlier by the citizens in Saint Omer and later thrown into the conflagration of the house where he had fled, was burned to ashes; being marked with the stigma of the treachery, he deserved to suffer such a death.[5] On the same day in Bruges the count gave Baldwin of Aalst four hundred pounds minus twenty[6] because by his strength and counsel he had done more for him in the county than anyone save the king.

On April 8, Friday, homages were done to the count in the same way.

On April 9, Saturday, the king set out to Wijnendale to speak

---

Normandy probably spoke only French. See Ganshof, *La féodalité*, p. 97, n. 5.

[3] Because of its precision and clarity, this passage has been frequently cited as a classic example of the ceremony by which the contract of vassalage was established. Galbert distinguishes the constituent elements of the rite; *homage* or self-surrender, symbolized by the "mingling" of the hands and expressed in the declaration of intention; and *fealty* or fidelity, which in Flanders included both a promise of loyalty (*securitas*), signifying the more primitive, negative aspect of fidelity, and an oath representing the positive side. In France these acts were frequently accompanied by a kiss, a striking symbolic gesture of confirmation. (The words *integre, integraliter*, translated here as "wholly," imply a primitive stage of vassalage, in which homage was complete and without reservation; a distinction between such "liege" homage and "simple" homage was soon to arise because of the multiplication of feudal relationships.) Galbert's account includes a third step, *investiture* with the fief, the creation of a property relationship between lord and vassal which generally supplemented the personal relationship of vassalage; the bestowal of the fief is also represented by a symbolic gesture. For a full analysis of these acts, drawn in part from Galbert's evidence, see Ganshof, *La féodalité*, pp. 98-106, 163-65, and "Les Relations féodo-vassaliques aux temps post-carolingiens," in *I problemi comuni dell'Europa post-carolingia*, pp. 67-114.

[4] He is named as a witness in a charter of 1126, *Actes*, no. 121, p. 280.

[5] In the charter of Saint Omer, Count William assures protection to those responsible for this murder; see c. 20 in *Actes*, no. 127, p. 298 (c. 21 in Espinas's revision, RN, XXIX, 43-49). In this case the community rather than the count (as in c. 10) is exercising the right to destroy a house; see Van Caenegem, *Geschiedenis van het strafrecht*, pp. 182-83.

[6] This large sum could not have come from the count's treasure because the king and Count William have not yet laid hands on any part of it; see c. 61.

to William of Ypres, that false count, in an effort to make peace between him and the new, true count. But it seemed most intolerable to the false count to enter into an agreement with the true count of Flanders or to make any peaceful settlement with him because he held him in contempt. The king, therefore, returned to us, resenting the proud and scornful attitude of the false count of Ypres, and scorning him in turn.

On April 10, Sunday, our count,[7] following the advice of the king and barons, set out for Saint Omer, but because there were few whom he trusted along the way he returned to us at night.[8]

[57] *William of Ypres has Bertulf put to death, April 11, 1127*

On April 11, Monday, the provost Bertulf was handed over[1] to that false count who had taken great pains and made every effort to find out where he was hiding so that when he had once captured him and let it be known that he had seized the provost of Bruges, he could effectively restore his own reputation and authority by inflicting a harsh vengeance on him. For, as we have noted above,[2] at the height of the treachery, he had openly sent greetings to the provost and his kin from Ypres, and in so doing he had made his name vile and traitorous throughout the length and breadth of the realm. Therefore when he had seized the provost, now a refugee and exile in his own fatherland and among his kin, he had difficulty in thinking up a suitable way of putting to death someone whose treachery he was accused of being accessory to. And although that false one seemed to prove his innocence by crafty and cunning evidence, nevertheless God, whom nothing can resist, by whose authority it is said, "There is nothing hidden which will not be revealed,"[3] made clear to

---

[7] The "new" count has become the "true" count and finally "our count" in Galbert's eyes.

[8] It is clear that William Clito's position is by no means secure.

[1] By Alard of Warneton, according to Walter, c. 38, who secured the account of Bertulf's humiliating journey to Ypres from one of the clerics present. Bertulf is last mentioned by Galbert in c. 46 as hiding near Warneton on March 17.

[2] In c. 25.

[3] Matthew 10.26; the phraseology is not that of the Vulgate.

his faithful this inhuman turpitude and revealed the betrayers of such a great prince, and He damned and proscribed them and cast them down.

There was so much tumult and clamor and such a great concourse of people from Ypres and the whole vicinity around that one captive that there is nothing to which we can compare it. It is said that they went before and followed after the provost, leaping, dancing, applauding in various ways, and pulling him with long ropes from the left and right so that the line of pullers could move alternately forwards and sidewise; in this way that man, once so respected and powerful, could be insulted shamefully and ignominiously by everyone. He was pulled along nude except for breeches, the target of mud and stones.[4] Except for the clergy and a few who had formerly known him as a religious man, no one took pity on him. Exhausted by so many insults and wounded by so many taunts and blows, he saw the punishment of death approaching him; and he could with justice have called up before his mind's eye everything he had done, if the mob, rushing him headlong to his death, had granted him any time to live. He could indeed have remembered, if he had wished, how after asserting himself forcibly and imposing himself unjustly while the provost Ledbert[5] was still alive—an honorable man who endured everything for the sake of God—he had, contrary to God, usurped the prelacy in the Church of God, and in the heresy of simony had trafficked in the prebends and equipped his nephews for all kinds of evil deeds with the revenues of the Church;[6] and now finally he was admitting in

---

[4] Walter, c. 38, adds "heads of marine fishes," which were plentiful in those parts. He gives a more vivid account of the injuries and insults Bertulf now suffered, and even with patience, although formerly he had wondered why Christ willingly endured the torments of His passion and had said that under similar circumstances he would resist.

[5] There are certain unsolved problems in connection with the dates of Ledbert's provostship, but according to Vercauteren's hypothesis, Ledbert became provost soon after October 31, 1089, as successor to Ranier, after having been chaplain (in 1087) and canon; see *Actes*, pp. liii-liv and pp. 28-29. The "canon Bertulf," named as witness in the charter of October 31, 1089 (*Actes*, no. 9, p. 32), was undoubtedly the future provost who must have seized the provostship *ca.* 1091 since Galbert, in this same chapter, refers to his tenure of thirty-six years in that office.

[6] According to Pirenne (ed. Galbert, p. 91, n. 3), a charter of 1115 in which

the agony of his punishment that he had betrayed to death either by his assent or counsel[7] the most noble and Catholic prince Charles, sprung from a line of kings, whom he could have saved from the treachery, if he had wished. He could indeed have pictured in his mind how much grace, how much honor, fame, wealth, power, and esteem had been freely bestowed on him as a cleric by God whose dispensing grace he had not remembered while he enjoyed its benefits, acting as if they were his by right; for he had been so entangled in all these virtues and vices for thirty-six years that it seems impossible to explain. If anyone considers the number of his clan and the greatness of their deeds, the more marvelous seems God's attack on them and the destroying hand He turned against them. (And although I may seem to have a convenient place here to recount his genealogy, nevertheless, it seems to me I should let the work I have undertaken suffice and omit such an account, for I have set out to relate the outcome of the siege and not the adulterous origin of the family of the provost and his kin.)[8]

And so that man went along, once glorious but now ignominious, once respected and now disgraced, his face immobile and his eyes turned to Heaven, and, unless I am mistaken, he was invoking the aid of God; not with his voice but in the depths of his soul he called upon him, the compassionate, with mercy towards that human condition which He had assumed when He reigned over men in the kingdom of the world. Then one of his persecutors, striking his head with a stick said, "Oh, you proudest of men, why do you scorn to look at us and to speak to the barons and us who have the power of destroying you?" But he did not trouble to look at them, and he was hanged on a gallows[9] in the middle of the market place at Ypres, like a thief or

Bertulf, to expiate his misdeeds, gave lands to Saint Donatian corroborates Galbert's words. On the conception of simony as heresy see J. Leclercq, "Simoniaca heresis," *Studi gregoriani*, I (1947), 523-30.

[7] Galbert here seems to admit two possibilities, either that Bertulf advised the treachery or that he consented to it.

[8] But Galbert later rectifies this omission in c. 71, one of the interpolated chapters written soon after May 22, 1127, when he believed his work was done. *Adulterinus*, the same word which Galbert applies to William of Ypres in the sense of "false," probably means literally "adulterous" here; see c. 71.

[9] Concerning the form of medieval gallows see Enlart, *Manuel d'archéologie*

robber. They took off his breeches so that his shameful parts could be seen, and there was nothing vile or shameful he did not undergo in his punishment. His arms were stretched out like a cross on the gibbet and his hands inserted, and his head thrust through the hole of the gibbet, so that the rest of his body, suspended by his own members, as if by a kind of noose, would expire by suffocation.

When that man was first suspended there and was still supporting his body slightly on the gallows by the joints of his feet so that he could at least prolong the span of his pitiable life in this way, that false count, William, came to him in the midst of the thousands who were throwing stones and making thrusts at him, and calling for silence from everyone, spoke to him:

"Now tell me, provost, for the salvation of your soul I call you to witness; tell me, I say, who, besides you and Isaac and the other obvious traitors, are the ones guilty and culpable in the murder of my lord, Count Charles, but whose names are still secret?"

And the provost answered before everyone, "You know as well as I!" Then William, seized with rage, ordered stones and filth to be hurled at the provost and directed that he be killed. And now without delay those who had come to the market to buy fish set about destroying the body of the man with iron hooks, clubs, and stakes; and they did not allow him to sustain himself any longer by the aid of the gallows on which he was supporting himself by the joints of his feet but pushed him out from this support and so brought his life to an end by hanging in the shadow of the most bitter death. Now as he died the provost brought charges of treachery against Walter,[10] a knight of Zarren and his vassal, who had betrayed him to the very death he was now suffering; he had deceived him when he should have lent him guidance. Then the people of Ypres, thirsting for the death of the provost, twisted the viscera of a dog around his

IIème partie, tome I, pp. 363-69. This one, situated in the market place, must have been a simple, wooden structure. According to Enlart (p. 367), gallows, as distinct from pillories, were generally located outside towns for reasons of health.

[10] This Walter is named in the Inquest; see MGH, SS XXV, 441.

neck, and placed the muzzle of a dog next to his mouth, now drawing its last breath, thus likening him and his deeds to a dog.[11]

[58] *Guy of Steenvoorde is defeated in single combat and hanged, April 11, 1127*

At the same time, Guy,[1] a famous and strong knight, who had been one of the chief counselors of the counts of Flanders, had conspired in the very same treachery because he had married the niece of the provost, that is, Isaac's sister. For this reason Herman the Iron, a strong knight, immediately after the murder of Count Charles, had, in the presence of that false count of Ypres, challenged Guy to single combat because he had vilely betrayed his lord. But Guy asserted that he was ready at any time to defend himself against the charge of treason. And the day was set for their conflict, the same on which the provost had borne the torments of his death. As soon as the provost was dead, everyone present went out to the manor[2] where the combat between Herman the Iron and Guy had been called and where both sides fought bitterly. Guy had unhorsed his adversary and kept him down with his lance just as he liked whenever Herman tried to get up. Then his adversary, coming closer, disemboweled Guy's horse, running him through with his sword. Guy, having slipped from his horse, rushed at his adversary with his sword drawn. Now there was a continuous and bitter struggle, with alternating thrusts of swords, until both, exhausted by the weight and burden of arms, threw away their shields and hastened to gain victory in the fight by resorting to wrestling. Herman the Iron fell prostrate on the ground, and Guy was lying on top of

[11] Galbert's rational interpretation of this act as symbolic may indicate his ignorance of the persistence here of elements of old Germanic ritual; see Van Caenegem, *Geschiedenis van het strafrecht*, p. 173 and n. 3.

[1] Guy of Steenvoorde, last mentioned in c. 39 as giving a refuge to Isaac on March 17. He is named among the guilty in the Inquest, p. 441.

[2] At Reningelst in the environs of Ypres, according to Walter (c. 39), who gives a much briefer account of the fight.

him smashing the knight's face and eyes with his iron gauntlets. But Herman, prostrate, little by little regained his strength from the coolness of the earth, as we read of Antaeus,[3] and by cleverly lying quiet made Guy believe he was certain of victory. Meanwhile, gently moving his hand down to the lower edge of the cuirass where Guy was not protected, Herman seized him by the testicles, and summoning all his strength for the brief space of one moment he hurled Guy from him; by this tearing motion all the lower parts of the body were broken so that Guy, now prostrate, gave up, crying out that he was conquered and dying.

Then the count,[4] wishing above all to look after his own reputation in this fight, ordered Guy to be hanged next to the dead provost on the same gallows so that just as they had been equals in treachery so they should die as equals in torment. After this they placed the bodies of both men on the wheel of a cart, fastened to a high tree, and exposed them to the gaze of all the passers-by; bending their arms around each other's necks as if in a mutual embrace, they made those dead men look as if they were plotting and conspiring for the death of their lord, the most glorious and pious Count Charles, even after they had been dead for three days.[5]

So it was related by a squire who came to us and in the presence of the king told us of their fate; he had been present on that day and had seen the provost and Guy hanged at Ypres. Those who were besieged in the tower were at once informed by shouting how their lord the provost had been captured and put to death and told that nothing now remained to them except to surrender to the king to be dealt with according to their evil deeds. Then sorrow and anxiety, lamentations and sighs, prevailed among those wretches, now deprived of all hope of life; fear and desperation assailed them more effectively than the barons of the siege.

---

[3] The mythical Libyan giant, invincible in wrestling because he could recover his strength by contact with his mother, the earth.

[4] Galbert usually calls William of Ypres the "false" count.

[5] Walter, c. 39, says the bodies hung on the gallows for a while until the stench began to corrupt the air; the burghers then had them removed and put on the wheel, sewed up in hides. After a few days the bodies were secretly carried off and buried.

On this same day Gervaise[1] had ordered the carpenters to take
apart the wooden tower[2] which had been constructed earlier for
storming the walls and now stood idle; he had ordered that the
strongest beam, separated from the others, should be made into
a battering ram by means of which the wall of the church could
be breached. Now when the bowmen among the besieged were
aiming their arrows at the workmen from their position on the
summit of the tower and the strings of the drawn bows were
vibrating, a certain bow with its arrow in place fell from the
hands of a bowman just in the act of drawing. This was observed
by the knights, who were standing by with their shields close to
the work of the artisans to protect them as they skillfully
operated the engines of war, such as rams, sows, projectile machines,[3] ladders, and the like which are used customarily to
destroy walls and stone structures; and they prophesied a most
unlucky consequence of the fall of the bow and arrow from the
besieged.

On the same day, in the evening, a serious disturbance broke
out between Gervaise and his men and our citizens. For on the
order of the king,[4] and at the command of the barons of the
siege, who were trying to speed up the destruction of the besieged, and who had been put to great expense throughout the
whole course of the siege, and had exerted themselves un-
ceasingly in watching and fighting—by their common counsel
and by royal edict, I say—a general decree had been issued, to
the effect that no one from the whole crowd of the siege should

---

[1] Gervaise, now castellan of Bruges (c. 54), is assuming direction of the
military tactics by virtue of his office.

[2] The engine made by the men of Ghent, see c. 35, 40.

[3] The "sow" (*sus*) was a kind of inclined portable "roof" made of boards or
skins, designed to protect the assailants working at the walls. The "ram" (*aries*)
was a battering-ram often suspended on a rolling foundation. Various kinds of
projectile engines might be implied by Galbert's word *jactatoria*, such as ballistae
and catapults. See Enlart, *Manuel d'archéologie*, IIeme partie, tome II, pp. 479 ff.

[4] The dominant role of the king, rather than the count, both in the siege and
in the military operations throughout Flanders, reveals his novel attempt to
exercise direct authority within a great fief even after the election of a new count;
see Ganshof, "Le Roi de France," RHDF, XXVII (1949), 214-215.

dare to approach the tower and speak to the besieged for fear that the latter might get some idea of how they were going to be taken. The law[5] also provided with respect to transgressors that if anyone violated this command, he should be thrown into captivity and punished by the common judgment of the barons.

Now one of the citizens who had married a sister of a certain knight[6] among the besieged went secretly to the tower, to get back from his brother-in-law the vessels and clothes he had lent him, and the latter gave him back the vessels. When that citizen was crossing the market place on his return, one of the vassals of Gervaise who had taken on the responsibility of enforcing the law of the king and barons and of his own lord,[7] and also the authority of seizing transgressors of the order, followed the citizen, and seizing him, led him captive with him to the count's house. Immediately a great tumult arose among the citizens. Hastening to arms, they attacked the house of the count and the household[8] of Gervaise which was defending itself strongly from within. They cried out that they did not intend to suffer the lordship of anyone at all, and that on the contrary, it was within their own power to correct this misdeed.[9] And when the uproar

[5] The formulation of a special law at the scene of the siege, intended to isolate the traitors from their friends and partisans, is implied in the action of the barons on March 11 (c. 31). It now receives the sanction of the king and becomes more explicit; it is later elaborated and is called by Galbert "the law of the siege" in c. 88.

[6] An interesting example of intermarriage between burgher families and knights.

[7] Presumably Gervaise.

[8] The word *familia*, here translated as "household," does not necessarily imply only serfs or ministerials, according to E. Champeaux, who sums up discusssion of this term in his review of Ganshof's *Étude sur les ministeriales*, in RHDF, VI (1927), 748-49. Galbert's use of the term here and in c. 11 seems to support Champeaux's interpretation.

[9] There seems little doubt that the citizens are here asserting the right to the jurisdiction of their own urban tribunal or *échevinage* and repudiating other jurisdictions, specifically that of the count's court, composed of his knights and barons, to which the enforcement of the "law of the siege" had been entrusted. This highly coveted privilege was very likely gained by the burghers of Bruges in their charter of April 6, according to Ganshof, "Le Droit urbain," RHD, XIX (1951), 395, and perhaps verbally, since it is not mentioned explicitly by Galbert. The only explicit grant of this kind in 1127 was that made to Saint Omer in c. 1 of the charter of April 17. To what extent the right to the sole jurisdiction of their own *échevins* (chosen by the count but from their own class, and independent of the territorial *échevinage* as well as of the count's court) existed before 1127 among the Flemish towns is a moot point and has been much debated. Ganshof has summed up current opinion in the article cited above; he believes that before

had gone on for some time, Gervaise, in their midst, spoke as follows:

"You know, citizens and my friends, that in accordance with your request, the king and count recently installed me as viscount[10] of your place, and it was according to the order of the king and barons that my knight just now seized the citizen, your neighbor, as a violator of the order; by this act you have personally shown contempt for my office, you have attacked the count's house and my household who are in it, and finally, without reason you have risen up in an armed band in the presence of the king. Therefore, if you wish, I will give up the viscountship, because of the injury done to me; I will dissolve the faith and loyalty affirmed between us, so that it may be clear to all of you that I do not seek to obtain lordship over you. If it pleases you, let us put aside arms and go into the king's presence so that he may judge between us and you."

And when he had finished his speech, they went together into the presence of the king, and they were again bound to each other in faith and friendship as before.[11]

[60] *The siege continues; the king and barons make a new plan of attack, April 12, 1127*

On April 12, Tuesday, the king with the more experienced[1] men and his counselors went into the brothers' dormitory to determine

---

1127 Arras and Grammont undoubtedly possessed this privilege, Ghent probably, Ypres and Douai possibly. See esp. pp. 388-89, 394-97.

[10] The castellans were literally "viscounts" because they exercised the full authority of the count within their own territories, but they were rarely called viscounts at this time. Only three examples occur in the charters, in 1085, 1117, 1119 (*Actes*, "Table des termes techniques," p. 392). The title "castellan" came into general use with the radical reform of the administration by Baldwin V. 1035-67, and the creation of new territorial units known henceforth as castellanies. Perhaps Galbert's use of "viscount" is an archaism, like his frequent use of "consul" for count. See J. Dhondt, "Note sur les châtelains de Flandre," *Études . . . Rodière*, pp. 43-51.

[11] This clever speech of their favorite, Gervaise, wins the citizens over and restores peace, but it seems unlikely that they gave up their claims since the principle of the competence of the *échevins* seems to be reaffirmed in the future (c. 88, c. 102, c. 110). These cases will be discussed in due course.

[1] Presumably among the barons but perhaps also experts from the lower ranks. The "men of Ghent" were experts in scaling ladders, see c. 33.

carefully in advance exactly where the attack on the church should be made. For since the dormitory was next to the church, the experts could prepare inside the building the machines to be used in breaking through the wall of the church and gaining access to the besieged. When those wretches had been unable to hold the lower parts of the church, they had blockaded with wood and stones the stairs[2] leading to the gallery so that no one could go up and they themselves could not come down, planning to defend themselves only from the gallery and the towers of the church.[3] They had in fact set up between the columns[4] of the gallery lookouts and fighting posts made out of piles of chests and benches, from which they could throw stones, lead,[5] and all kinds of heavy things down on the invaders of the church. They had also hung tapestries and mattresses in the openings of the windows in the tower[6] so that missiles and weapons could not by any chance be hurled inside when the tower was being attacked from without. At the very summit of the towers stood the younger men among the besieged who could crush with heavy stones those who were moving about in the court of the castle. And so, having set their affairs in order in such a disorderly way, they were awaiting their end in death, showing no honor or respect to the blessed corpse which lay buried among them in the gallery,[7] except in one respect; that is, although they scarcely called to mind the lord whom they had betrayed, they had placed a candle[8] at his head which burned continuously in honor of the

[2] In the two small towers, flanking the great west-work, which gave access to the gallery.

[3] Meaning the smaller towers and the central west-work or tower.

[4] The character and function of these columns are not revealed. At Aachen, the model for Saint Donatian, the corresponding columns are ancient, brought from Rome and Ravenna, and purely decorative. P. Rolland, "La Première église Saint Donatien," RBA, XIV (1934), 105-6, believes these were likewise without structural function. It seems clear that the gallery was equipped with some kind of an open balustrade, the openings in which the besieged had to block up both for offense and defense.

[5] Concerning the use of lead in the church see c. 41, 43.

[6] "Tower" here in the singular refers to the whole west-work.

[7] See c. 22. The count's body had apparently been buried in a tomb in the floor of the gallery, a fact which proves that the lower part of the church must have been vaulted, probably with rib-vaulting, according to Rolland, "La Première église," RBA, XIV (1934), 108.

[8] Was the candle placed to "honor the count" or to furnish the light needed

good count from the first day of the siege to the day when their attackers gained access to them. For they had laid out around the tomb of the count the flour and legumes[9] which they consumed daily to sustain life.

And when the king and his companions were carefully investigating and were marking the place to pierce the church, Robert the Young, sticking his head out one of the windows of the church,[10] spoke to the knights of the king and begged them to be his messengers to the king, saying humbly that he wished to submit to the judgment of the princes of the land and the barons of his lord, the king,[11] so that according to their law he could deserve either to live, by virtue of his defense, or to be destroyed by the punishment of condemnation if he could not absolve himself. But none of the men dared to go as messengers with these words to the king, because he was so filled with anger against the traitors that he hated even the sight of them. Our citizens, however, and the king's knights, and all who had heard with what humble language the young man had implored the lord king, suffered with him, dissolved in tears, praying that his lord would take pity on him.

[61] *The king hunts for the treasure, April 13, 1127*

On April 13, Wednesday, the besieged made up a story about Borsiard's death, to the effect that in a quarrel that sprang up between him and Robert the Young, he had fallen pierced by a sword; they hoped in this way to appease the severity of the barons so that they would not attack so fiercely in the future. They called out from the tower that Borsiard was dead, spreading this word mendaciously; others said that he had escaped.[1]

---

to get at the food? In c. 64, Galbert also says to "honor" him.
    [9] Peas and beans, a fundamental food at this time; see c. 3. See c. 90 about the rite of eating on the tomb.
    [10] Probably in the west-work.
    [11] The distinction between these two categories is clear: the "princes of the land" are the Flemish barons; the barons here are the French.

    [1] Walter, c. 40, 41, gives a full account of Borsiard's wanderings with a few

Hearing this, the king realized that the besieged were already losing confidence in themselves, that they were succumbing to fear and anxiety, and so, resolute in mind, he ordered his knights to arm themselves and attack the church. This was done in the hope that the besieged, weakened and exhausted by the fight, could not in the future sustain so many assaults and attacks but would rather give up and hand over the place in Christian victory to the Catholic king, Louis, and his knights. There was, in fact, heavy fighting on both sides; the hurling of stones and throwing of javelins went on from noon until evening.

On that day the king received from the dean, Helias,[2] the keys to the sanctuary of the church of Saint Christopher[3] because he had been told that the treasure of Count Charles had been placed in that sanctuary. But when the king entered he found nothing but the relics of the saints. It is true that the provost had received from his nephews as a kind of gift when the loot was divided, a golden goblet with its own lid, and a vessel, or rather a silver container for wine,[4] and that he had presented these vessels to God for the service of the church in order to save his soul. Then when the siege was going on and the brothers were carrying the relics and shrines of the saints out of the castle, they had borne out those two vessels which had been secretly placed in a certain chest under the guise of relics along with the true relics of the saints. The dean had entrusted that chest to the care of a certain simple priest, Eggard, in the church of the Holy Savior,[5] indicating that it should be venerated as though it contained the most precious relics. How devoutly, in fact, that simple priest

----

companions, his vain attempt to escape in a boat which Divine Providence immobilized, his consequent penitence and confession of sins, his unwitting betrayal when his serf tried to secure "delicate bread" for his starving master.

[2] He was dean of the chapter of Saint Donatian, the official just below the provost in rank; his name appears several times as witness to charters, from 1110 to 1127; see *Actes,* Index. His own interest in the treasure becomes clear later, c. 83, 85. Walter names him in c. 31 as one of those who informed him about events at Bruges after the murder.

[3] The church in the market place where the relics were deposited on March 17; see c. 35.

[4] Perhaps the vessel which the count had bought at the fair at Ypres; see c. 16.

[5] Probably the first urban parish church, lying to the south of the castle.

had received the chest and how, having placed it in the sanctuary, he poured forth prayers and begged for the salvation of his soul, was revealed by his fellow-priests in the same church; every night he placed before it tallow candles, wax candles, and lights and lighted lamps, believing he could not venerate those relics enough. (That priest had really done enough to deserve a drink or more of good wine from those vessels when they were handed over to the new count!)[6]

Then the king, in pursuit of the treasure, sent out agents and spies in all directions to gather up secretly the treasure of Count Charles, but he had no success. That is why the king on the second day before his departure for France[7] had Robert the Young beaten with whips so that he would tell the king who was in possession of any part of the treasure, if he could re-member anything about it. Thanks to his disclosure, on the same day the new count and the king secured the vessels, as we are about to tell.[8] Some of the besieged announced that Borsiard had fled, hoping by this lie to moderate the force of the attack.[9]

[62] *The besiegers breach the wall of the church, April 14, 1127*

On April 14, Thursday, the battering ram, designed to drive a hole through the wall of the church, was brought into the brothers' dormitory, a hall which was adjacent to the place where the good count's body was lying in its tomb,[1] commended to God. And immediately the artisans who had made the ram erected high slanting approaches,[2] like stairs, and after tearing

---

[6] It sounds as if Galbert were poking fun at Eggard.

[7] May 4, since the king left on May 6; see c. 82. It was Robert who told the count about Helias and the cups, before he left Bruges with the king; see c. 83.

[8] The vessels were given up to the count on May 7, see c. 83; it is clear that this item of information was added later to c. 61.

[9] This repetitious statement, one of several, reveals that Galbert did not work over his text.

[1] The dormitory must have been lofty, since its wall was high enough to be adjacent to the gallery where the count lay buried and ample enough to contain both ram and scaling equipment.

[2] *Ascensoria graditiva*: probably crude "stairs" made of loose stones, not ladders (called *scala* in c. 35, 40).

down the wooden wall of the dormitory, which had stood next to the church, they placed the top of these "stairs" in such a way that those who dared could ascend armed to the wall of the church. For the workers had laid bare a window[3] of the original structure of the church in the old stonework against which they had now placed the stairs. But they lowered the approaches of the equipment temporarily so as to direct the blows of the ram below the window and, once the stone wall was pierced, to secure the window as an entrance, almost like an open door, for the steps were so broad that ten knights could stand on them fighting side by side at the same time.[4]

When these were in place, they adjusted the great beam, suspended by ropes, so that it would pierce the church in that very place, above the stairs; and they attached nooses to it and also placed by the nooses armed men who were to draw it back from the church, raised on high, and, once it was pulled back with all their force and strength, to hurl it skillfully and effectively against the wall of the church. Over the heads of those ascending the stairs, coverings of green branches were woven together and inserted in the beams so that if the roof of the dormitory should by some device be broken through by the besieged, those who were driving the ram would be safe under the shelter of the branches. And wooden "walls" had also been placed before them as a protection so that they would not be wounded by arrows or spears coming from inside. Then, having pulled the ram back from the church wall by means of the nooses as far as they possibly could with outstretched arms, all together, with one impetus and one cry, they drove the great mass and weight of the ram against the church with their maximum strength and effort. At each blow a great heap of stones fell to

[3] The dormitory was probably built later than the church since its wall covers up one of the windows of the church gallery. The wooden wall was doubtless added to exclude dampness, according to Pirenne, ed. Galbert, p. 101, n. 2.

[4] The size of this window, apparently wide enough to admit ten men in a row, has led to ingenious reasoning concerning the shape and size of the church on the part of H. Mansion, "À propos de l'ancienne église Saint-Donatien à Bruges," RBA, VIII (1938), 108-9. His conclusion that the church must have been polygonal, not circular, is supported by the recent (1955) excavations of Dr. J. Mertens; see the Appendix.

the ground until the whole area of the wall was perforated in
the place where it was pounded. They had equipped the beam
in the head of the ram with a very strong piece of iron so that it
could not suffer any damage except what it incurred as a result
of its own weight and force. The work of ramming was long
drawn out; begun at noon it was not finished until after evening
had come.

[63] *The church is now invaded by the besiegers, April 14,*
    1127

Meanwhile the besieged, realizing that the wall was weak and
would quickly be breached, were undecided and uncertain what
to do; finally they fixed up coals, burning inside, and besmeared
with pitch, wax, and butter which they threw onto the roof of
the dormitory. And in a moment the coals, adhering to the
roofing, vibrated with flames as the wind blew, so that enormous
flames shot up and spread all over the roof. Now from the
upper part of the tower they were throwing mill stones onto the
roof of the dormitory over the place where the ram was battering
the church, both in order to prevent anyone from extinguishing
the fire thrown on the roof, and also to guard themselves
against the danger of a breach in the wall by hurling down stones
from on high to crush those who were breaking through into
the church. But neither the number nor size of the stones hurled
down could impede the drivers of the ram. For when the knights
saw the flames vibrating over their heads, one of them went up
onto the roof and managed to extinguish the fire, in spite of the
stones and javelins that were being hurled. After so many
blows of the ram an enormous hole now lay open in the church
wall, which had been breached more quickly than one would
have believed, because since the time of the former fire[1] in the
church, the whole structure of the church had become almost

[1] The fire, apparently some years before Galbert's time, which had led to the
abandonment of a wooden roof and the construction of a fireproof vault out of
earthenware material; see c. 37.

rotten from the rain and infiltration of water, lacking, as it did, any wooden roofing.[2]

Then a great cry arose outside, and all who had fought against the besieged at the doors and in the lower part of the church and through the windows and in every place where they could secure access to them,[3] hearing that the church wall had been breached, were now attacking with greater zeal of spirit and with audacity greedy for victory. And, in fact, they had all fought continuously on both sides from noon to evening, almost succumbing from the exertion of the struggle and the weight of arms. But now, knowing about the opening made by the ram, they were refreshed and strengthened in spirit, as if they had rushed to arms for the first time, and they began to attack the besieged and to pursue them in earnest. The wretched besieged, however, though weak in numbers,[4] were even weaker in the fight because they had the disadvantage of fighting, not all in one place, but rather at all the points of access, that is, at the doors and windows, in the choir and especially in the place which the ram had now taken over. Having suffered to the bitter end the misfortunes of life, and now fighting separately on all sides, they were henceforth anticipating ruin and destruction at the hands of their enemies. Those in the church[5] who had been hurling stones, arrows, pikes, stakes, and all kinds of spears against the drivers of the ram were even more fearful because they were few in number and because, separated from their companions and almost succumbing from their day-long struggle, they were fighting against such a strong army. What is more, lacking arms, they did not have the means of defending themselves; they resisted, nevertheless, as much as they dared.

But when the drivers of the ram, and other knights of the king, and the young men of our place, armed and avid for conflict, finally saw the besieged opposite them, they summoned all

[2] The new covering must have failed to protect the church from rain as a wooden roof would have done, or at least so Galbert implies. See Rolland, "La Première église," RBA, XIV, 110.

[3] See c. 43.

[4] How many were left? The number of those who surrendered on April 19 was less than thirty; see c. 74.

[5] In the gallery, apparently.

their courage. They may have been picturing in their mind's eye how noble it would be to die for father and fatherland,[6] and what an honorable victory was set before the conquerors, and how infamous and criminal those traitors had been who had made a den for themselves out of the church of Christ, but in fact it seems more likely that they were intent on rushing against the besieged because they were avid and greedy to seize the treasure and money of the lord count, and that for this reason alone they were hastening forward. But regardless of motives, they hurled themselves through the middle of the opening in one rush, without order, without line of battle, without any thought for the arms they bore, so that by rushing in all at once they could prevent the besieged from having any time or place in which to fight and kill anyone. For they did not cease to rush in until they had transformed themselves into a kind of continuous bridge, and, by the marvelous dispensation of God, they advanced without mortal danger to their lives, some dashing, others stumbling, some pushed in forcibly, others falling down and trying to get up again, some in complete confusion, as is usual in such a great tumult. Not only the church but the whole castle and its vicinity was filled with the sound of their shouts and cries, with the noise of their passage, the crumbling of the wall and the clamor and clash of arms. Outside they were praising God and thanking him for this victory by which He honored the victors, glorified the king and his men, cleansed his church in part from the defilers, and made it possible at last for that glorious martyr, his count, to be mourned by the pious veneration of good men and to be sustained by the prayers of his faithful.

[64] *The besieged are driven from the gallery into the tower, April 14, 1127*

Now at last Fromold Junior[1] was able to do what had not been possible before and what he had long and ardently desired, to

---

[6] This sounds like a garbled version of the line from Horace, *Odes* III.ii: "Dulce et decorum est pro patria mori."

[1] Last heard of in c. 24 when he was departing for exile on March 5. The abrupt change of tone in the first part of this chapter, its poetic language and

offer prayers to God for the salvation of his lord, the count, to make a sacrifice in tears and contrition of heart, and to rejoice greatly in the sight of the place where his lord, buried, was resting in peace; and so for the first time he was preparing funeral rites for his lord whom he had not been able to see since he was buried, that is for forty-four days.[2] Since he could see not his body but only the outside of the tomb, he wished and implored with the prayer of both lips and heart that God on the day of common resurrection would permit him finally to see his lord and prince, Charles, raised to double glory[3] among the faithful rulers and highest princes of his present Church, and to stay with him and be blessed with him eternally in the glory of the contemplation of the Holy Trinity. Therefore he considered it a great boon to be able to mourn the death of his lord at his tomb, to lament the ruin of the fatherland, and to perform with the greatest love the last rites for one whom he had cherished in life, now betrayed by his serfs. He did so, indeed, not without tears. Oh God, how many prayers of your faithful you deigned to receive on that day! Whatever part of the divine cult had not been performed in that church was more than compensated for in that hour by the magnitude and multiplicity of the prayers of the just. A wax candle was standing at the head of the count, placed there by the traitors in honor and veneration of their lord.[4]

Now after they had rushed into the church against the besieged and a great clamor had arisen in the pursuit, those most wretched of men had retreated both from the hole in the wall and from

---

deep emotional feeling, has led to the ingenious hypothesis that Galbert is here paraphrasing a lost *planctus* or mourning poem written by his friend and fellow-notary, Fromold Junior, soon after his master's death, perhaps about Easter (April 3). The dating is predicated on the striking similarity between its phrase-ology and that of the Easter offices, especially the theme of longing to see the body of his lord which is strongly reminiscent of the words of the Holy Women at the Lord's tomb. See J. M. De Smet, "Bij de latijnsche gedichten over den moord," in *Miscellania . . . de Meyer,* I, 440-43. De Smet (pp. 430-34) believes that Fromold may also be the author of one of the surviving Latin poems written soon after the death of Charles beginning "Karole, tu mea cura manens"; this is given in Pirenne's edition of Galbert, pp. 184-85.

[2] Since March 4; see c. 23.
[3] Perhaps as martyr and as prince.
[4] See c. 60.

the doors[5] and defense posts[6] and, ascending the tower to defend themselves, they were resisting their attackers on the stairs.[7] Therefore the victors, the most Christian knights of the king of France,[8] hastened to obstruct and block up the stairs with stones and wood, with chests and beams and other bulky things so that none of the besieged could come down into the gallery where the count was lying. And now the king, coming to the church, mourned the death of his cousin, Charles, and placed a guard to watch the tower carefully; in alternating vigils the king's knights watched the tower where the besieged were. Whatever was found in that gallery which could be seized was anybody's loot.

Finally the canons of the church, climbing up on ladders[9] to the gallery from the choir, arranged for certain of the brothers to keep vigils every night around the count's tomb. Looking around, they saw that although the church vessels were shattered and nothing was as it had been before, the altars and altar tables by God's care had remained in place, and with great rejoicing the brothers took possession of whatever they found, not by right or merit, but only by the gift of God. Then God brought that day to its conclusion by closing up his enemies and giving victory to the faithful, exalting the name of his power to the ends of the earth. The besieged, however, did not desist from setting watches in the tower, sounding their horns and acting proudly in such straits as if they still possessed some authority, not recognizing how extremely wretched they were, for they were confirmed reprobates. Therefore whatever they did henceforth was not pleasing to God or men but was reprobate and hateful.

[5] Probably the doors to the stairways in the small towers; see c. 43, 63.

[6] Between the columns of the gallery; see c. 60.

[7] The stairs in the small towers leading up from the gallery to the ramparts of the west-work.

[8] The king's forces seem to be playing the leading part.

[9] The stairs in the small towers leading from the ground floor to the gallery must have been blocked up by the traitors on March 17; see c. 43.

[65] *The king is beseeched to save Robert the Young, April 15-16, 1127*

On April 15, Friday, the people of Bruges came together in the presence of the king, and, bent to the earth, they implored his royal dignity, out of consideration for their prayers and services, to grant Robert the Young freedom to leave the besieged, and to accept lawful proof of his innocence.[1] And the king himself agreed to accept their petition, with due regard, however, to his own honor and dignity and that of the barons of the land without whose counsel he had promised to take no action in this matter.[2]

On April 16, Saturday, the castellan of Ghent[3] with Arnold of Grembergen[4] and other leading men of his region who had joined them, came before the king, begging him in every possible way for the liberation of Robert the Young. The king said to him that he could not with honor agree to their request without the common agreement of the barons; for if he did so, he would violate his faith and oath.

[66] *The new count is welcomed at Saint Omer, April 16(?)*

On April 17, Sunday, "Surrexit pastor bonus,"[1] it was announced to the king that the new count of Flanders had been graciously received with honor in Saint Omer,[2] according to the custom of

---

[1] Perhaps by ordeal.

[2] This is, of course, a refusal. Ganshof believes that the barons at Arras had secured this extraordinary and exorbitant concession from the king in order to safeguard forever their possession of the goods confiscated from the traitors; he considers it a limitation of the king's authority in law as well as in fact; see "Le Roi de France," RHDF, XXVII (1949), 213-14.

[3] According to the Inquest (MGH, SS XXV, 442), Wenemar, castellan of Ghent, admitted openly that he had received part of the count's treasure from Robert.

[4] It is possible that this Arnold was the famous Arnold of Grimbergen in Brabant, but more likely he was simply an otherwise unknown knight of Grembergen near Dendermonde.

---

[1] The opening of the Introit of the Mass for that day.

[2] The count's itinerary presents certain problems. According to Walter, c. 45, after Easter (April 3) he went to Lille, to Bethune, stayed in "our city," Therouanne, for two days, and then went on to Saint Omer. Since Galbert, c. 56, says

his predecessors, the counts of the land. For youths bearing bows and arrows had come forth to meet him; agile and lively they advanced toward the count in companies, pretending they were going to resist, girded and ready with drawn bows and strings to shoot arrows at the count and his men, if they so wished. Seeing the approach of the boys, the count and his men asked them by messenger what they wanted from him. They announced to the count that what they wanted was a kind of "fief" which our boys had obtained formerly from his predecessors:

"It is our right to acquire this privilege from you, that is, on feast days of the saints and in the summer time to wander freely about the woodland glades, to snare small birds, to shoot arrows at squirrels and foxes, and spend our time in boyish play of this kind. We did these things freely in the past and now we wish to confirm the customs of our games for the future by receiving the same liberty from you."

In the same way, following them, the citizens advanced in an armed band, awaiting the return of their boys and the arrival of the new count. Then Count William, who was himself still flourishing in youth, hardly beyond the age of boyhood,[3] with good grace and affection[4] granted the boys their playful sports; and, applauding and joking, he entered into the spirit of play with them, seizing their standard and banner. They had begun

---

that he made an abortive departure from Bruges to Saint Omer on April 10, his actual departure must have taken place April 11, or 12, at the latest, for he was probably welcomed in Saint Omer on April 16, a day before the king heard of this event. He did not enter Saint Omer, however, until after the concession of the charter, which is dated April 14. It has naturally been assumed that the charter was signed and granted at Bruges because it is signed by the king, and by the great barons who were at Bruges, probably after negotiations at Bruges with emissaries from Saint Omer; see Luchaire, *Annales de la vie de Louis VI,* no. 384, and, *Actes,* pp. 293-94. But the count, who also signed it, could not possibly have been present in Bruges between April 11 and 16, since in that interval he visited Lille, Bethune, and spent two days at Therouanne. Ganshof seems to suggest a possible explanation, that the *negotiations* took place in Bruges but not the *concession* of the charter ("Le Roi de France," RHDF, XXVII [1949], 221, n. 2), and that the latter took place in Therouanne ("Le Droit urbain," RHD, XIX [1951], 391). But then how can one explain the signatures of the king and the great barons who were at Bruges?

[3] Born in 1101, William was now twenty-six years old, hardly a boy!

[4] Thomas corrects the adverb *morose* here to *amorose* (from popular Latin), and thus makes the sentence intelligible.

to sing his praises and to sound the signals for the dances, when the citizens looking on from afar saw the count coming toward them, now formally received by the boys and surrounded peacefully by their acclaim and respect. Then when the people and the count had come together, the clergy of the place came out in procession to meet him, bearing incense and candles, in exaltation of his honor and glory, as is customary on the reception of those who have just received the countship. Filling the air with the jubilation of their voices and the harmonies of their sweet singers, they received him, while all the citizens applauded, and led him solemnly into the church amid the same sweetness of song. And here the count, catholically elected, devoutly made the offering of prayer due to God, and at the same time the people and the clergy prayed in his behalf that, while he administered the county, God should so rule and protect it that henceforth they might render their dues to both count and God in peace and safety.[5]

[5] Neither Galbert's poetic account of the *joyeuse entrée* at Saint Omer, nor Walter's terse comment that the count was welcomed by the castellan and burghers but only on the basis of certain promises (c. 45), gives any idea of the extent and character of the rights that the citizens of Saint Omer gained as the price of their recognition of the count. Their charter has been intensively studied, first in the classic work of A. Giry, *Histoire de la ville de Saint-Omer* (Paris, 1877), and most recently by G. Espinas, *Deux fondations de villes dans l'Artois et la Flandre française: Saint-Omer et Lannoy-du-Nord* (Lille, 1946), who has also prepared a new edition, "Le privilège de Saint-Omer de 1127," RN, XXIX (1947), 43-45. See also *Actes*, no. 127. Espinas and his critics agree that the count was not granting wholly new liberties but rather, in many instances, confirming in writing customary practices which had been enjoyed *de facto* by the "community" of Saint Omer for some time, but they disagree as to whether or not Saint Omer should be called a "commune" (as Espinas believes, *Deux fondations*, p. 134) *before* 1127. It is certainly recognized as such in the charter of 1127 (c. 12, "Communionem autem suam, sicut eam juraverunt, permanere precipio . . ."), and thus conforms even to the narrow definition of "a commune" laid down by C. Petit-Dutaillis, that of a community united by an oath of mutual aid; *Les Communes françaises* (Paris, 1947), pp. 12 ff., esp. pp. 21, 37, 81. Though it has the form of a concession granted by the count, signed by the king, the count, and twenty-odd of the greater barons, castellans, and officials, and not by any representatives of the town, the charter is actually an agreement between the count and the burghers, the fruit of hard bargaining, and limits the count's authority in various respects. Of its twenty-one provisions, more than half are fiscal in character, relieving the burghers from various kinds of exactions, especially tolls, and granting them rights of minting money; others recognize and confirm the sole jurisdiction of the urban *échevins* and exempt the burghers forever from the proof of the judicial duel. For an analysis of its provisions in relation to the other privileges granted in 1127, see Ganshof, "Le Droit urbain," RHD, XIX (1951), 387-416. If Galbert had seen the charter, he gives little evidence of its contents. His account of the count's entry into Saint Omer may

After receiving the count they did homage and pledged loyalty to him. The count had, in fact, gone to Saint Omer from the city of Therouanne.

[67] *Aire and Oudenaarde are besieged, ca.April 17*

Also at this time Hugh of Camp d'Avène,[1] and Walter of Vladslo[2] had made an attack with their men on the castle at Aire[3] into which the false count of Ypres, William, and his men had withdrawn and where they had fortified both the place and the castle. For he had seized the count's authority and had forcibly secured by this time many castles and fortifications[4] in Flanders, namely, the castle of Ypres, the stronghold of Voormezele, the castle of Kassel, the castle of Veurne, the castle of Aire, and the whole region around these castles, and the castle

be based on an official account sent to the king, stressing as it does, the ceremonial aspects, according to Giry, *Histoire*, p. 50. The "fief" claimed by the boys may actually refer to the use of woods and commons granted to the burghers in the charter (c. 17 in *Actes*, p. 296; c. 18 in the revision of Espinas).

[1] Hugh III, 1118?-1141?, count of Saint Pol (one of the autonomous counties of southern Flanders), is often confused with his father, Hugh II, 1078-*ca.*1118, whose policy of aggressive territorial expansion and effective internal consolidation he continued, to the detriment of the counts of Flanders, until his death *ca.*1141. After conspiring with the Countess Clemence against Charles in 1119-20, he was pacified and appears in Charles's court as a witness at Arras in 1122 and 1123 (*Actes*, nos. 108, 109, pp. 250, 252); he resumed his aggression under William Clito and his successor, Thierry of Alsace. See P. Feuchère, "Les Origines du comté de Saint-Pol," RN, XXXV (1953), 125 ff., and "Regeste des comtes de Saint-Pol, 1023-1145," RN, XXXIX (1957), 43-48. Feuchère gives no evidence to confirm Pirenne's statement (ed. Galbert, p. 108, n. 1) that Hugh married Marguerite of Clermont, the widow of Count Charles.

[2] Last heard of in c. 52 as the spokesman of the king at Bruges on March 30.

[3] For its history see P. Bertin, *Une commune flamande-artésienne: Aire-sur-le-Lys des origines au XVIe siècle* (Arras, 1946). It was one of the few urban communities which had received recognition by the counts before 1127. The exact privileges secured by its *amicitia* are known, however, only from a confirmation of 1188; supposedly they date from the reign of Robert II (1087-1111) and were confirmed by Charles, William Clito (probably between April 25 and May 4) and his successors. See Ganshof, "Le Droit urbain," RHD, XIX (1951), 388-92, and *passim*.

[4] Galbert's use of terms here is not entirely clear, but he seems to distinguish between great castles and fortifications (*castra, castella, munitiones*) and a smaller stronghold (*oppidum*). At Aire "the place" probably means the "town" or urban settlement.

of Bergues and others.[5] For he was a bastard of the lineage of the counts, and he had expected to obtain the countship by virtue of this relationship.[6] The barons mentioned above unhorsed two knights and gained five horses. At the same time Baldwin of Aalst[7] and Razo[8] with a very strong army from Ghent had besieged the castle of Oudenaarde[9] which the Count of Mons[10] and his men had entered and fortified for the purpose of invading the realm of Flanders, which by right of kinship more justly belonged to him.

[68] *How Count Baldwin V (1035-67) had extended his power*

Now[1] in order to tell a little more about the origin of the counts, his predecessors, Count Baldwin the Bearded[2] was the first of the line of subsequent counts. When he died he was buried in Lille. Now he had two sons who were his heirs, Baldwin[3] and Robert.[4]

[5] Walter, c. 43, gives almost the same list, including Saint Venant and Bailleul, but omitting Voormezele.

[6] See c. 47.

[7] Last referred to in c. 56.

[8] Razo of Gavere, the butler, last mentioned in c. 33, as arriving at the siege with an army on March 15th.

[9] A stronghold at Oudenaarde, on the Flemish side of the Scheldt, the boundary between Imperial and French Flanders, had been built by Baldwin IV, *ca.* 1000, opposite the imperial fortress of Ename, as a weapon in his policy of eastern expansion. See J. Dhondt, "Het ontstaan van Oudenaarde," *Handelingen van de geschied- en oudheidkundige kring van Oudenaarde*, X (1952), 58; see also L. Delfos, "Oudenaarde en Pamele voor 1117," in the same journal, Feestnummer (1956), 74-92.

[10] Baldwin IV of Mons, who had been rejected by the king as a candidate at Arras, according to Herman, c. 35; see Galbert, c. 47, concerning candidates, though he does not name Baldwin until this chapter. Like William of Ypres he was receiving English support; see Walter, c. 45.

[1] The following chapters, 68 to 71, are an interpolation, obviously written after May 22, 1127, when Galbert thought his work was done, and added to provide essential information concerning the genealogy of the two families, that of the counts and of the Erembalds. See Genealogies.

[2] Galbert refers to Baldwin V, "of Lille," 1035-67, not his father, Baldwin IV, 989-1035, who is also called the "Bearded." The "first" ancestor of Baldwin of Mons was actually Baldwin I, "Bras de Fer," 862-79, who acquired the county of Flanders from the emperor, Charles the Bald. See the Genealogy and the Introduction, II.

[3] Baldwin I, count of Hainaut, 1051-70, after his marriage; he later became Baldwin VI, called "of Mons," count of Flanders, 1067-70.

[4] Robert I, called "the Frisian," count of Flanders, 1071-93.

The father ordered both sons to take wives while he was still living. He arranged for Baldwin to marry Richilda,[5] countess of Mons, by whom he begot two sons, one called Baldwin,[6] the other Arnold.[7] And Robert married Gertrude,[8] countess of Holland, by whom, after the treachery[9] was carried out, he begot the abbess of Messines,[10] and Gertrude, mother of Simon and Gerard, who in fact was duchess of Alsace; Duke Thierry had married her.[11] He also begot Adele, mother of Count Charles, whom he married to the duke of Salerno[12] after she lost her first husband. Her first husband, King Canute of Denmark, betrayed by his own men, and slain in church, now enjoys the crown of martyrdom with the saints since he died for the sake of justice.[13] And while that first father Baldwin the Bearded was alive, he had spread out his sons, one to the left, and one to the right,[14] like two wings

[5] Richilda was a daughter of the count of Hainaut, Renier V, and a widow of his successor, Count Herman. This marriage in 1051, which extended the authority of the counts of Flanders over another imperial fief, was a great political coup.

[6] Baldwin II, count of Hainaut, 1086-98.

[7] Arnold III, "the unfortunate," count of Flanders, 1070-71, dispossessed by his uncle, Robert the Frisian, and killed at the battle of Kassel in 1071.

[8] She was the widow of Florent I, count of Holland, who died in 1061, leaving a minor son whose interests Robert protected after his marriage to Gertrude in 1063, according to Verlinden, *Robert le Frison*, pp. 37-39.

[9] The treachery of Robert the Frisian, in 1071, recounted below in c. 69, is, of course, distinct from that of 1127.

[10] Ogiva. See a letter from Pope Pascal II to the abbess Ogiva, daughter of Robert the Frisian, in 1107, in M. Sdralek, *Wolfenbüttler Fragmente* (Münster, 1891), p. 113.

[11] Pirenne (p. 109, n. 9) corrects Galbert here. Simon was Thierry's son by his first wife; "Gerard" should probably be read "Gertrude," another child of Thierry by his first wife, who became countess of Holland, and mother of the Thierry VI of Holland whose tenuous claim to Flanders she supported in March, 1127 (see c. 34). Galbert fails to mention the fact that Gertrude, the daughter of Robert the Frisian, and her husband, Thierry II, duke of Lorraine, bore Thierry of Alsace, who was to become count of Flanders in 1128.

[12] Roger "Borsa," son of Robert Guiscard, and duke of Apulia and Calabria, 1085-1111; the marriage took place in 1092 according to Romoald, *Annales*, MGH, SS XIX, 412. Their son, William, 1111-27, who succeeded his father, is said to have died of sorrow on hearing the news of the death of Count Charles, according to Walter, c. 2. Both father and son were weak and incompetent rulers, unable to cope with their anarchic barons, though respected for their piety and liberality to the Church; see F. Chalandon, *Histoire de la domination normande en Italie et Sicilie* (2 vols.; Paris, 1907), I, 301 ff., 325.

[13] See Galbert, c. 6, n. 10.

[14] To the left, that is, over Holland; to the right, over Hainaut.

with which he could fly over all their lands; he himself reigned alone in the middle, that is, in Flanders.

[69] *How Robert the Frisian had secured Flanders by treachery in 1071*

And when he had died, full of good days, his elder son Baldwin,[1] count of Mons, together with his wife, Richilda, obtained the county of Flanders. Fearing that he and his sons might suffer from some disturbance or treachery on the part of his brother, Robert, he required Robert to do homage and pledge loyalty to him and his sons. When he had taken counsel with the barons about this, knowing that it would be advantageous both to the fatherland and to himself, he summoned his brother, Robert, "the aquatic count,"[2] and called his court[3] at Bruges, and also all the peers and barons of his whole county. In the presence of them all, he spoke these words:

"I, Baldwin, count of Flanders, wishing to safeguard this fatherland and my sons for the future against any trickery and treachery on the part of my brother, in order that the inhabitants of my land will not suffer any wrongs and my sons will not be disinherited, beg and command my brother Robert, 'count of the waters,' to swear fealty and loyalty to my sons after my death, so that he will use no force against my sons nor deceive them by fraud or stealth after my death, but will swear fealty to my sons, his nephews, in his own person and that of his men, and will keep it as long as he lives to the best of his ability. And I will give him many presents and gifts on this condition."[4]

---

[1] That is, Baldwin VI, count of Flanders, 1067-70.

[2] This title is probably a fanciful literary device of Galbert's. Verlinden (*Robert le Frison*, p. 31, n. 4) rejects Pirenne's suggestion (ed. Galbert, p. 110, n. 4) that it refers to Zeeland (literally "sea-land") which Robert might have received as an appanage from his father. It could just as well apply to "Frisia" from which Robert gained his epithet, and which is a more accurate name than "Holland" for the small region at the mouth of the Meuse which Richilda inherited and Robert strengthened and extended; see Verlinden, pp. 28-29, 95-100.

[3] Probably in 1069 or 1070, according to Verlinden, p. 43. Baldwin VI died in 1070.

[4] Verlinden (pp. 42-46) has weighed the apparently conflicting evidence pre-

Then the oath was sworn in the church of Saint Donatian at Bruges on a great many relics of the saints which Count Baldwin had ordered to be brought out, in the presence of all who at that time were peers and barons in the land, and after the gifts were received, the count departed.[5]

Now when Baldwin, the husband of Richilda, had died in Bruges, his son Arnold, to whom the fatherland belonged,[6] stayed near Kassel and Saint Omer and in those parts after his mother returned to Mons and the proximity of her mother. That youth had not yet received arms but he had attained the strength of knighthood.[7] Now Robert, count of Holland, had heard that the fatherland had been left to his nephews,[8] still of tender years, and that their mother had withdrawn from the region around Bruges; and so he had a favorable moment for treachery, and an opportunity for beginning it.[9] He sent word secretly and with evil intent to the barons and influential men of the region near the sea, that is, in Ijzendijke, Oostburg, Aardenburg, and Bruges,

---

sented by Galbert, Herman of Tournai, and Gislebert of Mons, *La chronique de Gislebert of Mons*, ed. by L. Vanderkindere (Brussels, 1904), concerning this oath, and cleared up the questions posed by Pirenne in his edition of Galbert, p. 110, n. 5. There were two oaths, not one. The first was sworn by Robert to his *father*, Baldwin V, at Oudenaarde between 1063 and 1067, the year of Baldwin's death. It was to the effect that Robert would "do no injury" to his brother, Baldwin, and the latter's heirs on Baldwin's succession to the whole county (Herman, c. 12), and was meant to insure respect for the principle of primogeniture, not yet firmly established. The second oath was sworn at Bruges by Robert to his *brother*, Baldwin VI, in 1069 or 1070 shortly before the latter's death. The persistent suspicion of Robert was to prove justified!

[6] That is, Robert, who apparently returned to his wife's land of Frisia, as he did after the first oath (Herman, c. 12). No territorial appanage was granted to Robert.

[6] As Arnold I he also succeeded his father as count of Hainaut, 1070-71; he was Arnold III of Flanders.

[7] He was about fifteen, according to *Flandria generosa*, c. 15, MGH, SS IX, 321, and hence of age, with no need for a guardian; see Verlinden, *Robert le Frison*, pp. 48-49.

[8] There is no question, however, that the whole inheritance, Flanders and Hainaut, had gone to Arnold; see Verlinden, pp. 46-47. Arnold had, moreover, been recognized as successor by Philip, king of France, and invested with the county of Flanders; see Herman, c. 13, and Monier, *Les Institutions centrales*, p. 31.

[9] The events of 1070-71 have been subject to conflicting interpretations. To Verlinden, Galbert's account is in general more objective and reliable than that of either the strongly Flemish partisans of Robert, represented by *Flandria generosa* (of the later twelfth century), or the devoted adherents of Richilda, particularly Gislebert of Mons (late twelfth century).

and to the maritime Flemings,[10] and he bound them to him by money and promise so that he could secure the countship of the fatherland with their aid and drive out his nephews, who seemed to be young and ineffectual. He had a certain cleric in his household who was a faithful intermediary in this treachery; because he came so often to Bruges and near the boundaries of Flanders, the rumor spread abroad that that cleric was a messenger of treachery. For once, when he was stealthily carrying the orders of his lord to the barons, he had pretended to be blind, following his guide with hands outstretched, tapping with his stick; and so, blind in heart and eyes, he carried out the treachery of death and blindness.

Then, when the count of Holland had won over all the barons of the fatherland,[11] and obtained their pledges of faith and loyalty, he came secretly to Flanders by boat with only a small force, and when all the traitors had been secretly summoned, they agreed on a signal with their accomplices, the burning of a house on a certain night at a place called Kapelle; they were to assemble there at the signal of the fire.[12] And when they had all assembled at this signal, they formed a numerous and powerful band, and they went off, openly in pursuit of the boy Arnold. At this time, ignorant of what had happened, he was staying at Kassel with a few[13] who were also accomplices in the treachery; they were urging their young lord to take up arms against his

---

[10] The susceptibility of these coastal regions to Robert's influence can probably be explained on economic grounds rather than in the traditional terms of an ethnic hostility between its inhabitants and the southern, inland people of Flanders. There must have been grievances against Richilda, perhaps a harsher domanial régime, in this region of the north, neglected by the last counts. But it is true that the maritime Flemings had long had a reputation for being a rude, restless, independent people, hostile to the peace efforts and centralizing policies of the previous counts. See Verlinden, *Robert le Frison,* pp. 50-56, also the Introduction, IV.

[11] Doubtless an exaggeration.

[12] That Walter, c. 12, refers to such "flare signals" in his description of the maritime Flemings is questioned by Van Caenegem, *Geschiedenis van het strafrecht,* p. 235, n. 2. Kapelle is identified by Verbruggen as a place north of the later Sluis; see *Die krijgskunst,* p. 508.

[13] Verlinden, *Robert le Frison,* p. 66, says that the castellan of Kassel, Boniface, was a partisan of Robert and that others in the castle with Arnold were probably the young Baldwin, Richilda (back from Mons), King Philip I of France, and William Osberne.

uncle, the traitor, and promising him that God would grant him victory because he would be opposing him justly. And so the boy Arnold was aroused and rushed to war with only a few knights. His own serving men, who had put on his armor[14] in the very tumult of battle and knew in advance the markings on his arms, unhorsed their young lord, and slew him with their own swords, as if they were strangers rather than servants.

After the betrayal of their lord, all who had fought on his side turned to flight. Some who were struck down expired on the spot; others, mortally wounded, suffered death in a few breaths of life. In fact, many died, many were wounded and many captured.[15] While Count Robert, feeling secure from the enemy, was moving about with his army, a certain Wulfric Rabel who had remained faithful to the boy, whose death he was ignorant of, courageously, with his own following, seized that traitor, Count Robert and threw him into captivity. When the tumult of the day[16] was over, all the peers of the fatherland came together and besieged the castellan Wulfric of Saint Omer on all sides and forced him to give up Count Robert; when he was surrendered, they established him as count of the fatherland.[17] And so Baldwin,[18] who survived his betrayed brother, Arnold, was the ancestor of the line from which comes that youth of Mons,[19] count and vigorous knight, the one who should by right

[14] Verlinden, p. 49 and n. 1, conjectures from this statement that Arnold had been dubbed a knight and received arms between the time of his father's death and the battle of Kassel.

[15] There is no sure evidence of the size of the forces at Kassel. Verlinden, p. 64 ff., believes the troops in conflict were not large, Robert's being smaller, and probably exclusively feudal, though it is possible that some of the northern towns where Robert had partisans (Bruges, Ghent, Ypres) may have furnished him with contingents.

[16] The date has been established with certainty as February 22, 1071; on this day in 1085 Robert founded a church and chapter of twenty canons to commemorate his victory (see *Actes*, no. 6, pp. 16 ff.).

[17] The several accounts of this battle and of Robert's capture and surrender differ considerably, but Verlinden (*Robert le Frison*, pp. 67-70) accepts Galbert's version on the whole, though he thinks it probable that the burghers of Saint Omer played a part in liberating Robert, who may have been exchanged for Richilda.

[18] Baldwin became Baldwin II, count of Hainaut, 1071-98.

[19] Baldwin IV, count of Hainaut, 1120-71; see Galbert, c. 67. According to Gislebert of Mons, c. 32, he was a small child when his father died in 1120; Vanderkindere says he was no more than eleven years, ed. Gislebert, p. 58, n. 1.

obtain Flanders, and who now, having heard of the betrayal of Count Charles, is demanding all of Flanders as his fatherland and inheritance by hereditary right. Therefore he is doing what he can, but his challenge to our new count does not seem effective. In connection with this deed the prophecy concerning past treachery should be noted:[20] "Since God is wont in the severity of his punishment to correct the iniquities of the fathers unto the third and fourth generation."

[70] *How Count Robert crushed the traitors who had once supported him*

And so that Robert[1] who betrayed his nephew is numbered "the first," and his son Robert,[2] who lies in Arras as "the second," in the succession and in the countship. After him, his son Baldwin,[3] who lies at Saint Omer, was the third. And after him, the best count of all the counts,[4] the star and bright luminary of earthly splendor, was the fourth; in his betrayal and martyrdom God brought to an end the punishment of the former treachery, and carried off to the place of the saints the one who had been killed in the cause of justice in the fatherland, in the very place where formerly the oath had been sworn.[5] And so God took care of two things in the second betrayal: He carried out vengeance for the earlier treachery, and He immediately received among the blessed martyrs the one who died for the sake of justice.

But after that Robert who had betrayed his nephew had become established[6] in the countship, he remained suspicious of

---

[20] A version of Exodus 20.5 or Deuteronomy 5.9. It is clear that Galbert, like Herman, c. 13, 36, considers the treacherous murder of Charles, the descendant of Robert the Frisian, as a punishment for the earlier treachery of Robert.

[1] For the principle dates of the lives of the counts of Flanders from 1071 to 1128, see Vercauteren, *Actes,* pp. xv-xix.

[2] Robert II, called "of Jerusalem," count of Flanders, 1087-1111, who participated in the First Crusade.

[3] Baldwin VII, count of Flanders, 1111-19.

[4] That is, Charles, count of Flanders, 1119-27.

[5] In Saint Donatian at Bruges where Robert the Frisian had sworn to respect the rights of his nephews; see c. 69.

[6] He strengthened his position by reaching a reconciliation with Philip I of

those traitors in Flanders who had handed over the county to him, and did not allow them to enter into his counsels at all.[7] When they saw themselves scorned and despised by their count, they decided secretly that they would by some trickery kill the count and take as count Baldwin, brother of the slain Arnold, as it was just to do because he was the more rightful heir of Flanders. And just as before, they came together in a deserted spot to consider how to go about killing their lord. But when they returned, after agreeing on a suitable time for the betrayal, one of the knights who had been involved in the treachery went to the count and kneeling before him accused of abominable treachery the other accomplices who had sworn the count's death. The accused were summoned to combat[8] by the count and convicted; some were beheaded, some condemned to exile, and many proscribed.[9] Finally, in the fourth or third line of descent, God subsequently avenged the earlier treachery in the family of the traitors by means of new dangers and a new kind of fall.[10] (This is hardly worth hearing but should be recorded if only out of wonder.)

[71] *The career of Erembald, ancestor of the provost*

Now it seems desirable to consider a bit more fully the origins of the family of the provost and his nephews. There was once

France and receiving investiture with the county of Flanders in March-April, 1071; see Verlinden, pp. 70-72. This peace was crowned by the marriage of his stepdaughter, Bertha of Holland, to King Philip of France; see Herman, c. 14.

[7] His ruthless and effective rule doubtless alienated his supporters, who had exchanged a weak for a strong suzerain, one who raised the count's power "à la hauteur d'une souveraineté," according to Verlinden, p. 167.

[8] This probably means trial by combat.

[9] Concerning the forms of punishment imposed in this early case of Flemish treachery see Van Caenegem, *Geschiedenis van het strafrecht*, pp. 137-59, *passim*. "Proscription" put the culprit outside the law; it implied death and loss of goods (see Galbert, c. 52). Exile was an entirely different form of punishment (see Galbert, c. 24). Decapitation was one of many forms of the death penalty; there are several examples in Galbert.

[10] This cryptic remark seems to imply that the members of the Erembald clan who betrayed Charles were descendants of the treacherous maritime Flemings. It also indicates that Galbert wrote this chapter after the traitors died by "falling" on May 5.

a castellan in Bruges named Boldran whose wife was called Dedda or Duva. This Boldran had a vassal and knight named Erembald, born in Veurne. Now the Flemings were ordered to take part in a certain expedition,[1] and they went by horse and by ship in defense of the fatherland to the place of danger where the land was attacked. When they were following the course of the Scheldt river in their ships, the castellan, Boldran, and Erembald, his vassal, whom he trusted more than anyone, and many others, who were all wearing their cuirasses and prepared to fight, night fell and they cast anchor in the middle of the stream to await day. Now that Erembald had often committed adultery with the wife of his lord, the castellan. That adulteress, it is said, had promised her adulterer the office of castellan, if by chance her husband should die soon; and therefore the adulterer was always plotting the death of his lord. When the silence of night had fallen, and the castellan had gone to the rim of the ship to urinate, Erembald, running up from behind, precipitated his lord into the depths of the rushing water, far from the ship. This was done, in fact, while the others were asleep, and no one but the adulterer knew what had become of that castellan who had been drowned without heirs.[2]

On Erembald's return he married the adulteress, and bought the office of castellan with the plentiful resources of his lord.[3] By this wife he begot the provost, Bertulf, and Hacket, Wulfric Cnop, Lambert Nappin, the father of Borsiard, and also Robert, castellan after him in the second place.[4] After Robert, his son

[1] This was probably the abortive expedition of 1055 led by Count Baldwin V and Godfrey, rebel duke of Lorraine, against Antwerp, center of the imperial march, according to G. Blancquaert, "L'Expédition flamande contre Anvers en 1055 et les premiers châtelains de Bruges," ASRA, XLVI (1942-43), 170.

[2] Blommaert, *Les Châtelains*, pp. 10-11, believes this story is an invention of Galbert's designed to discredit the family of the provost; but Blancquaert, pp. 168-169, thinks it was probably based on a popular story, which sprang up naturally out of the circumstances following Boldran's death.

[3] Erembald's acquisition of the office was facilitated by Duva's dual position, probably as daughter of the former castellan, Robert, as well as widow of Boldran, according to Blancquaert, p. 171, and Dhondt, "Note sur les châtelains," in *Études ... Rodière*, p. 50. Erembald's payment was probably that of a relief due on succession to the office; see Blancquaert, p. 171.

[4] Robert's name is used as partial evidence in supporting the theory that Duva was daughter of Robert, the former castellan, by both Blancquaert and Dhondt.

Walter[5] succeeded as heir to the office of castellan in the third place. After him, Hacket was castellan, in whose time Count Charles was betrayed. In this fourth degree, therefore, the earlier precipitation of Boldran was punished in the persons of Erembald's successors by this new precipitation which was accomplished from the battlements of the count's house in Bruges. And so, you might say, by the dispensation of God they were punished for the sins of their parents, as it is read in Exodus, where God speaks to Moses in the thirty-fourth chapter of the same Exodus where God gives out the laws for all, saying:[6]

"I, the lord your God, am a jealous God, visiting the iniquities of the fathers upon the sons, even unto the third and fourth generation of those who hate me."

[72] *The count of Mons repels the besiegers at Oudenaarde, ca.April 17, 1127*

Now we should go back to the narration of events[1] at Oudenaarde because the count of Mons, together with the burghers[2] of that place and a force of knights, made an attack on the men of Ghent and after putting them to flight, killed some, wounded others, and captured a great many. The greater number of those who fled were drowned in the very waters which had brought them in ships to prepare for the siege, for the count and his men had got the upper hand in those parts. He had also acquired the castle of Ninove, and had placed in it very strong and ardent supporters of his. On the same day at Bruges a squire slipped from the tower by a rope; he was immediately seized, and

---

All these sons are mentioned by Galbert, c. 55, except Robert, the father of Robert the Young. Lambert Nappin is clearly the same as Lambert of Aardenburg.

[5] Walter appears frequently as witness to charters, from 1110 to 1115 and is named in the text of one charter (see *Actes,* Index and no. 77, p. 175).

[6] Exodus 20.5 is a more exact reference, but a similar statement is found in 34.7 and in Deuteronomy 5.9.

[1] Which was suspended in c. 67.

[2] The act of the burghers of Oudenaarde in supporting the count of Mons marks their emergence as a self-conscious community, according to Dhondt, "Het ontstaan van Oudenaarde," *Handelingen . . . Oudenaarde,* X (1952), 71.

dragged off to prison, and once within he awaited, though unwillingly, the day of his destruction.

[73] *The besieged ask to surrrender, April 18, 1127*

On April 18, Monday, our citizens again implored the king, on
their knees, for the liberation of Robert. The king, indignant
because they were bothering him so often,[1] disregarded them and,
in anger, ordered his sergeants[2] to make haste and undermine the
tower with iron tools. And at ónce they set about demolishing
the lower part of the tower with iron tools. While they were
doing this, mortal fear struck the besieged so that they exerted
themselves immoderately, in a kind of stupor; their food and
drink seemed loathsome and all their senses became sluggish and
weak. And so, enervated by hunger and thirst, although they
actually had enough with which to sustain life, they kept calling
out to those whom they saw moving about in the court of the
castle, awaiting the fall and collapse of the tower which was
already partly cut down, that they were becoming parched from
extreme thirst, and also growing faint from hunger and famine.
By the marvelous dispensation of God it came about that their
wine now smelled bad to those traitors, like a sour and tasteless
drink and draught, their grain and bread tasted putrid, and the
insipid water did them no good, so that they had almost succumbed to hunger and thirst,[3] nauseated by the rotten taste and
foul odor. And therefore, forced by necessity, they asked permission to come out of the tower and go to some other place,
wherever the barons decided they should go. Those who were
undermining the tower had now torn away the stairs,[4] and only
a short time remained until after a little more cutting it would
come down in a tremendous crash and fall.

---

[1] They had made a similar plea on April 15; see Galbert, c. 65.

[2] *Servos* here probably means men of lower rank in the king's following.

[3] Walter, c. 46, says that it was the besieged who lost their power of taste, not
the wine its savor, and gives as proof the example of Robert's recovery of his
taste after surrendering.

[4] The stairs in the small towers?

[74] *Twenty-seven surrender, April 19, 1127*

On April 19, Tuesday, when they realized that the greater part of the tower had been demolished and the danger of collapse was imminent—for at the summit of the tower they felt the reverberation and swaying at each blow of the hammers, and it seemed as if the tower were shaking and quaking—they were consumed with fear, and decided to surrender to the power of the king rather than be buried in the crash and suffocated in the collapse of the tower. Therefore Robert the Young[1] called out that he and his accomplices would surrender to the king, on this condition, however, that Robert himself should not be held in captivity, although the others would be thrust into prison. When the king had consulted the barons about this, he granted the request of the besieged that they should be permitted to come out because it was most expedient to have them surrender voluntarily and without endangering the lives of the besiegers and demolishers of the tower. Then they came out, one by one, up to the number of twenty-seven,[2] in the direction of the provost's house, through a curving window on the stairs of the tower; those who were fatter, however, slid down by ropes from a bigger window of the same tower.[3] Robert the Young was turned over to the king's knights to be guarded in the upper hall of the count's house, and all others were thrown into prison.

The king, however, wanted to seem to do a great favor to our citizens and so he entrusted Robert the Young to them to be guarded in fetters and bonds, on condition that they would shortly hand him over to the king and count to be dealt with according to the judgment of the barons. The citizens considered

---

[1] Robert now seems to be the leader and spokesman since Hacket, Bertulf, and Borsiard have fled. At least two other members of the clan are still in the tower, however; see c. 81.

[2] Concerning numbers see c. 81.

[3] Roland ("La Première église," RBA, XIV, 104) believes that the first window named was a narrow slit in one of the two flanking towers containing the stairs, while the second was a true window in the façade of the west-work or "tower" in the larger sense.

it a great boon even on this condition to receive in custody the young man, still a youth![4]

[75] *The besiegers sack the tower, April 19, 1127*

It should be noted here how God had laid those traitors low, reduced them in respect to family and place. Before this crime the stronger and better ones of the same blood had died; it would take too long to name them. At last there survived only those wretches through whom the dispensation of God was accomplished, the treachery fulfilled, the fatherland desolated, pillage unleashed, the hand of each armed against all. For when they thought they had committed with impunity all they had treacherously done, and no man dared to inflict vengeance, vengeance was left to God alone who at once confined them and struck them with fear so that they did not dare to go out beyond the inhabited area[1] of our place but decided instead to enclose the area[2] and our town by palisade and ditch, as we have told above.[3] On the eighth day[4] after the count's death they were forthwith shut up in the castle by the siege; then when the castle was invaded by our men, they fled to the tower where they were more confined; finally thrown into prison, they were in such close quarters that they could not sit down at the same time unless at least three or four stood up. Darkness, heat, stench, and sweat undid them, and the horror of hopeless life and the shame of uncertain death to come. It would have been a gift of the greatest mercy to them if they had been permitted to die by hanging like thieves and robbers. Therefore, when they were preparing to go out from the tower, one of the young men had

---

[4] *Ephebus* denotes a youth between eighteen and twenty years; Robert's age is not known.

[1] *Vicus* here probably means the inhabited area of the town; it could not mean "village" as it generally does.
[2] *Villa* here, like *vicus*, seems to refer to the populated area. See H. Dubled, "Quelques observations sur le sens du mot villa," *Le Moyen Âge*, LIX (1953), 8-9.
[3] See c. 25.
[4] That is, on March 9; see c. 28.

the thought of leaping out of the upper window of the tower, with drawn sword, and he suddenly aroused himself to this course of action. His guilty conscience had condemned him but he was strong enough in spirit to pursue liberty at the cost of his body. The others held him back in the very act, and he allowed himself to go to prison with them. Many of our citizens wept as they saw the young man's dangerous attempt and the captives' misery because they could not see their lords[5] go captive into prison without tears. Finally those pale wretches came forth, their faces bearing the marks of treachery and discolored and distorted by hunger.

As soon as they had come out, an enormous number of people rushed into the tower[6] and carried off as loot everything they could find there. While our people were running around and making an uproar in the tower, Benkin,[7] the mercenary, slipped down from the tower on a rope and hid where he could until he could flee by night to the island in the sea called Wulpen.[8] They hunted for him with one accord, even in the sewers and dirty places, for they believed he was hiding. Almost all who had taken part in the siege struggled to climb up into the tower in the hope of gain and of getting some of the count's treasure. Then the castellan, Gervaise, posted his armed knights inside to control those making such an uproar and prevent any more from coming up. And he secured the best wine of the traitors, and also the mulled wine which was the count's, the bacon, twenty-two pieces[9] of cheese, legumes, wheat flour, also the best iron pans in which they baked bread, and all the equipment and the best

---

[5] The Erembalds were "lords" of "our citizens" as the family of the castellans.
[6] They must have got into the tower by ladders, since the steps had been destroyed.
[7] See c. 16, where he is called "one of our citizens," and c. 36.
[8] Wulpen is an island off the Flemish coast.
[9] *Pisas* refers to a unit of weight (cf. *pensas*) which was used primarily in relation to cheese and butter. A *pisa* (old French *poise*) was a weight of about 52 kilos according to P. Thomas, "Problèmes au sujet du Gros Brief de Flandre," *Bulletin de la Commission historique du Département du Nord*, XXXV (1938), 267. The Flemish word for *pisa* is *waghe* (literally "weigh"); the *waghe* of Bruges was 120 pounds in terms of "the pound of Bruges," which was not very different from the English pound. See L. Gilliodts-van Severen, *Inventaire des chartes de la ville de Bruges, Glossaire flamand* (Bruges, 1882), p. 764.

vessels they had been using. But no trace of the count's treasure was found there.

[76] *The canons cleanse the church, April 20, 1127*

On April 20, Wednesday, the king went to Aardenburg to see the lay of the land and how that Lambert[1] had fortified himself; for he was besieged there as one guilty of the crime and marked with the stigma of treachery. On this day God renewed the world about us with brightness of sunshine and sweetness[2] of air because He had expelled the traitors and defilers of the church and temple from the sacred place and shut them up in prison. The brothers of the church, gladdened by these gifts of God's grace, set about cleansing the pavement and walls and altars of the church with every kind of ablution, leaving nothing unwashed. They rebuilt the steps which had been destroyed, and when the church seemed as if it were renovated,[3] they provided their place[4] with new vessels and repaired the damages.

On April 21, Thursday, a deer skin was sewn up in which the body of the count was to be placed, and a chest was also constructed in which to place it and close it up.

[77] *The bishop of Noyon-Tournai celebrates the Mass of the Dead for Count Charles, April 22, 1127*

On April 22, Friday, when seven weeks[1] since his first burial had passed, the tomb[2] of the count in the gallery was broken open,

---

[1] A brother of Bertulf whose oppression the citizens of Aardenburg had recently complained of; see c. 55. Unlike his brothers he had not been caught in the castle, it seems.

[2] Thomas here corrects *levitate* to *lenitate*.

[3] This hasty repair work must have been superficial. More fundamental reconstruction took place later in the twelfth century when the church was transformed into a Romanesque structure. See B. Firmin, *De romaansche kerkelijke bouwkunst in West-Vlaanderen*, pp. 36-38.

[4] This may refer to their dormitory and other buildings damaged in the siege.

[1] That is, since Friday, March 4; see c. 23.

[2] This had been constructed on the order of the canons, or of Bertulf; see c. 23.

and his body was reverently removed, with thyme and frankincense and unguents. For the brothers of the church believed that the body was already rotting and that no one could stand the mortal stench, because it had been committed to the tomb from the day of burial in the gallery, on the first Friday, up to the Friday which came afterwards on April 22. Therefore they had arranged in advance that during the removal of the body from the tomb they would burn thyme and frankincense in a fire lighted close by the place where the body lay, so that if any stench arose from the tomb, it would be overcome by the strength of the salubrious odors. But when they removed the stone and smelt nothing bad,[3] they placed the body wrapped in the deerskin on a bier in the middle of the choir.[4] Then the king, together with a great crowd of citizens and all the people, waited in the church until the bishop,[5] together with three abbots,[6] should come in procession from the church of Saint Christopher with all the clergy bearing the relics of Saints Donatian, Basil, and Maximus, to meet the corpse and the king on the castle bridge, and they bore the blessed body back to the same church of Saint Christopher with tears and sighs. And there the bishop with the whole choir of priests celebrated the prayers for the dead and the Mass of all the faithful dead for the salvation of the good count's soul.

On the same day the mercenary, Benkin,[7] was captured; bound to a wheel, which was fixed to a tree, he suffered the loss of his life, a spectacle to all. He had certainly deserved to die wretchedly on that instrument of torture[8] at the Sands.

---

[3] Walter, c. 46, unlike Galbert, calls this a miracle. Herman, c. 35, confirms this story.

[4] That is, the nave, probably.

[5] Simon, bishop of Noyon-Tournai.

[6] Among them were Absalon, abbot of Saint Amand, 1124-46, who described the event to Walter (c. 47), and Herman, recently elected abbot of Tournai, according to his own account (c. 35).

[7] See c. 75.

[8] The wheel served as a kind of rack.

[78] *Saint Donatian is purified and Count Charles entombed there, April 25, 1127*

On April 23, Saturday, the king and barons issued an edict to the effect that the citizens[1] should proceed in arms to Ypres and Staden and prepare for a siege.

On April 24, Sunday, the church of the Holy Savior at Bruges[2] was reconsecrated, for it had been injured by fire and its altars broken.

On April 25, Monday, because the altars of the church of Saint Donatian had not been broken, the bishop celebrated the reconciliation of the church at daybreak. Then the king and people, with the bishop, the abbots, and all the clergy of the place going before, went in procession to the church of Saint Christopher, and when they had brought the body of the blessed count, our lord and father Charles, back to the church of Saint Donatian, they commended it solemnly to God and enclosed it properly within the tomb in the middle of the choir. When the funeral rites had been solemnly completed, the king and bishop invested Roger[3] with the office of provost in the midst of the brothers of the same church. On the same day the king and our castellan, Gervaise,[4] went over towards Staden and Ypres with a big army, together with our citizens.

The same day was the feast of Mark the Evangelist. And it should be recorded that God bestowed three great gifts on the

[1] Of Bruges, presumably. The citizens of Aardenburg had gained the privilege of certain limitations on their military service in the charter of April 5 (see Galbert, c. 55), and those of Saint Omer had secured much more radical restrictions (see charter, c. 4, *Actes*, p. 295). See Ganshof, "Le Droit urbain," RHD, XIX (1951), 410.

[2] Mentioned in c. 61 as the church of the priest, Eggard; it had been destroyed by fire in 1116, according to Firmin, *De romaansche kerkelijke bouwkunst*, p. 57.

[3] Roger, successor to Bertulf as provost and chancellor, is named as witness in a charter of September, 1127, (*Actes*, no. 128, p. 302) and in many charters up to 1156 (Vercauteren, *Actes*, p. lv). The king here asserts the right he claimed earlier to confirm and induct into office the canonically elected provost of Saint Donatian; see c. 55. The bishop probably invested him with his spiritual powers, the king with the temporalities. Herman, c. 35, calls Roger "a young cleric."

[4] Gervaise, as castellan, now leads the forces of the castellany, both knights and citizens, as Wenemar of Ghent had done earlier, c. 30 and 33. But the expedition was ordered by the king, still exercising his sovereign power in Flanders, as Ganshof notes, "Le Roi de France," RHDF, XXVII (1949), 222.

church of Saint Donatian on that day, since He deigned to reconcile that church to himself, permitted the body of the good
count to be buried there, and established Roger as provost in
the same church.

[79] *The siege of Ypres and the capture of William of Ypres,*
April 26, 1127

On April 26, Tuesday, the king and count[1] besieged Ypres with
a big army, and a bitter contest[2] and conflict between knights
took place when that false count William was fighting against
our new count at one of the gates with three hundred knights.[3]
Then those wretched men of Ypres,[4] as they had secretly agreed
with the king in another part of the town, let in the king and
his enormous army. Rushing in, they suddenly created a clamor
and started burning houses, and were plundering when the false
count William came up to attack the looters, not knowing that
the castle had been betrayed, as well as himself and his men.
Then the king and count seized him and took him off captive
to Lille to be guarded.

It was true that many, after the death of Count Charles, had
gône over to him, such as the chaplains and servants and mercenaries and serfs of the usual household of the count, because

----

[1] Count William, coming back from Saint Omer by way of Lille and Therouanne,
joined the king at Ypres, according to Walter, c. 45 and 48.

[2] *Tornatio* here doubtless means encounters between knights like those which
occurred in tourneys.

[3] Suger, c. 30 (ed. by Waquet, p. 248), confirms this number.

[4] Despite the fact that they are both adherents of the "new" count, William Clito,
Galbert and Walter agree in condemning those at Ypres who admitted the king
and his army. Walter, c. 48, calls them "burghers who had often sworn faith to
him" and vassals, and condemns them bitterly for treachery to their lord, William
of Ypres. Galbert indicates the presence of two groups who were supporting him
at Ypres, former members of Charles' household, loyal to the dynasty, and "men
of Veurne," whom Bertulf had ordered to support William immediately after the
murder (see c. 25). Which group is Galbert referring to as the "wretches" who
betrayed William? Ganshof believes he means the adversaries of the "men of
Veurne"; see "Le Roi de France," RHDF, XXVII (1949), 222; he also suggests
that the men of Bruges were very hostile to Ypres at this time, and had gone on
the expedition eager for booty. Suger, c. 30, says nothing about treachery in the
taking of the city.

that false count of Ypres was sprung from the line of the counts. The men of Veurne also fought on his side so that if by chance he should become established in the countship, they could destroy their enemies by his strength and power. But because God smites the minds of the evil, it happened otherwise. For their enemies, hearing that William of Ypres had been captured, made an attack on the possessions and dwellings and households hostile to them, and destroyed by fire and sword all the goods of those they hated. And so not only were those wretches captured but they suffered the loss of their possessions at home. Thus God pursued both on the field of battle and at home those traitors who had conspired with their count of Ypres for the death of the lord and advocate of the land. And so our count[5] obtained everything that William of Ypres had possessed, and he also captured some knights and drove many from the land.[6] And so it came out victoriously for our side that day, and they returned with rejoicing and an enormous amount of loot.

[80] *The death of Borsiard; the sack of Oudenaarde, May 1, 1127*

On May 1,[1] Sunday, we heard that Borsiard had been seized at Lille[2] and, bound to a wheel fixed to a tree, had survived that day and the following night, and then perished in this shameful manner of death. Indeed he deserved to die many times over, if one could die more than once, because on account of his crime so many after him were punished, proscribed, cast down, hanged,

---

[5] Galbert has now apparently accepted William Clito as "our count" and omits "new."

[6] William was captured by Daniel of Dendermonde as he fled, was taken by the king and count to the abbey of Messines, and then turned over to the castellan of Lille to be guarded, according to Walter, c. 49.

[1] Up to the last entry, that for April 26, Galbert has made an entry for almost every day. At this point the victory of William Clito seems assured and the entries become less frequent for May.

[2] See c. 61 and notes. Walter, c. 42, stresses his penitence which moved the bystanders to pity. He begged to have his right hand cut off or to be allowed to cut it off himself because it had performed the act of murder.

and beheaded! At the news of his death all the faithful offered thanks to God who had deigned to exterminate such a murderer from his Church. And it was a happy dispensation, in view of the past evils of our times, that God restored the boon of peace and order to our land in the amenity of the month of May, as soon as Borsiard had been hanged and his accomplices taken captive.[3]

Then the king, changing his course,[4] went by way of Ghent to Oudenaarde where the count of Mons had attacked our land. But our count had preceded the king and laid violent hands on the town, burning it as far as the stone tower;[5] many who had taken refuge in the church of that place were burned to death at that time, as many as three hundred, it is said.[6]

[81] The "precipitation" of those left in the castle, May 5, 1127

On May 4, Wednesday, the king returned to Bruges without the count.

On May 5, Thursday, about noon, the count came back to us.[1] On his return he was received for the first time by the brothers of the church of Saint Donatian in procession; after offering prayers and gifts to God at the altar, according to the custom of his predecessors, the count by his own right went up into the house of Count Charles and dined there. A commotion was

[3] After the capture of Ypres, the king and count had taken over Aire, Kassel, and the rest of Flanders which William had subjugated; see Walter, c. 49.

[4] That is, turning north again. Perhaps he went through Ghent in an effort to persuade the citizens of Ghent to send their forces back to Oudenaarde where they had been put to flight recently (c. 72), as Ganshof suggests, "Le Roi de France," RHDF, XXVII (1949), 222, n. 6.

[5] The "town" (*suburbium*) was Oudenaarde-Saint Walburgis. See Dhondt, "Het ontstaan van Oudenaarde," *Handelingen ... Oudenaarde*, X (1952), 71, n. 34. The "tower" probably means the castle, of which the tower was the central feature (Dhondt, p. 58).

[6] This dreadful act is attributed to the count of Mons by Herman, c. 35, who says about one hundred of both sexes were burnt to ashes in the church of Saint Walburgis.

[1] The count had apparently been in the south of Flanders since his departure about April 12; the last certain date is his presence in Saint Omer about April 16 (see c. 66).

going on as a great crowd was waiting outside and inside the castle to see what would happen to Robert and the captives. Then the king, leaving his quarters, came over to the count. Because his house was so full of people and servants and knights, the count went down into the open space and court of the castle, and everybody who had been in the hall followed him out. When he saw that the house was vacated, as he had planned, he had the doors of his house bolted and went up again, taking with him only the barons. Then they decided exactly how those traitors should be hurled from the tower of the house.[2]

When this had been determined, the king and count sent spearsmen to the prison who were craftily to call out first of all Wulfric Cnop,[3] brother of the provost, Bertulf; and the messengers deceived the captives, saying that the king was going to deal mercifully with them. With that hope of mercy, therefore, they came out of prison without delay. But not all were permitted to come out at the same time, for first they led out Wulfric. After leading the knight by inner passages of the house up to the highest battlements of the tower, with his hands bound behind his back, the spearsmen hurled him down as he was gazing down at the steep descent which meant his death. And that wretch, clad only in shirt and breeches, fell to earth broken and ruined in his whole body, with little life left in him. Breathing his last, he died at once, a spectacle and eternal disgrace to his family or rather to the whole land of Flanders, mourned by no one. Next they led Walter, the knight,[4] son of Lambert of Aardenburg, to the edge of the precipice, his hands bound in front and not behind, planning to push him over at that very moment. But in the name of God he begged the king's knights who were standing

---

[2] The summit of the house (*camera*) was 100 aunes in height, according to the later *Passio Karoli auctore anonymo*, c. 9, MGH, SS XII, 622. (Since the aune of Bruges is 70 cm., the tower was 70 meters according to this estimate, which seems excessively high.) Herman, c. 35, seems to believe, erroneously, that the captured traitors were thrown from the tower of the *church*.

[3] First mentioned in c. 27 as one of the conspirators. As the sole surviving member among the captured of Bertulf's generation, he has the honor of going first.

[4] Rarely mentioned; see c. 20 and 42. It is ironic that the members of the family who seem to have been least active in the crime are the ones who suffer "precipitation."

by to grant him time for praying to God, and, taking pity on him, they allowed him to pray. When he had finished, the young man, so handsome in appearance, was hurled down, and falling to earth, he met the peril of death and expired at once.

A knight named Eric was also brought out and thrown down; he fell on the wooden stairs and tore away a step of the stairs which was fastened with five nails. Marvelous to tell, he crossed himself with the sign of the Holy Cross while sitting on the ground although he had been cast down from such a height. When some women wished to care for him, one of the knights threw a big stone among them from the count's house and so prevented them from approaching him. He could not have lived much longer in his shattered condition, anyway, for what he lived after the fall was not so much life as the misery of dying. And—to avoid naming them in order—twenty-eight,[5] all those left, were thrown down in the same way, one by one. Some of them had indeed hoped to escape, because they were not guilty of the treachery,[6] but because fate had caught them,[7] or rather because Divine vengeance coerced them, they were cast down along with those who were guilty of the treachery.[8]

[5] In c. 74, Galbert says twenty-seven were left in the tower but one more, a squire, making twenty-eight, had just been seized as he was escaping, in c. 72. Walter, c. 50, speaks of Wulfric Cnop and "about twenty-eight others." Herman, c. 35, says "thirty."

[6] Walter, c. 50, agrees that all were not equally guilty, as Galbert, c. 36, has already indicated. Some who were clearly innocent had been allowed by the barons to come out on March 17; see c. 37.

[7] Virgil, *Aeneid*, V.709.

[8] The legal basis of this punishment, carried out without previous trial, was the decision reached in the king's court at Arras, and announced to the people of Bruges on March 30 (c. 52), according to which the traitors were condemned to death in advance and their confiscated goods assigned to the barons of the siege. The barons had bound the king by oath not to pardon anyone without their consent and he had remained faithful to his promise (c. 65), despite strong popular pressure to pardon Robert. The peculiar form of punishment may have been Norman in origin; see the Introduction, p. 47 n. 55. A realistic representation of a man falling, almost contemporary with this event, is to be found on one of the capitals of the nave of the cathedral of Tournai (from *ca.*1140); see Moreau, *Histoire de l'Église*, Vol. III, Plate XLVI, opposite p. 654.

[82] *The king departs, taking Robert, May 6, 1127*

On May 6, Friday, the feast of Saint John, when he was put in a jar,[1] the king, setting out for home,[2] left Bruges and took Robert the Young captive with him. On the departure of this youth, our burghers followed him with tears in their eyes and deep mourning because they had loved him very much; for it was not on account of any infamy of his that the men of our place dared to follow him! Seeing the mourning and compassion of the citizens, he spoke to them: "Oh my friends, though you cannot do anything to save my life, nevertheless, pray God that He will deign to have mercy on my soul." Not far from the castle the king ordered the knight's feet to be tied together below the belly of the horse he had mounted as a captive. After the count had furnished escort to the king, he returned to us in the castle.

[83] *The count recovers the gold and silver vessels, May 7, 1127*

On May 7, Saturday, the dean, Helias, handed over to the new count the silver vessel and the golden goblet, with the golden cover,[1] belonging to Count Charles which the provost, Bertulf, had entrusted to the dean when he took flight. Robert the Young had revealed the whereabouts of this treasure to the count before he left Bruges, because, they say, the king had him whipped until he told what he knew about where the count's treasure was hidden. Many people marveled at the artlessness of the dean Helias, how he had feigned the appearance of sanctity and sim-

---

[1] According to apocryphal tradition, on May 6 Saint John was cast into a cauldron of boiling oil but was unharmed by it. See *The Apocryphal New Testament*, trans. by M. R. James (Oxford, 1924), p. 229.

[2] The king now left Flanders after an apparently successful experiment in extending his direct authority over the internal affairs of one of his great fiefs, a bold policy which he had continued even after general acceptance of his candidate, William Clito, as count. He had, however, suffered some limitations of his own rights in yielding at various times to the demands of barons, clerics, and burghers that he swear oaths to guarantee certain privileges and rights which he had conceded as the price of their support; see Ganshof, "Le Roi de France," RHDF, XXVII (1949), 220-21.

[1] See c. 61.

plicity, for although he had lived heretofore as if he were
rigorous in sanctity, he had certainly strayed from the path in
receiving this loot, since it is forbidden by the authority of God:[2]
"You shall not touch the unclean." For he gave that treasure
up unwillingly to the count, showing in this way how much he
had loved the loot. He also said that the provost Bertulf had
given those vessels to Saint Donatian for the salvation of his
soul,[3] believing he could in this way plead his innocence. In this
matter we all knew perfectly well that the provost had received
the count's vessels for his own use in the division of the treasure,
and when he was unable to carry them with him in flight, he
left that wretched loot to his dean.

[84] *The penitence of the traitors*

It is well to add something here about the penitence of Borsiard
and of those who had betrayed the count with him, that is, Isaac
and the others. They say that Borsiard admitted his sin, and was
so full of grief and penitence that he begged all the spectators
of his punishment to cut off the hands with which he had killed
his lord, Charles. And he implored them all to intercede immediately with God and beseech God for the salvation of his soul,
since he had in no way merited salvation in this life, and to the
best of his ability he called on the omnipotent God to be pro-
pitious to him.[1] What is more, as those who were thrown down
were leaning forward on the battlements and looking down,
they signed themselves with the sign of the Holy Cross, and in
the very act of falling called out, invoking the name of Jesus
Christ. But because those traitors were excommunicated immediately after the crime,[2] in accordance with strict justice they were

2 Leviticus 5.2.
3 Galbert seems to believe this interpretation in c. 61.

1 Galbert here adds to his earlier account in c. 80, and confirms Walter's account,
c. 42. Borsiard is actually calling for a recognized punishment, the most common
form of mutilation, consisting of removing the right hand, which was imposed
for various offenses, including injury to the person of the count; see Van Caenegem, *Geschiedenis van het strafrecht*, pp. 192-93.
2 By Simon, bishop of Noyon-Tournai, on March 2 or 3; see c. 21.

not absolved by the bishop before or after their destruction, and therefore they lie buried outside the cemetery, at the crossroads and in the country.

Now Isaac, when he was hiding among the monks in monastic dress and saw the mob coming at him, spoke to the abbot:[3]

"My lord, if my mind were set on fighting, I would not allow myself to be taken without killing a lot of people, but because I confess I am guilty of the treachery, I embrace all misfortunes and earthly death itself so that at this time I may be punished for having sinned greatly against my lord."

Then the son of the advocate of Therouanne[4] came up and seized Isaac, throwing him in chains until that false count of Ypres should come and pass judgment on him. Isaac also was awaiting William, believing he could escape through him, because William had been accessory to the crime.[5] But when that count came, concealing the fact that his own conscience was guilty, he ordered Isaac to be hanged because he had betrayed Count Charles. Along the way to Aire, as he was being dragged to the hanging, Isaac openly confessed that he had betrayed his lord and begged the tumultuous mob to overwhelm him with mud and stones and sticks, believing he could never be punished enough in this life for having committed such a great crime. Therefore he did honor to the blows and stones and to all his tormentors, and thanked them because they deigned to destroy such a grievous sinner. Finally when he had reached the place of the hanging, he saluted the tree trunk, and kissed the noose and the tree, and tied the noose around his own neck, saying:

"In the name of the Lord, I embrace my punishment of death, and I beg you all to pray God with me that whatever I, wretch that I am, committed against my lord, may be punished in me by the harshness of this death."

And so drawn up he died shamefully, as he deserved.

[3] Of Saint John of Therouanne, according to Walter, c. 35, who gives a detailed account of Isaac's seizure and death, and mentions his final confession. See Galbert, c. 48.

[4] Arnulf, according to Walter, c. 35.

[5] See Galbert, c. 20, 25, 57.

As for Bertulf,[6] the provost, he had received many signs of his death from God. For once at Bruges when the sacristan of the church was lying sick in his room and the provost came in to visit him, immediately the beams broke which supported the roof right over his head, so that he thought he barely escaped from the room. At another time the great beam in his house at Bruges fell down, not through the agency of man or wind, exactly on top of the chair and the seats next to it where the provost was accustomed to sit in his power and arrogance—he himself was at Veurne at the time—and everything affected by the crash was smashed to bits. At another time, when the provost was passing through Ypres near the gallows in the market, where he was afterwards hanged, he said to his knights: "Almighty God, what did I dream last night? For I saw in a dream that I was fixed to that very gallows!" And he joked about this vision and made nothing of it. We have heard of his punishment but nothing about his penitence.[7] Robert the Young, taken as far as Kassel,[8] was beheaded by order of the king, but he confessed his sins and pardoned the executioner who was about to hand him over to death.

[85] *Disclosures concerning the lost treasure, May 21, 1127*

On May 21, the eve of Pentecost, Eustace,[1] recently installed as castellan at Veurne by the new count of Flanders, brought captive to Bruges Alger,[2] the former chamberlain of the provost Bertulf. He led him into the presence of the whole court of the count so that the captive could reveal to the count who among the canons and laity had obtained from the provost Bertulf, or from his nephews, any treasure or loot from the property of Count Charles. Alger then accused the dean, Helias, of having

---

[6] See Galbert's earlier account in c. 57.
[7] According to Walter, c. 38, Bertulf did, however, confess and show penitence.
[8] A safe distance from his supporters in Bruges!

[1] Galbert is the only source which mentions him, according to Vercauteren, "Étude sur les châtelains," in *Études ... Pirenne*, p. 445.
[2] See c. 35; he had escaped dressed as a cleric.

received three hundred marks;[3] Littera,[4] a canon, two hundred marks; Robert, sacristan of the church, mattresses, garments, and silver; Master Ralph,[5] six silver cups; Robert, son of Lidgard,[6] one hundred marks of silver. Alger had made up lies of this kind in order to win pardon for his escape. It seemed likely to many, however—seeing that the dean, Helias, had already, on the accusation of Robert the Young, handed over to the count the silver vessel of the weight of twenty-one marks and the golden goblet with the golden cover of the weight of seven gold marks—that the dean as well as certain canons of his were still in possession of a lot of silver, as it later became clear. Robert,[7] the sacristan of the church, who came and went freely among the traitors throughout the whole siege, received a great deal of money from them on condition that, if the traitors escaped, that priest and sacristan would give back to them what he had received in custody. Then after those wretches were condemned, the sacristan tried craftily to conceal the money. He pretended that he was about to go to Jerusalem, and he loaded three strong palfreys and a half, and went out of our castle very early in the morning; and so he carried off loot from the property of Count Charles, supposedly to be offered to Christ in Jerusalem. By this act of his the suspicion of everyone was thrown back onto those canons. On the same day Littera gave up to the count three marks of silver which he had held out from the provost's silver.[8]

[3] See c. 83; he had also received the gold and silver cups from Bertulf.

[4] A "Littera" is named as witness without title among the clergy of Saint Donatian in a charter of 1113; see *Actes*, no. 61, p. 147.

[5] Probably a canon and master of the school attached to the chapter. The school (*scholae*) is mentioned in c. 17 and 42, and students (*scholares*) in c. 12. A canon Ralph is named in a charter of 1110, *Actes*, no. 42, p. 118. According to J. M. de Smet ("Bij de latijnsche gedichten," *Miscellanea . . . de Meyer*, I, 434-35), Ralph may have been the author of a Latin epitaph on Charles, probably written at the order of the chapter, and inscribed on the tomb in Saint Donatian where Charles was buried on April 25; it is given by Pirenne (ed. Galbert, p. 190), beginning "Hic pupillorum pater."

[6] In the Inquest (MGH, SS XXV, 442), "Rolins," son of "Liegarde," is named as one who aided the traitors.

[7] A Robert is mentioned among the clergy of Saint Donatian in a charter of 1127, *Actes*, no. 128, p. 302.

[8] The size of the count's treasure must have been enormous, even if all these tales were not true. William of Ypres had received five hundred pounds (c. 49), and many are named in the Inquest as having shared in it.

On May 22,[9] the holy Sunday of Pentecost, the count and the castellan Gervaise and Walter of Vladslo and the knights of Flanders who were present swore that they would preserve the peace[10] to the best of their ability throughout the whole land of Flanders.

[86] *William of Ypres is brought to Bruges, after September 10, 1127*

After the feast of the nativity of the Virgin Mary, which falls on September 10, that is on Saturday, our count had William of Ypres, whom he had captured in the attack on Ypres,[1] brought to him at Bruges, and he imprisoned him in the upper room of the castle at Bruges with his brother, Theobald Sorel.[2] After they had remained for six days as fellow captives, Theobald was entrusted to a certain knight, Everard of Ghent,[3] to be guarded. Soon William of Ypres was forbidden to look out the windows[4] but he could move around to some extent within the house. Watches and guards were placed with him to keep a careful eye on him.

[87] *The count orders a sworn inquest, September 16, 1127*

On September 16, Friday, on the eve of Saint Lambert, the count ordered the best and most faithful men from among the citizens of Bruges and from all the vicinities around us[1] and also the

---

[9] The interval between these entries of May 21 and 22 and the preceding one, of May 7, is the longest since Galbert began. It marks the tapering off of his day-by-day account, which he was later to round out. See the Introduction, p. 64.

[10] That is, they reaffirm the count's "peace" which had collapsed during the crisis.

[1] See c. 79.

[2] Nothing is known about him. The Bollandists suggest that he was a uterine brother of William; see AASS, March 1, p. 211, note b.

[3] He is named as witness to a charter of 1120; see *Actes*, no. 97, p. 223.

[4] He may have had partisans at Bruges.

[1] Perhaps the *échevins* of the castellany of Bruges; see c. 51.

castellan, Gervaise, to swear that they would declare by true assertion, for the honor of the land, the names of those

who had killed Count Charles and

who had slain those who were killed along with the count and

who had seized as booty the property of the count and of those killed with him, and of his vassals and members of his household and

who had lent aid to those traitors after the death of the lord of the whole fatherland and

who had stood by those most impious men before or after the siege and

who had led out those traitors and their accomplices, without the permission of the barons who were besieging the castle and the very same men inside, and as reward had secretly received from them money and treasure belonging to Count Charles and

who had afterwards given them refuge and lent them aid

—all of whom the king and count with the common consent of the barons of the land had condemned and proscribed.[2] Then after taking the oath[3] they assembled in the count's house and they accused one hundred and twenty-five among us[4] and thirty-seven at Aardenburg together with Lambert,[5] whom they had marked with the stigma of treachery.

[2] At Arras the traitors proper had been condemned and proscribed; see c. 52. In c. 59 the "law of the siege" had been partly formulated.

[3] They now constitute a jury of accusation and proceed to a sworn inquest; this is apparently ,the earliest surviving example of the special Flemish process known as *durginga* or *franca veritas*, derived from the Carolingian *inquisitio*. See the full discussion of Van Caenegem, *Geschiedenis van het strafprocesrecht*, pp. 35-50. The complete findings of the jury, given in the so-called Chronicle of Baldwin of Avesnes, in French translation (MGH, SS XXV, 441-43), may have been used by Galbert as the basis for his brief summary. The longer account names 115 living persons in categories of guilt similar to those used by Galbert, and says that it was the "little people" who forced the count and barons to modify their original judgment that all the guilty should be treated alike, sentenced to exile and loss of goods. It states erroneously (p. 441) that the Inquest was held at Ypres, and before the king and count. Galbert's total is greater, 162 (125 plus 37).

[4] This seems to imply "at Bruges."

[5] Lambert, brother of Bertulf, is accused in the Inquest (p. 441) of participating in the murder of the castellan of Bourbourg; see Galbert c. 16, n. 1.

[88]   *Count William alienates the burghers of Bruges, September 17, 1127*

On September 17, Saturday, the day of Saint Lambert, the count demanded the toll from our burghers just as he was setting out for Ypres. The count was unfriendly towards them because his vassals had been enfeoffed with the revenues of the toll from the time of his predecessors, the counts. His vassals were plaguing the count because he had remitted to the people of Bruges the toll with which they had formerly been enfeoffed;[1] they asserted that the count had no right to remit it without the consent of his vassals, nor had the citizens the right to demand such a concession from the count.[2] This was the source of ill will between the citizens and the count and between the count and his vassals.

Now after the accusation[3] the count and his court were trying to act in accordance with the law of the siege[4] which the barons had decreed. The law and decree was to this effect: "Whosoever shall lead out any of the besieged against the will of the barons of the siege shall be condemned to the same punishment as that to be inflicted on the one led out." And since many of the besieged had been led out secretly for a price, the relatives of those who had been killed while besieging the traitors were now imploring the count, on their knees before him, to hand over to them, to be killed or punished, the ones who had secretly and slyly and treacherously led out the besieged, or to throw those "misleaders" out of the land. And so the count, bound by the rule, ordered the accused to come before him, intending to deal

---

[1] In the charter of April 6; see c. 55 and notes.

[2] The knights were right; the count's concession had constituted an "abridgement" of their fiefs, contrary to feudal law. Ganshof believes this illustrates the *droit revolutionnaire* of some of the provisions of the charters of 1127, such as the concession of minting money to the people of Saint Omer; see "Le Droit urbain," RHD, XIX (1951), 407, n. 55, and 413-14. William's military needs are now forcing him to placate his vassals and to rescind his earlier concession to the burghers of Bruges which had proved to be inexpedient. It was not renewed by his successor, Thierry.

[3] That is, the charges brought by the jury of accusation.

[4] See c. 59 for the first enunciation of the law of the siege, prohibiting access to the traitors and providing as punishment seizure and judgment by the barons.

with them according to the law of the siege. But they answered that they had not been accused lawfully but out of envy and hatred rather than on account of the inquest. They urgently begged the count to deal with them according to the judgment of the magistrates of the land[5] both with reference to the charge of treachery and with respect to any suspicion of it. And, in fact, many of the accused were reconciled to the count, but the nephews, sons, and relatives of those who had been killed in the siege were still after them because they had led out traitors who had betrayed Charles, the lord of the land and likewise their father. Such were the sons of the castellan of Bourbourg who lost no time in challenging, in the very presence of the new count, Everard of Ghent,[6] who for the sake of money had led out the ones among the besieged who had killed their father and brothers[7] along with the count of the fatherland. On hearing this, the greater number of the accused, whom their consciences were devouring, withdrew from the land. Then the count took counsel and, having summoned his barons, decreed that he would proscribe those among the accused who had done homage to Count Charles and who had also lent aid to the traitors with whom they were besieged, but he would allow some of the others to do satisfaction and would receive others back into his favor without any judgment.[8]

---

[5] It is likely that "magistrates" (*scabini*) here refers to both the newly recognized *échevins* of the town and the older *échevins* of the castellany because both inhabitants of town and country were certainly included. See A.-M. Feytmans, "Scabini terrae," RB, X (1931), 172. The infringement of the rights of the new urban *échevinage* by the castellan had already created trouble; see c. 59.

[6] Mentioned in c. 86 as custodian of Theobald, brother of William of Ypres. This charge is substantiated by the Inquest (MGH, SS XXV, 441-42) which names the murderers and what Everard got from them, a horse and halbert.

[7] See c. 16.

[8] The Inquest first gives specific charges against each individual named, arranging the accused roughly in the order given by Galbert in c. 87 and carefully distinguishing between vassals and non-vassals of the count; these were all to be condemned to exile and confiscation of goods. It next deals en masse with the hangers-on of those named, who had aided the accused but were not guilty of murder or pillage; these the count was to allow to remain in the land and keep their property although they were subjected to certain restrictions. Finally it states that the wife of Walter of Lissewege (daughter of Hacket) and the wife of Christian of Gistel (sister of Borsiard) were not to be disinherited, according to the king's will. (See Galbert, c. 54 and c. 117.)

[89] *God's punishment of Walter of Vladslo*

It came about by the severe and horrible judgment of God that Walter of Vladslo, one of the peers of the land, was hurled from his horse by its motion while he was on a certain knightly expedition and died after languishing for a few days in a shattered condition. It was certainly true that he had been accessory to the betrayal of his lord,[1] the father of the whole land of Flanders. In order to stand in with the traitors in the most binding way possible he had even married off to one of Bertulf's nieces a certain adopted boy, actually the son of a cobbler whom his wife had passed off as his own. For he had really believed that he was the father of the boy whom the "mother" pretended falsely to have borne as his wife. But the child whom she had borne had died at once at birth. Therefore she substituted the cobbler's son, who had been born about the same time, and secretly sent the dead child, whom she had borne, to the wife of the cobbler, giving her money so that she would claim to have given birth to the dead child and conceal what she had done from her husband. And when that stolen and "adopted" son had grown up, and everyone actually believed him to be Walter's son, the provost went and gave in marriage his niece, the daughter of the son of his brother, to that false son so that they would stand together firmly under all circumstances by reason of that marriage, and would become bolder, stronger, and more powerful.[2]

Now, after the death of Walter, his wife announced publicly that the boy was an adopted son and not his real son, whom Walter had put away in the home of a certain burgher in pledge for three hundred pounds. And so God's stratagem foiled the stratagem of the provost, who, when he wanted to exalt his family proudly and arrogantly by that marriage, joined it to the

---

[1] His complicity in the escape of the traitors is proved by Galbert's own revelations concerning Bertulf's escape (c. 42, c. 46) and by the Inquest (p. 441) which charges him with harboring one of the count's murderers and sharing in the treasure, but he had also played a leading role in the siege (c. 31, c. 45) and had served as the king's spokesman (c. 52). There is no evidence of his complicity, or that of any of the barons, in the murder itself.

[2] That is, the provost and Walter. This marriage seems to prove that there was no suspicion of the servile status of the Erembald clan on Walter's part.

son of a cobbler, deceived by the stratagem of God! It was true that no one dared to raise a hand against Walter although he was accessory to the treachery, for he was a peer of the land, and next after the count.³ But God, to whom his punishment was left, removed him by a lingering death from the sight of the faithful.

[90] *William of Ypres is taken to Lille, October 8, 1127*

On October 8, Saturday before the feast of Saint Richard, by the order of the count, William of Ypres was taken to Lille and entrusted to the castellan of that castle.¹ He was afraid that our citizens and also some of those exiled by proscription would try by some trick to release William from his captivity at Bruges and would storm the castle.²

It should be noted that after Count Charles was killed, Borsiard and his accomplices in the crime, on the night when Count Charles was first buried, followed the custom of pagans and sorcerers.³ Taking a vessel full of beer, and bread, they sat around the tomb and placed that drink and bread on the top of the tomb as if it were a table, eating and drinking over the body of the dead count in the belief that no one could in any way avenge him.⁴

[91] *God's punishment of Baldwin of Aalst, October 24, 1127*

On October 24, the second day before the feast of Saint Amand, Baldwin of Aalst died. He, also a peer of the peers¹ of Flanders,

---

³ Galbert uses this expression (*aliter a comite*) only of Walter. It seems to indicate high rank and position rather than intimacy with the count. Walter alone among those called "peers" by Galbert is an aulic official, a butler; he was also, as lord of Eine near Oudenaarde, one of the great barons of the land. See Galbert, c. 21, note 12. It is clear that even the new count does not dare bring him to justice.

¹ Roger II; see Galbert, c. 52, note 13.
² See c. 86.
³ Galbert mentions sorcery again in c. 110, c. 112.
⁴ According to J. M. Kervyn de Lettenhove, *Histoire de Flandre* (4 vols.; Brussels, 1847), I, 385-86, the Erembalds were following a pagan Saxon custom to appease the souls of the dead, called the *dadsisa*, condemned by the Church in 743 at the Council of Leptines. The question of the Saxon origins of the people of maritime Flanders, from which the Erembalds came, has been much debated.

¹ Whether this designation implies a special rank is debatable. It has been

was branded with the stigma of the betrayal of his lord, Charles.[2] Not long afterwards, in the full strength of life, he died from a trivial cause, that is, while he was blowing a horn. While the air was inflating his arteries within and all the strength of his head was straining in order to blow, suddenly the marrow of the brain, shaken loose from its natural place, burst out through a wound suffered long before in the forehead. When the inflation caused by the air and his own breath had broken this open, the inner parts which had lain in the brain boiled up so that they choked the passages of the nostrils, the eyes, and also the throat, and so, slain by the sword of God, he suffered mortal injuries. Finally, when he was breathing his last, he assumed the monastic habit and so departed from this world like a Christian knight.

And therefore after these two barons[3] of the land had died, not far apart in time or space, they were remembered and discussed by the inhabitants of the land; they talked about the sudden death of those whom God had deprived of life after the death of lord Charles by such a swift sentence and had ordained that they should die from such trivial causes. They had, in fact, acted contrary to Christian conduct in their dealings with the provost and the others whom they had led out from captivity. For after they had taken money from the provost[4] and his kin, whom they had helped to escape contrary to the decrees of the king and barons, they led them astray and deserted them, destitute and solitary in the country, until they were seized as they wandered and roamed about in the fields and villages,[5] and destroyed by the most wretched kind of death.

---

suggested that it merely designates Baldwin as equal to the peers in French Flanders since he was lord of the county of Aalst in imperial Flanders; see C. Piot, "Les Beers de Flandre," ASEB, XXVIII (1876-77), 121-22.

[2] Baldwin's complicity may have been first revealed to Galbert by the Inquest (MGH, SS XXV, 442) which accuses him of having aided Hacket who escaped on April 1, according to Galbert, c. 54. Up to this point Galbert has presented him as a loyal baron of the siege (c. 30, c. 52), to whom the new count felt greatly indebted (c. 56). Herman, c. 31, calls him the leader of the avengers, and Walter, c. 36, gives a similar impression. It is clear that the new count did not dare proscribe such a powerful figure.

[3] That is, Walter and Baldwin.

[4] It was Walter who had helped Bertulf escape, according to Galbert, c. 42, 46.

[5] See c. 46 concerning Bertulf's wanderings, c. 57 concerning his death.

[92] *Didier, brother of Isaac, dies, December 17, 1127*

On December 17, Saturday, the end of the third week in Advent, in the period of the four seasons of the same year,[1] Didier, brother of the traitor Isaac, died. As an accessory to the treachery,[2] he did not deserve to enjoy the felicity of life any longer. Now from the time of the siege he had never dared to show himself in the count's court except secretly, for there were many in our county who would have challenged him to combat and reviled him as someone guilty of treachery if he had appeared openly at court. The new count, moreover, had forbidden Didier, if by chance he should come to court, to serve him wine,[3] for he had been one of the servers of wine at the court.[4]

[93] *The citizens of Lille rebel, August 1, 1127*

On last August 1,[1] and so on the feast of Saint Peter in August,[2] at the time of the fair in Lille,[3] when the count wished to seize

[1] That is, in the fourth of the four periods or seasons of special fasting and prayer prescribed at the Council of Piacenza, 1095; in this case the "Ember Days" were the Wednesday, Friday, and Saturday following Saint Lucia's day, December 13.

[2] Perhaps Galbert was convinced of Didier's guilt by the charge brought against him by Robert the Young in c. 44. (In c. 29 he declared him innocent.) He is not named in the Inquest, however, and is treated as loyal by Walter, c. 34, c. 36.

[3] Was he a butler? See c. 10 concerning the ceremonial serving of wine at court.

[4] The fate of two conspirators (mentioned in c. 11) who had not been caught in the siege is related by Walter, c. 51, 52. Ingran of Esen, nephew of the castellan of Dixmude, fled the land and never returned. William of Wervik fled with part of the treasure and after various adventures entered a monastery in Hainaut, but he soon returned to the world and to arms!

[1] It is clear from what follows that Galbert resumed his narrative in February, 1128, after hopefully rounding out his account of the events from March 2 to May 22, 1127, by adding chapters 1-14, 68-71, and 86-92. (See the Introduction, VI). Revolts against the new count in Saint Omer and Ghent in February, 1128, must have led him to take up his pen, and he logically added as a beginning the revolt in Lille of August, 1127. *Retro* indicates that he refers to August of "last year," that is, 1127. The narrative again takes on the journalistic character of recording events day by day.

[2] The feast of Saint Peter's Chains (*in vinculis*), one of several feast days of the Apostle, and originally the dedication feast of the church of the Apostle, erected on the Esquiline Hill in the fourth century, where his chains were preserved.

[3] Galbert is the first to mention the fair at Lille, as well as that at Ypres (c. 16). Like Ypres, the castle, town, and fair of Lille first appear early in the second half of the eleventh century, probably as a result of a conscious policy on the part of

a certain serf of his in the market and had ordered him to be seized, the citizens of Lille rushed to arms and chased the count and his men outside the town.[4] They beat up some from the court, threw the Normans[5] into the swamps, and inflicted wounds on many more. And immediately the count besieged all parts of Lille and forced the citizens to hand over to him one thousand and four hundred marks of silver to see if they could at least be quieted down in this way. This was the source of such great ill will between those citizens and the count that henceforth both sides regarded each other with suspicion.[6]

[94] *The citizens of Saint Omer rebel, February 8, 1128*

On February 8, 1128, the sixth day after the feast of the purification of the Mother of God, the burghers of Saint Omer rose in rebellion against the count, because the count unjustly wished to set over them as castellan[1] of that place one who had violently seized the goods and substance of their citizens and was still trying to despoil them. The count also besieged Saint Omer with a big army. But by stealth the citizens let in Arnold,[2] a nephew

---

Baldwin V; see Dhondt, "Développement urbain," RN, XXX (1948), 150, 155-156, and also J.-A. Van Houtte, "Les Foires dans la Belgique ancienne," in *La Foire* (Brussels, 1953), pp. 182-83.

[4] The special peace enjoyed by fairs was an aspect of the "count's peace" which prevailed in Flanders. In this case the new count himself violates the peace, essential to the conduct of business, by trying to seize one of his own serfs at that time. Perhaps he was not fully aware that his predecessors had severely punished violations of this sort; see famous cases of harsh enforcement by Robert the Frisian, in Hariulf, *Vita Arnulfi*, lib. II, c. 16, MGH, SS XV[2], 888-89, and by Baldwin VII in Herman, c. 24. On the measures taken to ensure security of persons and roads throughout the period of the fair (and eight days before and after), see S. Poignant, *La Foire de Lille* (Lille, 1932), pp. 61-71.

[5] Galbert's first use of the epithet "Normans," implying that the count's men were "foreigners," is probably a sign of his growing disillusionment with the "new count."

[6] Herman, c. 36, praises the men of Lille for being the first to rebel against the count's extortions.

[1] Hoston, according to Blommaert, *Les Châtelains*, p. 171; he had been installed by William Clito in 1127 and was driven out by his successor, Thierry, in 1128.

[2] Arnold was the son of Charles's older Danish sister, Ingertha; see *Flandria generosa*, c. 29, MGH, SS IX, 324. He is mentioned by Walter, c. 44, as one

of Count Charles, and did homage and pledged loyalty to him so that if by chance the new count[3] persisted in the unjust siege they could adhere to Arnold. At this time snow and ice, and cold and the east wind coming all at once crackled above the surface of the land, and therefore they feared the count would attack, and they handed over six hundred marks of silver to reestablish peace. And this was the source of the greatest ill will between those citizens and the count, and henceforth they regarded each other with suspicion.[4]

[95] *The count's authority is challenged in Ghent, February 16, 1128*

On February 16, the fifth day before Septuagesima, the men of Ghent rose against their castellan[1] because he continued to deal with them unjustly and wrongfully. The castellan went to the count and brought him back to restore peace between himself and the citizens. Now the count, wishing to oppress the citizens[2] and to impose the castellan on them by force, stayed there for several days. Then the citizens, as they had pledged to do with the baron Daniel,[3] and Ivan,[4] the brother of Baldwin, called the count to a reckoning, and after summoning everyone in Ghent, Ivan was made spokesman for the citizens and spoke as follows:[5]

"Lord count, if you had wished to deal justly with our citizens, your burghers, and with us their friends, you would not have

---

of the claimants considered by the king at Arras, but not by Galbert at that time (c. 47).

[3] Galbert's resumption of this title indicates his troubled state of mind.

[4] It is likely that the burghers of Lille and Saint Omer were also alarmed at the economic effects of the measures taken by Henry I of England against his nephew, William Clito, according to Ganshof, "Les Origines du concept de souveraineté nationale," RHD, XVIII (1950), 144.

[1] Wenemar II, 1122-27; see c. 30.

[2] Galbert's hostility is now clear.

[3] Called a peer in c. 31.

[4] Concerning Ivan's important role earlier see c. 30 and c. 52. His brother. Baldwin, accused of treachery, had recently died; see c. 91.

[5] This interview with the count probably took place within the last two weeks of February; see Ganshof, "Les Origines du concept," RHD, XVIII (1950), 144, n. 1.

imposed evil exactions upon us and acted with hostility toward us but, on the contrary, you would have defended us from our enemies and treated us honorably. But now you have acted contrary to law and in your own person you have broken the oaths that we swore in your name[6] concerning the remission of the toll, the maintenance of peace and the other rights[7] which the men of this land obtained from the counts of the land, your good predecessors—especially in the time of lord Charles—and from yourself; you have violated your faith and done injury to ours since we took the oath to this effect together with you. Everyone knows how many acts of violence and how much pillage you have been responsible for in Lille, and how unjustly and wrongfully you have persecuted the citizens of Saint Omer. Now, if you can, you are going to maltreat the citizens of Ghent.

"But, since you are our lord and the lord of the whole land of Flanders, it is proper for us to deal with you reasonably, not violently or wrongfully. Let your court, if you please, be summoned at Ypres, which is located in the middle of your land, and let the barons from both sides, and our peers and all the responsible men among the clergy and people, come together in peace and without arms, and let them judge, quietly and after due consideration, without guile or evil intent. If in their opinion you can keep the countship in the future without violating the honor of the land, I agree that you should keep it. But if, in fact, you are unworthy of keeping it, that is, lawless and faithless, a deceiver and perjurer, give up the countship! relinquish it to us so that we can entrust it to someone suitable and with rightful claims to it. For we are mediators between the king of France and you to guarantee that you undertake nothing important in the county without regard for the honor of the land and our counsel. And now you have dealt wrongfully, not only with us, your guarantors to the aforesaid king, but also with the burghers of

[6] It sounds as if Ivan had been the count's spokesman in Ghent early in April, 1127, and had, together with other leading barons, guaranteed by oath a charter granted to Ghent at that time, just as he and other barons did in the case of Saint Omer; see Ganshof, "Le Droit urbain," RHD, XIX (1951), 393, n. 20.

[7] Nothing more is known about the contents of the supposed charter. The "other rights" may have included confirmation of the right to their own urban *échevinage*; see Ganshof, "Le Droit urbain," RHD, XIX, 396.

almost the whole of Flanders, contrary to the faith and oath sworn both by the king and yourself, and subsequently by all of us, the barons of the land."[8]

Then the count leapt forward and would have thrown back the *festuca* to Ivan,[9] if he had dared to do so in the midst of the tumultuous crowd of citizens, and said:

"I wish, then, to make myself your equal by rejecting the homage you have done to me, and to challenge you without delay to combat,[10] because as count I have thus far acted rightly and reasonably in every way."

But Ivan refused. And so they set the day, the Thursday at the beginning of the fasts,[11] March 8, when they should assemble peacefully at Ypres.[12]

Then the count went to Bruges, and summoning all his vassals in that region, he ordered them on the day fixed to proceed to that place with him in an armed band; he summoned the citizens in Bruges and protested to them that Ivan and his men were going to drive him from the land if they could, and he begged them to remain faithful to him. And they agreed to do so.[13]

[8] The radical implications of this speech have been much discussed, most recently by Professors Dhondt and Ganshof, who see in it a precocious and striking statement of the principle of "popular sovereignty" or "national sovereignty," in a sense limited to Flanders, of course. Although the components of the active group here are limited to two great barons and the burghers of one town (Ghent), they claim to act in the interests of Flanders as a whole, and they express in a practical form the idea that power pertains to the collectivity of free inhabitants and is delegated by it to the prince on condition that he prove a worthy ruler; see Ganshof, "Les Origines du concept," RHD, XVIII (1950), 147-49. As to the composition of the proposed representative assembly, its elements, barons, clergy, and people (urban primarily) suggest the groups that will later be called "estates," although Galbert may be using "clergy and people" loosely, as he often does, to mean simply "all the people," as Professor Dhondt warns, *Les Origines des États*, pp. 18-19. The "institutional framework" of the assembly is nothing new; it is obviously the traditional one of the count's court, with a larger and more heterogeneous composition than usual, as Professor Ganshof points out in the same article, pp. 148-49.

[9] This example of *exfestucatio* on the part of a lord toward his vassal may be compared to the case in c. 38 where the vassals of the traitors rejected their homage to them as their lords.

[10] A judicial duel could be engaged in only by equals.

[11] March 11 was the first Sunday of Lent; see c. 96.

[12] The count accepts the demand but under duress and not in good faith, as events prove.

[13] The altercation between the count and the burghers of Bruges over the remission of the toll must have been settled favorably to the citizens; see c. 88.

And so on the day set the count went to Ypres with an armed force, and filled it with knights and mercenaries, ready and girded for fighting. Ivan and Daniel also went towards Ypres, that is, as far as Roeselare, and sent messengers to the count saying:

"Lord Count! Because the day was fixed in the holy time of fasting, when you should have come reasonably, in peace, and not with evil intent, in arms, and you have not done so but on the contrary are getting ready to fight against your vassals, Ivan and Daniel and the men of Ghent send word to you that they will no longer delay in rejecting through us the homage,[14] which they have up to now maintained inviolably towards you, because you now come craftily to kill them."

And the messengers proceeded to throw away the *festuca* in the name of their lords and departed.

Ivan and Daniel had previously sent messengers with greetings to the towns[15] of Flanders saying:

"We will exchange hostages and guarantors with you, if you wish to live with honor in the land, so that if the count tries to attack you or us by force, we can come to each other's defense in any place whatsoever."

They agreed[16] that they would do this most willingly, if without violating the honor of the land and their own honor they could get rid of such an evil count, who was interested only in seeing how he could slyly oppress his citizens. And they added:

"See how the merchants and traders of the whole land of Flanders are hemmed in on account of that count whom you[17] have set up in the place of the most worthy father, Charles! And remember how we have been consuming our wealth throughout the whole year! And, moreover, whatever we earned in other times that count has taken from us or we have used up within

[14] In this case, Galbert uses the word *hominia* (homages) as the object of *exfestucare*.

[15] *Castra* undoubtedly means towns here.

[16] That is, the townsmen appealed to. Concerning the citizens of Bruges, however, see c. 98.

[17] The townsmen, whoever they are, seem glad to throw the whole responsibility for choosing William upon the barons.

this land since we are shut in and besieged by his enemies.[18] Think, then, how we can get rid of our plunderer and oppressor, taking into account, however, the honor of the land and your honor."

Meanwhile the count was lying in wait for Daniel and Ivan at Ypres, gathering around him all the knights of the land.

[96] *"So many lords!" Thierry of Alsace appears in Ghent, March 11, 1128*

On March 11, the first Sunday in Lent, the news, which was true, reached us that the young Thierry,[1] a cousin of Count Charles, had come from Alsace to Ghent and was waiting there until he himself should be received as count, once that count and his Normans had been driven out. And it is amazing that Flanders could receive and be ready to accept so many lords, at one and the same time the boy from Mons,[2] and Arnold[3] who had been secretly admitted to Saint Omer, and the one now waiting at Ghent, and that oppressive count of ours. For the castellan Thierry[4] and his kinsmen and friends were hastening to support that Norman, our count, while those in Saint Omer were trying to set up Arnold as count; those in Arras and its vicinity were for the count of Mons; Ivan and Daniel for that Thierry.[5]

---

[18] The economic losses suffered by the burghers, in England and in the lands of Stephen of Blois, are implied in sections 7 and 16 (or 7 and 17 in the revised text of Espinas) of the charter of Saint Omer; see *Actes*, no. 127, pp. 296-97. Stephen of Blois became count of Boulogne in 1125; with his uncle, Henry I, he opposed William Clito.

[1] See c. 47 and the Genealogy.
[2] Baldwin of Hainaut; see c. 67. He was supported by Oudenaarde, according to Galbert, c. 72, 80.
[3] The nephew of Charles; see c. 94.
[4] Thierry of Dixmude; see c. 31.
[5] The theme of "so many counts" recurs in Galbert, c. 96, c. 99, c. 121, and in other sources. It reveals Galbert's distress and confusion of mind; he has already turned against William Clito but has not yet taken a firm stand for one of the other claimants.

[97] *Count William drives out Arnold, March 21, 1128*

On March 16, Friday, the citizens of Bruges ran into the castle, trying to find out if Fromold Junior[1] had filled the count's house with grain and wine and other foodstuffs, for they wanted to see what Count William was doing. On the same day, hearing that the count was coming to the town of Bruges, they closed the gates on him in case he should come to attack them, for they no longer wished to consider him as count.[2]

On Saturday in the four seasons,[3] after the first full week of fasting was over, on March 17, the feast of Gertrude the Virgin, the castellan Gervaise ordered everyone who lived in his viscounty[4] to prepare themselves to set out ready for action[5] to Torhout on the fourth day after that Saturday; they were to wait there until our count, William, should lead them to fight against Daniel and Ivan.[6]

On March 21, the feast of Benedict the abbot, our castellan, Gervaise, returned to Bruges from Torhout with his men, and reported that Arnold, the nephew of Count Charles, had been fraudulently let into Saint Omer for the second time[7] by some of the citizens. On hearing this, Count William of Flanders rushed from Ypres to Saint Omer with a strong force and drove Arnold, who was surrounded, into the church of Saint Bertin, meaning to burn up the church;[8] and he forced Arnold and also those who had been besieged with him to abjure Flanders hence-

---

[1] Last heard of in c. 64, preparing the obsequies of Count Charles. Fromold, as a notary, would be one of those responsible for receiving the count's domanial revenues in kind. Perhaps the citizens fear that the count is making ready to defend himself in the castle.

[2] Contrary to their promise to remain faithful to him in c. 95.

[3] That is, the Ember Day following the first Sunday in Lent.

[4] "Castellany" is more generally used by Galbert.

[5] It is Gervaise's right as castellan to summon all able-bodied free men of the castellany to serve the count as well as to act as commander of the knights of his castellany (see c. 75, 109, 113) and of the urban forces (see c. 114). See Blommaert, *Les Châtelains*, pp. 20-21.

[6] Daniel and Ivan are near Ypres, the count is in Bruges; Torhout is on the road to Ypres from Bruges.

[7] See c. 94.

[8] Simon of Saint Bertin (*Gesta abbatum*, lib. II, c. 190, MGH, SS XIII, 659) reports, on the contrary, that the count prevented his soldiers from burning the church.

forth. And on the same day the count returned to Ypres, preparing on the next day to attack Ivan and Daniel with the forces sent to Torhout. On the same day, that is, Wednesday, our citizens and our maritime Flemings swore with one another that they would stand together in the future to protect the honor of the place[9] and the fatherland.

[98] *The movement against Count William grows, March 23-24, 1128*

On March 23, Friday, the men of Ghent together with Ivan and Daniel sent word to our burghers by means of letters that they should make up their minds by the next Monday whether they intended from now on to stand by the men of Ghent and reject their homage[1] to the count, or to stand by Count William and oppose the men of Ghent and their lords and friends. For they no longer wished to remain in doubt about the men of Bruges beyond the day fixed.[2]

On March 24, Saturday, "Dixit Rebecca,"[3] the people of Bruges heard that the count was planning to come to Bruges from Aalter; they forbade both the place and the castle to him. They sent word to the count by the castellan, Gervaise, that he should go elsewhere until he had rooted his enemies out of Flanders, and then only would they turn over to him the place and the castle at Bruges. They also demanded of the same castellan, Gervaise, that he should declare openly whether he had

---

[9] "The place" here seems to mean the whole castellany of Bruges, not merely the town and castle of Bruges as it often does in Galbert's narrative. This action, reminiscent of the regional solidarity between town and country expressed on March 27, 1127 (see c. 52), marks a temporary phase of "armed neutrality" on the part of the people of Bruges; see Ganshof, "Les Origines du concept," RHD, XVIII (1950), 150.

[1] *Exfestucare.*

[2] The people of Bruges are obviously uncertain what course to follow. After swearing to be faithful to William late in February (c. 95), they shut the gates in his face on March 16 (c. 97).

[3] The Saturday before the Sunday of Lent when in the Mass part of chapter 27 of Genesis is read in place of the Epistle, according to the Bollandists, *Vita Beati Caroli,* AASS, March 1, p. 212.

decided henceforth to stand by them in the same faith and loyalty or to withdraw from them along with his count.[4] On the same day toward evening they saw the count crossing over near Maldegem in our direction, and immediately our citizens rushed to arms and would have resisted the count face to face at the gates if he had come to Bruges; they barred the gates against him on all sides. On the same day, Cono,[5] the brother of Walter of Vladslo, who was now dead, came into our citizens, and in the middle of the market he swore in the presence of all that he would stand faithfully by the citizens with his following. And these knights were supporters of our citizens: Walter of Lissewege[6] and his men, and those men from Oostkerke, and Hugo Snaggaerd[7] and his brothers.

[99] *Thierry of Alsace invites support from Bruges, March 25, 1128*

On March 25, on the Sunday of the Annunciation to the Virgin Mary, the Gospel was read, "Every kingdom divided against itself shall be laid waste."[1] The countess of Holland[2] and her brother Thierry, the "adopted" count of the men of Ghent and of our citizens,[3] sent greetings to us in Bruges, both to the clergy and to the people of our vicinity as follows:

[4] Pressure from Ghent apparently weighs the scales against William, who is now "his" count, not theirs.

[5] Cono is named in a charter of 1119 to which he was also witness (*Actes*, no. 94, pp. 211 ff.); he is witness also to one of William's reign in 1127-28 (*Actes*, no. 129, p. 303).

[6] The rich knight, Walter Crommelin, who had married Hacket's daughter (c. 54). The Inquest (MGH, SS XXV, pp. 441-42) charges him with helping Hacket escape and receiving part of the treasure.

[7] Named by the Inquest (p. 442) as one of the count's vassals who shared in the treasure. Both he and Walter apparently hope to save their skins by supporting the movement against William.

[1] Mark 3.24. Galbert's version here is not that of the Vulgate.

[2] Gertrude is now supporting her half-brother, Thierry of Alsace, instead of her son, Thierry VI of Holland, whose chances had never been very good. See c. 34.

[3] This is Galbert's first admission that the citizens of Bruges, who had already rejected William, have now openly espoused the cause of Thierry. He still refers to William as "count," however.

"Whatever you hold lawfully from the counts our predecessors, you will keep more securely through me if you will put me in the countship in place of William. I will grant your merchants both peace throughout Flanders and free transit for trading, and my sister, the countess, will also grant the same,[4] on this condition, however, that we exchange pledges to the effect that you will receive me and that I will grant you freedom of commerce."

The castellan, Gervaise, went at once to the count at Maldegem, advising him to go towards Ypres because he would be practically besieged in Maldegem if by any chance the men of Ghent should attack him. And the men of Bruges at once sent word to Daniel to come with his following to them in Bruges. Meanwhile, supported by Henry,[5] the castellan of Bourbourg, Arnold, whom they had formerly received as count in Saint Omer, was trying to secure the county of Flanders with the aid and counsel of the king of England. And so the land of Flanders was divided, because some, still observing faith and homage to Count William, were fighting with him; others such as Daniel, and Ivan, and the men of Ghent and Bruges were siding with Thierry; others were supporting Arnold, such as the people in Saint Omer and that region; others thought the count of Mons should be preferred. And therefore the land lay desolate, so greatly divided!

[100] *Gervaise leaves Bruges and Thierry arrives there, March 26, 1128*

On March 26, Monday, the castellan, Gervaise, decided he would stay no longer with our people in Bruges because they had forbidden the place and his castle to Count William, and had barred the gates against him, and, moreover, had put Thierry in his

---

[4] This concession, involving free navigation of the Scheldt, was an alluring bait to the burghers of Bruges. The count of Holland controlled the mouth of the Scheldt.

[5] The son and undoubted successor of Themard, castellan of Bourbourg, whose father and two brothers were slain on March 2, 1127 (see c. 16). His name appears several times as witness to charters, including the famous charter to Saint Omer (see *Actes*, no. 127, p. 298). See Vercauteren, "Étude sur les châtelains," in *Études ... Pirenne*, pp. 434-35.

place as their count. Therefore Gervaise sent for the leading citizens and spoke to them as follows, outside the castle at Bruges:

"Because I still keep faith with my only lord, Count William, from whom, according to secular law,[1] I cannot be separated without loss of honor, I am no longer free to stay with you, who have shown such contempt for the count. But because I love you, I will go to the count and plead your cause at length so that he may be persuaded not to do you any injury before next Sunday. If I can reconcile you to the count, I will so do; if not, I will warn you of any injury which the count intends to inflict on you, if I know about it in advance. I beg of you, take honorable care of my wife, my sons and daughters, and my goods, which are still inside the castle, until the day fixed."

And all our citizens agreed that they would faithfully respect his wishes.

On the same day Stephen of Boelare[2] came over to us with about forty knights. Our knights made a sortie before Thancmar's[3] house. On the same day Ivan and Daniel brought Thierry of Alsace to Bruges so that he could be received as count. Our citizens ran out to meet him, applauding his arrival.

[101] *The burghers of Bruges question Ivan and Daniel, March 27, 1128*

On March 27, Tuesday, at dawn, Thancmar and his nephews burned up their own house and dwellings[1] at Straten because if they had not done so, Daniel and Ivan with their Thierry would have burned them. We learned, in fact, that Ivan and Daniel had not yet done homage and pledged loyalty to that Thierry but

---

[1] That is, according to feudal law, which forbade a vassal to do anything harmful to his lord, such as aiding his enemies.

[2] He appears as a witness in several charters, all before 1102; see *Actes*, Index.

[3] Last heard of in c. 45 when he and his nephews were thrown out of Bruges by the citizens. The hostility of the people to Thancmar persists even in the midst of such important events.

[1] *Domum et mansiones:* probably the stronghold and outlying dwelling houses.

were inducing the people and knights to choose him as count by taking him through the towns of Flanders. For Ivan and Daniel had not been able to carry out the election without the permission and consent of the duke of Louvain;[2] they had both pledged their faith to the duke not to elect Thierry as count without his consent.

On the same day we heard that William of Ypres,[3] released from captivity, had gone to Courtrai in order to help with his advice and forces Count William, who had been expelled from Bruges and Ghent. Now because Ivan and Daniel, two of the peers and barons of Flanders, had received many gifts from the king of England and were about to receive more in return for the expulsion of his nephew, that is, our Count William, they had decided to do nothing without the advice of the king or without the advice of the duke of Louvain whose daughter[4] the king of England and the duke were about to give in marriage to Arnold, nephew of the most pious Count Charles, whom meanwhile the people of Veurne and the castellan of Bourbourg had received as count, with the counsel and aid of the king of England. Finally our citizens questioned Ivan and Daniel:

"Why, then, did you bring Thierry around to us if all of us are not going to pledge faith and loyalty and do homage to him, you first and we second?"[5]

They replied:

"Because when he came to Bruges, he came with us and we

---

[2] Godfrey I, count of Louvain from 1095, and from 1106 to 1140 duke of Lower Lorraine, whose daughter Alix had married Henry I of England. Ivan and Daniel were his vassals for lands held in Brabant.

[3] William of Ypres had apparently gained his freedom in return for promising to help Count William, now in great need. His military gifts became apparent in his later career as a famous mercenary captain, employed with other Flemish mercenaries by Stephen of Blois in England during the Anarchy, and made "Count of Kent" for his services. His English career is related in many English sources; see G. Dept, "Les Marchands flamands et le roi d'Angleterre," RN, XII (1926), 304, n. 3. He wept when he was thrown out of England on the accession of Henry II, according to the *Vita sancti Thomae,* c. 10, in Vol. III of *Materials for the Study of Thomas Becket,* ed. by J. C. Robertson, Rolls Series, no. 67, pp. 18-19.

[4] Possibly Ida by name, according to Pirenne, ed. Galbert, p. 147, n. 1. Henry I, in his eagerness to circumvent William Clito, is aiding the leading pretenders without distinction. His aid to Thierry is mentioned by many contemporary writers, English, Norman, and Flemish; see Pirenne, p. 146, n. 4.

[5] The burghers are trying to get the barons to commit themselves first.

with him so that he could see the lay of the land, and find out in what mood the people of Bruges would receive him and who were joined to them securely in friendship and loyalty."

On March 29, Thursday, those knights from Oostkerke, with their names inscribed on parchment, sent a message on behalf of themselves and many others, to Count William in Ypres, and they renounced the faith and homage[6] they had formerly pledged to that same count.

[102] *The barons and burghers elect Thierry as count at Bruges, March 30, 1128*

On March 30, Friday, the people of Bruges were expecting the return of Daniel and Ivan who earlier had gone out of the town secretly with their vassals. For they had agreed upon this day with our citizens as the time when they would do homage and pledge loyalty to Thierry of Alsace, and also the people of Ghent and of Bruges and those who had sworn with them. Now this day was Friday in this bissextile year whereas it was Wednesday before Easter in the previous year.[1] On the same day, at evening, Ivan and Daniel returned to us in Bruges, and with them came Hugh of Saint Pol.[2] And it was reported that the captive William of Ypres had been given his liberty by Count William the Norman.[3] Immediately after eating, the barons and the people came together at the exit of the town, at the Sands, and there they all[4] elected Thierry of Alsace as count of all Flanders, and

[6] *Exfestucaverunt;* this rejection of homage simply by written message rather than by rite in the presence of their lord seems to express the contemptuous attitude of the knights towards Clito.

[1] That is, March 30 fell on Friday in 1128 but on Wednesday in 1127. The year 1128 was a "leap year"; the intercalated day, *bissextum,* was inserted before the 6th of the Kalends of March, which in common years was February 24. See Poole, *Medieval Reckonings of Time,* p. 23.

[2] See c. 67.

[3] Galbert resorts to this title for William Clito in desperation, perhaps.

[4] "All the people," probably refers to the various elements which have gradually formed a kind of coalition, the burghers of Ghent, the burghers and clergy of Bruges, and representatives of the castellany (c. 97), a group of knights from northern Flanders (c. 98), and several other barons besides Ivan and Daniel

Ivan and Daniel did homage to him in the presence of everyone. And the law was laid down for all who had been proscribed on account of the betrayal of Count Charles, that they might return to the court of this new count,[5] and, if they dared, offer satisfaction according to the judgment of the barons and feudatories of the land, that is, anyone who was a knight and had belonged to the count's court; anyone else who was accused could purge himself according to the judgment of the magistrates of the land.[6] In addition the count granted to his barons and to the people of the land, the right to amend all the laws and judgments and customs and usages of the inhabitants of the land in matters concerning the common welfare and the honor of the land.[7]

And it should be noted that on the very same day, in the year before, the barons of the siege had returned from Arras, the ones who had gone out from us to elect the count of the land according to the counsel and order of King Louis—Ivan of Aalst and his brother Baldwin, Walter of Vladslo, and other peers of the land. Coming back to us in happy spirits, they had announced to us that they, together with the king of France, had elected the young William of Normandy freely and lawfully as count and lord of our whole land.[8] And it should be noted that while Count William was sitting with his barons in a certain gallery

---

(c. 100, 102). It is noteworthy that barons and knights are now acting in cooperation with popular elements, urban and rural, in electing Thierry, and not separately, as in the election of William.

[5] "This new count" is used to distinguish him from Count William, who was "the new count" in 1127.

[6] See c. 88, n. 5; Galbert probably means again the magistrates (*scabini*) of both the urban and territorial *échevinages*. Galbert makes clear in this passage as in c. 110 the difference in status between knights, subject only to the count's jurisdiction in *matière répressive*, such as this, and other free persons, subject only to the jurisdiction of the *échevins* in most cases. See Ganshof, *Recherches sur les tribuneaux*, pp. 37 ff. and "Les Transformations de l'organisation judiciaire," RB, XVIII (1939), 46-49. It is clear that Thierry's action amounts to a virtual amnesty for the partisans of the Erembald clan who have developed a kind of solidarity of their own. See J. Dhondt, "Les Solidarités," *Annales*, XII (1957), 551-52.

[7] This privilege, interpreted by Ganshof ("Les Origines du concept de souveraineté," RHD, XVIII [1950], 151), as the right of lords and communities to amend freely their customary law, far exceeds the earlier concession made to Bruges, and Bruges only, by William Clito (c. 55).

[8] See c. 52. Galbert's tone is perhaps more nostalgic than ironic; he longs for the time when there was only one count in the land.

at Ypres, considering what he should do against the newly elected
Thierry, count only of the people of Ghent and Bruges and their
confederates, the gallery fell to the ground and also all those
sitting in it, so that one of them almost died of suffocation in the
crash.

[103] *Thierry is acknowledged as count at Bruges, March 31*
and April 1, 1128

On March 31, Saturday, the clergy[1] and people returned to the
Sands, and the count took an oath on the shrine of Saint Donatian, as we have said above, and Ivan and Daniel were named as
pledges between the count and the clergy and people, to make
sure the count would fulfill everything he had sworn and not
consciously violate anything. Then the men of Ghent swore
fealty to the count and then the men of Bruges, and they performed homages.[2] On the same day Lambert of Aardenburg
came to Bruges in order to clear himself of the charge of treachery.[3]

On April 1, Sunday, "Laetare Hierusalem," in the middle of
Lent, Thierry was acknowledged as count, and he went in procession to the church of Saint Donatian in Bruges and entered in,
according to the custom of the counts, his predecessors, and he
dined in the hall and house of the counts, and throughout the
whole day our men of Bruges were laying plans to bring back
the castellan Gervaise whom they had loved faithfully. There
were some men of Bruges, however, even vassals of Gervaise
himself, who were plotting evilly against him, having secretly
entered into dealings with a certain Walter,[4] son-in-law of the

---

[1] The clergy are probably canons of the chapter of Saint Donatian.

[2] The solidarity of the burghers of Bruges and Ghent, which first developed
in 1127 (c. 53), has now been completely reestablished, for they have participated
jointly in the election and formal recognition of Thierry. On this occasion, however, they do not perform homage until *after* the count has sworn to be faithful
to his engagements (cf. c. 54).

[3] See c. 87 concerning the charges against him.

[4] Walter Crommelin of Lissewege; see c. 98. As the son-in-law of the previous
castellan, he is probably asserting an hereditary claim to the office which had
passed out of the Erembald family when it was given to Gervaise (c. 54).

castellan Hacket, whom they were trying to put in Gervaise's place.

[104] *Gervaise comes over to Thierry, April 2, 1128*

On April 2, which last year was the Holy Saturday of Easter but now in fact was Monday, the castellan Gervaise came into the castle at Bruges to see Count Thierry in the midst of his knights and of the burghers who had faithfully loved him, and standing before them all he said:

"Lord Count Thierry! if God had granted us and the fatherland the favor of your presence right after the death of our lord and your cousin Charles, we would have acknowledged no one but you in the countship. Therefore I now give notice to all that I break completely with Count William, that I renounce the homage and faith and loyalty I have observed towards him up to now because the peers of the land and all the people have condemned that one who is still wandering about the land lawless, faithless, without regard for the justice of God or men, and they have acknowledged you with honor and love as the natural[1] and rightful lord of the land. I wish, therefore, to do homage and pledge my faith to you, as to the natural lord of the land and the one with whom we are in agreement; I wish to receive from you the office[2] and fiefs that I formerly held from your predecessors. If anyone claims the viscountship at my expense in the name of Hacket, the last castellan before me,[3] I am ready to give

---

[1] Meaning lawful, legitimate.

[2] Gervaise had been chamberlain to Count Charles (c. 16), but he is probably referring to his office as castellan (c. 54). Both these offices were actually held as fiefs.

[3] The future of Hacket in relation to the office of castellan has been disputed. It is clear from a charter of Count Thierry in 1133, in which he restores to the abbey of Saint Peter lands usurped by Hacket, that he had survived the "purge" and that two branches of the family, his own and that of his brother, Lambert of Aardenburg, had recovered some of their lands. See A. Van Lokeren, *Chartes et documents de l'Abbaye de Saint Pierre au Mont Blandin* (Ghent, 1868), no. 214, pp. 131-32. But whether or not Hacket was restored to his former office as castellan of Bruges in 1130 (when Gervaise is last named) and held it until 1134 (when a new line assumed the office) is disputed. On Thierry's accession, Hacket's son-in-law, Walter Crommelin, had tried to displace Gervaise but failed (see

satisfaction in your presence and that of the peers of the land."

And so when he had finished the speech he became the vassal of Count Thierry. Then throughout the rest of the day all who were bound to become enfeoffed in the county did homage to the count, and for several days afterwards.[4] The count immediately set to work to establish peace throughout his county among those who had been heretofore engaged in discord and strife and serious conflict.[5]

[105] *The citizens of Ypres approach Thierry, April 9, 1128*

On April 6, Friday, Lambert of Aardenburg in the presence of Count Thierry cleared himself by the ordeal of hot iron of the charge of betraying and putting to death the lord Count Charles.[1] Daniel and Ivan were not present.

On April 9, Monday, certain men of Ypres came before Count Thierry on the balcony[2] of his house in Bruges; they declared that the count should come to the aid of the citizens of Ypres,

Galbert, c. 103). Contrary to the opinion of Blommaert (*Les Châtelains*, pp. 14-15) that Hacket never again became castellan, is the evidence that he is always referred to as "castellan of Bruges" in the charter mentioned above and is referred to as castellan in another of 1133 (F. d'Hoop, *Chartes du prieuré de Saint-Bertin à Poperinghe* [Bruges, 1870], no. 13); this use of the title, however, might have been simply honorary. In support of Blommaert's opinion is the fact that neither Hacket's son, Robert, nor his son-in-law, Walter, is ever named as castellan, and that no signature of Hacket from this period has ever been found, not even in the charter edited by Van Lokeren. Professor Dhondt suggests that Hacket may have recovered his office on condition that he renounce hereditary right to it, or that he regained the office and his son died before he did.

[4] See c. 56 for the ceremony followed in April, 1127.

[5] In "Les Origines du concept de souveraineté," RHD, XVIII (1950), 152-53, Ganshof interprets the preceding events as demonstrating that the coalition of barons, knights and communities has translated the principle of popular sovereignty into a reality by rejecting one count and freely electing another whom they acknowledge formally as count only after he has granted privileges affecting the land as a whole. This action, however, as he points out, does not give birth to any organ which could give permanence to this expression; after the collective process of choice, the members of the coalition carry out separately the formalities binding themselves to the new count, the burghers as communities, the barons, castellan, and knights as individuals.

[1] In the Inquest (MGH, SS XXV, 441), "Lambins Nypa" is charged with the murder of the castellan of Bourbourg.

[2] *Lobium* is used in c. 42 to mean balcony.

on this condition, that if the citizens expelled Count William from Ypres, Count Thierry would come at once on the next day to the aid of the citizens.

[106] *The burghers of Bruges defy the king of France, April 10, 1128*

On April 10, Tuesday, Count Thierry with his vassals[1] and the burghers of Bruges made an attack on his enemies who had settled down in Oudenburg and Gistel,[2] but because they were strongly fortified for defense on all sides, he turned back with the citizens when only half-way.

On the same day, the king of France[3] sent a letter to our citizens to this effect:

"I wish you to send to me at Arras on Palm Sunday[4] eight responsible men; and I shall in fact summon the same number of wise men from each of the towns[5] of Flanders. In their presence and that of all my barons, I want to reconsider rationally the point at issue and the cause of conflict between you and your count, William, and I shall try at once to bring about a peaceful settlement between you and him. If anyone of the citizens does not dare to come to me, I will grant him a safe conduct for coming and returning."[6]

[1] *Feodati*, literally those enfeoffed by him, doubtless referring to those who had just received their fiefs in c. 104. Galbert generally uses *homines* to mean vassals, sometimes *milites*.

[2] Both towns are in the vicinity of Bruges.

[3] Doubtless in response to a desperate plea from William Clito, who late in March had humbly implored his suzerain for aid against the machinations of his uncle and mortal enemy, Henry I. See his letter in *Epistolae Ludovici VI regis francorum*, in Bouquet, RHF, XV, 341. Since Henry had landed in Normandy, Louis did not dare take military action but attempted to reassert his direct authority in Flanders by peaceful means. See Ganshof, "Le Roi de France," RHDF, XXVII (1949), 223-24.

[4] That is, on April 15.

[5] *Castra*; it is possible that the king's order contained this word in the sense of towns; it is so used in acts of the royal chancellery, according to Ganshof, "Trois mandements perdus," ASEB, LXXXVII (1950), 131.

[6] This is the last of three lost *mandements* or royal orders concerning Flanders which have been analyzed by Professor Ganshof. Galbert here gives no indication of the protocol or of the *exposé* but reproduces the gist of the *dispositif*, perhaps more literally than in the other two cases; see "Trois mandements perdus,"

The citizens at once began to argue and deliberate about sending a reply, saying:

"The king has perjured himself because he swore before the recognition of Count William that he neither wished to receive nor was entitled to receive any payment or relief[7] for the election of that count, but afterwards he openly received one thousand marks as payment and relief. Also, he has used force to violate his word about the remission of toll to the citizens, which he and the king swore to observe inviolably. And although that count gave hostages[8] to confirm everything that he had either remitted or granted to the citizens, he broke his word to those hostages. Then when he had finally set a day for us and the peers of the land to come to Ypres in order to settle his differences with us, as all the inhabitants of the land well know, he took that town in advance with an armed band so that he could use force against us and coerce us into doing whatever he wanted. And he has shut us up in this land, contrary to reason, contrary to the law of God and men, so that we cannot trade; on the contrary, whatever we once possessed we have consumed, being deprived of money, trade, and the ability to acquire goods.[9] For this reason we have just cause for expelling him from the land!

"Now we have chosen as our count a more rightful heir, the son of the sister of Count Charles's mother,[10] a man faithful and wise; raised to power in accordance with the custom of the land, and strengthened by our faith and homage, he is worthily imitating the character and customs and deeds of his predecessors. Therefore we give notice to all, both to the king and his barons, and also to those present and to our successors, that the king of

---

pp. 130-32. This use of the *mandement,* according to Ganshof (p. 133), strengthens the impression that the Capetian monarchy was at this time more advanced in its development than is generally believed.

[7] This is the first evidence of William's having paid a feudal relief to the king, an act which the citizens at Bruges had apparently tried to prevent, knowing the dangerous implications of such a precedent, both political and economic. (Galbert does not mention any such oath by the king in c. 55.) There is, so far as I know, no evidence that a relief was ever paid to the king by William's predecessors.

[8] There is no reference to pledges in c. 55.

[9] The same complaint was expressed in c. 95.

[10] That is, Thierry, son of Gertrude who was the sister of Adele, Count Charles's mother.

France has nothing to do with choosing or setting up a count of Flanders, whether the previous count has died with or without heirs. The peers of the land and the citizens have the power of electing the nearest of kin as heir to the count's authority, and they have the privilege of raising him to the countship. When a count dies his successor shall give to the king, for the right to those lands which the former held in fief from the king, only a relief of arms[11] for that same fief. The count of the land of Flanders owes nothing beyond this to the king of France, nor does the king have any right by virtue of his authority to impose a count on us for a relief or for a price, or to prefer one candidate to another. But because the king and the counts of Flanders were formerly joined together by the bond of kinship, the knights[12] and barons and citizens of Flanders, out of consideration for this fact, gave their assent to the king concerning the election and installation of that William as their count. But what is due on account of kinship is one thing, and what is well established by the ancient tradition of the predecessors of the counts of Flanders and by law is quite another thing."[13]

[11] The word used is *armatura*, the meaning of which is made clear by Ganshof in "Armatura," *Archivium Latinitatis Medii Aevi* (*Bulletin du Cange*), XV (1941), 179-93. The burghers, although recognizing the feudal bond between their count and the king of France, audaciously reduce the obligation of feudal relief to a payment which was little more than symbolic, thus affirming the principle of the autonomy of Flanders. The *armatura* was a peculiar form of relief, possibly a survival of some early custom by which the arms of the defunct vassal, and perhaps also his horse, were surrendered to his lord. Though there is no evidence earlier or later of this practice in Flanders, it was known in other areas, including western Lorraine. The citizens probably assert that it is the "customary" relief because in that case it would be both fixed in character and modest in value, whereas the amount of relief paid by William, 1,000 marks. was probably arbitrary and certainly extortionate on the part of the king.

[12] The first time Galbert explicitly mentions the knights (*milites*) as a distinct participating group.

[13] Pirenne points out (ed. Galbert, p. 153, n. 1) that Galbert probably conveys the sense rather than the text of the answer to the king; and also that this passage was used in later struggles between the counts of Flanders and the kings of France. The revolutionary nature of its content is discussed by Ganshof, "Les Origines du concept," RHD, XVIII (1950), 155-58. He sees in it a striking reaffirmation of the principle of "national sovereignty," notable because it is formulated in opposition to well-established principles of feudal law and royal sovereignty, and because it expresses clearly and practically the notion of contract between a ruler and his subjects. He stresses also the dynamic role of the urban communities in the progressive development of the concept of "national sovereignty" which reaches its climax at this point; he believes their action in forming

[107] *The struggle continues, April 11 and 23, 1128*

On April 11, Wednesday, the day of Pope Leo, the nephews of Thancmar[1] made a surprise attack on the people of Bruges at the Sands, challenging the citizens and trying to induce them, although they had hardly eaten, as well as Count Thierry and his knights, to come out and fight. But when the sacristans of the churches rang the bells and the knights sounded the trumpets, they were put to flight far from Bruges. Later some of our swifter knights and citizens again made an attack on their enemies in Gistel and compelled certain ones to agree to do homage to our Count Thierry,[2] if by chance they should be permitted to do so, and to give pledges to this effect so that they would not go back on their word.

On April 23, the Monday after Easter Sunday, our Count Thierry went by horse to Lille, and secured that region. Meanwhile Lambert of Wingene[3] with a few knights made an attack against Bruges, and at the same time the nephews of Thancmar burned up the house[4] of Fromold Junior, notary of the count, a fortified house which had stood at Beernem.[5] Now Count William at this time had gone to see the king of France at Compiègne, which is located in France, in order to receive aid and

---

alliances among themselves, and with barons and knights, is nothing but an extension of the practice of "sworn union" which had earlier led to the creation of communes and gilds. Dhondt (*Les Origines des États,* pp. 17 ff.) sees in the action of the towns in 1127-28 the emergence of an urban "order" asserting itself as a new "power" (*puissance*) in opposition to that of the knights and barons. He interprets these manifestations, however, primarily as those of "powers" rather than those of "orders" in the usual corporative sense; their basis was simply the sworn oath, renewed before each step of common action, and the composition of groups was shifting and sometimes interlocking. See also his "Ordres ou puissances," *Annales,* V (1950), 291-95.

[1] Last heard of in c. 100, and c. 101. Are they supporting the enemies of Bruges or acting simply in their own interests in this period of anarchy?

[2] Galbert's first use of "our count" with reference to Thierry; he has now completed his shift to the new allegiance, for the time being, at least.

[3] Named as a witness to a charter of William Clito; see *Actes,* no. 129, p. 303.

[4] Is this the splendid house built by the count for Fromold, according to Galbert, c. 19? The house he left as an exile in c. 24 may have been within the castle; see c. 24.

[5] Beernem is 13 kilometers from Bruges.

counsel from the king[6] and in this way keep his hold on Flanders. He freely returned to our bishop, Simon of Noyon, the twelve parish churches[7] which he had received in fief so that he might appear as the advocate and defender of the churches of God in Flanders, with this understanding, that the bishop, by the ban and word of excommunication should condemn all citizens[8] whatsoever of the land of Flanders who had received Thierry as count and elevated him to the power of the countship and had forcibly and unlawfully substituted him for Count William. Therefore, according to this agreement,[9] the bishop sent a letter to Ghent and suspended divine services in the churches there.[10]

[108] *Lambert of Aardenburg dies in battle, April 30, 1128*

On April 30, Monday, Lambert of Aardenburg, who had been under the stigma of treachery until he had done satisfaction to Count Thierry by the ordeal of hot iron,[1] besieged his enemies at Oostburg with a very powerful force, for he had summoned to his aid about three thousand[2] vassals and friends and kinsmen from the islands of the sea all around. But the people of Aardenburg[3] had assembled a strong band of both foot and mounted

[6] To which he was entitled as vassal of the king; this phrase confirms the belief that William Clito had already done homage to the king, at Arras or earlier; see Ganshof, "Le Roi de France," RHDF, XXVII (1949), 211, n. 1.

[7] *Altaria*, or churches in private hands, an abuse which the Gregorian reform was attacking; see Fliche, *La Réforme grégorienne*, pp. 411-13. Concerning these churches see *Liber de restauratione S. Martini Tornacensis continuatio*, c. 16, MGH, SS XIV, 324; according to this, Thierry confirmed the cession, but since the barons who were enfeoffed with the churches objected, the cession was of no avail.

[8] This blow is directed against the townspeople in general, the major support of Thierry.

[9] Ganshof, "Le Roi de France," RHDF, XXVII (1949), 225-26, believes that the king arranged this "deal" between the count and bishop as a peaceful means of strengthening William's position. Louis's own problems prevented him from undertaking military action.

[10] That is, he imposed an interdict.

[1] See Galbert, c. 105.

[2] These forces, though probably not as large as 3,000, must have been large enough to make a great impression on Galbert, for he repeats the number below.

[3] Their hatred of Lambert is apparent in c. 55.

soldiers against him. Now when they had approached each other, some to besiege and others to liberate the besieged, a messenger of Count Thierry, the castellan Gervaise, intervened, trying to put off the battle until they could be reconciled in the presence of the count. But because Lambert and his men were bent on killing the besieged, they absolutely refused to put off attacking the besieged. Then while so many thousands were engaged in the assault, and the besieged were ably defending themselves, suddenly the knights from Aardenburg, who in another place had been awaiting the outbreak of fighting to come to the aid of the besieged, rushed up in arms, some on horse, some on foot, but few in numbers compared to the besiegers. And immediately those who had rushed up, by filling the air with tremendous noise and clamor, so utterly surprised and terrified the besiegers that they took flight; casting aside their shields and weapons they prepared to flee on foot. Then the besieged, coming out in the strength of their arms, and also the men from Aardenburg, pursued them from the rear as they fled and cut down the chiefs and leaders of all those enemies; as for the footsoldiers, they slew whomever they wished. The number of those wounded was infinite and so was the number of men slain.[4]

It should be noted that in this battle Lambert, who had recently cleared himself by hot iron of the charge of having betrayed Count Charles, was now killed. For as long as he acted humbly towards God, God forgave him for having taken part in the murder of his lord. But, after being cleared by the ordeal, that Lambert and his men had arrogantly, without any sense of mercy, used a force of three thousand men to besiege a handful; wholly determined as he was not to spare them, he had refused to put off the fight and the slaughter of the besieged, without any regard for God or for the oath he had sworn to Count Thierry not to stir up any discord either in his own person or through his men.[5] And so he deserved to be killed since he

---

[4] The text, *occisorum liberorum virorum,* must be faulty here; it seems wise to omit *liberorum.*

[5] An allusion, probably, to the oath taken recently by the nobles of Flanders to maintain the peace; see c. 104.

disregarded the mercy of God and the dispensation by which He had saved his life when he was about to be killed with the others, on condition, however, that he should carry out worthy acts of penitence, as he had promised God and the Church. For when a servant acts humbly towards his lord because of an offense of which he is accused, the lord forgives him if he is acting in accordance with the law of penitence. When a man acting justly brings action against another man acting evilly, and God is called upon as judge between them, God supports the faith of the one acting justly, casting down the unjust man in his suit and confounding him in his obstinacy. So it happens that whilst in battle the guilty one is slain, in the judgment of water or iron the guilty one, if he is penitent, does not succumb.[6]

It should be noted, in fact, that those who were killed at Oostburg had by their counsel and trickery originally supported the cause of Count Thierry in Ghent and Bruges and put him in the place of Count William. And although Thierry is a legitimate heir to Flanders and a just and pious count, and William is, in fact, a dishonorable count of Flanders and an oppressor of the citizens of the land, nevertheless, those who now miserably lie dead did not advise him rightly; and they can not be called innocent of the betrayal of their lord since Count William as a result of their false counsel and guile is now a wanderer in his own land of Flanders.[7]

[6] It is clear that Galbert is troubled by the fact that Lambert, now justly killed in battle, had previously been cleared in the ordeal by hot iron. Generalizing from this incident, he seems to conclude that proof by iron or water, in which God suffers even a guilty man to survive if he is penitent, is not as satisfactory as proof by battle in which the guilty one is simply slain, thus removing all doubts about his guilt. See R. C. Van Caenegem, *Geschiedenis van het strafprocesrecht*, pp. 136-39.

[7] Galbert's increasingly equivocal attitude toward Thierry can probably be attributed to conflicting emotions, a lingering loyalty to William as the lawfully chosen successor to Count Charles, a sense that he had been treated unjustly by his original supporters, and perhaps growing doubt about the success of Thierry's cause to which he, Galbert, along with the people of Bruges had gone over.

[109] *The supporters of Count William at Ghent resist, May 2, 1128*

On May 2, Wednesday, at night, those who were still held shut up in the count's castle in Ghent by the citizens because they persisted in supporting Count William, came out in the streets and burned many houses. And while the citizens were at work trying to put out the fire, they cut down with axes the hurling machines,[1] that is, the mangonels, with which the citizens were destroying the stone house and tower where the besieged were holding out. On the same day, Wednesday, the castellan of Bruges, Gervaise, with his knights tried to besiege the supporters of Count William at Wingene.[2] But those vigorous knights attacked Gervaise and wounded him, and they seized two squires and acquired horses and palfreys.

[110] *Anarchy prevails in Flanders; the king summons his count at Arras, May 6, 1128*

On May 5, Saturday, after the revolution of a year, there came about the anniversary day of all those who had been hurled from the tower on account of the murder of Count Charles. And it should be noted that in the same week Lambert,[1] the son of Ledewif, was killed at Oostburg and with him more of those by whose counsel and treachery Thierry of Flanders was forcibly put in the place of William the Norman.

In this same week, on Sunday, "Misericordia Domini," May 6, the king of France was engaged in summoning archbishops, bishops, and all synodal persons among the clergy, and abbots, and the most responsible persons from both the clergy and people, counts and barons and other leading men to come to him

---

[1] The mangonel was a projectile machine, constructed on the counterweight principle rather than on the spring principle of the ballista or catapult. See Enlart, *Manuel d'archéologie*, IIeme partie, tome II, p. 491.
[2] See c. 107.

[1] Named as witness in a charter of 1114; see *Actes*, no. 64, p. 153.

at Arras[2] where he was about to hold a council concerning those two counts and decide which of them he should drive out by his royal authority and which he should establish. At this time Thierry was in Lille and William was wandering about at Ypres. Now in truth the whole land was so torn by dangers, by ravaging, arson, treachery, and deceit that no honest man could live in security.[3] For on both sides they were waiting to see what decision or judgment would be reached in the court and assembly of so many wise and responsible men, and what perils they should fear for the future since they feared that all kinds of perils were about to descend on them.

And it should be noted that almost all of those to whom the land of Flanders had been forbidden on account of the betrayal of Count Charles, in accordance with the judgment of the leaders and barons of the land, came back to the land at this time. They craftily pretended, in case anybody dared to challenge them about the treachery, that anyone who was challenged would answer either in the count's court, if he was a knight, or in the presence of the magistrates or judges of the land, if he was of inferior status. But up to this time no one has been challenged or has responded![4]

And it is worth remembering that when Count Thierry first went to Lille, a certain sorceress ran towards him, going into that body of water[5] which the count was about to cross over by the bridge close by the soothsayer, and she sprinkled the count with water. Then, they say, Count Thierry sickened in heart and

[2] Galbert apparently knows little about the action of the great judicial court summoned by the king, entirely different from the consultative assembly of burghers he had tried to call on April 10 (see c. 106). The council was actually dual in character, the ecclesiastics forming a provincial synod, and the vassals a *cour plenière*; see Ganshof, "Le Roi de France," RHDF, XXVII (1949), 226. The archbishop of Rheims excommunicated Thierry, who refused to appear, and all his followers, and laid an interdict on Lille where Thierry was staying; the king ordered him to leave Flanders and return to his own land, according to Herman, c. 36. Here again, says Ganshof (p. 227), the king is using both his rights as feudal seigneur and the plenitude of his royal power.
[3] A similar impression is given by Simon, *Gesta abbatum S. Bertini*, lib. II, c. 123, MGH, SS XIII, 659.
[4] Their return seems to be in accordance with the law of amnesty laid down by Count Thierry in c. 102; Galbert's evident bitterness probably springs from his certainty that no one will dare to challenge them.
[5] The Deule river.

bowels so that he loathed food and drink. And when his vassals grew anxious about him they seized the sorceress, and binding her hands and feet, placed her on a pile of burning straw and hay and burnt her up.[6]

From that time up to May 9, Cono of Vladslo at Wijnendale and those who had borne arms with Lambert against Count Thierry and his men at Wingene did not cease ravaging the villages around them and violently carrying off peasants[7] together with their goods. Now the people of Bruges encircled themselves with new ditches,[8] and defended themselves by their own watches and ambushes and those of their knights. At this time the village of Oostkamp was completely sacked by the knights of Count William.

[111] *The partisan conflict continues, May 14-15, 1128*

On May 14, Monday, the men of Bruges[1] made an attack on Wingene and many were wounded on both sides, and some were killed. The stronghold of the besieged was not destroyed, however.

On May 15, Tuesday, Count William, assembling his knights, attacked the magistrate[2] in Oostkamp, and chased him into the church of the same village and besieged him, shut up inside; he set fire to the doors of the church and burned them up. Meanwhile our burghers in arms came against him in Oostkamp, but when they saw the count and his knights, and the flames in the church, they fled in fear, and many were taken captive on that day. Then while the count made a sally to pursue and overtake our citizens, the magistrate of Oostkamp with a few men rushed out of the church and escaped the peril of the fire; and one of

---

[6] This was the recognized form of punishment for witches; see Van Caenegem, *Geschiedenis van het strafrecht*, pp. 163-64.

[7] *Rustici* is used here, as always by Galbert, to denote country folk.

[8] See c. 25; on March 6, 1127, they surrounded the town with a palisade, but do not seem to have dug the ditches which were also ordered by Bertulf at that time.

[1] Led by Gervaise, c. 109.

[2] *Praeco*, an inferior official of justice in the tribunal of the castellany; see c. 50.

the knights who came out of the church in this escape was seized. Our burghers fled, overcome by fear and alarm, and also because they knew in their hearts that they had unjustly expelled the same Count William and had betrayed him;[3] and certain of them hid themselves in rural ovens[4] from which they were pulled out and led off captive.

[112] *Count William gains in strength, May 21-31, 1128*

On May 21, Monday, the news reached us from Lens that the king of France had fled from Lille where he had besieged our Count Thierry[1] for four days.[2] At the same time the men of Ghent eviscerated a certain sorceress and carried her entrails around their town.[3]

On May 29, Tuesday, Count William, with a very strong band of knights and foot-soldiers, attacked Bruges and carried his assault boldly and courageously up to the gates and fortifications and within our ditches;[4] some were killed on both sides, many more wounded. Finally, at evening, he returned to Jabbeke.

On May 30, Wednesday, Count William with his armed men again seized peasants and knights at Oostkamp and carried them off forcibly to Wijnendale and Oudenburg.

On May 31, the day of the Ascension of the Lord, Count William from Oudenburg[5] sent a certain monk named Basil to

[3] Galbert's sense of guilt about the rejection of Count William now includes "our citizens" as well as the supporters of Lambert (see c. 108).

[4] *Furnos:* either open fireplaces or big ovens used by the peasants, called *ast* in Flemish.

[1] Thierry is now "our count" to Galbert, but William is still "count."

[2] Herman, c. 36, says the king, with William, laid siege for six days and then withdrew to Arras, and to "France." He never returned to Flanders after this failure to maintain his candidate there and the collapse of his effort, successful earlier, to exert his direct sovereignty as well as his feudal suzerainty in this great fief of the crown.

[3] This is a unique instance in Flemish penal law of this old German custom, according to Van Caenegem, *Geschiedenis van het strafrecht*, pp. 168-69.

[4] The quotation from Herman, c. 36, which Pirenne (ed. Galbert, p. 159, n. 4) applies to Bruges, seems rather to apply to Lille above. New ditches had just been dug at Bruges; see c. 110.

[5] About 18 kilometers from Bruges, southwest.

order his notary, Basil,[6] to come to him at once because the
overseers of the sheep runs and keepers of his farms and revenues had come into his presence, ready to render account of
what they owed him.[7] But that monk was detained in Bruges by
Ivan and Gervaise, the castellan, and Arnold, the nephew of
Count Charles, who had come to Bruges from Bourbourg on the
previous day. At the same time Count William ordered Oudenburg to be surrounded by fortifications and strengthened by
ditches; he had planned that he and his forces would withdraw
to that place. Therefore no countryman around us was secure;
everyone had either fled in hiding to the woods with all their
chattels or had come into Bruges, although even there they were
hardly safe in person or goods.[8]

[113] *Thierry comes to Bruges, June 10, 1128*

On June 10, the Holy Sunday of Pentecost, Count Thierry came
to Bruges after taking all the villages lying around Ghent, and
was received by our people with great joy.

On June 11, Monday, the knights and certain bandits who
were on Count William's side, came out of Jabbeke and, acting
as if they meant peace, began exchanging words and greetings

---

[6] The third notary named by Galbert: himself, Fromold, and now Basil. The
count summoned him to come from Bruges.

[7] This passage has often been cited because of its significance in revealing the
basic function of the count's notaries, that of taking charge of the domanial revenues,
many of them paid in kind, and keeping the accounts (*brevia*) of these revenues.
The fiscal area of Bruges was so important that it was divided into six units
(*officia*), largely because the counts were, by right, proprietors of the coastal land
which was rapidly being recovered from the sea; it was first exploited as sheepruns (*bercaria*), later as pastures, then partly as arable. These *bercaria* appear
frequently in the charters of the counts, especially after 1100, often as donations
to the new monastic foundations in maritime Flanders; they were evidently bestowed
with the aim of stimulating its economic development. See especially Monier,
Les Institutions financières, pp. 7-10 and 39-41, and F. Vercauteren, "Note sur la
valeur et l'importance économique des donations faites par les comtes de Flandre
au XIe et XIIe siècles," RB, XVI (1937), 938-39. The death of the provost,
who, as chancellor, was chief of the notaries, and the ensuing anarchy had probably
disrupted the well-organized fiscal administration of the county. The importance
of the notarial records is revealed by the fact that some were rescued from the
castle along with the relics of the saints on March 17; see c. 35.

[8] The complete collapse of the count's "peace" could hardly be better expressed.

with a certain knight who was on our side. Now the house of
this knight of ours was fortified and very strong; into it all those
in the vicinity and many citizens from Bruges had brought their
goods, believing they would be safer there.[1] Then they seized
that knight[2] as he was going about safely on his farm and struck
him down, overcome by wounds, and took forcible possession
of the house, having thrown out the knight. Count Thierry went
out at once joyfully with an enormous crowd, laid siege and
forced the besieged to surrender. He let them go out, however,
safe in members, and successfully restored the knight and lord
of that house to his own home on Tuesday, that is, June 12.

On the same day, June 12, the knights of Count William, who
had held Oudenburg and Jabbeke and Straten in order to prepare
ambushes for our Count Thierry and our knights, hearing that
Thierry with his whole following had laid siege to some remote
villages outside Bruges, sent about sixty scouts to burn a house
next to the castle at Bruges, hoping to lure out our citizens whom
they might be able to seize in this way. They attacked us all the
more in the hope of recalling Count Thierry from the siege by
means of the smoke and flames. Then the castellan, Gervaise,
coming up to attack the scouts with his knights, seized two
vigorous knights, Walter, the nephew of Thancmar, who was
responsible for all the strife and conflict which sprang up between Thancmar and Borsiard, that betrayer of Count Charles;
and he captured another knight with Walter. And this Walter
was mortally wounded while he was being captured.

Now the citizens of Bruges clapped their hands with joy,
hardly able to express their high spirits over such a great success.
For finally, after so many evils, so much looting and burning of
houses, and so many murders which had been inflicted on us,
we had captured that Walter who was the source and beginning
of all the misfortunes of our land, by whose cunning Count
Charles had been betrayed; not that he himself had betrayed him
but he had forced his enemies, Borsiard and his men, to the act

---

1 Evidence of a surprising sense of insecurity in the town.
2 Galbert's word here is *eques* instead of the more usual *miles* for knight.

of betrayal.[3] I say this in accordance with the feeling of the people and with the rage of spirit of those who would have hanged that captive Walter without delay or destroyed him by some new and unheard-of kind of death, if the count had permitted it. For Count Thierry, seeing the fire close to Bruges, was already coming back from the siege and approaching with the whole crowd, but before his arrival those two were seized and the other scouts had fled. On the same day Walter of Zomergem,[4] and the knights and foot soldiers with him who were fighting on our side, were captured at Aalter. On the same day Daniel and Ivan at Rupelmonde captured fifty knights from the duke of Louvain.[5]

On hearing all this news, the citizens of Bruges attributed Thierry's successes and good fortune to a certain priest of his who by his anathema had excommunicated Count William and his partisans. But at Ypres a certain provost, Hildfred, was daily excommunicating all those who sided with or aided our Count Thierry. In this interchange, however, the anathema of our priest prevailed, and I do not think our priest intends to desist from the anathema until he has forced Count William with his supporters and his provost, Hildfred, into exile. And it is marvelous that a priest can cast a spell on God in such a way that, whether God wishes it or not, William may be thrown out of the countship![6] On the same day the men of Ypres sent a letter secretly to the men of Bruges, saying that they wanted some of our responsible men and theirs to assemble privately and in a safe place, and to take proper steps for the honor of the county.[7]

---

[3] Galbert's belief in the responsibility of the Straten family (see c. 9) seems to have grown until he now shares the popular prejudice, especially against Walter, never before named. See c. 45 where he first expresses this sentiment.

[4] He is named in two charters of 1122 as the brother of Baldwin of Zomergem (*Actes*, no. 106, 107, pp. 243, 247). Baldwin is mentioned in c. 34.

[5] They have violated their promise to their lord, the duke of Lorraine, in supporting Thierry without his permission; see Galbert c. 101, and c. 118.

[6] The passage beginning "On hearing all this news" and ending at this point, is one of those which Pirenne believed (ed. Galbert, p. xxiv) the Bollandists suppressed in their original edition of Galbert's work, AASS, March 1 (Antwerp, 1668), pp. 179-219. Concerning the debate between Pirenne and the Bollandists on this subject see the Preface, p. x, n. 5.

[7] They had approached Thierry on April 9; see c. 105.

[114] *Thierry is defeated in the battle of Axspoele, June 21,*
    1128

On June 18 and 19, Count Thierry went with Count Frederick[1]
to Ghent, and he assembled a very large army from Axel and
Boekhoute and the country of Waas and those parts; he also
brought projectile machines with which to reduce the fortified
houses and strongholds of his enemies. He took a strong force
to Tielt and besieged the house of Folk, a knight. Then on June
20, Wednesday, the men of Bruges came to the count with their
castellan, Gervaise, and an enormous number of Flemings[2] who
had made a sworn compact with them. On the following night
they settled down for the siege around the house. Now Count
William, following close after, looked over the army which had
besieged his vassal to see how much of it was a band of auxilia-
ries and how much a real army;[3] he was very angry because of
that insult and the growing arrogance of the besiegers. For
Count William had chosen to die rather than endure such a great
dishonor. Therefore on June 21, Thursday, and the fourth day
before the feast of Saint John the Baptist, in Oudenburg, about
dawn, he devoutly received the sacrament of penance from the
abbot of that place,[4] a devout and wise man, and vowed solemnly
to God that he would henceforth be the protector of the poor
and of the churches of God. In the same way all his vigorous
knights took vows; after cutting off their hair and casting off
their ordinary garments, they put on linen shirts and cuirasses
and took up arms.[5]

Advancing to battle with humble prayers to God and fiery

[1] Unknown, perhaps a German kinsman of Thierry, says Pirenne, ed. Galbert,
p. 162, n. 2.

[2] From maritime Flanders, probably.

[3] *Turba et exercitus:* Galbert probably distinguishes between the town forces,
workers of the machines, and the like, all on foot, and the "army proper" of
mounted knights. See the comments of J. F. Verbruggen, "La Tactique militaire
des armées de chevaliers," RN, XXIX (1947), 161-80, who analyses the following
battle of Axpoele in detail.

[4] The abbot of Oudenburg was Hariulf, 1105-43, author of the chronicle of
Saint Riquier and of the life of Saint Arnulf.

[5] In this stage of the war between the two claimants, a curious mixture of
"magical" practices and religious austerities appears; see the comments of J. Dhondt,
"Une Mentalité du douzième siècle," RN, XXXIX, 105-7.

zeal, they came to the top of a hill which overlooked the army of Count Thierry, and there they arranged themselves for combat. Then Count William divided his forces into three corps of horsemen, taking over the first line which, under his command, was to make the first attack. On the other side, Count Thierry similarly[6] drew up his lines; in one of these he and Gervaise, the castellan, were leaders, in the other Count Frederick. With lances drawn back, they advanced little by little on both sides, making their way by lance and sword, and great numbers fell. Both the counts were fighting as if they offered themselves to death, rushing into the midst of hostile arms;[7] they had decided beforehand to die in battle rather than be expelled from the countship.

Now in the first attack Daniel, commander of Count Thierry's knights, was trying to force his way into Count William's lines; and there Count Frederick was unhorsed and opposite him Richard of Woumen[8] was taken prisoner in this first contact of the lines; the number of those joined in conflict was infinite! Finally they resorted to swords. But when part of Count William's forces and that formation in which he himself was fighting, began to give way, he turned in flight, and Daniel pursued him with his men.[9] While they were struggling on both sides, some fleeing, some pursuing, the second part of the detachment of Count William which was hiding in ambush, rushed out in the face of Daniel and his men. And because they were stimulated by fresh energy and common purpose, and had been instructed in how to fight, they did not hesitate a moment, but

---

[6] That is, in two units, like the visible army of William, but a third corps of the latter was lying in ambush behind the hill, as appears later. As to numbers, Verbruggen estimates that William's army, composed largely of knights, numbered about 450 while Thierry had about 300 knights plus the town forces of Ghent and Bruges, perhaps 1500 *fantassins*; that is, William's force was superior in quality, Thierry's in numbers. See "La Tactique militaire," RN, XXIX (1947), 170.

[7] That is, the two advancing lines of knights have merged, each trying to dismount the other. The footsoldiers come behind, probably to capture the dismounted knights.

[8] See c. 16 and c. 31. Verbruggen, p. 171, thinks he was head of William's second corps.

[9] Verbruggen, pp. 171-72, interprets this retreat as a feint of William's to draw out the enemy and to save his own corps of knights from the greater numbers of the enemy.

intercepted the pursuers with their lances and swords.[10] Then Count William, rallying quickly from flight, turned back with his forces; he urged them on, bold in spirit and strong in body, to attack the enemy furiously and disperse them in one onslaught.[11] When Count Thierry's men saw the imminent perils of battle they cast aside their arms and fled without protection in all directions, so that only ten knights remained with their count. Then at last Count William and his men, throwing off their cuirasses and thus riding more easily, secured the fruits of their victory; they killed some of the enemy and captured others.

About midnight Count Thierry returned to Bruges; but how Count William returned we have not heard. Then our place was full of mourning; wives mourned their lost husbands, sons their fathers, serfs and handmaidens their lords. Trying to understand the calamity and misfortunes of the war, they spent the whole night weeping and sighing. Now at dawn when our people went out to find their dead, more captives were seized by William's knights. Never before in our region had such an outrage of war been heard of as this dreadful pursuit and capture of so many of our people! And in fact such an enormous amount of money was paid out to redeem our captives from Count William and his men that in a certain sense our land was again despoiled. When our own people[12] finally heard that Count William, before going into battle, had dedicated himself humbly to God, and had received the sacrament of penance, and that he and all his men, after his misfortunes in war, had cut off their hair and cast off their superfluous garments, our citizens together with their Count Thierry, removed their hair and clothes.

And now those priests of ours, following the example of the enemy, finally preached penance, and after so much injury, loss, and captivity had been inflicted upon us, they called for a universal fast. And they bore the crosses and reliquaries of the

[10] Verbruggen, p. 173, stresses the element of conscious planning on William's side, his use of real military "tactics," as seen in his early reconnaissance, the planting of the reserve, the feigned retreat, and sudden recovery with the use of the trained reserves.

[11] Thomas corrects *corporum* to read *corporis* and suggests the omission of *armorum* in this difficult sentence.

[12] *Nostrates,* an unusual term, is here used.

saints into the church of the Holy Virgin in Bruges[13] and there all the priestly clergy of Bruges excommunicated by name William, count of the Normans: that is, Thancran the dean, and the priests Eggard, Sigebod, Heribert, Fromold Senior, and Thierry.[14] And they made Count Thierry swear in the presence of all that if any people came over to him from Ypres he would receive them mercifully, and he would act similarly towards any one in the whole county who came over to him, and he would not disinherit them.

Here[15] it should be noted that the excommunications by our priestly clergy and those on the other side, by our archbishop and his suffragan bishops,[16] were conflicting with each other, because our priests were excommunicating William, and the archbishops and bishops of the same priests were excommunicating our Count Thierry. However, while the archbishop and his bishops believed that divine offices had been suspended at Bruges by the ban, and that our dead had not been buried in holy ground, we, in fact, contrary to the command of our metropolitan and our bishop, were carrying on divine services and were burying those

---

[13] The erroneous belief that divine services were being held *only* in the church of the Holy Virgin as a result of the episcopal ban laid on Bruges (c. 107) has led to two conflicting hypotheses. Pirenne (ed. Galbert, p. 164, n. 1) believes that the church was not subject to the ban because, by a special ecclesiastical arrangement of 1122, it was subject to the jurisdiction of the bishop of Utrecht, not of Noyon-Tournai, while Ganshof ("Iets over Brugge," NH, I [1938], 288 and n. 47) believes the church was unaffected by the ban because it lay outside the town proper. According to the recent interpretation of Professor Dhondt, however, the church lay inside the town; see "De vroege topografie van Brugge," HMGG, XI (1957), 28-29. Galbert's own statement, moreover, proves that services were going on in all the churches of Bruges and not merely in that of the Holy Virgin; see the last sentences of c. 116, as well as the end of this chapter. It is true, however, that the church of the Holy Virgin and her mother-church at Sijsele (southeast of the town), were subject to the chapter of Saint Martin of Utrecht by virtue of a donation made by Count Baldwin I to the bishop of Utrecht at the time of his quarrel with Hincmar, archbishop of Rheims; see the article of J. Noterdaeme, "Studiën over de vroegste kerkgeschiedenis van Brugge: I, Sijsele en het Sint-Maartenskapittel te Utrecht," *Sacris Erudiri,* VI (1954), 180-88.

[14] Eggard was a priest of the church of the Holy Savior; see Galbert, c. 61. Fromold Senior was a canon of Saint Donatian; he was last mentioned in c. 35.

[15] This paragraph is another of the passages suppressed in the Bollandist edition, according to Pirenne.

[16] The suffragan bishops of the province of Rheims with jurisdiction over Flemish territory were those of Therouanne, Arras, Noyon-Tournai (to 1146) and Cambrai.

killed in battle in holy ground, and we struck with anathema William and his supporters by name.[17]

[115] *The strange incident of the cross, June 24, 1128*

On June 24, Sunday, on the feast of Saint John the Baptist, in the church of the Holy Virgin, a crucifix which was standing on the floor to be adored by the faithful rose up from the place where it had been firmly fixed, by itself and through the power of God; and it would have fallen to the pavement if one of the sacristans of the church had not caught it in his hands as it fell. This sacristan placed the crucifix again in its usual place, but when he had left, again, just as before, it rose up from its stand and began to fall. Then all who were standing around in worship ran up and set it in its place again, thinking that the fall had come about from the carelessness of the one who had placed it. But on looking around they were satisfied that no lack of care could account for this. Again[1] our priests had the stupidity to say[2] that the priest from Aartrijke and the priest from Koekelare and the cleric Odfrid had put Count Thierry and his men to flight in the battle by incantations, when in fact it is God who disposes and ordains all things!

[116] *Count William tries to seize Oostkamp, July 4, 1128; the people of Bruges become demoralized*

On July 4, Wednesday, the day of the translation of Martin, bishop of the church of Tours, Count William the Norman with

---

[17] Galbert's use of "we" here does not necessarily imply that he was a priest as Pirenne suggests, ed. Galbert, p. ii, and n. 3; he seems, rather, to be identifying himself with the people of Bruges as a whole. See the Introduction, VI.

[1] From this point on, the passage is another of those believed by Pirenne to have been suppressed by the Bollandists.

[2] In his debate with the Bollandists, Pirenne admitted that the reading *idiote* should probably be corrected to *idiotae*. *Revue générale*, XXVIII (1892), 524, n. 5.

a strong army besieged the house of the chief magistrate[1] in the village of Oostkamp, bringing up projectile machines,[2] a mangonel and a *pyrrira,* with which to destroy the house. But Count Thierry with citizens of Bruges and men of Flanders from around Bruges, and also Arnold Wineth,[3] were opposing him inside the ditches and palisades of that house. Now the two armies were divided by the river[4] which served to fortify the house on the east. But on the side where William made the attack that house was well defended by palisades and ditches. Many, therefore, on both sides were killed or wounded in the onslaught and in the fighting against each other, but the house and its ditches and palisades stood firm. Finally they set up towers[5] on the two sides opposite each other, and fought even more fiercely when they had mounted them. Then, because the west wind was blowing strongly on the enemy forces opposite the army of William, he ordered hay, grass, the roofs of houses, brush, and all kinds of stuff to be brought to fill up the ditches so that they could pass over to the enemy opposite. But those inside threw on the machine[6] pieces of pitch and old ointment and wax, burning lightly, and so everything that had been piled up was consumed by fire. The smoke of the burning machine, however, driven by the strong winds, blew into the eyes of those who had hurled the fire from within. Many succumbed, wounded by lances and spears and arrows.

Then William continued that siege[7] for six days, and during those days how many deeds of knighthood, how many encounters[8] those knights in both armies engaged in! For, although the river

---

[1] See c. 50, where a *magnus praeco* is mentioned.

[2] *Magnella* (*mangonel*) was a counterweight machine; the *pyrrira* (probably a *perrière*) was a spring machine. See Enlart, *Manuel d'archéologie,* IIeme partie, tome II, pp. 486, 491.

[3] An Arnold of "Windeke" appears several times as witness in charters of Count Charles; see *Actes,* Index.

[4] The stream of Oostkamp.

[5] "Towers" were a common siege equipment. They were wooden structures, usually on rollers, with projecting platforms to reach the top of the walls; they were sometimes called *belfragia* ("belfreys"). See Enlart, *Manuel d'archéologie,* IIeme partie, tome II, pp. 480-82.

[6] The tower, apparently.

[7] This is mentioned as a classic example of a siege by Enlart, IIeme partie, tome II, p. 475.

[8] *Tornationes* (tourneys), used as in c. 79 to mean real conflicts.

between the enemies was deep, throughout the whole siege William's knights sought out the shallows and crossings in the river which they used promptly, eager for conflict and fighting, since they were stronger in arms and greater in numbers. On the sixth day, which was July 9, Monday, towards evening, William, seeing that there was no profit in the siege of that house, ordered four hundred knights to cross the shallows of the river, and they burned down the house of the knight, Ansbold,[9] and the houses of his brother and sisters; then his army withdrew. But our people[10] fled into Bruges, and those who lived in the vicinity around us came in to us at Bruges, fleeing with all their furniture and flocks, overcome with fear and trembling; they passed a sleepless night. On the same day one of the cells of the monks of Saint Trond near Oostkamp[11] was so completely sacked that neither a book nor chalice of the Mass was left there.

It should be noted, certainly, that no intelligent man among us at Bruges dared to speak the truth about the calamity and misfortune and our flight. For if anyone uttered a word of the truth, they defamed him as a traitor to our place and a supporter of Count William and threatened him with sudden death. And it was no wonder, because God was hardening their hearts so that they did not want to hear the truth at all. By following the crosses and processions led by the clergy through the churches they actually provoked God to wrath rather than appeasing him, because they had freed themselves from the power set over them by God in their obstinacy of soul, evil doing, pride, and strife. "Let every soul be subject to every power" says the apostle.[12] Therefore, if in that place where the most wicked treacheries had come forth, there came to pass misfortunes, war, sedition, homicide, and the eternal disgrace of all Flanders, did not that place rightfully deserve all those evils? And if the church of the brothers in Bruges suffered, was it not deservedly because the provost of that church bore responsibility for the evils? And

---

[9] Ansbold and the chief magistrate had been acting together earlier; see c. 50.

[10] *Nostri:* the burghers of Bruges.

[11] See c. 21, n. 10.

[12] I Peter 2.13; one of Galbert's favorite sentiments. See also his introduction and c. 118.

although no one dared to announce publicly the ban and anathema of our archbishop and bishop and of his other suffragan
bishops, we heard and we knew for a fact that we had been
deservedly placed under the ban and prohibition of divine services because we had substituted one count for another and had
thus been responsible for an infinite number of deaths. Our
priests and the clergy of our place had taken their stand in the
fight with the people and the crowd, not remembering that they
should stand like a wall for the house of Israel.[13]

[117] *Hostages are exchanged at Bruges, July 11, 1128*

On July 11, Wednesday, the day of the translation of Benedict
the abbot, Christian of Gistel[1] and the brothers of Walter *Pennatum-mendacium*[2] came to Bruges by the arrangement of Daniel.
And Christian gave his son as hostage, and the two brothers
remained as hostages for their brother Walter, who was shackled
in the count's house in Bruges. Then Christian and his knights
carried off Walter with them to see whether he would get well
or die, for he seemed to be dying of wounds.

[118] *The vicissitudes of Bruges, July 12-25, 1128*

On July 12, Thursday, the duke of Louvain[1] besieged Aalst with
a strong army, and Count William of Flanders came to his aid

---

[13] Ezekiel 13.5.

[1] Not named in the count's charters 1071-1128. The Inquest (MGH, SS XXV,
p. 443) reveals that he had married Borsiard's sister, who was one of those not
disinherited.

[2] He is doubtless the nephew of Thancmar, recently wounded and captured
(c. 113) to the joy of the people of Bruges, who now treat him as a traitor. Perhaps
the identity of his name with that of one of the nephews of Bertulf (c. 81)
contributed to the growth of the popular legend which fastened the blame for the
murder on the unpopular family of Straten. See the interesting interpretation of
Count F. van der Straten Ponthoz, *Charles-le-Bon, causes de sa mort, ses vrais
meurtriers* (Metz, 1853), pp. 40-43.

[1] Godfrey is besieging in Aalst his vassal, Ivan, who contrary to his promise,
is supporting Thierry. See Galbert, c. 101, 113. The hostile policies of the emperor,
Lothair, and of Simon, duke of Upper Lorraine, who was the brother of Thierry,

with four hundred knights. Meanwhile at Bruges many lies were circulating about the affair of the recent siege.[2]

It happened meanwhile that a mill at Bruges[3] which had sunk into the water and collapsed now gave way completely, and the water which had defended the castle and town of Bruges on the southern side, where the mill had held in the waters, almost all flowed out. The citizens in alarm rushed to work and obstructed the escaping water with dung, wood, and earth. Then they charged that the undermining of the mill had been done secretly by their enemies so that after the water flowed off the castle and their town would lie open to enemy attack. There were many soothsayers, both laymen and priests, who were flattering our citizens, foretelling whatever they knew the citizens wanted to hear. In fact, if anyone knowing the truth about the affair of the siege and the dangers threatening the place and the citizens spoke the truth, they brought base charges against him and he was silenced.

But it proved to be a good thing for those fawning priests![4] Although in the holy time of Lent they had permitted the citizens to eat twice on a day when all Catholics were observing fast, and now, at the time of the siege of the duke (on the second day before the vigil of Saint Jacob, the apostle, and Saint Christopher, the martyr) they had enjoined fasting on bread and water for everyone in our place, including children above seven years and all persons of both sexes, those priests received a reward for bearing crosses and anathematizing Count William—candles and pennies and other offerings suitable only for bellies! They acted as if they could bend God himself to injustice by such fasting and offerings, although the citizens were still persisting in their

---

probably impelled Godfrey to oppose Thierry and hence support William, as Galbert implies in c. 120.

[2] That is, the siege at Oostkamp; see c. 116.

[3] The exact location of this mill has been a matter of dispute. For the most recent interpretation, that of Professor Dhondt, consult the Plan of Bruges and "De vroege topografie," HMGG, XI, 9; the mill was probably located on the watercourse running just south of the castle, connecting the Fullers' Stream and the Reie.

[4] The following paragraph is the last of those passages which Pirenne believed to have been suppressed by the Bollandists.

obstinacy by refusing absolutely to recognize their lord. As we have often said, "Let every soul be subject to every authority"[5] for the love of the Lord, and the Lord himself answered Pilate (who was himself set over the Jews of Jerusalem by the Romans) at the very time of the Lord's Passion, "You would not have any power over me, if it had not been given to you from above by my Father";[6] and again, "Render unto God the things that are God's and unto Caesar the things that are Caesar's."[7] The citizens were, indeed, acting unjustly in that while their lord was still alive they had put another lord in his place, and neither was the one justly cast down nor the other justly set up.[8] A certain one of the priests took counsel with his fellow-vicars as to whether on the feast of Saint Christopher in Bruges he should excommunicate Count William and all his supporters regardless of rank.[9] How clear it became that iniquity sprang forth from the elder judges who were supposed to rule over the flock of the Lord! But our citizens still struggled on, extorting money from each other which they sent to Count Thierry to carry on the siege mentioned above. And those in Ghent did likewise. The ones besieged at Aalst were Ivan and Daniel and Count Thierry with a strong band of knights well proved in fighting.

On July 25, Wednesday, the feast of Saint Christopher, Walter *Pennatum-mendacium* was brought back to captivity in Bruges; and the hostages were handed over which had been given for him and had been held up to this time.

[5] I Peter 2.13; none of these quotations follows exactly the language of the Vulgate.

[6] John 19.11.

[7] Luke 20.25.

[8] Although he accepted Thierry once he was "elected" as "our count" (c. 107) and as the "natural and just count of Flanders" (c. 108), Galbert shows an increasing concern for Count William as the victim of injustice from c. 108 on, and persists in calling him "Count William." Now he seems to accept neither as rightful count! He does not again call Thierry "our count" until after William's death; see c. 119. In c. 121 he tries to resolve his dilemma.

[9] But according to c. 114, this had already been done.

[119] *The death of Count William, July 27 or 28, 1128*

On July 27, the sixth day after the Transfiguration of the Lord on Mount Tabor, the Lord deigned to bring an end in a certain manner both to what he had foreseen and to what we had suffered in this strife, for Count William the Norman was unhorsed when he exposed himself to the enemy in the assault during the siege at the castle of Aalst. He regained his feet, but when he was stretching his right hand towards his weapons a footsoldier rushed out from the enemy, and, piercing the palm of the count's right hand with his lance, he drove it through the middle of the arm adjacent to the hand, thus inflicting a mortal wound.[1] His knights gathered round him, seeing that their lord was dying so pitiably; concealing his death from his enemies throughout the whole day, they held back the words and sounds of sorrow, without mourning and lamentation, in great anguish and confusion of spirit. Then the duke of Louvain made an effort to reach an agreement between himself and his men and our Count Thierry, and he commended the case of all the discord between them to the judgment of Ivan and Daniel and the king of England.[2] After this offer of agreement was received with praise on both sides, he asked our Count Thierry to grant Count William the freedom of returning peacefully from the siege with his men; and when Count Thierry had given his consent to the duke, the latter spoke: "Alas! Count William, whom you are pursuing with all your strength as a great enemy, lies dead of a mortal wound!" Then everyone on both sides started up, some to mourn the fall of such a great and famous knight, others to arouse the enemy by exultation, others to denounce those who had stayed at home, so concerned for the safety of their goods that they would do

[1] Pirenne (ed. Galbert, p. 171, n. 2) points out that the other sources do not agree wholly with each other or with Galbert as to the exact date of William's death or the interval of time between his injury and death. Herman, c. 36, simply says in the "month of August"; according to him the wound was slight, "under the thumb," but a swelling of the arm followed, aggravated by the heat. Galbert seems to imply that he died the same day, but other sources say after "three" or "five" days. Vercauteren (*Actes*, p. xix) believes he died on July 27 or 28.

[2] According to Herman, c. 36, the duke, on the advice of the dying William, pretended to act as mediator between Thierry and William, and beat a retreat before sending back word that William was dead.

nothing except with caution and deliberation. Now the rumor and news of the death of that prince spread about, and those who had fought for that count in faith and loyalty, took themselves off to safer places. Then with the sound of infinite mourning filling the air they bore the body of the brave knight on a bier to Saint Omer to be buried.[3]

[120] *Count Thierry extends his authority, July 29, 1128*

Count Thierry was now pursuing his enemies in all directions and using fire to ravage and capture and destroy them, unless they won his favor by money or some other means beforehand. Therefore Count Thierry went to Ypres on July 29, Sunday, with an enormous force of knights and took Ypres. The citizens of Bruges and their knights and mercenaries came out and sacked the village of Ruddervoorde and burnt the houses. And so Lambert of Ruddervoorde[1] and Lambert of Wingene[2] and Folk of Tielt,[3] and many others in our region who had fought in aid of Count William, withdrew into the stronghold of Wijnendale.[4] Also those citizens at Ypres who had supported William fortified themselves with Isaac at Voormezele[5] where large forces were made ready.

And it should be noted that when the town of Bruges stood in such great peril that the citizens believed there was no remedy possible except through God's aid and therefore appeased God by penitence of heart, He came to their rescue with his customary dispensation. For He slew Count William by the sword of His

---

[3] At the abbey of Saint Bertin.

[1] Named as witness in the charter of Count William to Saint Omer; see *Actes*, no. 129, p. 303.

[2] See c. 107, 110; he is a witness to the same charter, *Actes*, no. 129.

[3] See c. 114.

[4] It seems clear that William's chief support had lain among the knights whereas many burghers, together with some of the great barons, supported Thierry. See Verbruggen, *Die krijgskunst*, p. 371, and Dhondt, *Les Origines des États*, p. 18, n. 42.

[5] He appears as witness to a charter of Count William, *Actes*, no. 128, p. 302, as well as to several charters of Count Charles.

justice but in such a way that he died fighting not in his own cause but in that of another, that is, he was giving aid to that duke.[6] Consequently we people of Bruges were considered guiltless of his death since in fact none of us had inflicted death on him; on the contrary, at the very time when he departed this life, we were afraid that he was certainly going to besiege us. And yet those knights from Oostkerke[7] who were on our side and Count Thierry's charged us with being traitors and withdrew from us on the very day the count died.

Meanwhile a messenger came to us at Bruges to announce the death of Count William. On hearing the news the citizens and all of us[8] gave thanks to God for such a great liberation of their persons and their goods. For it was a marvelous dispensation of God which arranged for that prince to die in such a way that he went outside our county[9] to aid the duke at the siege of Aalst. And although he was fighting on the side against our count and us, the responsibility for the siege and the conflict rested on the duke and no one else. And although Count William fought against us willingly on any occasion whatsoever, and for this very reason had gone to the aid of the duke, his fight and his death there, predetermined by God, cannot be attributed to anyone but the duke. For he was the duke's knight in this respect, that he died there fighting not primarily for the countship but for the honor and safety of the duke, just like any mercenary.

Some argue that our own people, after expelling Count William, substituted Count Thierry for him, and that after establish-

---

[6] That is, on the side of the duke of Lorraine. Since the duke was besieging Ivan of Aalst, William's leading enemy, it is hard to accept Galbert's reasoning as valid. His attitude toward the people of Bruges has grown more tolerant or conformist since c. 111 and c. 118; William's death has simplified the situation.

[7] See c. 98. These knights seem to have shifted back to what they now believed to be the winning side, but just at the wrong moment.

[8] *Cives et omnes nostrates.* This is the first time Galbert has used such an expression; "all of us" seems to include those who were not burghers, such as the clergy and knights of the castle.

[9] Pirenne (ed. Galbert, p. 173, n. 3) explains this statement by saying that Aalst was not at this time a "fief" of the county of Flanders like the other parts of Imperial Flanders, but an "allod"; this interpretation, however, is not tenable. It is certainly curious that Galbert should refer to Aalst as "outside our county" since he calls the barons of Imperial Flanders "peers of the realm." Perhaps it simply suits his argument to distinguish here between the original Flanders, held of the French crown, and the later acquisitions.

ing the latter in the towns and all the places they could get hold of by means of silver and persuasion and in every possible way by use of influence and money, they set him to resisting William. For, according to this argument, they can not be proved innocent of his death. Others contend that the duke had attacked Count Thierry because he foresaw that if Thierry should by chance rule in Flanders and remain in the countship, he could inflict much harm on him in the future and perhaps even drive him from his duchy, or straightway seize the dowry on account of which Count Thierry was trying to challenge the duke in the presence of the emperor.[10] Count William for a similar reason was fighting in the duke's siege against Count Thierry because he knew the latter was striving by every possible device to drive him out of the countship. And yet he knew that Thierry had been put in his place unjustly and treacherously. And therefore on both sides they could argue rationally, on the one hand that Count William rightly succumbed there both in support of the duke and as a result of his own injurious acts, and on the other that Count Thierry fought there against the duke and Count William for the sake of the dowry which was justly demanded from the duke, and for the sake of the countship which had been handed over to him but not in a proper way.[11]

[121] *How can God's dispensation be explained?*

It may well be asked why, therefore, when God wished to restore the peace of the fatherland through the death of one of the two, He preferred that Count William should die, whose claim to rule the land was more just, and why on the contrary Count Thierry did not die who seemed unjustly put in his place; or by what justice God granted the countship to the one who forcibly seized

[10] The extensive dowry that Clemence, widow of Count Robert II of Flanders, had brought to Godfrey in marriage. Walter, c. 8, says it comprised "twelve strong-holds"; according to *Flandria generosa*, c. 32, MGH, SS IX, 324, it included about one-third of Flanders.

[11] Galbert's involved attempt to justify the actions of both counts reveals his own inner conflict; see the Introduction, pp. 70-72.

the office. If, indeed, neither of them rightfully received the countship, by right both of them should have been removed. And yet, because the countship pertained by hereditary right to Count Thierry, he holds it by right; and if he seems to have seized it unjustly, nevertheless, because before the election of that William, who is now dead, he had claimed that it belonged to him by letters sent to the barons of Flanders—although at that time they did not listen to him—he did right in seeking and conquering his heritage which had been unjustly taken away from him and sold unjustly by the king of France.[1] Therefore, after so much controversy, we consider the more just cause to be that of Count Thierry who cannot be called unjustly substituted for Count William; on the contrary, that dead count was most unjustly substituted for Thierry and given the authority of the count by the authority of the king in return for a relief. And so God rightfully preserved the life of Count Thierry in accordance with ancient justice, and restored him to his heritage, and removed by death from the countship the other one, who, as long as he had the power, laid waste the whole land and provoked all the inhabitants of the land to civil war and confounded the laws of God and men; on the basis of his merits God determined, by strict law, that he should go the way of all flesh, not without misfortunes. For Count William will confess, among the shades which he sent before him to the places of punishment, that nothing remains to him of all he possessed in life except fame: for he was called good in knighthood.[2]

Therefore God righted such a great wrong, which no human power could or would correct, in accordance with the line of strict examination.[3] He turned the flails of his wrath against the men of Flanders for this reason, because earlier it had been within the power of everyone to consider and foresee and discuss, and seek out with all care the one whom they would set up as lord

[1] A reference to the large sum, 1,000 marks, paid as relief by William to the king; see c. 106.
[2] Pirenne points out (p. 175, n. 1) that all the sources agree in recognizing his courage. Lambert (*Genealogia comitum Flandriae*, c. 12, MGH, SS IX, 312) calls him "the best knight in thousands" (*optimus miles in milibus*).
[3] Perhaps from Amos 7.7?

over themselves and the fatherland, and whom they would love and venerate once he was elected. And by contrition of heart and uprightness of mind they could have pleased God in this matter. But because they neglected this, they had to endure the one whom they had received as lord so rashly, as a tyrant and despoiler and evil exactor; and after his election and elevation to the countship, the barons and officials and counselors of the land did not guide him in the right path or teach him the honorable customs of the counts his predecessors, but instructed him in pillaging and in crafty and deceitful pretexts by means of which they could demand vast sums of money from the citizens and burghers of the land and extort it from them by violence whenever they wished.

[122] *Count Thierry is confirmed in power*

Therefore Thierry, marquis of Flanders, reigned from the time of William's death, and after visiting all the towns,[1] that is Arras, Therouanne, Saint Omer, Lille, Aire, where he was received with respect, according to the custom of his good predecessors, by the clergy and the people, and was confirmed by faith and homage, he finally went to the kings of France and England to receive from them fiefs and royal gifts.[2] For our Count Thierry was acceptable to the kings of both realms, France and England, and they freely granted him investiture with the fiefs and benefices which the most holy and pious Count Charles had held from them.[3]

[1] That is, those towns which had not yet received him.

[2] The exact date of Thierry's recognition as count of Flanders by the king of France is not known. Herman, c. 36, confirms Galbert's statement. The fief received from Henry I was undoubtedly a renewal of the money-fief, granted first to Robert II in the year 1101, renewed in 1110, suspended during Baldwin VII's anti-English reign, and apparently renewed during Charles's reign (though Galbert is the only direct authority for this). See G. Dept, *Les Influences anglaise et française dans le comté de Flandre au début du XIIIe siècle* (Ghent, 1928), pp. 19-20. Nothing is said of Thierry's enfeoffment with imperial Flanders by the emperor.

APPENDIX

GENEALOGY OF THE COUNTS OF FLANDERS
from 1035 to 1128

BALDWIN VI, "of Mons"
m. Richilda, widow of Herman I,
count of Hainaut, 1051–70, as Baldwin I
count of Flanders, 1067–70, as Baldwin VI

BALDWIN V,
"of Lille"
count of Flanders,
1035–67
m. Adele,
daughter of
Robert, king of
France

ROBERT I, "the Frisian"
m. Gertrude, widow of
Florent I, count of Holland,
d. 1061, by whom she
bore .... **THIERRY V** ———— **FLORENT II**
count of Flanders,   of Holland,   of Holland,
1071–93   d. 1091   d. 1122

MATHILDA
d. 1083
m. William, duke of Normandy,
king of England, 1066–87

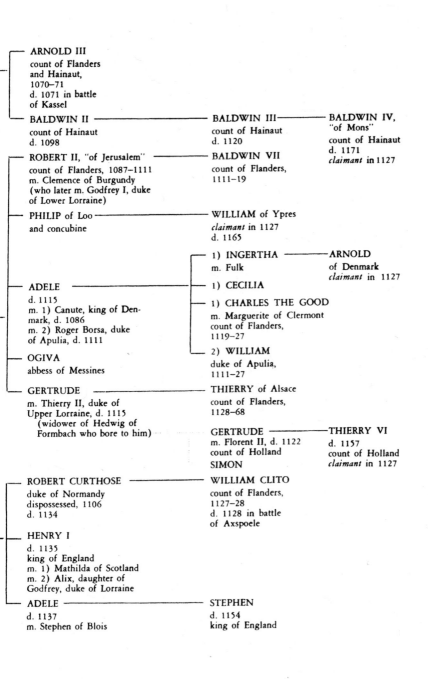

ARNOLD III
count of Flanders
and Hainaut,
1070–71
d. 1071 in battle
of Kassel

BALDWIN II ─────────────── BALDWIN III──────── BALDWIN IV,
count of Hainaut   count of Hainaut   "of Mons"
d. 1098   d. 1120   count of Hainaut
                                                  d. 1171
ROBERT II, "of Jerusalem" ──────── BALDWIN VII   *claimant* in 1127
count of Flanders, 1087–1111   count of Flanders,
m. Clemence of Burgundy   1111–19
(who later m. Godfrey I, duke
of Lower Lorraine)

PHILIP of Loo ─────────────── WILLIAM of Ypres
and concubine   *claimant* in 1127
                             d. 1165

                             ┌─ 1) INGERTHA ────── ARNOLD
                             │ m. Fulk   of Denmark
                             │   *claimant* in 1127
                             ├─ 1) CECILIA
ADELE ───────────────────────┤
d. 1115   ├─ 1) CHARLES THE GOOD
m. 1) Canute, king of Den-   │ m. Marguerite of Clermont
mark, d. 1086   │ count of Flanders,
m. 2) Roger Borsa, duke   │ 1119–27
of Apulia, d. 1111   │
                             └─ 2) WILLIAM
OGIVA   duke of Apulia,
abbess of Messines   1111–27

GERTRUDE ─────────────────── THIERRY of Alsace
m. Thierry II, duke of   count of Flanders,
Upper Lorraine, d. 1115   1128–68
   (widower of Hedwig of
   Formbach who bore to him)   GERTRUDE ───────────THIERRY VI
                                 m. Florent II, d. 1122   d. 1157
                                 count of Holland   count of Holland
                                 SIMON   *claimant* in 1127

ROBERT CURTHOSE ─────────────── WILLIAM CLITO
duke of Normandy   count of Flanders,
dispossessed, 1106   1127–28
d. 1134   d. 1128 in battle
                               of Axspoele
HENRY I
d. 1135
king of England
m. 1) Mathilda of Scotland
m. 2) Alix, daughter of
Godfrey, duke of Lorraine

ADELE ─────────────────────── STEPHEN
d. 1137   d. 1154
m. Stephen of Blois   king of England

GENEALOGY OF THE EREMBALD CLAN

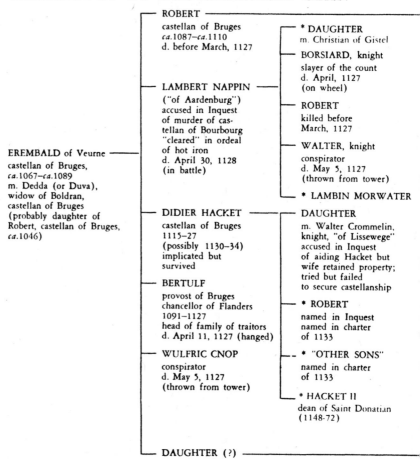

EREMBALD of Veurne
castellan of Bruges,
ca.1067–ca.1089
m. Dedda (or Duva),
widow of Boldran,
castellan of Bruges
(probably daughter of
Robert, castellan of Bruges,
ca.1046)

ROBERT
castellan of Bruges
ca.1087–ca.1110
d. before March, 1127

— * DAUGHTER
m. Christian of Gistel

— BORSIARD, knight
slayer of the count
d. April, 1127
(on wheel)

— ROBERT
killed before
March, 1127

— WALTER, knight
conspirator
d. May 5, 1127
(thrown from tower)

— * LAMBIN MORWATER

LAMBERT NAPPIN
("of Aardenburg")
accused in Inquest
of murder of cas-
tellan of Bourbourg
"cleared" in ordeal
of hot iron
d. April 30, 1128
(in battle)

DIDIER HACKET
castellan of Bruges
1115–27
(possibly 1130–34)
implicated but
survived

— DAUGHTER
m. Walter Crommelin,
knight, "of Lissewege"
accused in Inquest
of aiding Hacket but
wife retained property;
tried but failed
to secure castellanship

— * ROBERT
named in Inquest
named in charter
of 1133

— * "OTHER SONS"
named in charter
of 1133

— * HACKET II
dean of Saint Donatian
(1148-72)

BERTULF
provost of Bruges
chancellor of Flanders
1091–1127
head of family of traitors
d. April 11, 1127 (hanged)

WULFRIC CNOP
conspirator
d. May 5, 1127
(thrown from tower)

DAUGHTER (?)

* Persons whose names are derived from sources other than Galbert's narrative.

WALTER
castellan of Bruges
*ca.*1110–15
d. before March, 1127

ALBERT
conspirator
(fate unknown)

ROBERT THE YOUNG
conspirator
d. May 7, 1127
(decapitated)

DIDIER
court servant (?)
conspirator (?)
d. Dec. 17, 1127

ISAAC ──────────────── * GERVAISE and
(widow* Inmie named ────── GILBERT
in Inquest)   both accused
chamberlain and vassal   in Inquest of
of count   aiding traitors
"head of the conspiracy"
accused in Inquest of
murder of castellan of
Bourbourg
d. March 23, 1127
(hanged)

DAUGHTER (?) ──────── SONS
m. Fromold, notary,   (nephews of Isaac)
favorite of count

DAUGHTER
m. Guy of Steenvoorde,
knight, counselor of count
accused in Inquest of
murder of castellan of
Bourbourg but wife
retained property
d. April 7, 1127 (killed
in single combat)

Other Nieces of Bertulf, Parentage Unknown

* BRIARDIS (?)
m. Robert of Crecques, "free knight"

(grandniece m. "son" of Walter
the butler, peer of Flanders)

* AGANITRUDE
m. 1) Baldwin, castellan of Saint Omer
*ca.*1092–*ca.*1097 ·· GILBERT
m. 2) Alard of Warneton,   castellan of Bergues
accused in Inquest of   *ca.*1125–53
sheltering Bertulf   suspected, cleared himself

THE CHURCH OF SAINT DONATIAN
AT BRUGES

by Joseph Mertens

In his account of the murder of Charles the Good (March 2, 1127), Galbert gives an interesting description of the edifice in which the crime was committed, that is, the church of Saint Donatian. From his description it is clear that this church was a building constructed on a central plan, provided with an upper gallery and a very massive west-work or tower; these details are confirmed by a Flemish writer of the thirteenth century, Jacob van Maerlant, who adds that the church was built on the model of the cathedral of Aachen. Galbert also gives us details concerning the interior of the church, its vaults, windows, furniture, and the like.

In order to illuminate the earliest history of the city of Bruges and at the same time to test the accuracy of these texts, we carried out a systematic examination of the site where the church of Saint Donatian, the castral chapel erected in the middle of the "Bourg," once stood. In the course of two series of excavations, completed in 1955,[1] almost the whole of the original edifice was brought to light and examined; unfortunately only the foundations survive, but they provide ample evidence for the reconstruction of the ground plan in all its details.

The church was oriented with its choir to the east.[2] It is composed of three essential parts, a rectangular choir, a central-type nave composed of an octagonal core supported by eight massive piers, and a circular ambulatory of sixteen sections to which the choir and the west-work are attached. The west-work comprises a central tower, squared and massive, flanked by two smaller towers; the foundations of the latter are rectangular in plan. We shall consider briefly these different parts of the church.

The choir opens into the whole width of a bay of the central octagon. Its interior measures 5.12-5.20 meters long, and 3.37 meters (west) and 3.61 meters (east) wide; the lateral walls have a thickness of 1.37-1.46

---

[1] The excavations were undertaken under our direction by the Service des Fouilles (Musées Royaux d'Art et d'Histoire, Brussels) with financial assistance from the city of Bruges.

[2] In the course of the excavations we even found the wooden axial marker which was used to outline the plan of the edifice.

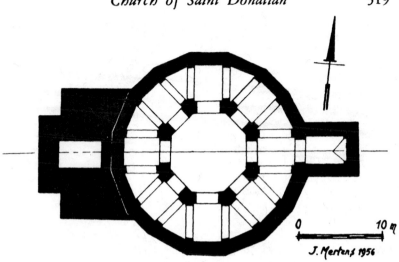

SCHEMATIC RECONSTRUCTION OF THE CHURCH BASED ON
THE EXCAVATIONS OF 1955

meters, while the front wall is only 1.25 meters thick. This sanctuary was probably vaulted, to judge from the angle pilasters which were obviously intended to support a vault.

The central octagon, very regularly laid out, has an interior diameter of 8.89 meters, with sides of 3.63 meters. The width of the foundation which forms the octagon and on which the piers of the central nave rest, varies from 1.65 to 1.72 meters. At each angle stood a pier, the configuration of which we were fortunately able to discover. They were very massive, from 1.95 to 1.60 meters thick, formed of four engaged pilasters; two of these (87-84 centimeters wide) faced the aisle, while the other two (1.25 meters wide) faced the pier of the octagon. The distance between the piers of the octagon averaged 3.19 meters.

An aisle or ambulatory, 4.62-4.68 meters in width, encircles the octagon; to each section of the octagon correspond two exterior sides, so that a polygon of sixteen sides is formed. The thickness of the wall varies from 1.75 to 1.91 meters. On the outside there are no buttresses; on the inside, pilasters, 86-95 centimeters wide, correspond to the pilasters of the piers of the octagon. The distance between the pilasters on the wall is 3.30 meters, a measurement which thus determines the length of an inner side of the polygon. These pilasters as well as masonry angles on the central piers prove that the aisle was vaulted, like the choir. In the foundation all the pilasters of the aisle are connected with the octagon (see Plan).

The west-work is a very massive construction comprising a central tower and two smaller towers, just as Galbert describes it. The total length is 16.05 meters; the central part, extending beyond the lateral towers by 2.45 meters, measures 10.65 meters (east-west) by 9.69 meters (north-south). In the center there is an empty space, 2.58 by 5.11 meters, indicating the passage-way. The foundations of the lateral towers containing the stairs are rectangular, but this does not preclude the possibility that they were surmounted by circular turrets like those at Aachen.

Some technical details are of great interest. In the walls of the choir, of the tower and of the aisle, local greenish sandstone is used for the most part, set in a very hard white mortar. In certain places the stones are arranged in herring-bone pattern (*opus spicatum*); here and there we find a very hard blue limestone and even some reused stones and bricks, coming from earlier Roman buildings. The octagon is constructed almost wholly of the hard limestone of Tournai, very well dressed.

The whole edifice, being constructed on marshy ground, rests on very deep foundations, which broaden at the base to a width varying from 2.20 to 2.70 meters. In order to ensure stability in this boggy soil, the architect placed under all the walls, even under those of the connecting links, a thick flooring made of two superimposed layers of great trunks of beech trees placed horizontally along the whole width of the wall. This wood was amazingly well preserved by the water.

The masonry of the west-work was not joined to that of the polygon but was placed against it. This is an ingenious device, designed to avoid cracks in the superstructure, since the thrust of the heavy west-work was not the same as that of the lighter ambulatory.

We found no trace of the vaulting in bricks and earthenware mentioned by Galbert in his description of the building.

Because of local topographic conditions, the excavations could not be extended to the buildings adjoining the church which Galbert also mentions. Many of these must have been demolished when the church was transformed into a Romanesque church, and later into a Gothic one.[3]

At present, a fragment of wall has been restored on the site of the former choir, and the outline of the polygonal edifice is preserved on the pavement of the Place du Bourg.

November, 1957

Trans. by J. B. R.

---

[3] The edifice, transformed after the murder of Charles the Good into a Romanesque church of basilican plan and then into a Gothic sanctuary — well known to us from numerous pictures and drawings of the eighteenth and nineteenth centuries — ceased to be used as a church after the French Revolution and was completely demolished about 1800. Today the site has become a public square, in front of the Town Hall of Bruges.

BIBLIOGRAPHY

EDITIONS AND TRANSLATIONS OF GALBERT'S RECORD

Editions

Henschen, G., and D. Papebroch, eds. Acta sanctorum, March I (Antwerp, 1668), pp. 179-219: *Vita B. Caroli boni comitis Flandriae, auctore Galberto notario ex aliquot mss.*

The four MSS on which this edition was based are all lost. One was probably contemporary with Galbert; nothing is known about the age of the other three. Of these one was used by André Duchesne who published some fragments in his *Histoire généalogique des maisons de Guines, d'Ardres, de Gand et de Coucy*, Paris, 1631. (The Bollandist edition is reprinted in Migne, *Patrologia latina*, CLXVI, 943-1046.)

Langebek, J., ed. Scriptores rerum Danicarum medii aevi, IV (Copenhagen, 1776), 110-92: *Historia vitae et passionis S. Caroli comitis Flandriae, auctore Galberto notario.*

A faulty reproduction of the Bollandist text.

Köpke, R., ed. Monumenta Germaniae historica, Scriptores XII (Hanover, 1856), 561-619: *Passio Karoli comitis auctore Galberto.*

This edition is based on the Bollandist text, with some corrections, with more regular orthography and better division into "chapters," but unfortunately the text was used in the faulty reimpression of Langebek.

Pirenne, Henri, ed. *Histoire du meurtre de Charles le Bon, comte de Flandre (1127-1128) par Galbert de Bruges suivie de poésies latines contemporaines publiées d'après les manuscrits.* Paris, 1891. "Collection de textes pour servir à l'étude et à l'enseignement de l'histoire."

A new critical edition of the Latin text based on the two sole surviving manuscripts, both of the sixteenth century: Arras, Bibliothèque de la ville, 115 (paper), and Paris, Bibliothèque nationale, MS Baluze 43 (fol. 200 to 318, paper). It contains passages heretofore unpublished in chapters 113, 114, 115, and 118.

Translations

Guizot, F. P. G., trans. "Vie de Charles le Bon, comte de Flandre, par Galbert, syndic de Bruges, in *Collection des mémoires relatifs à l'histoire de France depuis la fondation de la monarchie française jusqu'au XIIIᵉ siècle*," VIII (Paris, 1825), 237-433.

A free and often inaccurate translation.

Delepierre, O., and J. Perneels, trans. In *Histoire de Charles le Bon.* Brussels, 1850.
> Very defective.

La légende du bienheureux Charles le Bon, comte de Flandre. Recit du XIIᵉ siècle par Galbert de Bruges. Paris: Hachette, 1853. "Bibliothèque des chemins de fer."
> An abridged and somewhat altered form of Guizot's translation.

LIST OF WORKS CITED[1]

Actes des comtes de Flandre, 1071-1128. Ed. by Fernand Vercauteren. Brussels: Palais des académies, 1938. "Commission royale d'histoire. Recueil des actes des princes belges."

Acta sanctorum quotquot toto orbe coluntur. Begun by J. Bollandus. Antwerp, 1643-.

Anna Comnena. Alexiade. Ed. by Bernard Leib. 3 vols. Paris: Société d'édition "Les belles lettres," 1937-45. "Collection byzantine, publiée par l'Association Guillaume Budé."

Baldwin, Marshall W., ed. A History of the Crusades: The First Hundred Years. Philadelphia: University of Pennsylvania Press, 1955. Vol. I of *A History of the Crusades,* ed. by Kenneth M. Setton.

Bernhardi, Wilhelm. Lothar von Supplinburg. Leipzig: Duncker and Humblot, 1879. "Jahrbücher der deutschen Geschichte."

Bertin, Paul. Aire-sur-la-Lys des origines au XVIᵉ siècle: une commune flamande-artésienne. Arras: Brunet, 1946. "Commission départmentale des monuments historiques du Pas-de-Calais: Études historiques," 3.

Blanchard, Raoul. La Flandre: étude géographique de la plaine flamande en France, Belgique et Hollande. Paris: Armand Colin, 1906.

Blancquaert, G., "L'Expédition flamande contre Anvers en 1055 et les premiers châtelains de Bruges," Appendix IV, pp. 167-71, to "Les Origines de la Flandre impériale," by F. L. Ganshof, *Annales de la Société royale d'archéologie de Bruxelles,* XLVI (1942-43), 99-137.

Bloch, Marc, "Un Problème d'histoire comparée: la ministérialité en France et en Allemagne," *Revue historique de droit français et étranger,* VII (1928), 46-91.

——— La Société féodale: la formation des liens de dépendance. Paris: Albin Michel, 1939. "L'Évolution de l'humanité," No. 34.

——— La Société féodale: les classes et le gouvernement des hommes. Paris: Albin Michel, 1940. "L'Évolution de l'humanité," No. 34 bis.

Blockmans, Frans, "De oudste privileges der groote Vlaamsche steden," *Nederlandsche Historiebladen,* I (1938), 421-46.

---

[1] If the primary sources cited in the notes have been drawn from the great source collections found below, they are not listed separately in this bibliography.

Blockmans, Frans. Het gentsche stadspatriciaat tom omstreeks 1302. Antwerp: De Sikkel, 1938. "Rijksuniversiteit te Gent: Werken uitgegeven door de faculteit van de wijsbegeerte en letteren," fasc. 85.

Blommaert, W. Les Châtelains de Flandre: étude d'histoire constitutionelle. Ghent: E. van Goethem, 1915. "Université de Gand: Recueil de travaux publiés par la Faculté de philosophie et lettres," fasc. 46.

Bonnaud-Delamare, R., "La Paix en Flandre pendant la première croisade," *Revue du Nord*, XXXIX (1957), 147-52.

Borchgrave, Émile de. Histoire des colonies belges qui s'établirent en Allemagne pendant le douzième et le treizième siècle. Brussels: C. Muquardt, 1865.

Bosl, Karl. Die Reichsministerialität der Salier und Staufer; ein Beitrag zur Geschichte des hochmittelalterlichen deutschen Volkes, Staates und Reiches. Part I. Stuttgart: Hiersemann, 1950. "Schriften der Monumenta Germaniae historica," Vol. X.

Bouquet, Martin. *See* Recueil des historiens des Gaules et de la France.

Boussard, Jacques, "Les Mercenaires au XIIe siècle: Henri II Plantagenet et les origines de l'armée de métier," *Bibliothèque de l'Ecole des chartes*, CVI (1945-46), 189-224.

———— "La Vie en Anjou aux XIe et XIIe siècles," *Le Moyen Âge*, LVI (1950), 29-68.

Boutruche, Robert, "Histoire de France au moyen âge, V-XV siècles: publications des années 1947-1953," *Revue historique*, CCXIII (1955), 47-80.

Callewaert, Camillus A., "Les Origines de la collégiale Saint-Donatien à Bruges," *Annales de la Société d'émulation de Bruges*, LVI (1906), 395-408.

———— "Les Origines du style pascal en Flandre," *ibid.*, LV (1905), 13-26, 121-43.

———— "Nouvelles recherches sur la chronologie médiévale en Flandre," *ibid.*, LIX (1909), 41-62, 153.

The Cambridge Economic History of Europe from the Decline of the Roman Empire. Planned by the late Sir John Clapham and the late Eileen Power. 3 vols. Cambridge: The University Press, 1941-63.

"Catalogue des reliques conservées à l'église Saint Donatien à Bruges au XIIIe siècle," *Le Beffroi*, IV (1872-73), 199-202.

Chalandon, Ferdinand. Histoire de la domination normande en Italie et en Sicile. 2 vols. Paris: A. Picard et fils, 1907.

Champeaux, Ernest, review of F. L. Ganshof's *Etude sur les ministeriales* in *Revue historique de droit français et étranger*, VI (1927), 744-56.

Cipolla, Carlo M. Money, Prices and Civilization in the Mediterranean World, Fifth to Seventeenth Century. Princeton: Princeton University Press, 1956.

Coens, Maurice, "La Vie ancienne de sainte Godelive de Ghistelles par Drogon de Bergues," *Analecta Bollandiana*, XLIV (1926), 102-37.

IXᵉ Congrès internationale des sciences historiques. Vol. I: Rapports. Paris: Armand Colin, 1950.

Coornaert, Émile, "Draperies rurales, draperies urbaines: l'évolution de l'industrie flamande au moyen âge," *Revue belge de philologie et d'histoire*, XXVIII (1950), 59-96.

Corpus chronicorum Flandriae. Ed. by J. J. de Smet. 4 vols. Brussels: M. Hayez, 1837-65. "Collection de chroniques belges inédites," ed. by J. H. Borgnet *et al*, No. 3.

Curschmann, Fritz. Hungersnöte im Mittelalter: ein Beitrag zur deutschen Wirtsschaftsgeschichte des 8 bis 13 Jahrhunderts. Leipzig: B. G. Teubner, 1900.

Delatouche, Raymond, "Agriculture mediévale et population," *Études sociales*, XXVIII (1955), 13-23.

Delcourt, André. La Vengeance de la commune. L'arsin et l'abattis de maison en Flandre et en Hainaut. Lille: Raoust, 1930. "Bibliothèque de la Société d'histoire du droit des pays flamands, picards et wallons," No. 3.

Delfos, Leo, "Oudenaarde en Pamele voor 1117," *Handelingen van de geschied- en oudheidkundige kring van Oudenaarde*, Feestnummer (1956), 74-92.

Dept, Gaston G. Les Influences anglaise et française dans le comté de Flandre au début du XIIIᵉ siècle. Ghent: Van Rysselberghe and Rombaut, 1928. "Université de Gand: Recueil de travaux publiés par la Faculté de philosophie et lettres," fasc. 59.

——— "Les Marchands flamands et le roi d'Angleterre (1154-1216)," *Revue du Nord*, XII (1926), 303-24.

Dereine, Charles, "Vie commune, règle de S. Augustin et chanoines réguliers au XIᵉ siècle," *Revue d'histoire ecclésiastique*, XLI (1940), 365-406.

De Smet, J. M., "Bijdrage tot de iconographie van de Glz. Karel de Goede, Graaf van Vlaanderen," *Album English* (1952), 117-57.

Despy, G., review of L. Génicot's *L'Économie rurale namuroise au bas moyen âge*, in *Revue belge de philologie et d'histoire*, XXXI (1953), 890-91.

Doehaerd, Renée. L'Expansion économique belge au moyen âge. Brussels: La Renaissance du livre, 1946. "Notre passé."

——— "Un Paradoxe géographique: Laon, capitale du vin au XIIᵉ siècle," *Annales*, V (1950), 145-65.

——— Les Relations commerciales entre Gênes, la Belgique et l'Outremont d'après les archives notariales génoises au XIIIᵉ et XIVᵉ siècles. 3 vols. Brussels: Palais des académies, 1941-52. "Institut historique belge de Rome: Études d'histoire économique et sociale," Nos. 2-4.

Dictionnaire de droit canonique. Begun under the direction of A. Villien and E. Magnin, continued under the direction of A. Amanieu *et al.* Paris: Le Touzey, 1935-.

Dictionnaire d'histoire et de géographie ecclésiastique. Ed. by A. Baudrillart *et al.* Paris, 1912-.

Dhondt, Jan (Jean), "Développment urbain et initiative comtale en Flandre au XIe siècle," *Revue du Nord*, XXX (1948), 133-56.

———— "Essai sur l'origine de la frontière linguistique," *L'Antiquité Classique*, XVI (1947), 261-86.

———— Études sur la naissance des principautés territoriales en France (IXe-Xe siècle). Bruges: De Tempel, 1948. "Rijksuniversiteit te Gent: Werken uitgegeven door de faculteit van de wijsbegeerte en letteren," fasc. 102.

———— "Une Mentalité du douzième siècle: Galbert de Bruges," *Revue du Nord*, XXXIX (1957), 101-9.

———— "Het ontstaan van Oudenaarde," *Handelingen van de geschied- en oudheidkundige kring van Oudenaarde*, X (1952), 50-80.

———— " 'Ordres' ou 'puissances': l'exemple des États de Flandre," *Annales*, V (1950), 289-305.

———— Les Origines des États de Flandre. Louvain: E. Nauwelaerts, 1950. "Anciens pays et assemblées d'états: études publiées par la section belge de la Commission internationale pour l'histoire des assemblées d'états."

———— "Petit-Dutaillis et les communes françaises," *Annales*, VII (1952), 378-84.

———— "Les Solidarités médiévales: une société en transition, la Flandre en 1127-1128," *Annales*, XII (1957), 529-60.

———— "De vroege topografie van Brugge," *Handelingen der maatschappij voor geschiedenis en oudheidkunde te Gent*, XI (1957), 3-30.

Dhondt-Sevens, Léa, "Les Premiers seigneurs d'Alost, de Bornem et de Termonde," Appendix III, pp. 161-65, to "Les Origines de la Flandre impériale" by F. L. Ganshof, *Annales de la Société royale d'archéologie de Bruxelles*, XLVI (1942-43), 99-137.

Dubled, Henri, "Quelques observations sur le sens du mot *villa*," *Le Moyen Âge*, LIX (1953), 1-9.

Duchesne, Louis M. O. Fastes épiscopaux de l'ancienne Gaule. 3 vols. Paris: Thorin et fils et A. Fontemoing, 1894-1915.

Enlart, Camille. Manuel d'archéologie française depuis les temps merovingiens jusqu'à la Renaissance. 2d ed. rev. Paris: A Picard et fils, 1920-32. Ière Partie: Architecture religieuse. Tome 1, Périodes mérovingienne, carolingienne et romane (1919; 3d ed. rev., 1927); Tome 2, Période française, dite gothique style, flamboyant, renaissance (1929); Tome 3, Table alphabétique et analytique des matières, by Rémy Delauney (1924). IIème Partie: Architecture civile et militaire. Tome

1, Architecture civile (1929); Tome 2, Architecture militaire et navale, by Jean Verrier (1932).

Espinas, Georges. Deux fondations de villes dans l'Artois et la Flandre française (Xᵉ-XVᵉ siècles): Saint-Omer, Lannoy-du-Nord. Lille: Raoust, 1946. Vol. III of *Les Origines du capitalisme.*

——— "Les Origines urbaines en Flandre," *Le Moyen Âge,* LIV (1948), 37-56.

——— "Le Privilège de Saint-Omer de 1127," *Revue du Nord,* XXIX (1947), 43-49.

Études d'histoire dédiées à la mémoire de Henri Pirenne par ses anciens élèves. Brussels: Nouvelle société d'éditions, 1937.

Études historiques dédiées à la mémoire de M. Roger Rodière. Calais, 1947. "Mémoires de la Commission départementale des monuments historiques du Pas-de-Calais," Vol. V, fasc. 2.

Feuchère, Pierre. Essai sur l'évolution territoriale des principautés françaises (Xᵉ-XIIIᵉ siècle): étude de géographie historique," *Le Moyen Âge,* LVIII (1952), 85-117.

——— "Histoire sociale et généalogie: la noblesse du Nord de la France," *Annales,* VI (1951), 306-18.

——— "Les Origines du comté de Saint-Pol," *Revue du Nord,* XXXV (1953), 125-49.

——— "Pairs de principauté et pairs de château," *Revue belge de philologie et d'histoire,* XXXI (1953), 973-1002.

——— "Regestes des comtes de Saint-Pol, 1023-1205. 1ᵉʳᵉ partie (1023-1145)," *Revue du Nord,* XXXIX (1957), 43-48.

Feytmans, Anne-Marie, "Scabini terrae," *Revue belge de philologie et d'histoire,* X (1931), 170-74.

Firmin, B. De romaansche kerkelijke bouwkunst in West-Vlaanderen. Ghent: Universitaire stichting van België, 1940.

Fliche, Augustin. La Réforme grégorienne et la reconquête chrétienne (1057-1123). Paris: Bloud and Gay, 1946. Vol. VIII of *Histoire de l'Église,* ed. by A. Fliche and V. Martin.

La foire. Publié avec le concours de la Fondation universitaire de Belgique. Brussels: Éditions de la librairie encyclopédique, 1953. Vol. V of *Recueils de la Société Jean Bodin.*

Gailliard, Édouard. Inventaire des archives de la ville de Bruges: Glossaire flamand. Bruges, 1882. See Gilliodts-van Severen.

Ganshof, François L., "Armatura," *Archivium Latinitatis Medii Aevi (Bulletin du Cange),* XV (1941), 179-93.

——— "Coemptio gravissima mansionum," *ibid.,* XVII (1943), 149-61.

——— "Le Droit urbain en Flandre au début de la première phase de son histoire (1127)," *Revue d'histoire du droit,* XIX (1951), 387-416.

——— Étude sur les ministeriales en Flandre et en Lotharingie. Brussels: M. Lamertin, 1926. "Mémoires de l'Académie royale de Belgique: Classe des lettres et des sciences morales et politiques," Vol. XX, fasc. 1.

———— Étude sur le développement des villes entre Loire et Rhin au moyen âge. Brussels: Éditions de la librairie encyclopédique, 1943: Paris: Presses universitaires de France, 1943.

———— La Flandre sous les premiers comtes. 3d ed. rev. Brussels: La Renaissance du livre, 1949.

———— "Iets over Brugge gedurende de preconstitutionelle periode van haar geschiedenis," *Nederlandsche Historiebladen,* I (1938), 218-303.

———— Le Moyen Âge. Paris: Hachette, 1953. Vol. I of *Histoire des relations internationales,* published under the direction of Pierre Renouvin.

———— "Note sur le premier traité anglo-normand de Douvres," *Revue du Nord,* XL (1958), 245-57.

———— "Les Origines du concept de souveraineté nationale en Flandre," *Revue d'histoire du droit,* XVIII (1950), 135-58.

———— "Les Origines de la Flandre impériale," *Annales de la Société royale d'archéologie de Bruxelles,* XLVI (1942-43), 99-137.

———— Qu'est-ce que la féodalité? 3d ed. rev. Brussels: Office de publicité, 1957.

———— Recherches sur les tribuneaux de châtellenie en Flandre avant le milieu du XIIIᵉ siècle. Antwerp: De Sikkel, 1932; Paris: Champion, 1932.

———— "Le Roi de France en Flandre en 1127 et 1128," *Revue historique de droit français et étranger,* XXVII (1949), 204-28.

———— "Les Transformations de l'organisation judiciaire dans le comté de Flandre jusqu'à l'évènement de la maison de Bourgogne," *Revue belge de philologie et d'histoire,* XVIII (1939), 43-61.

———— "Trois mandements perdus du roi de France Louis VI intéressant la Flandre," *Annales de la Société d'émulation de Bruges,* LXXXVII (1950), 117-33.

Gebhardt, Bruno. Handbuch der deutschen Geschichte. Ed. by R. Holtzmann. 2 vols. 7th ed. Stuttgart: Union deutsche Verlagsgesellschaft, 1930-31.

Génicot, Léopold, "Le Premier siècle de la 'curia' de Hainaut (1060 env.-1195)," *Le Moyen Âge,* LIII (1947), 39-60.

———— "Sur les origines de la noblesse dans le Namurois, premiers jalons," *Revue d'histoire du droit,* XX (1952), 143-56.

———— "Sur les témoignages d'accroissement de la population en occident du XIᵉ au XIIIᵉ siècle," *Cahiers d'histoire mondiale,* I (1953), 446-62.

Gesta Stephani. Trans. from the Latin with introduction and notes by K. R. Potter. London: T. Nelson and Sons, 1955. "Medieval Classics."

Gilliodts-van Severen, L. Inventaire des archives de la ville de Bruges. 8 vols. Bruges, 1871-85.

Giry, Arthur. Histoire de la ville de Saint-Omer et ses institutions jusqu'au XIVᵉ siècle. Paris: F. Vieweg, 1877. "Bibliothèque de l'École des hautes études: Sciences philologiques et historiques," fasc. 31.

Gislebert de Mons. La Chronique de Gislebert de Mons. Nouvelle ed. Ed. by Léon Vanderkindere. Brussels: Kiessling, 1904. "Commission royale d'histoire: Recueil de textes pour servir à l'étude de l'histoire de Belgique."

Gottschalk, Maria K. E. Historische geografie van Westelijk Zeeuws-Vlaanderen tot de St Elisabethsvloed van 1404. Assen: Van Gorcum, 1955 (With a French summary).

Grand, Roger. L'Agriculture au moyen âge de la fin de l'empire romain au XVIᵉ siècle, avec la collaboration de Raymond Delatouche. Paris: E. de Boccard, 1950. Vol. III of *L'Agriculture à travers les âges*.

Grierson, Philip, "The Relations between England and Flanders before the Norman Conquest," *Transactions of the Royal Historical Society*, 4th Series, XXIII (1941), 71-112.

―――― The Translation of the Relics of St. Donatian to Bruges," *Revue Bénédictine*, XLIV (1937), 170-90.

Guibert de Nogent. Histoire de sa vie (1053-1124). Ed. by G. Bourgin Paris: A. Picard et fils, 1907. "Collection de textes pour servir à l'étude et à l'enseignement de l'histoire."

Gysseling, M., "Étymologie van Brugge," *Bulletin de la Commission royale de toponymie et dialectologie*, XVIII (1944), 69-79.

Hagenmeyer, Heinrich, ed. Epistulae et chartae ad historiam primi belli sacri spectantes ... (Die Kreuzzugsbriefe aus den Jahren 1088-1100, eine Quellensammlung). Innsbruck: Wagner'sche Universitäts-buch-handlung, 1901.

Hefele, Charles J. von. Histoire des conciles d'après les documents originaux. Trans. from the 2d German ed. by Dom H. Leclerq. 8 vols. Paris: Letouzey et Ané, 1907-21.

Héliot, Pierre, "Sur les résidences princières baties en France du Xᵉ au XIIIᵉ siècle," *Le Moyen Âge*, LXI (1955), 27-61, 291-317.

Histoire des institutions françaises au moyen âge. Published under the direction of Ferdinand Lot and Robert Fawtier. Vol. I: Institutions seigneuriales. Paris: Presses universitaires de France, 1957.

Huyghebaert, N. N., "Abt Giselbrecht van Eename en de Gelukzalige Karel de Goede: nota over Herman van Doornik, Liber de restauratione, hk. 28-29," *Sacris Erudiri*, I (1948), 225-31.

Karolingische und ottonische Kunst: Werden—Wesen—Wirkung. Wiesbaden: Franz Steiner, 1957.

Kervyn de Lettenhove, Joseph M. B. C. Histoire de Flandre. 4 vols. Bruges: Beyaert-Defoort, 1874.

Keys, Ancel, "Human Starvation and Its Consequences," *Journal of the American Dietetic Association*, XXII (1946), 582-87.

Kienast, Walther. Unterteneneid und Treuvorbehalt in Frankreich und England. Weimar: H. Böhlaus Nachfolger, 1952.

Kinsky, Georg, ed. A History of Music in Pictures. Ed. with the collaboration of Robert Haas *et al.* London: J. M. Dent and Sons, 1930.

LaMonte, John L., "The Lords of Sidon in the Twelfth and Thirteenth Centuries," *Byzantion*, XVII (1944-45), 183-211.

Laurent, Henri. Un Grand commerce d'exportation au moyen âge: la draperie des Pays-Bas en France et dans les pays meditérranéens (XIIe-XVe siècles). Paris: Librairie Droz, 1935.

Leclercq, Jean, "Simoniaca heresis," *Studi gregoriani*, I (1947), 523-30.

Lemaire, Raymond. De romaanse bouwkunst in de Nederlanden. Brussels: Paleis der academiën, 1952. "Koninklijke Vlaamse Academie voor wetenschappen, letteren en schone kunsten van België, Klasse der schone kunsten." Verhandeling No. 6.

Lesne, Émile. Les Écoles de la fin du VIIIe siècle à la fin du XIIe. Lille and Paris: Facultés catholiques, 1940. Vol. V of *Histoire de la propriété ecclésiastique en France;* Fasc. 50 of "Mémoires et travaux publiés par des professeurs des Facultés catholiques de Lille."

Lestocquoy, Jean, "Les Dynasties bourgeoises d'Arras du XIe au XVe siècle," *Mémoires de la Commission historique du Pas-de-Calais*, V (1945), 172 ff.

——— Histoire de la Flandre et de l'Artois. Paris: Presses universitaires de France, 1949. "Collection que sais-je?"

——— "Les Origines du patriciat urbain. Henri Pirenne s'est-il trompé? La thèse," *Annales*, I (1946), 143-48.

——— Les Villes de Flandre et d'Italie sous le gouvernement des patriciens. Paris: Presses universitaires de France, 1952.

Luchaire, Achille. Histoire des institutions monarchiques de la France sous les premiers Capétiens (987-1180). 2 vols. 2d ed. Paris: A. Picard, 1891.

——— Louis VI le gros: annales de sa vie et de son règne (1081-1137). Paris: A. Picard, 1890.

Lyon, Bryce D. From Fief to Indenture. Cambridge: Harvard University Press, 1957.

——— "Medieval Real Estate Developments and Freedom," *American Historical Review*, LXIII (1957-58), 47-61.

Lot, Ferdinand. L'Art militaire et les armées au moyen âge en Europe et dans le proche orient. 2 vols. Paris: Payot, 1946.

McKisack, Mary, "London and the Succession to the Crown during the Middle Ages," in *Studies in Medieval History Presented to F. M. Powicke*, ed. by R. W. Hunt *et al.* Oxford: Clarendon Press, 1948, 76-89.

McLaughlin, Terence P., "The Prohibition of Marriage against Canons in the Early Twelfth Century," *Medieval Studies*, III (1941), 94-100.

Mâle, Émile, "L'Église d'Aix-la-Chapelle et son influence dans la vallée du Rhin," *Mémoires de la Société nationale des antiquaires de France*, LXXXIII (1954), 127-29.

Manitius, Max. Geschichte der lateinischen Literatur des Mittelalters. 3 vols. Munich: C. H. Beck, 1911-31. "Handbuch der Klassischen Altertumswissenschaften," Abteilung IX, Teil II, Bände I-III.

Mansi, Giovanni D., ed. Sacrorum conciliorum nova et amplissima collectio. 31 vols. Florence and Vienna, 1759-98.

Mansion, H., "À Propos de l'ancienne église Saint-Donatien à Bruges," *Revue belge d'archéologie et d'histoire de l'art*, VIII (1938), 99-112.

Massiet du Biest, Jean, "Les Origines de la population et du patriciat urbain à Amiens (1109-XIVᵉ siècle)," *Revue du Nord*, XXX (1948), 113-32.

Mélanges d'histoire du moyen âge dediés à la mémoire de Louis Halphen. Paris: Presses universitaires de France, 1951.

Mélanges d'histoire offerts à Henri Pirenne par ses anciens élèves et ses amis à l'occasion de sa quarantième année d'enseignement à l'Université de Gand, 1886-1926. 2 vols. Brussels: Vromant, 1926.

Mélanges Julien Havet. Recueil de travaux d'érudition dediés à la mémoire de Julien Havet (1853-1893). Paris: E. Leroux, 1895.

Mertens, Joseph, "De opgravingen in de Sint-Donaaskerk te Brugge," *Streven*, IX (Part I, 1955-56), 57-60.

Migne, J. P., ed. Patrologiae cursus completus. Series latina, 221 vols. Paris: J. P. Migne, 1844-64.

Miscellanea historica in honorem Alberti de Meyer. 2 vols. Louvain and Brussels: Bibliothèque de l'université, 1946.

Monier, Raymond. Les Institutions centrales du comté de Flandre de la fin du IXᵉ siècle à 1384. Paris: Éditions Domat-Montchrestien, 1943.

———— Les Institutions financières du comté de Flandre du XIᵉ siècle à 1384. Paris: Éditions Domat-Montchrestien, 1948.

Monumenta Germaniae historica (500-1500). Ed. by G. H. Pertz et al. Hanover and Berlin, 1826-.

Moreau, Édouard de. Histoire de l'Église en Belgique. 3 vols. Brussels: L'Édition universelle, 1945. 1st edition of Vol. III; 2nd edition of Vols. I and II.

Mortet, Victor, ed. Recueil de textes relatifs à l'histoire de l'architecture et à la condition des architectes en France au moyen âge, XIᵉ-XIIᵉ siècles. Paris: A. Picard, 1911. "Collection de textes pour servir à l'étude et à l'enseignement de l'histoire."

Noterdaeme, Jérome, "De graven van Vlaanderen en hun domeinen rond Brugge," *Handelingen der maatschappij voor geschiedenis en oudheidkunde te Gent*. VIII (1954), 31-39.

Noterdaeme, Jérome, "Studiën over de vroegste kerkgeschiedenis van Brugge: I, Sijsele en het Sint-Maartenskapittel te Utrecht," *Sacris Erudiri*, VI (1954), 180-88.

——— "Studiën over de vroegste kerkgeschiedenis van Brugge: II, De fiscus Weinebrugge en de herkomst van St-Salvatorskerk te Brugge, *ibid.*, VII (1955), 131-39.

Nowé, Henri, "Une Étude récente sur l'évêché de Térouanne," *Revue du Nord*, XIII (1927), 45-56. (An extensive French summary of H. Van Werveke's *Het bisdom Terwaan*, Ghent, 1924).

Otto of Freising. Chronica sive historia de duabus civitatibus. Ed. by A. Hofmeister. Hanover, 1912. "Scriptores rerum Germanicarum in usum scholarum."

——— The Two Cities, a Chronicle of Universal History to the Year 1146 A.D. Trans. by C. C. Mierow. New York. Columbia University Press, 1928. "Records of Civilization. Sources and Studies," No. 9.

Ordericus Vitalis. Historiae ecclesiasticae libri tredecim. Ed. by Auguste le Prévost. 5 vols. Paris: J. Renouard, 1835-55.

Oppolzer, Theodor Ritter von. Canon der Finsternisse. Vienna, 1887. "Denkschriften der kaiserlichen Akademia der Wissenschaften, mathematischnaturwissenschaftliche Classe," 52.

L'Organization corporative du Moyen Âge à la fin de l'Ancien Régime. Études présentées à la Commission internationale pour l'histoire des assemblées d'états. Vol. III. Louvain: Bibliothèque de l'université, 1939. "Université de Louvain: Recueil de travaux publiés par les membres des conférences d'histoire et de philologie." Sér. 2, fasc. 50.

Pergameni, Charles. L'Avouerie ecclésiastique belge des origines à la période bourguignonne, étude d'histoire ecclésiastique. Ghent: Société cooperative, 1907.

Perroy, Édouard, "Les Origines urbaines en Flandre, d'après un ouvrage recent," *Revue du Nord*, XXIX (1947), 49-63.

Petit-Dutaillis, Charles. Les Communes françaises, caractères et évolution des origines au XVIIIe siècle. Paris: A. Michel, 1947. "Évolution de l'humanité," No. 44.

Piot, Charles. "Les Beers de Flandre," *Annales de la Société d'émulation de Bruges*, XXVIII (1876-77), 94-139.

Pirenne, Henri. Les Villes et les institutions urbaines. 2 vols. Paris: Felix Alcan, 1939; Brussels: Nouvelle société d'éditions, 1939.

——— Histoire économique de l'occident mediéval. Preface by E. Coornaert. Bruges: Desclée de Brouwer, 1951.

(The monographs in these volumes, published originally in periodicals or collections, are indispensable to the student of Flemish society. Since Pirenne's ideas, however, have been absorbed into the general current of historical thought, and in many cases modified in the process, it does not seem necessary to cite particular works here or in the notes, except in a few cases.)

———— Letter to the Editors, under "Correspondance," *Revue générale,* XXVIII (1892), 521-26.

This is Pirenne's reply to "Une Leçon d'honnêteté scientifique donnée aux Bollandistes," published in the same issue (pp. 341-45).

———— "Tanchelm et le projet de démembrement du diocèse d'Utrecht vers 1000," *Bulletin de la classe des lettres de l'Académie royale de Belgique,* 5e série, XIII (1927), 112-19.

Poerck, G. de, "Enceintes castrales et urbaines à Bruges," in *Premier Congrès international de géographie historique.* Vol. II: *Mémoires.* Brussels, 1931. Pages 79-88.

Poignant, Simone. La Foire de Lille: contribution à l'étude des foires flamandes au moyen âge. Lille: Raoust, 1932. "Bibliothèque de la Société d'histoire du droit des pays flamands, picards et wallons," No. 6.

Poole, Reginald L. Medieval Reckonings of Time. London: Society for Promoting Christian Knowledge, 1935. "Helps for Students of History," No. 3.

Post, Gaines, "Two Notes on Nationalism in the Middle Ages," *Traditio,* IX (1953), 281-320.

I Problemi comuni dell'Europa post-carolingia. Spoleto: Presso la Sede del Centro, 1955. Vol. II of *Settimane di studio del Centro Italiano di studi sull'alto medioevo,* April 6-13, 1954.

Recueil des historiens des croisades. Académie des inscriptions et belles lettres. Historiens occidentaux, 5 vols. Paris, 1844-95.

Recueil des historiens des Gaules et de la France. Ed. by Dom Martin Bouquet *et al.* 24 vols. Paris: Aux dépens des librairies associées, 1738-1904.

Regesta regum anglo-normannorum 1066-1154. Vol. II, Regesta Henrici primi 1100-1135, ed. by Charles Johnson and H. A. Cronne. Oxford: The Clarendon Press, 1956.

Reinhardt, Hans, and Étienne Fels, "Étude sur les églises-porches carolingiennes et leur survivance dans l'art roman," *Bulletin monumental,* XCII (1933), 331-65; XCVI (1937), 425-69.

Rolland, Paul, "L'Origine des châtelains de Flandre," *Revue belge de philologie et d'histoire,* VI (1927), 689-724.

———— "La Première église de Saint-Donatien à Bruges," *Revue belge d'archéologie et d'histoire de l'art,* XIV (1944), 101-11.

Rousset, Paul, "La Croyance en la justice immanente à l'époque féodale," *Le Moyen Âge,* LIV (1948), 225-48.

———— "Le Sens du merveilleux a l'époque féodale," *Le Moyen Âge,* LXII (1956), 25-38.

Runciman, Steven. A History of the Crusades. 3 vols. Cambridge: The University Press, 1951-54.

Russell, Josiah Cox. Late Ancient and Medieval Population. Philadelphia, 1958. *Transactions of the American Philosophical Society,* Vol. XLVIII, Part 3.

Sabbe, Étienne, "La Réforme clunisienne dans le comté de Flandre au début du XIIᵉ siècle," *Revue belge de philologie et d'histoire,* IX (1930), 121-38.

Sanderus, Antonius. Flandria illustrata sive provinciae ac comitatus huius descriptio. 3 vols. The Hague: C. Van Lom, 1732.

Sarton, George. Introduction to the History of Science. 3 vols. Baltimore: Williams and Wilkins, 1927-48.

Schaeffer, Herwin, "The Origin of the Two-Tower Façade in Romanesque Architecture," *The Art Bulletin,* XXVII (1945), 85-108.

Schaten, Nicolaus. Annales Paderbornenses. 2 vols. Neuhaus, 1693-94.

Schrijver, Hippoliet de. De oude landmaten in Vlaanderen. Ghent: F. Dujardin, 1936.

Sdralek, Max. Wolfenbüttler Fragmente. Analekten zur Kirchengeschichte des Mittelalters aus Wolfenbüttler Handschriften. Münster, 1891.

Smith, E. Baldwin. Architectural Symbolism of Imperial Rome and the Middle Ages. Princeton: Princeton University Press, 1956. "Princeton Monographs in Art and Archaeology," No. 30.

Straten Ponthoz, F. van der. Charles-le-bon, causes de sa mort, ses vrais meurtriers. Metz, 1853.

Strubbe, E. I., "De parochies te Brugge voor de XIIᵉ eeuw," *Album English,* 1952, pp. 355-80.

Sturler, Jean de, "Note sur l'emploi de poteries creuses dans les édifices du moyen âge: À propos de la première église de Saint-Donatien à Bruges," *Le Moyen Âge,* LXIII (1957), 241-65.

Suger. Vie de Louis VI le gros. Ed. and trans. by Henri Waquet. Paris: H. Champion, 1929. "Les Classiques de l'histoire de France au moyen âge," No. 11.

Thomas, Paul, "Problèmes au sujet du Gros Brief de Flandre," *Bulletin de la Commission historique du Département du Nord,* Vol. XXXV (1938).

Translatio S. Jonati. Excerpt from MS included in E. Sakur, "Reise nach Nord-Frankreich im Frühjahr 1889," *Neues Archiv der Gesellschaft für ältere deutsche Geschichtskunde,* XV (1890), 439-73.

Van Caenegem, R. C. Geschiedenis van het strafrecht in Vlaanderen van de XIᵉ tot de XIVᵉ eeuw. (With a French résumé.) Brussels: Paleis der academiën, 1954. "Koninklijke Vlaamse Academie voor wetenschappen, letteren en schone kunsten van België, Klasse der letteren." Verhandeling No. 19.

——— Geschiedenis van het strafprocesrecht in Vlaanderen van de XIᵉ tot de XIVᵉ eeuw. (With a French résumé.) Brussels, 1956. Same series, No. 24.

Vanderkindere, Léon. La Formation territoriale des principautés belges au moyen âge. 2 vols. Brussels: Hayez, 1902. Vol. I, 2d ed.

Van Drival, Eugène, "Mémoire liturgique et historique sur Saint Maxim," *Mémoires de l'Académie des sciences, lettres et arts d'Arras,* XIV (1883), 312-34.

Van Houtte, Hubert. Essai sur la civilisation flamande au commencement du XIIᵉ siècle, d'après Galbert de Bruges. Louvain: C. Peeters, 1898.

Van Lokeren, A. Chartes et documents de l'Abbaye Saint Pierre au Mont Blandin à Gand depuis sa fondation jusqu'à sa suppression. Ghent: H. Hoste, 1868.

Van Werveke, Hans. Het bisdom Terwaan van den oorsprong tot het begin der XIVᵉ eeuw. Ghent, 1924. "Rijksuniversiteit te Gent: Werken uitgegeven door de faculteit van de wijsbegeerte en letteren," fasc. 52.

—— Bruges et Antwerp: huit siècles de commerce flamand. Brussels: Éditions de la librairie encyclopédique, 1944.

—— "Comment les établissements religieux belges se procuraient-ils du vin au moyen âge?," *Revue belge de philologie et d'histoire,* II (1923), 643-62.

—— Monnaies, lingots ou marchandises? les instruments d'échange au XIᵉ et XIIᵉ siècles," *Annales d'histoire économique et sociale,* IV (1932), 452-68.

Verbruggen, J. F. De krijgskunst in West-Europa in de middeleeuwen (IXᵉ tot begin XIVᵉ eeuw) (With a French résumé). Brussels: Paleis der academiën, 1954. "Koninklijke Vlaamse Academie voor wetenschappen, letteren en schone kunsten van België. Klasse der letteren." Verhandeling No. 20.

—— "Note sur le sens des mots castrum, castellum et quelques autres expressions qui désignent des fortifications," *Revue belge de philologie et d'histoire,* XXVIII (1950), 147-55.

—— "La Tactique militaire des armées de chevaliers," *Revue du Nord,* XXIX (1947), 161-80.

Vercauteren, Fernand, "Note sur la valeur et l'importance économique des donations faites par les comtes de Flandre au XIᵉ et XIIᵉ siècles," *Revue belge de philologie et d'histoire,* XVI (1937), 938-39.

—— *see also* Actes des comtes de Flandre.

Verhulst, A., "Différents types de structure domaniale et agraire en Basse et Moyenne Belgique pendant le haut moyen âge: un essai d'explication," *Annales,* XI (1956), 61-70.

Verlinden, Charles. Robert 1ᵉʳ le Frison, comte de Flandre: étude d'histoire politique. Paris: E. Champion, 1935.

La ville. 3 vols. Brussels: Éditions de la librairie encyclopédique, 1954-56. Vols. VI-VIII of *Recueils de la Société Jean Bodin.*

Vincent, Jacques, "Au sujet de la tour et du *solarium* de l'ancienne église Saint-Donatien à Bruges," *Revue belge d'archéologie et d'histoire de l'art*, XIV (1944), 47-55.

Vredius, Olivarius. Historiae comitum Flandriae. Bruges, 1650.

Wattenbach, Wilhelm. Deutschlands Geschichtsquellen im Mittelalter: deutsche Kaiserzeit. Ed. by Robert Holtzmann. Vol. I. Tübingen: Dr. M. Matthiesen, 1948.

William Fitzstephen. Vita sancti Thomae Cantuariensis archiepiscopi et martyris, auctore Willelmo filio Stephani, in Vol. III of *Materials for the History of Thomas Becket*, ed. by J. C. Robertson. London, 1877. "Rolls Series," No. 67.

William of Malmesbury. Willelmi Malmesbiriensis monachi de gestis regum anglorum libri quinque. Ed. by William Stubbs. 2 vols. London, 1887. "Rolls Series," No. 90.

William of Tyre. A History of Deeds Done beyond the Sea. Trans. and annotated by E. A. Babcock and A. C. Krey. 2 vols. New York: Columbia University Press, 1943. "Records of Civilization, Sources and Studies," No. 35.

SUPPLEMENT TO BIBLIOGRAPHY

De Smet, J. M., "De monnik Tanchelm en de Utrechtse Bisschopszetel in 1112-1114," in *Scrinium Lovaniense. Mélanges historiques Étienne van Cauwenbergh*. Louvain, 1961. "Université de Louvain: Recueil de travaux d'histoire et de philosophie," 4ᵉ série, fasc. 24. Pages 207-34.

———— "Charles le Bon," Dictionnaire d'histoire et de géographie ecclésiastique, Vol. XII (Paris, 1953), cols. 483-86.

Diplomatic Documents Preserved in the Public Record Office. London, Her Majesty's Stationery Office, 1964. Vol. I, 1101-1272, ed. by Pierre Chaplais.

Duby, Georges, "Au XIIᵉ siècle: les 'jeunes' dans la societé aristocratique," *Annales*, XIX (1964), 835-46.

Ganshof, François L., "Bemerkungen zu einer flandrischen Gerichtsurkunde," in *Festschrift P.E. Schramm*, ed. by P. Classen and P. Scheibert. 2 vols. Wiesbaden: F. Steiner, 1964. Vol. I, 268-79.

Génicot, L., "Bibliographie: La noblesse dans la société médievale, à propos des dernières études relatives aux terres d'Empire," *Le Moyen Âge*, LXXI (1965), 539-60.

Graboïs, Aryeh, "De la trève de Dieu à la paix du rois: étude sur les transformations du mouvement de la paix au XIIᵉ siècle," in *Mélanges offerts à René Crozet*. Poitiers: Societé d'études médiévales, 1966.

Hollyman, K.-J. Le Développement du vocabulaire féodale en France pendant le haut moyen âge: étude sémantique. Geneva: Droz, 1957.

Huyghebaert, N. N., "De abdis van Origny en de stervende burggraaf," in *Album archivaris Jos. de Smet.* Bruges, 1964. Pages 191-97.

———— "Thémard, châtelain de Bourbourg, et l'abbesse d'Origny," *Revue d'histoire ecclésiastique,* LX (1965), 444-57.

Kleinbauer, W. E., "Charlemagne's Palace Chapel at Aachen and Its Copies," *Gesta* (International Center of Romanesque Art), IV (1965), 2-13.

Koch, A. C. F., ed., "Actes des comtes de Flandre de la période de 1071 à 1128," *Bulletin de la Commission royale d'histoire,* CXXII (1957), 261-78. (Supplement to *Actes des comtes de Flandre,* ed. F. Vercauteren, comprising four charters, of 1093, 1114, 1126, 1119-1127.)

Ladner, G. B., "Greatness in Mediaeval History," *Catholic Historical Review,* L (1964), 1-26.

Mertens, Joseph, "Quelques édifices religieux à plan central découverts récemment en Belgique," *Genava,* N.S., XI (1963), 141-61.

Noterdaeme, Jérome, "De ridders van Straten," *Het Brugs Ommeland,* I (1961), 23-30.

Pacaut, Marcel. Louis VII et son royaume. Paris: SEVPEN, 1964.

Ross, J. B., "Rise and Fall of a Twelfth-Century Clan: the Erembalds and the Murder of Count Charles of Flanders, 1127-1128," *Speculum,* XXXIV (1959), 367-90.

Verhulst, Adriaan, "Die binnenkolonisation und die Anfänge der Landgemeinde in Seeflandern," *Vorträge und Forchungen vom Konstanzer Arbeitskreis für mittelalterliche Geschichte,* VII-VIII (1964), 447-60.

———— "Historische geografie van de Vlaamse Kustvlakte tot 1200," *Bijdragen voor de Geschiedenis der Nederlanden,* XIV (1959-60), 1-37.

———— "Les Origines et l'histoire ancienne de la ville de Bruges (IXe-XIIe siècle)," *Le Moyen Âge,* LXVI (1960), 37-63.

Verplaetse, André, "L'Architecture en Flandre entre 900 et 1200 d'après les sources narratives contemporaines," *Cahiers de civilisation médiévale,* VIII (1965), 25-41.

INDEX

348 *Index*

Walter of Vladslo, peer and butler, 29; wife of, 48, 262 f.; relations with Bertulf, 136, 177, 262 f.; baron of the siege, 158, 183, 195 ff.; spokesman for Louis VI, 195 ff.; and William Clito, 230, 258, 279; death of, 262 f.

Walter of Zomergem, 296

Walter *Pennatum-mendacium,* see Walter, nephew of Thancmar

Warneton, 185; *see also* Alard of Warneton; John of Warneton

Water transport, 132*n*

Weather: inclement cold, 42, 85*n*, 267; coming of spring, 245, 250

Week, days of, 118*n*, 137*n*

Weight, units of, 244*n*; see also *Pisa*

Wenemar II, castellan of Ghent, 29; and siege of traitors, 156 f.; and Robert the Young, 227; rebellion against, 267 ff.

Weriot, knight, 165 f.

West-work (western façade on "tower" of Saint Donatian), 59, 168*n*, 177 f., 192*n*, 217*n*

Wheel, torture by, 46, 246, 249

Whipping, as punishment, 220

Wijnendale, stronghold, 207, 293, 308

William, castellan of Saint Omer, 191

William, count of Burgundy, 95*n*

William, duke of Apulia, 13 f.

William Clito, count of Flanders: claim to duchy of Normandy, 12, 196*n*; and burghers of Flanders, 28, 260 f., 265 ff., 284; acts of arson, 46, 272, 292; and Louis VI, 69, 194 ff., 284, 286 f.; Galbert's argument on legitimacy, 72, 309 ff.; elected by barons to countship, 195 ff.; accepted by men of Bruges and Ghent, 198 f.; charters granted by, 201 ff.; homage to, at Bruges, 206 f.; welcomed at Saint Omer, 227-30; and William of Ypres, 248 f., 258, 277 f.; precipitation of traitors, 250 ff.; recovery of count's

vessels, 253 f.; oath to preserve peace, 258; and inquest, 258 f.; challenge to authority, 267 ff.; and Arnold, nephew of Charles, 272 f.; loss of supporters, 273, 278, 281 f.; sacrament of penance, 297; victory at Axspoele, 298 ff.; excommunication, 300; siege of Oostkamp, 301 ff.; and Godfrey, duke of Louvain, 304 f.; death, 307 f.

William of Tyre, 93*n*

William of Wervik, knight, 33, 108 f., 143, 265*n*

William of Ypres: claimant to countship, 15, 134*n*, 144 ff., 162, 181; and Bertulf, 133 f., 143 ff., 190 f., 208-12; forces homage of merchants, 133 f, 144, 200*n*; illegitimacy, 187, 231; and fate of Isaac, 189*n*, 255; and William Clito, 196*n*, 208, 277 f.; and Guy of Steenvoorde, 213; besieged at Aire, 230 f.; captured, 248 f.; imprisoned at Bruges, 258; taken to Lille, 263; later career, 277*n*

William the Conqueror, 11 f., 81*n*

Wine: price control of, 88; serving of, 107, 265; of the traitors, 241, 244

Wingene, siege of, 290, 292 f.

Woltra Cruval, 190

Wulfric Cnop, brother of Bertulf, 109*n*, 150, 206, 239; leader of besieged, 177; death by precipitation, 251

Wulfric Rabel, 236

Wulpen, island, 244

Ypres, town: merchants at fair, 25, 123, 133, 144; news of count's death, 123 f.; execution of Bertulf, 209 ff.; *échevinage,* 216*n*; and William of Ypres, 230, 248 ff.; and William Clito, 270, 284; and Thierry of Alsace, 282 f., 296, 308

Yser, river, 23

Zeeland, 194*n*, 233*n*

Zwin, river, 23